Marxism and Social Science

Marxism and Social Science

Andrew Gamble
David Marsh
and
Tony Tant

Editors

University of Illinois Press
Urbana and Chicago

First published 1999 by
MACMILLAN PRESS LTD
Houndmills, Basingstoke, Hampshire RG21 6XS
and London
Companies and representatives
throughout the world

UNIVERSITY OF ILLINOIS PRESS edition, 1999

Library of Congress Cataloging-in-Publication Data

Marxism and social science / edited by Andrew Gamble,
    David Marsh, and Tony Tant.
      p. cm.
    Includes bibliographical references and index.
    ISBN 0–252–02501–6 (cloth : alk. paper)
    ISBN 0–252–06816–5 (pbk. : alk. paper)
    1. Communism and social sciences.   I. Gamble. Andrew.
II. Marsh, David, 1946–   .   III. Tant, Tony.
HX541.5.M346   1999
335.4'1—dc21   98–48308
                                CIP

This book is printed on acid-free paper.

1 2 3 4 5 c p 5 4 3 2 1

Printed in Hong Kong

Contents

v

vi *Contents*

Notes on the Contributors

John Barry teaches in the Department of Politics at Keele University. His main interests are green political and ethical theory, ecofeminism, theories of political economy, democratic theory and debates within contemporary political philosophy. He has two forthcoming books: *Environment and Social Theory* and *Rethinking Green Politics: Nature, Virtue and Progress*. He is currently working as co-editor on the *International Encyclopaedia of Environmental Politics* to be published with Routledge in 2001. He also has an interest in the history and politics of Ireland and Northern Ireland, and the relationship between literature, national identity and politics.

Simon Bromley is Senior Lecturer in Government and Politics at the Open University, UK. His research interests are in the field of international political economy and publications include *American Hegemony and World Oil* and *Rethinking Middle East Politics*. He is currently working on questions of sovereignty, globalisation and governance, focusing on the place of the South in the emerging frameworks of global governance.

Glyn Daly has written numerous articles on post-Marxism, post-structuralism, psychoanalytic theory and its consequences for the study of politics and ideology. He is the author of a forthcoming book *Post Marxism*.

David P. Dolowitz is a Lecturer at the University of Liverpool. His current research focuses on how political systems influence each other. He is particularly interested in the development and operation of workfare. He is author of *Learning from America: Policy Transfer and the Development of the British Workfare State* and has published in journals such as *Political Studies*, *Governance* and *Parliamentary Affairs*.

Andrew Gamble is Professor of Politics at the University of Sheffield and Director of the research programme on the political economy of the company funded by the Leverhulme Trust and the Anglo–German Foundation at the Political Economy Research Centre. Recent publications include *Hayek: the Iron Cage of Liberty* and (with Gavin Kelly) *The New Politics of Ownership* and *Owners and Citizens*.

Daryl Glaser is a Lecturer in the Department of Government, Strathclyde University. He was born in South Africa. He obtained his BA(Hons) (1983) and MA (1988) at the University of Witwaterstrand and his PhD at the University of Manchester (1994) He has lectured at the Universities of Witwaterstrand, Natal and Strathclyde. His main areas of interest are radical political thought, democratic theory and South Africa. He is currently working on books in these areas.

Colin Hay is a Lecturer in the Department of Political Science and International Studies at the University of Birmingham. He is the author of *Re-Stating Social and Political Change* (winner of the Philip Adams Memorial Prize), *Labouring Under False Pretences?* and co-author of *Postwar British Politics in Perspective*. He is also co-editor of *Theorizing Modernity* and *Demystifying Globalization*. He is on the Editorial Board of *Sociology* and, with David Marsh, is series editor for *Globalization and Governance*.

Stevi Jackson is Professor of Women's Studies and Director of the Centre for Women's Studies at the University of York. She is the author of *Childhood and Sexuality* (1982) and *Christine Delphy* (1996) and co-editor of *Women's Studies: A Reader* (1993), *The Politics of Domestic Consumption* (Wheatsheaf, 1995), *Feminism and Sexuality* (1996) and *Contemporary Feminist Theories* (1998).

Jim Johnston is completing a PhD at the University of Birmingham. His research interests include post-war British politics and Britain's relative economic decline. His other published work includes *Post-war British Politics in Perspective* (co-author).

Michael Kenny is a Lecturer in Politics at Sheffield University. He is the author of *The First New Left: British Intellectuals after Stalin*, co-author of *Western Political Thought: A Bibliographical Guide to Post-war Research*, and joint editor of *Planning Sustainability?* and *Rethinking British Decline*. He is currently preparing a book on political theory and the question of identity.

David Marsh is Professor of Politics and Head of Department in the Department of Political Science and International Studies at the University of Birmingham. He has published widely on British politics, political sociology and political economy.

Charlie McMahon has taught at the University of Strathclyde, University of Glasgow, Glasgow Caledonian University, University of Paisley and the Open University in the areas of social theory, philosophy, political philosophy, philosophy of the social sciences and cultural theory.

Chris Pierson is Professor of Politics at the University of Nottingham. He has written extensively on the problems of social democracy and the welfare state. His latest publications include *Beyond the Welfare State?*, *Developments in British Social Policy* (edited with Nick Ellison) and *Making Sense of Modernity: Conversations with Anthony Giddens*.

Trevor Purvis has recently completed his doctoral dissertation at Lancaster University. The dissertation focuses on the failure of Western conceptions of nation and sovereignty to accommodate aboriginal peoples' political aspirations. He has also recently published articles relating to discourse and ideology and citizenship and the politics of identity. He teaches in the Law Department at Carleton University in Ottawa.

Neil Robinson is Lecturer in Russian politics at the University of Essex. His publications include *Ideology and the Collapse of the Soviet System*, *Post-Communist Politics* (co-author) and articles on Soviet and post-Soviet Russian politics.

Tony Tant is Senior Lecturer in the Department of Politics at the University of Plymouth. He received his PhD from the University of Essex in 1986, having previously been an undergraduate there. Before taking up the position at Plymouth he taught in both Government and Sociology Departments at Essex. His teaching, research and publications focus upon the relationship between beliefs/ideas and structures, conventions/behaviour.

1

Why Bother with Marxism?

ANDREW GAMBLE

Marxism is widely perceived to be in crisis, and many believe the crisis is terminal. Marxism it is said has had a long run and now its energies are spent and its usefulness is long past. It is time to return Marx to the nineteenth century where he belongs. For most of this century a critical engagement with Marx and Marxism was an essential part of social science, and even anti-Marxists owed Marx a great debt in formulating their ideas. Today a new generation of social scientists is growing up which has little or no contact with Marxist ideas and Marxist methods of analysis, and for whom Marxism, with its antiquated concepts and obscure concerns, seems increasingly to belong to a past era. This book asks whether Marxism, either as theory or as doctrine, has anything left to contribute to the understanding of our circumstances at the end of the twentieth century, or whether like the Soviet Union it has ceased to be part of our political present and political future and should now only be of concern to historians and archivists.

Crises are not new to Marxism. The doctrine which placed the explanation of crisis so close to the centre of its concerns and promised to lay bare the iron laws of social development which made crises inevitable has periodically suffered its own internal crises of belief. The relationship between theory and practice has been central to Marxism, and external events and changes which have affected the political prospects for Marxism have often triggered reassessments of Marxist theory.

Nothing quite as cataclysmic however has occurred before in the history of Marxism as the collapse of communism in eastern Europe and the Soviet Union between 1989 and 1991. Its significance for Marxism must not be underrated. Despite the ossification of Marxism as a doctrine in the Soviet Union, and the open repudiation of the

1

Soviet system by Marxists in many other parts of the world, the extent
to which in the previous seventy years the meaning of Marxism and of
socialism had become inextricably bound up with the fate of the Soviet
Union had not been fully appreciated.

Why was the Soviet Union so important for Marxism? The
Bolshevik Revolution in 1917 created the first major socialist experiment, the first workers' state. From the outset it split the Marxist
movement, and in subsequent years there were to be many further
splits. Nevertheless, although its legitimacy as a *Marxist* regime was
endlessly disputed, the fact of its continued existence did transform
twentieth-century world politics by creating the ideological image and
practical example of an economic and social system based on different
principles to those of capitalism. The ideological battle between left
and right in the twentieth century became focused on the issue of
socialism against capitalism, public versus private ownership of
property, and planning versus markets. The possibility of transcending
a capitalist economy and organising the economy in a different
manner was a theoretical one when Marx first formulated it; the
existence of the Soviet Union gave it some substance and historical
validity, however unusual (in classical Marxist terms) had been the
circumstances surrounding its origins. Marxists had expected the
transition to socialism to take place in the most developed rather than
the least developed capitalist economies. Many Marxists justified the
seizure of power in Russia as providing a potential catalyst for
revolution in Europe, particularly Germany, but few believed that a
socialist society could be successfully constructed in a single country,
and one as backward in economic terms as Russia was.

The survival of the Soviet Union and the economic progress which
was apparently being achieved under the five year plans (many of the
costs were concealed) contrasted with the worldwide depression which
affected the capitalist world. The victory of the Soviet Union against
Nazi Germany in the Second World War further increased the prestige
of the Russian model, and for twenty years after the war the possibility
that a planned economy would outperform the market economies of
the West was treated seriously. In the last thirty years all that has been
stripped away, and the hollowness of the pretensions of the Soviet
system, even of its most efficient sectors like the East German
economy, to be a serious competitor or alternative to capitalism has
been exposed.

The collapse of communism in Europe is not an isolated event.
Although communist regimes survive in many other parts of the

world, particularly China, the turn to the market there was already pronounced even before the political changes in Europe. In the developing countries of the Third World the possibilities of pursuing a third way between capitalism and socialism have largely been discounted. The need to accept capitalist institutions and methods and full integration into the capitalist global market has become the new universal wisdom. At the same time the neo-liberal offensive against even mild forms of state intervention and planning within capitalist economies remains strong, often fuelled by a discourse about globalisation and the need for all countries to accept the disciplines of competing in the world market.

These developments have forced not just Marxism but all forms of socialist thought and practice onto the defensive. The unity of the global capitalist economy has been restored, after seventy years in which it was divided by fierce ideological, political, economic and military confrontation between two rival alliances. But Marxists cannot simply pick up where they left off before the events of the First World War and the Bolshevik seizure of power in Russia. The world has changed in many other ways as well: the spread of democracy, the break-up of the old colonial empires, the enlarged role of the state in managing capitalist economies, new forms of technology and communication, and with them a new structure of work and jobs. The mass labour movements of European social democracy, many of whom embraced Marxism in the decades before 1914, are now much weaker. They have abandoned Marxism and have steadily shed, not just socialist objectives on common ownership, but increasingly social democratic objectives on employment, welfare and redistribution as well.

In this new world Marxism as a system of thought is in danger of going down with the discredited regimes which used a corrupted version of it as their official doctrine. Marxists have been painfully grappling with the new realities, and in particular with having to think what Marxism still means when so many of the links between theory and practice which were once taken for granted have been broken.

Marxism almost from the very beginning was a highly diverse movement and set of theories. There was never one Marxism; even Marx himself disavowed some of the earliest varieties. What developed was an extremely rich and variegated intellectual tradition which interacted with politics and political movements, but which increasingly developed its own autonomy, direction and status within the academy. One of the questions which this book seeks to explore is what now happens to this tradition. There are two obvious possibilities. It might linger on like mediaeval scholasticism, based on textual exegesis of sacred texts, with no observable connection to anything in the real world, or Marxists might simply merge their identity entirely within mainstream intellectual currents, no longer bothering to distinguish either themselves or their approach as Marxist. The label 'Marxist' would disappear, applied either to individuals or to particular analytical approaches.

This may well be Marxism's fate, but if it is something valuable will have been lost. There is an intellectual core to Marxism which is worth preserving and which is capable of further development. Marxism continues to pose key questions about the origins, character and lines of development of the economic and social systems of the modern world. The foundations of Marxism in the nineteenth century lay in Marx's critique of political economy and political liberalism and the doctrines of class struggle and historical materialism which developed out of it. Marx's criticism of liberalism was so profound because he took the strongest arguments and assumptions of liberalism and showed how even then liberalism would fail to deliver what it proclaimed as its ideals.

The last hundred years have been dominated by the clash between liberalism and Marxism, but this is not a clash of opposites, but a clash between two doctrines which have many of the same ideals and the same conception of modernity. Marxism does not represent the negation of liberalism so much as the attempt to fulfil it. The collapse of Marxist political regimes has led some observers to declare the conflict between liberalism and Marxism to be over. Liberalism has triumphed and Marxism has been finally discredited not just politically but intellectually too. The idea of an end of history popularised by Fukuyama at the end of the 1980s resurrects a kind of historicism, but this time a liberal historicism, not the Marxist historicism which Karl Popper had sought to demolish. One of the ironies of the end of history debate is that most currents of Western Marxism had long since abandoned the historicist framework with its emphasis on progress and the imputation of an objective meaning to history. Fukuyama argued that all the ideological problems of modern society have been solved, because no alternatives have been found to the institutions of capitalism and democracy. History is at an end, not because there will no longer be any events or conflicts, but because there are no longer fundamental disputes over different principles of social and economic organisation. The issues which 'history' was about have been settled.

The end of history had been a Marxist concept, appropriated from Hegel, to indicate that stage of society when the transcendence of the social relations of capitalism would signify the disappearance of exploitation and with it the material basis for class modes of production. In the Marxist tradition this was variously interpreted, either in a utopian manner as signalling the arrival of a stage of universal bliss and harmony or more pragmatically as marking the ending of that stage of human development which for ten thousand years had been dominated by successive class modes of production. What seems clear at the end of the twentieth century is that neither conception any longer has credibility. Whether this will always be so is uncertain. Faith in the possibility of alternative forms of economic and social organisation may well revive at some point in the future, but if it does it will not be based on historicist assumptions.

One of the most difficult questions for Marxism now to address is the status of its concepts once the historicist framework is abandoned. Does a Marxist intellectual tradition make sense when the link with practice has been mostly severed and there is no longer a clear conception of an alternative and feasible non-exploitative mode of production beyond capitalism? If capitalism is now the horizon of economic and social possibility what role does a critical analysis of the workings of this society and this economy still play?

The purpose of this book is to explore a variety of answers to these questions, looking at the strengths and the weaknesses of the Marxist tradition in a number of fields, but also seeking to demonstrate the extraordinary richness and diversity of the Marxist intellectual tradition and the way in which it has absorbed so much material from other traditions in social science. Marxism has become increasingly eclectic in its readiness to borrow methods and insights from outside its own tradition. It has proved highly flexible in responding to criticism and also in being highly self-critical. One consequence, as the contributions to this book make clear, is that it is very hard to define *the* Marxist approach, although many social science textbooks have no such qualms. There are some basic differences in the Marxist tradition over the status of Marxism as a form of knowledge (is it science or discourse or critique?) as well as over methodology.

Obviously this diversity means that any assessment of the utility of the approach has, to an extent, to remain open. Many Marxists now call themselves post-Marxists rather than Marxists. Others have dropped the label 'Marxist' altogether because it is no longer clear what it signifies. One of the strengths of Marxism was that it was instinctively interdisciplinary and sought the most comprehensive and universal explanations. It had no patience with artificial discipline boundaries or with investigation of trivial and marginal questions. It always wanted the big picture. This metanarrative has been much criticised, particularly for some of the unargued assumptions that underlay it. Many of the intellectual constructions Marxists have erected in the past have not survived and do not deserve to have survived. Criticism has reached back to Marx himself, and many of the assumptions, for example on the environment, which went unexamined in his writings.

The areas in which Marxists have shown most interest are also subject to change. At different times history, political economy, philosophy, political science or sociology have commanded most attention. After the great upsurge of interest in Marxist political economy in the 1970s, the emphasis has switched to state theory, ideology and culture. The older controversies on the theory of value and the theory of crisis seem for the moment to have run their course. Marxist economists have for the most part abandoned the attempt to provide a comprehensive alternative analytical framework to mainstream economics. Instead they have contributed to a range of heterodox economic approaches, whose common feature has been to emphasise the complex institutional foundations of capitalism, how economic and social relations are reproduced, and in particular how the state and the economy interact. Two key areas of interest to Marxist political economy have been firstly how different regimes of accumulation become established within national and regional economies and are reproduced, and secondly the significance of recent changes in the way capitalism is organised as a global economy. For this reason Marxist political economy is represented in this volume most directly by the chapters on globalisation and on regulation theory. But in a more general sense it underpins all the chapters, because of the central importance of Marx's original critique of political economy to his understanding of the nature of power, class, ideology and the state. If Marxism has a future as an intellectual perspective it is always likely to return to that original critique of political economy, which remains the foundation for the interdisciplinary approach of Marxism and its continuing critique of the inadequacy of the assumptions of mainstream economics, sociology and political science.

Events also play their part. The enormous dynamism of capitalism as an economic system also makes it highly unstable and prone to crises. The turmoil in the global economy at the end of the twentieth century demonstrates once more just how difficult it is to regulate capitalism. Marx used to worry that he might not have time to finish *Capital* before the final crisis of capitalism struck. The scale and the frequency of crises has changed greatly since he wrote, but the need for crisis as an essential means by which the capitalist economy renews and restructures itself has not. The re-emergence of crisis does not prove that Marx was right all along, but it will perhaps reawaken interest in a theory of the capitalist economy which takes instability and crisis to be fundamental to the way it operates, and not just incidental.

Ultimately it is Marx's writing and the extraordinary breadth and richness of his conception of social and economic change which has provided the inspiration for generations of Marxist intellectuals, and still provides so many fertile ideas, even for those who disagree strongly with them. Few Marxists would now claim that Marxism has all the answers, or even most of the answers. In many areas it has been found deficient and inadequate. But there is a legacy of critical social theory and analysis which remains a key resource for today's social scientists. The political horizon may have changed markedly since Marx was writing *Capital*, but the social and economic system which he described and which was still then in only its early stages, is still recognisably the same system in its core features today. A critical engagement with Marxism and with the best that this intellectual tradition has to offer remains important for the further development of contemporary social science.

The Structure of the Book

This book addresses the questions raised in the introduction and attempts to establish how Marxism engages with other theoretical positions, how it has changed in response to these engagements and changes in the world it studies, and what it has to offer contemporary social science. The book is divided into two parts. Part One considers the engagement of Marxism with other perspectives in social science: feminism, the new right, regulation theory, postmodernism, and ends with a consideration of the extent to which Marxism can be considered scientific. Part Two assesses the utility of the Marxist approach to a broad span of substantive issues: the state, welfare, democracy, culture, class, globalisation, ecology, nationalism and communism. The conclusion provides an overview of the main themes of the book. All authors were asked to follow certain guidelines in their consideration of the topic for their chapter. In the case of the chapters on critical engagements in Part One each author was asked to examine the way in which certain key approaches in contemporary political science (for example discourse analysis) had criticised Marxism, how Marxists had responded to this critique, and how successful the response had been. A similar pattern has been followed in the chapters on substantive analysis. Each author begins with a consideration of the development of the Marxist perspective in relation to the particular topic, then examines contemporary criticisms of the Marxist position and finally assesses with what success Marxism has responded to those criticisms, and what the Marxist perspective still has to offer.

PART ONE

CRITICAL
ENGAGEMENTS

2

Marxism and Feminism

STEVI JACKSON

This chapter charts the engagement between Marxism and feminism from the early 1970s to the mid-1990s, outlining the major feminist perspectives on Marxism to emerge during this time. In the early part of this period Marxism was central to feminist debates, but it has since become far less prominent. In part its declining significance is attributable to the difficulties of welding feminism to Marxism, but this trend also reflects shifts in feminism – and social theory more generally – away from materialist analysis. However, while Marxist feminism as such is less influential than it once was, there is still a vigorous materialist current within feminism which owes much to Marxist methods of analysis.

The first section begins by examining the ways in which feminists sought to extend and modify Marxism and the problems they encountered in so doing. It then explores the reasons for the move away from materialist analysis on the part of many Marxist and socialist feminists during the 1980s, as they began to embrace poststructuralist and postmodernist perspectives. The second section covers some materialist alternatives and responses to postmodernism, while the final section assesses the state of play today. It will be argued that, despite the continued influence of postmodernism, materialist feminism has retained a foothold in academic debate and that there are signs that it is beginning to reassert itself.

Feminist Engagement with Marxism

During the 1970s and into the 1980s, most feminist theory was addressed to a single basic question: why are women oppressed? Many looked to variants of Marxism for answers; not only those who

11

identified as Marxist or socialist feminists, but also many who called themselves radical feminists. The women's movement emerged during a period of widespread radical political activism. Many feminists were drawn from the ranks of left groups and campaigns and already had Marxist sympathies. Marxism's central rationale was an explanation of oppression. Furthermore it analysed oppression as systematic, built into the structure of society. This made it attractive to feminists since it held out the promise of an explanation of women's subordination as social in origin; as neither given by nature nor an accidental feature of relations between men and women. Yet women's subordination could not be easily incorporated into existing Marxist theory. Marxism was developed to explain class relations and required considerable modification to accommodate gender relations.

Feminists sought in a variety of ways to extend, modify or reformulate Marxist ideas, giving rise to a series of debates on the relationship between capitalism and male domination, often referred to as the patriarchy debate (see, for example, Stacey, 1993). The differing positions taken on this issue were related to political differences among feminists, particularly on the relationship between women's liberation and class struggle. Many textbooks on feminist theory give the impression that feminists were split into two opposing camps: Marxist or socialist feminists versus radical feminists. In fact the theoretical divisions which emerged in the course of the 1970s were far more complex. Rather than there being a split between two distinct variants of feminism, there was a continuum between those who saw women's subordination as a consequence of capitalism and those who saw it as a consequence of patriarchy or some other form of systematic male dominance.[1] Theorists at both ends of the spectrum drew upon Marxism, but in rather different ways: while the more orthodox sought to fit feminist analysis into existing Marxist conceptual frameworks, others experimented with more radical reworkings of Marxism, taking from it only what seemed productive for feminism.

Within these debates patriarchy was a highly contentious concept. Hardened Marxists insisted that women's oppression was part and parcel of capitalist social relations, resisted the idea of feminist struggle existing independently of class struggle and damned feminists as 'bourgeois'. Some sections of the left maintained this position well into the 1980s (see, for example, Petty *et al.*, 1987). Marxist feminists did not generally reduce women's subordination to a side-effect of capitalism, but even those who saw male domination as a systematic feature of modern society were often reluctant to accept that patriarchy could exist side by side with capitalism. Many worried that the concept of patriarchy was ahistorical, some felt that it aptly described past societies based literally on the rule of fathers, but was not applicable to our own (Rubin, 1975; Barrett, 1980). Others, however, defined patriarchy more broadly as a system of male domination and sought to historicise it (for example, Walby, 1986a). Some shared Sheila Rowbotham's (1981) concern that positing the existence of patriarchy as a system which long pre-dated capitalism might lead feminists into a fruitless search for its pre-historic origins. Yet not all those who used the concept of patriarchy were interested in unearthing its origins, while some of those opposed to the term, such as Gayle Rubin (1975), were engaged in attempts to establish the genesis of male dominance.

Another source of concern was the difficulty of establishing the central dynamics of patriarchy. Among those who have used the term 'patriarchy', whether from a Marxist perspective or not, there is no consensus on how to define or theorize it (see Beechey, 1979; Barrett, 1980; Walby, 1986a). These disagreements entailed another set of differences, cutting across the capitalism–patriarchy continuum, concerning the level of the social formation at which women's subordination was said to be located. Many Marxist feminists argued that, rather than being rooted, like class, in relations of production, women's subordination was either a consequence of specific relations of reproduction or was primarily ideological. Some theorists at the radical feminist end of the spectrum also drew on Marxist perspectives to develop analyses of reproduction and sexuality. The range of feminisms this produced is represented diagramatically in Figure 2.1.

In outlining these perspectives we will first deal with those who concentrated on economic analysis, on productive relations, then with those who focused on reproduction and finally with theories focusing primarily on ideology. Ideology figures to some degree in all feminist theories, hence its location at the centre of the vertical axis in Figure 2.1. Certain perspectives on ideology, however, proved particularly significant for the development of feminist perspectives in the 1980s, ultimately producing a shift away from materialist analysis on the part of many Marxist feminists.

Relations of Production: Capitalist or Patriarchal?

Just as Marxist analysis takes the productive relations of a given society as its point of departure, so too did many feminists. A wide

Explanations emphasising	Capitalist relations	Patriarchy+capitalism	Male dominance or patriarchal relations
Material factors.	Traditional Marxism Barrett (UK): Marxist feminist (not reducible to capitalism, but concept of partiarchy inappropriate)	Some Marxist feminists e.g. *Hartmann* (USA) Materialist dual systems theory *Walby* (UK)	Materialist radical feminists e.g. *Delphy* (France)
Culture/ideology		Psychoanalytic Marxist feminism e.g. *Mitchell* (UK)	Heterosexuality as a class relation e.g. *Wittig* (France) Subordination through sexuality: *MacKinnon* (USA)
Sexuality & reproduction		Relations of production v. relations of reproduction. Some Marxist feminists e.g. *McDonough & Harrison* (UK)	Male control over reproduction as basis of sex class: *Firestone* (USA) Differing male & female relationships to reproduction: *O'Brien* (Canada)

FIGURE 2.1 *Explanations for women's subordination*

Source: This figure taken from S. Jackson and J. Jones (eds) (1988) *Contemporary Feminist Theories* (Edinburgh University Press).

range of theorists sought explanations for male domination in terms of the exploitation of labour, from orthodox Marxists seeking to attribute women's subordination to capitalism to radical feminists arguing that the productive processes of modern society entail both capitalist and patriarchal relations. This form of analysis was founded on two aspects of women's economic situation. First, women's position in the labour market differs from that of men in that they tend to be lower paid, concentrated into fewer occupations and employed less continuously than men and frequently on a part-time basis. Second, in addition to any paid employment women undertake, they are typically also engaged in unpaid domestic work outside capitalist relations of production.

For those with orthodox Marxist preoccupations, the most obvious line of enquiry was to relate these facts to the capitalist economy. The conditions of women's employment, particularly its intermittent character, led to women being dubbed a 'reserve army of labour', which could be called on when needed by capital and laid off at other times. Women workers satisfied capitalism's need for a pool of cheap, flexible and disposable labour, suited to the cycles of boom and slump to which capitalist economies are subject. There are a number of problems with this model, which appears applicable to some situations but not others (see Bruegel, 1979; Walby, 1986a). For example, women very clearly were used as a reserve army of labour during the two world wars, when they took over men's jobs only to be returned to the home or to low-paid 'women's work' once peace returned. In other circumstances, however, the model has less empirical validity. If women are employed because their labour is cheaper than that of men, why are they not always given jobs in preference to men? Women may be a flexible labour force, but that flexibility is not utilised in such a way that they are potential replacements for male workers. Indeed women rarely do the same jobs as men and are employed instead in a different range of occupations. At a conceptual level, this approach does not explain why it should be women who constitute the reserve army, except insofar as it is taken as given that women's primary role is a domestic one and that this renders them marginal to the wage economy.

Women's domestic labour was itself the subject of much debate. Marxists theorised housework in terms of the contribution it made to capitalism, within what became known as 'the domestic labour debate' (DLD), which dominated theoretical discussions on housework in many Western countries, particularly in Britain and Canada, throughout the 1970s.[2] The debate was premised on capital's need for a constantly replenished labour force. Marx observed that workers' wages were converted into fresh labour power and also provided for their children: the workers of the future (see Marx, 1976: 275, 717–18). He himself ignored the domestic work this entailed – the cooking of meals and washing of shirts necessary to make the worker ready for each new day – and the fact that this work was done largely by women. Marxist feminists initially sought to establish that this work was socially necessary, essential to the functioning of capitalism (see, for example, Benston, 1969). The DLD thus began from feminists' attempts to challenge the orthodox Marxist view that housework was marginal to capitalism, but it subsequently became a highly technical discussion about Marx's theory of value.

Those associated with the Wages for Housework campaign argued that housework was productive labour and a hidden source of profit for capitalism (Dalla Costa and James, 1972). In Marxist terms productive labour is that which produces 'surplus value'. If housewives produce labour power and labour power is the source of surplus value, then housework could be seen as indirectly producing surplus value and hence as productive. Most Marxist feminists, however, contested this interpretation, resisting the extension of the term 'productive labour' to work which did not directly produce surplus value. A further, and related, point of contention was whether housework itself could be said to have value or create value. Marxists generally see domestic labour as socially useful, but as having no 'exchange value' – it is not exchanged for a wage. Similarly the products of housework, viewed by Marxists as 'use-values', have no exchange value because they are not exchanged for cash. However, labour power is seen as a commodity with an exchange value – the wage paid for it. So, does a housewife produce a commodity after all: her husband's labour power? If that commodity has an exchange value (the man's wage), does the wife's labour power have a hidden exchange value incorporated into her husband's wage?

Marxists were soon tied in knots trying to answer these questions (see, for example, Coulson *et al.*, 1975; Gardiner *et al.*, 1975; Smith, 1978a; Molyneux, 1979). The problems proved insoluble because domestic labour, unlike wage labour, is not directly exchanged for set remuneration and does not involve a fixed quantity of labour power. It cannot, therefore, be explained in terms of a theory designed to analyse wage labour. By the end of the 1970s it had become clear that this was not a fruitful line of feminist enquiry. Participants in the domestic labour debate took divisions of labour between men and women for granted: they never paused to consider why it was women who performed domestic labour or why men apparently 'needed' to have it done for them. The competing claims made about the value of domestic labour were entirely contingent upon the position of the housewife's husband within the capitalist economy. It was in terms of his labour that her work was conceptualised. Yet relations between husbands and wives, particularly inequalities between them, were largely ignored. For most Marxists it was unthinkable that working class men might be oppressors in their own homes or that 'bourgeois' women might also be oppressed (Delphy and Leonard, 1992).

From the early 1970s a rather different approach to domestic labour was being developed by French materialist feminists, particularly Christine Delphy. According to Delphy, the peculiarities of housework arise from the social relations within which it is performed. She argues that these relations are patriarchal and that within families men systematically exploit and benefit from women's labour within a domestic mode of production (Delphy, 1976; 1977; 1984). Women's domestic work is undertaken as a personal service to a male head of household. He effectively appropriates her whole person and the labour she embodies, so that the work she does is potentially limitless and depends on his requirements. Hence housework has no fixed job description and does not directly involve the exchange of a set number of hours or an agreed amount of work for a given return. The maintenance a wife receives is not related to the work she does, but is determined by her husband's income and his generosity. The direct appropriation and non-exchange of women's labour is particularly clear when a wife is also in employment, earning enough to meet her own maintenance costs, but is still expected to do the housework. In this situation she is clearly working for nothing. Delphy argues that, within the domestic mode of production, men constitute a class of exploiters while women are an exploited class.

Delphy says little of the relationship between patriarchal and capitalist modes of production, but others, notably Sylvia Walby, have explored this further. Walby concentrates less on the direct benefits men gain from their wives' work and more on the ways in which these benefits are mediated through the exchange of labour power. She argues that a man realises value of the domestic labour he has appropriated when he exchanges his labour power – which his wife's work has produced – for a wage which he controls. This, for

Walby, is the main mechanism of exploitation within the patriarchal mode of production (Walby, 1986a).

The idea of a domestic or patriarchal mode of production, and Delphy's analysis in particular, generated some very hostile responses from Marxist feminists. Some critics questioned whether two modes of production can co-exist within one society, seeing this as antithetical to Marxism (Kaluzynska, 1980; Molyneux, 1979), a view contested by Walby (1986a). Many Marxists and Marxist feminists conceded that housework is subject to relations of production distinct from those of capitalism. They were, however, unwilling to entertain the possibility that these relations were patriarchal, or that they might be part of a distinct mode of production, or that women were exploited.[3] These objections are not, at root, merely technical ones, but spring from a refusal to accept that men benefit directly from the work their wives do (see, for example, Barrett, 1980: 216–17). Yet men do not, as Barrett would have it, simply 'evade' their share of housework: they have their share done for them and it is done to suit their routines and tastes.[4] Moreover, a wife is not merely a 'dependant' whom her husband is obliged to support from his wage, but contributes to his ability to earn that wage (Walby, 1986a).

Neither Delphy nor Walby see women's exploitation within the domestic mode of production as the sole basis of their subordination. Another, obviously material, aspect of women's situation is their disadvantaged position in the labour market. As we have seen, this is not directly explicable in terms of ready-made Marxist concepts. Marxism cannot explain why women and men should not be exploited equally in the capitalist economy. By extending materialist analysis, however, it may be possible to explore the interconnections between capitalism and patriarchy in the structuring of labour markets. This is a theme explored by the American Marxist feminist, Heidi Hartmann (1976; 1981) and subsequently developed by Walby (1986a).

Although recognised as Marxist feminist, Hartmann's perspective is not dissimilar to Delphy's. Both argue that patriarchy existed as a distinct system of inequality alongside capitalism and that patriarchy was founded upon male control of women's labour. Hartmann differs from Delphy in that she devoted more attention to women's paid work outside the home and sought to establish the interconnections between patriarchy and capitalism. Using historical analysis she argues that the development of capitalism within societies which were already patriarchal had consequences for gender divisions in both the home and the workplace. During the nineteenth century, organised working class men used their social advantage to exclude women from well paid, skilled occupations and to marginalise them in the labour market. A vicious circle was established, such that women's disadvantage in the labour market constrained them into dependence on marriage for survival. Within marriage they exchange domestic services for maintenance, and housework and childcare become their primary responsibilities. Because of the burden of domestic work they cannot compete in the labour market on equal terms with men, thereby compounding their original disadvantage.

This suggests some interesting possibilities for grounding theory in history, but history is itself contested terrain. Marxist feminists have often been concerned to reassert the primacy of class relations in history (see, for example, Humphreys, 1977). Michèle Barrett (1980) was less inclined to reduce women's subordination to class relations and saw in historical research a means of resolving questions about the interrelationship between capitalism and women's subordination. She argues that women's subordination is not a product of the logic of capitalist development, but is nonetheless now thoroughly enmeshed in the material structures of contemporary capitalist societies. The research which accumulated during the 1980s, however, swung the balance towards a recognition of the importance of patriarchal relations and the resilience of male domination under changing historical conditions (see Walby, 1986a; Jackson, 1992a).

Relations of Reproduction and the Control of Women's Sexuality

An alternative to locating women's subordination in productive relations was to suggest that it was located in social relations of reproduction. This was one logical outcome of the DLD, which produced a covert consensus whereby housework continued to be regarded as reproducing labour power; to suggest that it produced anything became almost taboo. Housework is thus talked of as reproducing, but not producing, labour power or as 'reproduction' in some general, unspecified sense. This distinction between production and reproduction is spurious, nonsensical – something cannot be reproduced without first being produced – and runs counter to Marx's position that every process of production is simultaneously a process of reproduction (Beechey, 1979; Walby, 1986a). It also raises the problem of conflating social reproduction, the reproduction of the labour force and biological reproduction (Edholm *et al.*, 1977; Delphy,

1980). When women's work is said to 'reproduce' the proletariat or capitalist social relations, the implication is that they do this work because they have babies. Hence all the complex ways in which capitalist social relations are reproduced, as well as women's subordination itself, are reduced to women's reproductive capacities (Delphy and Leonard, 1992). Sometimes this connection was made explicit. For example, Michèle Barrett and Mary McIntosh, in criticising Delphy's emphasis on the exploitation of women as wives, suggest that greater priority should be given to motherhood:

> An analysis of childcare and women's position with regard to the reproduction of the species would lead to an analysis of the role of women in reproducing labour power, and the forces and relations of production more generally. (Barrett and McIntosh, 1979: 102)

It might seem rather curious for feminists to succumb to such blatant biological determinism, to reduce women's oppression to their reproductive capacities without questioning women's responsibility for childcare, but this is a common means of theorising the relationship between capitalism and women's oppression among Marxist feminists. The idea that women's subordination is rooted in reproduction also has a respectable history within Marxism, deriving from Engels' thesis that the 'world historic defeat of the female sex' occurred with the rise of private property and the establishment of patrilineal descent.

Modern anthropology has revealed a number of errors in Engels' basic assumptions about the sexual division of labour and the organisation of kinship. His work also suffers from conceptual problems. The empirically false assumption that women have always been excluded from productive work and confined to child rearing was based on the assumption of a 'natural' sexual division of labour. There is also a less obvious form of essentialism implicit in Engels' proposition that once men owned individual property they would want to pass it on to their children, providing the motive for overthrowing 'mother-right'. This presupposes an innate male desire to transmit property to their biological offspring, and reduces the social relations of patrilineal descent to a 'natural' male urge towards genetic continuity. Whatever principles kinship and descent are based upon, they always entail social rather than natural continuity. A fundamental tenet of materialism is that it examines the ways in which given human needs – to eat or reproduce – are transformed through social relationships. Treating such social relations as natural thus undermines materialism.

These flaws in Engels' reasoning have not deterred Marxist feminists from using his work to authorise a search for the roots of women's subordination in relations of reproduction. For example, Roisin McDonough and Rachel Harrison locate patriarchy in men's control of women's sexuality and procreative functions. They suggest that this transhistorical subordination of women can be historicised through examining the differing ways it is mediated within given modes of production, and also by relating it to class relations. They suggest that the emergence of social classes divided women into two groups: 'those who procreated heirs (future owners of the means of production) and those who procreated future . . . labourers'. Thus women perform 'two economic functions necessary to perpetuate the social relations of capitalist production' (McDonough and Harrison, 1978: 34). The assumption that the reproduction of the capitalist class has to be accomplished through biological paternity closely echoes Engels' presupposition of men's innate urge to endow their progeny.[5] Once again the reproduction of class relations is reduced to biology, an error compounded by the classic functionalist teleology: projecting current functions into the past and treating them as causal origins.

The attraction of the idea of relations of reproduction is that it keeps Marxist analysis of productive, class relations intact while simultaneously providing a means for arguing that patriarchy currently exists to service capitalism. Other Marxist feminists, however, are wary of leaving the Marxist perspectives on productive labour relations untouched by feminism, and are therefore sceptical of arguments based only on reproduction (see, for example, Beechey, 1979). It is not only those who wish to avoid troubling Marxist conceptualisations of capitalism who concentrate their efforts on reproduction. This has also been a strategy adopted by some who seek to displace class relations from the privileged place they occupy in Marxism, and concentrate on the significance of gender relations in the progress of human history.

One of the best known examples of this tendency is Shulamith Firestone, (1972). Often taken as an exemplar of radical feminism, Firestone's analysis is in fact highly individual and idiosyncratic. She attributes women's subordination directly to their reproductive functions. 'Unlike economic class, sex-class sprang directly from biological reality: men and women were created different, and not equal' (Firestone, 1972: 16). Although Firestone claims to employ Marx's dialectical method, in her hands this amounts to little more than overturning the Marxist view of history as class struggle, entailing a succession of modes of production in favour of an alternative view of history as founded upon 'the division of society into two distinct biological classes for procreative reproduction, and the struggles of these classes with one another' (1972: 20). She claims that the organization of the biological family is the crucible of all forms of domination and inequality, and that this is the motor of history, but there is nothing in her model to explain how such historical changes come about.

A far more sophisticated account of the historical development of relations of reproduction is offered by Mary O'Brien (1981). She argues that feminists need a theory of reproduction and male domination analogous to Marx's analysis of production and class domination (which she endorses but sees as only a partial explanation of human history). O'Brien's conceptualisation of reproduction includes the biological processes of conception, gestation and nurture and the social relations involved in nurturing a child. She establishes reproduction as a legitimate object of materialist analysis far more convincingly than either Firestone or McDonough and Harrison, arguing that paying attention to reproduction is no more biologistic than Marxist accounts of production.[6] Both production and reproduction start from basic human needs: to eat and breed, to survive as individuals and as a species. The point is that in satisfying these basic human needs we enter into social relationships, and it is these which shape the conditions under which we produce and reproduce, which bring these activities into the sphere of human consciousness and which have, historically, produced structural inequalities of class and gender.

O'Brien also suggests mechanisms for social change in the sphere of reproduction, and posits two major historical transformations: the discovery of biological paternity and the recent development of technologies of fertility control. The outcome of the latter is still uncertain and is a site of feminist struggle. The discovery of paternity, however, presaged the beginnings of patriarchy. This knowledge simultaneously included men in reproduction and excluded them from it. Men became aware of their alienation from their own seed and lack the experiential sense of generational continuity. To establish their place in the succession of generations they needed to appropriate the fruits of women's reproductive labour as their own, co-operating with other men to maintain their individual rights. O'Brien thus supplies what is missing in analyses deriving from Engels, an explanation of why men should seek to pass on property to their biological offspring; but whether she does, in fact, avoid biological reductionism is a moot point.

Whereas O'Brien treats sexual acts primarily as moments in the reproductive cycle other radical feminists have focused on sexuality itself. Catherine MacKinnon begins by establishing parallels between the object of Marxist analysis, labour, and the object of feminist analysis – in this case sexuality. 'Sexuality is to feminism what work is to Marxism: that which is most one's own, yet most taken away' (MacKinnon, 1982: 515). She does not use the term 'class' to denote gender relations, but nonetheless treats the two sexes as analogous to classes, constructed through sexual rather than labour relations. 'Sexuality is that process which creates, organizes, expresses and directs desire, creating the social beings we know as women and men' (ibid., p. 516). The division of gender is founded on 'the social requirements of heterosexuality, which insitutionalizes male sexual dominance and female sexual submission' (ibid., p. 533). Unlike O'Brien, MacKinnon does not leave Marxism secure in its own territory. Rather she sees feminism as superseding Marxism, turning it 'inside out and on its head' (ibid., p. 544). Feminism, she maintains, challenges the fundamentals of materialism, in that feminist theory springs from a collective consciousness of shared experience rather than a scientific perception of an objective world external to experience.

While MacKinnon offers useful insights into sexuality, she ignores much of the material reality of women's lives and overly privileges sexuality. An alternative analysis is offered by Monique Wittig who began developing her analysis of heterosexuality in the late 1970s. Drawing on Delphy's work on the exploitation of women's labour within marriage and Guillaumin's conceptualisation of the public and private appropriation of women's bodies and labour, she analyses heterosexuality as a class relationship which is founded upon both sexual and labour relations (Wittig, 1992; Delphy, 1984; Guillaumin, 1995). She likens lesbians to runaway slaves; as fugitives from their class they are no longer 'women'. Wittig's analysis is a contentious one, and rejected by some other French materialists, particularly Delphy, for implying that it is possible to escape patriarchy by opting out of heterosexuality.

The work of O'Brien, MacKinnon and Wittig has had a lasting impact on feminist theory and politics. The influence of more orthodox Marxist feminist analyses of relations of reproduction, on the other hand, has proved to be less durable. Among Marxist feminists, the most significant developments have taken place in the sphere of ideology and culture.

Ideology, Discourse and the Turn to Culture

Since the 1970s many of those who once saw themselves as Marxist feminists have turned their backs on materialist analysis in favour of a focus on language, discourse and representation. Michèle Barrett (1992) has characterized this trend as a 'cultural turn', a shift in the objects of feminist analysis from 'things' to 'words' – a turn of phrase borrowed from Foucault (1972). In the process there has been a move away from social scientific perspectives within feminist theory towards those deriving from literary and cultural studies. Not only have macro-level models of social structure, of patriarchy and capitalism, disappeared from many feminist analyses, but so have familiar 'things' such as poverty, housework, labour markets and sexual violence. This trend can be traced, for example, in the pages of the Marxist feminist journal, Feminist Review, which was established in 1979. Issues such as welfare provision, education and women's work, accounted for a large proportion of its content in the early 1980s, but have now vanished from sight. Marx was commonly cited in its early years, but now his place as intellectual mentor is taken by Lacan, Foucault or Derrida.

The cultural turn became increasingly evident in the 1980s, but its origins can be discerned in the late 1970s, presaged by Marxist feminist interest in ideology and psychoanalysis. At first, this was accomplished through an Althusserian framework drawing in the arguments of Lacan and Lévi-Strauss, an approach pioneered by Juliet Mitchell (1975). Althusser's reformulation of the traditional base-superstructure model, his theorization of ideology as relatively autonomous, having its own effectivity and materiality, was potentially attractive to feminists. If ideology no longer had to be seen as a mere superstructural reflection of the economic base of society, this created a space to theorise women's subordination without having to relate it to the capitalist mode of production or engage in spurious distinctions between production and reproduction. Indeed, sexuality and procreation could be reconceptualized as implicated in processes now deemed to be ideological. Mitchell's analysis uses Althusser to define women's subordination as ideological, draws on Lacan's reading of Freud to explain how ideology is reproduced in our psyches and brings in Lévi-Strauss to account for the origins of patriarchy.[7] She argues that women's subordination once had a material base, rooted in the social ordering of kinship. With the rise of capitalism, kin ties are no longer a fundamental form of social and economic organisation and women's subordination is now ideological, guaranteed only by the continual replaying of the oedipal drama between generations. For Mitchell, the struggle against patriarchy must take the form of a 'cultural revolution' (Mitchell, 1975: 414).

Mitchell's analysis is still a structural one, although its relation to Marxism is problematic. Lévi-Strauss's analysis of the incest taboo and the exchange of women as a prerequisite for all human culture and the universalism of psychoanalysis do not sit well with Marxism's insistence on the historical specificity of both social structure and human consciousness. Although Mitchell argues that the exchange of women no longer has more than a symbolic significance in modern society, she gives us no clues on how we are to break out of the cycle by which a universal oedipal drama determines our psychic functioning. Mitchell's work was important insofar as it rehabilitated psychoanalysis, which many feminists had rejected, introduced English speaking feminists to the work of Jacques Lacan, and was indicative of a growing interest in the structuralist tradition of French theory.

Other Marxists and Marxist feminists were also experimenting with combinations of Althusserian theory, linguistics and semiology, particularly the idea that ideology is effective through the capacity of language to shape our thoughts and desires (see Coward and Ellis, 1977). Once Foucault's ideas were added to this mixture, the emphasis shifted from linguistic and semiotic structures to a more fluid notion of discourse and power was reconceptualised as diffuse and dispersed rather than concentrated into the hands of ruling classes. Moreover the concept of ideology itself became untenable as 'truth' was declared to be an effect of discourse, so that ideology could no longer be seen as 'false', with effects discoverable by 'scientific' Marxism. The one, fragile, link which had moored these new analyses of the symbolic realm to the material world was severed. Gradually these new forms of feminist theory developed in the direction of poststructuralism and postmodernism.

The influence of these ideas on feminism was felt early and first among Marxist feminists. In part this was a response to the perceived failure of Marxism to deal with issues which were important to feminist analysis, such as subjectivity and sexuality. Moreover those who had sought to explain women's subordination within Marxism, whether in terms of productive relations, reproduction or ideology, faced the difficulty of explaining why women should occupy particular niches within the social hierarchy. They often found themselves sliding into universalistic and biologistic accounts at odds with both materialism's emphasis on the primacy of the social and their desire as feminists to avoid identifying women's subordination with 'nature'. These new forms of theory offered perspectives which were radically anti-essentialist and could potentially avoid some of the pitfalls Marxist feminists had found themselves stumbling into.

The British journal *m/f*, launched in 1978, was at the leading edge of these new developments, and its first editorial provides a clear statement of both the growing dissatisfaction with conventional Marxist models and the move towards cultural analysis. The editors situate themselves firmly within Marxism, still expressing a wish to engage with class politics, but are explicitly critical of materialist explanations of women's subordination. They define their project as follows: 'We are interested in how women are produced as a category; it is this which determines the subordinate position of women' (Adams *et al.*, 1978: 5). Psychoanalysis is seen by them as essential to an understanding of gendered subjectivity, but so too is discourse.[8] Their next editorial brought the category 'women' into question, arguing that there is no unity to 'women', or to 'women's oppression' and that differing discourses construct varying definitions of 'women' (Adams *et al.*, 1978). This deconstruction of 'women' was to become a central theme in some of the most celebrated works of postmodern feminism (for example, Riley, 1988; Butler, 1990).

In this context the immediate concern was to counter the idea of 'women' as a fixed, natural category, to emphasise its historical, cultural and contextual specificity. There was, however, another, and compelling, reason for questioning the category 'women', in that it often served to conceal differences among women. The analyses of women's oppression which shaped feminist debate were framed almost entirely from a white Western perspective. By the end of the 1970s white feminists found themselves confronted by black women, Third World women and women of colour, angrily denouncing those who had excluded them or unthinkingly subsumed them under the banner of 'sisterhood', without allowing them to speak for themselves. Hazel Carby summed this up when she asked of white feminists, 'what exactly do you mean when you say WE?' (Carby, 1982: 233) As the clamour of critique grew in the 1980s it became abundantly clear that 'women' was not, and could not be, a unitary category, and that any theory attempting to distil women's subordination into a single explanation was doomed to exclude the experiences of the majority of the world's female population (Flax, 1990). Moreover attention was increasingly being drawn to the complexities of women's lives in a postcolonial era with its global economy, its history of colonial diasporas and its current labour migrations and displacements of refugees.

All of this was taken by some feminists as a further mandate for postmodern theorising, seen as a means of avoiding the exclusions of an assumed universal womanhood and the simplifications of causal models of oppression (see, for example, Riley, 1988). Some critics have suggested that postmodernists are simply taking refuge in an impenetrable elitist theory which does not require them to confront the realities of racism (Modleski, 1991). However there are feminist postcolonial theorists who speak from the position of the previously marginalised 'other', and hence from a rather different location from that occupied by white theorists (Spivak, 1988; Trinh, 1989). Whether postmodernism is the only means of coping with the complexities of gender in a postcolonial world, or whether materialism still has something to offer, is a question to which we will return.

Materialist Responses to Postmodernism

Taken to its logical conclusion the cultural turn implied the abandonment of analyses of the material conditions of women's lives, the denial of any overarching systems of power and a move towards a focus on culture and the discursive construction of difference. Once it was under way, the continued defence of Marxism's relevance was left to those materialist feminists whose affiliations were closer to radical than to Marxist feminism. In some ways these theorists were better placed than traditional Marxist feminists to defend materialist methods. Since they had never slavishly endorsed the whole Marxist conceptual framework as if it were divine truth, their theorising had been less fettered by the need to fit feminism into existing Marxist formulations. As a result, they did not take gender divisions themselves for granted and had been less inclined to endorse monocausal models of the kind which tended towards reductionist and essentialist conclusions. Those who invested in the turn to culture were concerned with the ways in which gender is constructed and with the differences among women which cut across gender divisions. Yet there is no reason why a materialist analysis, provided it is not crudely reductionist, should be unable to deal with the fact of gender difference or with diversity among women.

The inability of Marxist feminists to develop an adequate theorisation of gender without resorting to idealist formulations derives from their unwillingness to entertain the possibility of a materialist analysis of male dominance itself. In France, however, materialist feminists had developed just such a formulation. The year before *m/f* was launched in Britain, French materialist feminists began to produce their own theoretical journal, *Questions Féministes* (*QF*). They too were interested in how women are produced as a category and identified ideology as playing a role in this, but unlike the *m/f* group, they did not see this process as entirely ideological. Nor did they locate the reproduction of the categories men and women in our individual psyches and most of them were sceptical of psychoanalysis. In their first editorial they argued that radical feminism must refuse any notion of 'woman' that is unrelated to social context.

> The corollary of this refusal is our effort to deconstruct the notion of 'sex differences' which gives a shape and a base to the concept of 'woman' and is an integral part of naturalist ideology. The social mode of being of men and of women is in no way linked to their nature as males and females nor with the shape of their sex organs. (*QF* collective, 1981: 214–15).

Like many postmodern feminist theorists, materialist feminists are critical of those who see gender as built upon a foundation of biological sex and have continued to elaborate upon this critique (Delphy, 1984; 1993; Wittig, 1992).[9] Both perspectives bring the existence of gender categories themselves into question, arguing that the terms 'women' and 'men' are constructs defined in relation to each other which have no meaning outside that relation. The grounds on which this case is made, however, differ. Where postmodernists see gender categories as products of language and discourse, materialists see them as rooted in the material realities of male domination.

The materialist feminist position on gender follows from the conceptualisation of men and women as existing in a class-like relationship. Patriarchal domination is not based upon pre-existing sex differences, rather gender exists as a social division because of patriarchal domination. Hence hierarchy precedes division. As Delphy and Leonard put it: 'For us "men" and "women" are not two naturally given groups who at some time fell into a hierarchical relationship. Rather the reason the two groups are distinguished socially is because one dominates the other' (Delphy and Leonard, 1992: 258). This argument is in keeping with a Marxist method of analysis. For Marxists classes only exist in relation to one another: conceptually and empirically there can be no bourgeoisie without the proletariat and vice versa. Similarly 'men' and 'women' exist as socially significant categories because of the exploitative relationship which both binds them together and sets them apart from each other. Conceptually there could be no 'women' without the opposing category 'men', and vice versa. As Monique Wittig says, 'there are no slaves without masters' (1992: 15). The political goal of feminist struggle is therefore analogous to that of class struggle: to do away with gender division. This does not mean women becoming like men, since 'men' as we know them would no longer exist. 'If women were the equals of men, men would no longer equal themselves' (Delphy, 1993: 8).[10]

Where materialist feminism has an explanation of gender at the level of social structure, it has not yet produced an analysis of the construction of gender at the level of our individual agency and subjectivity. Furthermore the ways in which gender intersects with other forms of inequality, especially those founded on racism and colonialism, have been undertheorised. Some materialist feminists have paid attention to the construction of 'race' as a category (Guillaumin, 1995) and to women's location within the global division of labour (Mies, 1986), but this has not been sufficient to answer the postmodernists' accusation that materialist analysis cannot capture the multiplicity of differences among women, that the term 'patriarchy' conceals such differences, that the concept 'women' itself denies diversity of experience. Moreover racism can no longer be understood as a power dynamic between black and white, since ethnic, religious, national and cultural differences are themselves so complex and context-specific.[11]

Sylvia Walby (1992) has contested such postmodernist claims, in particular the tendency to fragment the categories of 'women', 'race' and 'class'. While accepting that postmodernists have much to offer in sensitising us to varying cultural constructions of gender, she argues that they go too far. In neglecting the social context of power relations, and in viewing power as diffuse and dispersed, postmodernism fails to recognise that systematic oppressions of gender, class and race persist. Seeing these in terms of 'difference' serves to deny inequality. Moreover, while Walby accepts that gender relations are culturally and historically variable, this is not in her view sufficient to justify the abandonment of attempts to explain them. There are also cross-cultural regularities and historical continuities in gender relations.

The signifiers 'woman' and 'man', she maintains, 'have sufficient historical and cross-cultural continuity . . . to warrant using such terms' (Walby, 1992: 36). She recognises that many feminist theories have not dealt adequately with historical change and cultural variations, but this she attributes to unicausal analyses rather than the concept of patriarchy per se. Similarly she is critical of traditional Marxist models which reduced all relations of inequality to class. She argues that, rather than abandoning attempts to explain inequality, we should be developing theories of gender, class and ethnicity which recognise the intersections between them and which place them in the context of the international division of labour. To do so we need to retain the structural concepts of patriarchy, capitalism and racism. She concludes:

> We do not need to abandon the notion of causality in the face of the complexity of the social world. We do not have to move from analysis of structure to that of discourse to catch that complexity; neither do we have to resort to capitalism as the sole determinant in order to have a macro-social theory. (Walby, 1992:48–9)

It is easy to get the impression that all progress on theory in the 1980s and 1990s was being made via studies of culture, that materialists were simply fighting a rearguard action against the encroachments of poststructuralism and postmodernism. This is not in fact the case, since a number of major theorists were continuing to build theories of materialist foundations throughout the 1980s (for example, Pateman, 1988; Walby, 1986a & b; 1990). Having outlined Walby's critique of postmodernism, we will take her as just one example of an active exponent of materialist theorising.

Walby draws upon both Delphy (1984) and Hartmann (1976; 1981) to defend a 'dual systems' perspective within which patriarchy and capitalism are conceptualised as developing in dynamic articulation with each other. Although she devotes considerable attention to the material, economic bases of patriarchy in men's control over women's labour in the home and workplace, she does not root patriarchy exclusively in these sites. Rather she suggests that patriarchy is located in six relatively autonomous structures: domestic production, paid employment, culture, sexuality, male violence and the state. All of these structures change historically, and the relative salience of each of them varies from one historical era to another. For example, Walby suggests that in the nineteenth century patriarchy was rooted primarily in the private sphere of domestic production, while today it is the public spheres of employment and the state which are the dominant patriarchal structures. While the details of this shift from private to public patriarchy can be questioned (Delphy and Leonard, 1992), Walby's model does have the advantage of flexibility. She contends that identifying several causal bases of patriarchy enables us to account for variations in forms and degrees of patriarchal domination over time and from one context to another (Walby, 1990). Furthermore these various structures affect differently specific groups of women and might all allow for a more sensitive appraisal of the differing structural locations of, for example, white British, Asian–British and Afro-Caribbean British women.

The Current State of Play

In the 1990s materialist feminist analyses are not particularly fashionable in academic circles. Somewhat prematurely, and groundlessly, a theoretical tradition little more than twenty-five years old has been declared by some to be outmoded. There is a tendency in some recent feminist writing to assume that theories which emerged in the first decade of second wave feminism have now been superseded, and that feminists who continue to work within these theoretical frameworks are no longer producing relevant work. In particular, feminist postmodernists constantly warn us against these older theoretical traditions, implying that they claim to have discovered the ultimate cause of women's oppression or that they assume universal applicability for theories generated from a particular historical and social location (see, for example, Flax, 1990). Such accusations are not always just. Some feminists were always critical of attempts to construct totalising theories of women's oppression and sceptical of transhistorical, universalistic explanations (Delphy, 1984; Walby, 1990).

While warning of totalising tendencies in feminist theory, Jane Flax (1990) also indicates some points of convergence between feminism and postmodernism. She is substantially correct to say that feminists have always been sceptical about claims to 'objectivity' and 'truth', since these so often turned out to be very particular truths constructed from an androcentric perspective. We have also long been aware that language and discourse are not transparent media of communication, that they construct rather than reflect meaning. We have also recognised that the idea of a unitary, fixed, rational self is not tenable, that it does not match the complexities and contradictions of our lived experience as women and as feminists. Since postmodern theories speak to these concerns, it is perhaps not surprising that feminists have been attracted to them. Materialist feminists, too, have sometimes drawn on aspects of postmodern theorising but have remained wary of its tendency to discount the world of 'things' in favour of 'words' (Jackson, 1992b). Since materialism presupposes a 'real' world outside and prior to discourse, it will always be irreconcilable with much postmodernist thinking.

There are signs, though, that some feminists are retreating from the extreme anti-materialist implications of postmodernism, and are edging back towards accepting the existence of structural inequalities. In this context the term 'materialist feminism' has been reinvented by American theorists such as Rosemary Hennessy (1993) and Donna Landry and Gerald MacLean (1993). Both texts claim some Marxist antecedents and both are motivated by the wish to avoid the politically disabling consequences of postmodernism consequent upon the denial of any material reality outside language and discourse. Hence Hennessy argues that materialist feminism needs to retain a 'critique of social totalities like patriarchy and capitalism' (1993: xii). Neither of these texts has a very clear idea of what materialist feminism has been and is in the European context, and both see it as a form of Marxism infused with postmodernism. Hennessy comes close to defining it in this way, saying that materialist feminism 'is distinguished from socialist feminism in part because it embraces postmodern conceptions of language and subjectivity' (ibid., p. 5). Whatever its failings, if this work represents a trend towards a more materially grounded discourse analysis, it is to be welcomed.

In the meantime, older forms of materialist analysis have not disappeared, despite imputations of their irrelevance in these supposedly postmodern times. While some have taken on postmodernism directly, countering charges of essentialism and oversimplification (Jackson, 1992b; Walby, 1992), others continue to demonstrate that material factors shape women's lives in determinate ways. Materialism continues to be drawn on as a framework for empirical work and is proving relevant to a new generation of social researchers (see, for example, Van Every, 1995; Adkins, 1995). Many of those with materialist sympathies would concur with Walby that no 'grand theory' can explain women's subordination and cope with the complex differences among women. Mary Maynard (1995) has suggested that the way forward lies in developing what some sociologists have called 'middle range theories'. Such theories emphasise the specifics of given social contexts, institutions and relationships, offering grounded generalisations rather than universalistic, totalising models of entire societies and are more easily integrated with empirical research. Middle range theories would enable us to use materialist methods of analysis without constructing huge, theoretical edifices which are remote from everyday life and insufficiently flexible to account for the varying life patterns of differing groups of women. A materialist analysis is as relevant now as it ever was. While accepting that traditional Marxism had little to say about gender divisions, that one theory cannot explain the whole of human life, the method of analysis Marx left us remains useful. There are good reasons why materialist perspectives remain necessary to grapple with the complexities of a postcolonial world, with the intersections of gender, ethnicity and nationality. It seems evident that the material foundations and consequences of institutionalised racism, the heritage of centuries of slavery, colonialism and imperialism and the continued international division of labour are at least as important as culturally constituted difference. We live our lives now within a global system characterised by extremely stark material inequalities. Even within the wealthy Western nations the material oppression suffered by women has not gone away, and for many women the situation is worsening as a result of unemployment and cuts in welfare provision. Intersections between class, gender and racism are clearly important issues here, too, and need to be pursued in terms of structural patterning of inequality as well as multilayered identities. The continued vitality of approaches which deal with such inequalities is crucial for feminist politics and theory.

Notes

1. In general, where I am not referring to a specific theorist, I use the term 'patriarchy' descriptively to mean systematic male dominance, and theories of patriarchy refer to any formulation which assumes the existence of such a system.
2. For summaries of the debate from a range of perspectives see Rushton (1979), Kaluzynska (1980) and Walby (1986a).
3. One partial exception is Harrison's (1973) analysis of the 'housework mode of production'. Although his formulation attracted criticisms (see, for example, Molyneux, 1979), it was treated as a serious contribution to Marxist debate and did not provoke the outrage which greeted Delphy's

work. Unlike Delphy, he saw the housework mode as a client mode through which capitalism extracted labour from the wife of the proletarian. Hence capital, rather than the husband, was the beneficiary.

4. There is now considerable empirical evidence to support this claim (see, for example, Finch, 1983; Charles and Kerr, 1988; Brannen and Wilson, 1987).

5. Capitalism requires only that classes are reproduced: its logic does not dictate precisely how class continuity is to be ensured. A ruling class does necessarily have to reproduce itself through strict genetic inheritance. In following Engels in assuming that class gave rise to monogamy in order to ensure biological paternity, McDonough and Harrison also replicate his error of pre-supposing what needs to be explained: why men should want to pass their property to their sons rather than anyone else.

6. A similar point is made by Anne Ferguson (1989), a self-defined socialist feminist who examines reproductive, sexual and intimate relations within what she calls 'sex affective production'. In arguing that a separate system of production exists alongside capitalism, her work has something in common with that of Delphy and Walby, but because she locates this production in sexual and reproductive realms her analysis is in many respects closer to those which focus on relations of reproduction.

7. This linkage is not coincidental. Lacan's version of Freud, which gives primacy to symbolic representations of kinship relations such as the incest taboo and the law of the father, owes much to Lévi Strauss and more to the structural linguistics of Saussure which forms the basis of Lévi-Strauss's analysis. Althusser appropriated Lacan to explain how ideology constitutes subjectivity. Another analysis which draws upon Lévi Strauss and Lacan is Gayle Rubin's (1975) conceptualisation of 'sex/gender' systems. Rubin, does not, however, link this up with ideology.

8. Like many theorists of this ilk, those associated with *m/f* assume that two theories which are antithetical to each other – Lacanian psychoanalysis and Foucauldian discourse analysis – are complementary. This despite Foucault's contention that psychoanalysis is no more than a discourse, another disciplinary regime of truth.

9. For this reason most French materialists use the term 'sex' rather than 'gender'. Delphy is the exception, preferring the term 'gender' since it carries with it the sense of divisions between men and women being social in origin, whereas 'sex' is difficult to divest of its essentialist connotations (see Delphy, 1984; 1993). Fuller discussion of this and other aspects of the French materialist perspective on sex differences can be found in Adkins and Leonard (1995) and Jackson (1996).

10. Interestingly the insights of materialist feminism here have been appropriated (and torn from their materialist roots) by some influential postmodern theorists, notably Judith Butler (1990), whose radical deconstruction of gender as a 'regulatory fiction' leans heavily on Wittig's analysis. (See Jackson, 1995).

11. For a good discussion of the issues this complexity raises for feminist theory and politics, see Avtar Brah (1992).

3

Marxism and Regulation Theory

Michael Kenny

The ideas associated with the regulation 'school' have grown in influence in the last two decades and now comprise one of the most important approaches to the study of contemporary political economy. In many ways, the regulationist research paradigm has achieved recognition and a degree of legitimacy beyond the domain of neo-Marxist scholarship. In terms of the survival or demise of Marxist analyses of the political economy of contemporary capitalist states, the history and applicability of the regulationist approach is equally significant. However, its devotees claim to build upon the insights embedded within Marx's own work while avoiding some of the pitfalls into which Marxist social analysis has fallen. The viability of this critical perspective will play an important part in determining whether an analytical input into social science research can be maintained by Marxists.

Yet some serious interpretative differences divide proponents of regulationist ideas, while the extent and usefulness of their application remain contentious (Dunford, 1991). Rather than conceiving regulationists as a unified methodological 'school', the principal thinkers associated with this approach are better regarded as the producers of interwoven, overlapping lines of enquiry. Analysts who use these ideas deploy a common intellectual framework to interpret a range of phenomena. Regulationist thinking has made greatest headway amongst economists, geographers and sociologists in France, Germany and Britain, but variants of these ideas can be found in the USA (for example, in the work of theorists analysing the social structures of accumulation (Bowles et al., 1986)) and have been applied in a number of non-European contexts, for instance by Japanese economists (Peck and Miyamachi, 1994) and Latin American social scientists. This chapter offers an abbreviated account of some of the central ideas associated with regulationist theorising and assesses the principal usages to which these ideas have been put. In particular, debates surrounding the categories of Fordism and post-Fordism – which are associated with this perspective – are examined. We then point to several theoretical tensions underlying the ideas of some of the principal advocates of this approach and, finally, consider the significance of the spread of the regulationist paradigm for neo-Marxist thinking in the social sciences.

The force of regulationist thinking lies in its stress upon the 'integration of the role of political and social relations (state action and legislature, social institutions, behavioral norms and habits, political practices) . . . into the conception of capitalist reproduction and crisis' (Tickell and Peck, 1992, p. 192). This key theme was initially expressed in the French word 'régulation', a term which, as Bob Jessop suggests, is better translated into English as 'normalisation' or 'regularisation' rather than the more limited conventional sense of regulation (Jessop, 1995, p. 309). Much of the distinctiveness of regulationist analysis lies in this central claim that 'crucial features of the trajectory of the capital accumulation process, over a long time period, are the product of the supporting role played by a set of social institutions' (Kotz, 1990, p. 7). Thus the economism which has characterised some forms of classical Marxist analysis is supposedly displaced by a more contingent conception of socioeconomic change which reflects the provisional and open nature of historical processes. Simultaneously the prevailing paradigms within orthodox economics are also rejected as overly narrow in their conception of how economic behaviour occurs. Regulation theory purports to describe and explain the socially embedded and regularised nature of economic activities.

For those unfamiliar with these ideas, one of the most off-putting aspects of this approach is its devotees' use of a fairly technical economic vocabulary and occasionally unthinking dependence upon neo-Marxist categories. But to dismiss the ideas on these grounds would be a mistake. Regulationists have helped disseminate some of the key concepts of today's intellectual and political debates and, for all its flaws, this approach seeks to transcend one of the most pervasive and disabling binary divides within the contemporary social sciences – that between 'political economy' as traditionally conceived and the interpretation of cultural change and patterns of social identification.

Regulationist analysis needs to be understood therefore as one contemporary attempt to rectify the analytical boundaries institutionalised by the separation of economics from other social science disciplines which characterised the history of the social sciences from the late nineteenth century (Gamble, 1995). Like other comparable theoretical schools – for example institutional and neo-Schumpeterian economics, and some forms of governance theory – the aim is to construct an 'integral economics', in which artificial distinctions between, for instance, economic development and social institutions are supplanted. Regulationist thinking has also been deeply shaped by the turn towards the superstructural within Western socialism as the intellectual underpinnings of classical Marxism have come under powerful theoretical and political attack.

The most important notions that regulationists have helped popularise are Fordism, post-Fordism and flexibility. These have achieved a fairly wide usage in different intellectual quarters and have even figured in the discourse of politicians and political parties. But, as is often the case when popularisation occurs, these ideas have come to carry different meanings from those with which they were invested by the inner circle of regulationists. It is worth, therefore, briefly stating the central aspects of regulationist research before examining the most important categories deployed in greater depth.

This school's approach has developed against the background of what Mike Rustin terms:

> the post-war stabilization of this system [capitalism], on both economic and political levels [which] required that a new attention be given to the enhanced role of the state, to mass consumption, to processes of socialization, and to the ideological role of the information industries in the 'consumer societies'. (Rustin, 1989, p. 54)

As we shall see, regulationists have found an audience by propounding a fairly overarching account of the crises facing industrialised states in the 1970s, and offering some important insights into the social paradigm taking shape thereafter, commonly labelled 'post-Fordism'. These thinkers range across a number of domains and debates, though their central concerns remain broadly macroeconomic. Their work has been deployed to assess phenomena as diverse as contemporary social movements, political regimes and the interface between local economies and global forces, as well as more conventional economic questions.

The Origins of Regulationist Thinking

While the literature on the ideas of some of the principal advocates of this school is now bountiful, less consideration has been given to where and how regulation theory fits into the corpus of neo-Marxist thought. In part this is because French regulationists drew inspiration from different sources, including the ideas of the Annales school of historians, and in some cases the thinking of the philosopher Louis Althusser. Like many other intellectuals, the founding group of regulationist economists were, to varying degrees, uneasy with core tenets of classical Marxist economic thought, and were especially critical of the absence of an account of the extra-economic dimensions of accumulation (Aglietta, 1979). But unlike other Marxists who also rejected Althusser in the 1970s, regulationists did not resort to what Jessop labels the 'simplistic celebration of militant class instincts' or ultra-leftist piety (1995, p. 310). Significantly, they have been attacked for failing to ground their rhetoric of class struggle in their theory of how crises of capital accumulation occur (Clarke, 1986). In fact, regulationists have been concerned with the ways in which 'particular institutional or structural forms delimit the forms and intensity of class struggle for more or less extended time periods' (Jessop, 1995, p. 310). In the 1970s, several leading regulationists drew inspiration from one of the other central figures of the Western Marxist tradition, Antonio Gramsci. Their most obvious debt concerns the notion of Fordism which he used in his pioneering essay 'Americanism and Fordism' to describe the institutionalisation of a whole new way of life around the industrial paradigm being constructed in the USA in the 1920s (Gramsci, 1971a). In a more indirect sense, Gramsci has offered insight into the interpenetration of values, morals and cultural practices with socioeconomic change. Equally significant was the desire of French economists like Michel Aglietta to contest the hegemony of neo-classical accounts of the general equilibrium which supposedly resulted from unfettered, 'free' market exchanges. Aglietta, and other sympathetic economists like Alain Lipietz and Robert Boyer, became interested in the processes whereby capitalism's inherent contradictions were repeatedly vitiated and the process of accumulation was able to continue, if on a new footing.

Other commonalities bound together the group of French economists who first developed regulationist analysis. Lipietz points to a shared set of experiences that the more theoretical commentaries on this school have rarely pinpointed (1987b, p. 20). Many were 'polytechnicians', civil servants and advisers who had worked within a particular policy paradigm which was premised upon high levels of government intervention in the economy and the belief in state-orchestrated economic growth. In this sense these economists played an active part in dealing with the problems stemming from the crisis of Fordism in France. In this group Lipietz includes Robert Boyer, Michel Aglietta, Bernard Billaudot, Huges Bertrand, Jacques Mistral and himself.

Early Figures in Regulationist Research

Against the background of the destabilisation of existing patterns of economic activity, as well as the common perception that the established social order faced numerous threats, new lines of research were pursued across the social sciences in the 1970s. In 1974 Aglietta, who had written his doctoral thesis on the American economy, returned to France with a new research agenda (Aglietta, 1979). He focused less upon the causes of the contemporary crisis and more on why no rupture had occurred beforehand. In particular, he broke Marx's theory of accumulation into a shorter temporal epoch, talking of different patterns of accumulation. Aglietta's findings were supplemented by the research of a body of scholars from the French institution CEPREMAP (the Centre for Mathematical Economic Forecasting Studies Applied to Planning) who reassessed some of the central features of French economic history, pointing to the rise and decline of a succession of different regimes of accumulation – characterising these as 'ancien régime', extensive and intensive. Some of the figures involved in this collective research programme have become leading advocates for these ideas. Alain Lipietz developed an important study on inflation and economic crisis, whilst Robert Boyer and Jacques Mistral completed an analysis of the different ways of regulating what they termed 'the wage relation', and Boyer produced an extensive study of the dynamics of French capitalism and other industrialised states (Lipietz, 1987b; Boyer, 1986; Boyer and Mistral, 1982). Lipietz's recent work on the international division of labour and the debt crisis, as well as the increased focus of this school's thinkers on the international dimensions of political economy, have become highly influential and mark a change of tack in regulationist research (Lipietz, 1986b, 1987a). The core ideas of this approach have been applied to a number of non-European states and to international economic phenomena (Ruccio, 1989). This represents perhaps the most troubling and fruitful area for the future development of this paradigm, raising questions about the applicability of its prognoses beyond the industrialised West, and indeed of the possibility of a regime of accumulation organised on a transnational level (Lipietz, 1986b).

Regulationist ideas quickly found a resonance beyond France, a process that culminated in the first international conference on this paradigm, held in Barcelona in 1988. This approach has been assimilated by numerous West European intellectuals to the point where some commentators have begun to speak of nationally based regulationist schools (though this may overstate the degree of coherence shared by scholars in particular countries). In Germany, Joachim Hirsch has incorporated the regulationist analysis of Fordism into his theorisation of the changing nature of the modern state, deploying the notion of a 'Fordist security state' to explain a number of social and political developments in the 1970s and 1980s (Hirsch, 1983). More recently he has conceptualised the political configurations particular to post-Fordism in terms of the emergence of a national competition state (Hirsch, 1991). In the USA, this approach has been drawn upon by political economists working within the 'social structures of accumulation' paradigm, and has clearly influenced some leading sociologists in their account of the re-emergence of a craft mode of production in the wake of the crisis of 'mass production' in the 1970s and 1980s (Kotz, 1990; Piore and Sabel, 1984). Several British academics have derived insights from regulationist research, and have juxtaposed these ideas and other theoretical traditions such as discourse and governance theory (Hay, 1995a). Scholars beyond these Western contexts have applied and refined these ideas too, as we shall see. As these different research programmes have developed, some core regulationist ideas have been reformulated, making this approach less the preserve of a small French intellectual circle. Whether the coherence and central analytical claims of this perspective can survive these different adaptations is far from clear.

The Regime of Accumulation

Regulationist research revolves around a number of central categories founded upon some highly important and, according to critics, tendentious assumptions. The most important of these is the idea of a regime of accumulation. This provides, in essence, an alternative periodisation of the historical development of capitalism to that lodged in the classical Marxist imagination. This concept has helped regulationists present the narrative of the reproduction of capitalist social relations and accumulation drives at a lower level of abstraction than that favoured by Marx. It also makes central the role of non-economic phenomena in ensuring the possibility of capitalist reproduction. Rather than deploying the language of modes and relations of production, these theorists have focused upon the institutional mechanisms and social forms through which capitalist development has been assured and stabilised.

A regime of accumulation (RA) has generally been taken to mean the particular configuration of production and consumption relationships which prevail at the macroeconomic level within a given national economy (though not all regulationists regard the national economy as the central structural locus in this way). Robert Brenner and Mark Glick describe the RA as typically constituted in the following way:

> Each regime of accumulation represents a distinct pattern of economic evolution which, though limited in historical time, is relatively stable. The immediate source of the dynamic specific to each regime of accumulation is a particular series of regularities which include: (i) the pattern of productive organization within firms which defines the wage-earners' work with the means of production; (ii) the time horizon for decisions about capital formation; (iii) the distribution of income among wages, profits and taxes; (iv) the volume and composition of effective demand; and (v) the connection between capitalism and non-capitalist modes of production. (Brenner and Glick, 1991, p. 47)

The RA consists of both these regularities and the processes which develop historically to ensure its reproduction in the medium or long term – commonly referred to in this literature as the mode of social regulation (MSR). The MSR works by accommodating, mediating and normalising the inherent crisis tendencies of capitalist accumulation (Dunford, 1991, pp. 306–8). But the RA provides the primary unit of analysis, and commits regulationists to the view that the 'logic of accumulation' remains central to the developmental trajectory of a particular society. This concept is frequently deployed to generate an analysis of capitalism as a succession of different regimes which periodically become ascendant but are likely to fall. Regulationist thinking is in fact an extended account of socioeconomic crisis, even if the emphasis is generally upon the avoidance of social rupture and economic breakdown (Kotz, 1990; Aglietta, 1979). Two particular types of crisis recur according to the literature. The first is typically seen as a cyclical kind resulting from an imbalance in the accumulation process causing periodic economic ruptures which are 'corrected' within the existing system of institutions and norms. These are generally short-term and less serious dislocations, like the impact of the First World War on the British economy. The other kind is a structural crisis which involves a significant reduction in the rate of accumulation over a prolonged period of time. This is caused by a substantial deterioration in the relationship between the accumulation process and the institutional fabric. This kind of rupture, exemplified by the Great Depression of the 1930s, inevitably undermines the coherence and balance of the prevailing RA. Lipietz argues that a crisis indicates that 'the mode of regulation is not adequate to the regime of accumulation' because either 'the emergence of a new regime is being held back by outdated forms of regulation' or 'the potential of the regime of accumulation has been exhausted given the prevailing mode of regulation' (Lipietz, 1987a, p. 34). This theory of structural crisis is rooted in a dichotomy criticised by Alain Noel. He points to the underlying assumption amongst these analysts that periods of stable accumulation can be dissected using the analytical techniques appropriate to macroeconomic analysis, whilst in moments of crisis it is assumed that political parties and figures are granted a significant amount of autonomy (Noel, 1992).

But for regulationists, the ways in which crises unfold and the different resolutions to each still depend greatly on the kind of regime that has been predominant. Here regulationist writers have specified two particular kinds within the recent history of industrialised states.

Extensive Regimes

In delineating different accumulation regimes, the regulationist debt to Marxist categories is important. Marx's understanding of political economy revolved around his theory of how surplus value was created in the processes of commodity production under capitalism. In essence, surplus value arose from both the value of products and the value of the capital involved in the production process. The latter was constituted by what Marx termed 'constant and variable capital'. He defined surplus value as the product of the ratio between the two. In historical terms, capitalists generally resorted to two different ways of increasing the rate of surplus value they could extract from workers:

first, through an increase in what Marx termed 'absolute surplus value', by making workers work for longer hours or by expanding the size of the workforce. Both of these processes had obvious limitations in terms of productivity growth. The second method posited by Marx, therefore, involved an augmentation of 'relative' surplus value, through the more complex process of reducing the socially necessary labour time taken by the worker to produce the same quantity of use values. This generally involved improving productivity through revolutionising production methods and technological advance. This dichotomy has been carried into the analysis of capitalism offered by leading regulationists. An extensive regime came to mean one in which accumulation depends upon a relatively unchanging labour process and technological environment. 'Extensive accumulation occurs basically through extension of the workweek and expansion of the supply of wage labourers' (Kotz, 1990, p. 11). This label has been applied, for instance, to the British economy in the nineteenth century.

Intensive Regimes

This description is used to designate a regime under which the labour process is transformed and productivity increases fairly continuously (expanding increases in 'relative' surplus value in Marx's schema). In the postwar period in western Europe, the most commonly cited intensive regime in this literature – the Fordist accumulation system – depended upon the configuration of mass forms of production with new kinds of collective consumption. Fordism was sustained by some powerfully entrenched norms of social consumption, as wages increased for many social groups and domestic consumer durables were available at affordable prices. Equally the reorganisation of the labour process which was enabled by the diffusion of the new scientific techniques of Taylorism played a key role in permitting a more intensive process of accumulation to occur. The Taylorist quantification of work tasks in the factory was, in fact, merely one element of the 'rationalisation' of the work process in a number of industrial sectors in the 1920s and 1930s. According to regulationists like Aglietta, the Fordist system was first established in the USA in the prewar years and was stabilised around the productivity increases which stemmed from the new modes of manufacturing, collective bargaining arrangements hammered out between the state, capital and labour, and the social programmes adopted by different states from the 1930s onwards (Aglietta, 1979). The latter have critically raised the level of social consumption and sustained a higher level of economic output. The accumulation regime labelled 'Fordism' takes its name from the production systems installed at Henry Ford's motor car factories throughout the 1920s and 1930s.

Some regulationists have interpreted rising living standards in the conditions of the long boom of the 1950s and early 1960s in western Europe, as well as the expansion of welfare provision, as integral components of the system of accumulation which reached its apogee in these years (Lipietz, 1987a, pp. 29–46). In western Europe, they argue, macroeconomic policies which can be designated as broadly Key-nesian sustained the new Fordist compromise, whilst the military commitments developed in the Cold War era unleashed the rapid development of a host of new technologies that fed back into the rise in labour productivity (Jessop, 1995, pp. 321–4).

But the validity of using this distinction between relative and absolute surplus value to characterise different phases in the history of capitalist states has been questioned by Mark Glick and Robert Brenner. Looking carefully at the economic development of the USA, the key example in much regulationist research, they find little empirical support for the idea that a 'qualitative, once-and-for-all transformation in the balance of class forces and the nature of technical change . . . occurred at the time of the Taylor-Ford revolu-tion. . . . such an extreme and discontinuous account of the develop-ment of control over the labour process would appear impossible to sustain'. They go on to argue:

> The Regulationists appear largely to ignore the general fact that, ever since the Industrial Revolution, if not before, the capitalist labour process has been transformed and re-transformed through new techniques that have brought greater profitability to individual firms by providing greater efficiency (greater outputs for given inputs), not merely by – and often irrespective of – eliciting more intense or more protracted labour inputs. (Brenner and Glick, 1991, p. 58)

They question not only the empirical applicability of the regulationist schema, but the assumption of some who use this approach that the nature of capital accumulation can be understood without 'specifica-tion of the broader system of social-property relations in which they are embedded' (ibid., p. 111). Equally they have cast doubt on the interpretation of analysts such as Michel Aglietta that in the 1930s 'competitive wage regulation' can be said to have acted as a fetter upon intensive accumulation, thus precipitating a structural crisis (ibid., p. 114). As they put it:

> The question that needs to be asked is, on what basis can the Regulationists posit an entire, normal, initial phase of institutionally determined development – an entire epoch – in which capitalist social-property relations have been fully established, yet which operates predominantly by intensifying labour and lengthening the working day, keeps working-class wages and aggregate consumption from rising, and finds the road to mass production blocked by restricted mass consumption? (Brenner and Glick, 1991, p. 54)

Clearly the notion of a regime of accumulation is the conceptual springboard for the different kinds of claims regulationists have made about socioeconomic change. In most accounts, regimes appear as the 'partial, temporary and unstable result of embedded social practices rather than the pre-determined outcome of quasi- natural economic laws' (Jessop, 1993, p. 26). Yet the concept of an accumulation regime – a theoretical abstraction rather than an observable entity – remains, in certain respects, problematic. The general idea is that the schema of reproduction remains an abstract possibility without the requisite MSR (Lipietz, 1986a, p. 19). What is meant by a schema of reproduction is not always apparent, and the precise nature of the causal relationship between the RA and MSR is frequently obscured. Though rarely discussed in this way, one would deduce that most regulationists assume some kind of interactive causality between them (Tickell and Peck, 1995, pp. 359–63). But the status of this central theoretical relationship remains cloudy in regulationist analysis. There is, for instance, little consideration of what evidence we should accept as demonstrating that stabilisation has actually occurred in this paradigm. The designation of the regime is frequently taken for granted and some fairly loose historical periodisation accompanies its application – the question of how one defines a 'regime' of accumulation is closely related to the problems of 'dating' its rise and fall in any precise fashion. Moreover the emphasis of regulationist research on the 'structural coupling' of the regime and its accompanying mode of regulation has distracted from close examination of how the various dynamics of accumulation actually interrelate (Peck and Tickell, 1992,

p. 347). The question here is whether the stress upon coherent regimes of accumulation can properly convey the often troublesome co-evolution of different production styles, consumption norms and practices that characterise capitalist development.

The Mode of Social Regulation

The other major category central to this research programme is the mode of social regulation (MSR) which is said to accompany and, on the whole, stabilise a given accumulation regime. The MSR allows regulationists to focus attention upon 'the complex interrelations, habits, political practices, and cultural forms that allow a highly dynamic and consequently unstable, capitalist system to acquire sufficient semblance of order to function coherently at least for a certain period of time' (Harvey, 1989, p. 122).

When the 'coupling' between a system of accumulation and an MSR achieves a level of stability in terms of its reproducibility, the way is prepared for the predominance of a particular accumulation regime. The key questions here are which elements in concrete historical situations constitute this mode of social regulation (and which do not – a rather neglected feature of this research programme), how these are articulated into a relatively coherent social infrastructure, and how the coupling with the RA is best understood: as a process of mutual 'selection', as the search for a fit between prior accumulation drives and a supporting institutional structure, or as a more contingent, if not random, series of experiments conducted by human agents?

The focus of much regulation theory is on the institutional forms and practices within a given mode which guide the processes of accumulation, but also provide the 'atmosphere' within which individuals and social groups act. Thus the MSR is understood to articulate the social behaviour of individuals with the requirements of accumulation. As a number of commentators have observed, this thesis is not wholly dissimilar to the Marxist conception of the relationship between the forces and relations of production at the heart of the materialist account of human history. A key difference is that, for most regulationists, the fit between the regime and the regulatory system is complex, open-ended and potentially conflicting, even if those features of the regulatory system are likely to prevail which most abet the accumulation process. On occasions, regulationists treat this central relationship as if it were unproblematic: 'We might say that the mode of regulation constitutes the "scenery", the practical world, the superficial "map" by which individual agents orient themselves so that the conditions necessary for balanced economic reproduction and accumulation are met in full' (Lipietz, 1994, p. 339).

Here the relationship looks dangerously functionalist, with the implication that individual behaviour can be ultimately explained according to the prior demands of the processes of accumulation. But on the whole, as B. Jessop suggests, regulationists seem committed to the idea that the objects of regulation are only constituted as such as the processes of regulation occur. In other words, the relationship between accumulation and regulation is integral, not functional (1995, p. 326). This central problem – the causal relations between the RA and MSR – spills over into two other kinds of interpretative problems within this research paradigm.

Institutions and Structural Forms

As critics have noted, the rather cumbersome terminology deployed by analysts within this school is actually open to very different interpretations, raising problems in terms of its application to concrete historical situations. Some of these concepts conflate different kinds of theoretical arguments: causal claims are frequently blurred with metatheoretical exposition or macroeconomic description in this literature. This conceptual looseness is well illustrated by the ways in which the notion of 'institutions' is invoked. These are interpreted very broadly by some analysts to signify regularity in certain social practices, or sometimes a 'norm' for social interaction and relationships rather than the narrower sense that other economists might give to this term. Regulationists seek to elaborate the 'institutional complementarities . . . that sustain an accumulation regime' (Jessop, 1995, p. 319). Jessop, for instance, points to five 'institutional complexes or structural sets' which are fairly common in this literature and which are taken to make up a '(social) mode of (economic) regulation' – the wage relation, the money form, competition, the state and international regimes (Jessop, 1995, p. 319). The notion of structural forms is continually invoked by authors like Boyer to describe 'a codification of one main social relationship', the idea being that 'the same invariant and abstract relationship might have very different precise configurations . . . through time or across countries'

(Boyer, 1990, p. 21). As David Kotz observes, the absence of standardised usage here masks some important interpretative differences:

> This problem is akin to the problem of defining an industry, for the purpose of analyzing competition . . . As defined in the literature, an institution could mean any social process or event which has more than an instantaneous lifetime . . . the range of phenomena that can qualify is extremely broad. (Kotz, 1990, p. 21)

This terminological confusion matters because these terms are meant to designate the various social and cultural practices and traditions that regulationists consider central within socioeconomic reproduction. This problem relates to the ambiguity noted above about the significance to be accorded to non-economic phenomena in explaining socioeconomic change. But for some analysts one of the strengths of this set of ideas stems from the insights they offer into the relationship between the experiences and identities of individuals and groups and broader economic imperatives. This approach has been invoked as a useful way of understanding the changing patterns of collective action and social identification which appear to characterise contemporary industrialised societies. Rejecting macrosocial theories which regard new kinds of social movement as inherently cultural and oppositional in nature, Margit Mayer and Roland Roth suggest that today's urban social movements might be regarded as organically connected with and indeed precursors of wider economic and organisational developments (Mayer, 1991; Mayer and Roth, 1995). But critics remain unconvinced, for reasons that are connected with the above discussion. This kind of argument, according to George Steinmetz, conceals an underlying attachment within this paradigm to a conceptual hierarchy which privileges the regime of accumulation as the ultimate source of explanation of change, relegating other factors to an ultimately epiphenomenal role (Steinmetz, 1994). Could one, for instance, employ this theoretical apparatus to comprehend phenomena like the changing patterns of racial identification and conflict in an industrialised state? Interestingly, within this paradigm a more explicit concern with the constitution of social identities and interests has become apparent, though one might argue, as Jessop does, that even 'early regulationist work on Fordism was concerned with the manner in which workers and consumers had been transformed through struggles around new norms of production and consumption and the associated development of a new mode of societalization' (1995, p. 315).

The Breakdown of a Mode of Social Regulation

An equally important objection lodged by critics concerns the absence of clear causal explanations of when and why a particular MSR proves inadequate and how its replacement happens (Hay, 1995a). In very general terms, this question appears in all regulationist research, yet these analysts are sometimes imprecise about the causal mechanisms which produce breakdown. Quite often the creation of a new MSR is presented as an outcome of the evolution of the RA. Aglietta's reading of the emergence of a new regulatory mode in US society after 1918 is a good example of this (Aglietta, 1979). Yet, if this is so, the MSR can only relate to the RA in a functionalist, if not teleological, fashion, a view which undercuts one of the foundational claims of regulationist theory.

In part, the problem is that what critics perceive as latent functionalism is a product of the regulationist preference for macroeconomic description. This is the conceptual level favoured by nearly all researchers in this tradition and tends to provide the framework within which social and cultural change is assessed. Alain Noel has perceptively pointed out that, in the work of the more 'orthodox' economists using this approach, like Robert Boyer, some of the assumptions underpinning macroeconomic analysis clash with aspects of the regulationist approach:

> As economists, they wished to construct an approach that would be respectable in a discipline that views the construction of formal approaches as the prime scientific activity. . . However, in order to define verifiable models, they had to assume the existence of systems of econometric relations that were complete and relatively stable . . . situations that could be adequately rendered by a limited number of simultaneous equations. (Noel, 1992, p. 108; my translation from the original French)

In this sense, Noel argues, regulationists are as much 'les fils respecteux de l'économétrie' ('respectful sons of econometrics') as they are 'rebellious sons of Althusser' (Alain Lipietz's designation of them (Noel, 1992, p. 108; Lipietz, 1987b). Ultimately, Noel suggests, this kind of analysis risks reintroducing the dichotomy that many regulationists claim to have transcended – between the economic and political (Noel, 1992, p. 112). In the periods characterised (caricatured?) as epochs of stability in terms of economic growth and capital accumulation, the danger arises that, for all the stress upon the contingency and complexity of the 'institutional complementarities' that one finds in the literature, these phenomena are theoretically subservient to the imperatives of accumulation. In this sense, Jessop is right to note that the regulationists' emphasis upon the MSR acts in many cases as a heuristic device rather than a fully elaborated causal theory (Jessop, 1995, p. 318). Regulationists have yet to develop a language which expresses their supposed commitment to the view that social processes and political struggles have played an integral part in determining the nature of accumulation.

Applications of Regulationist Ideas

Fordism

Regulationist ideas have been applied to a broad range of phenomena across the social sciences. Perhaps the most influential, and in some ways controversial, contribution to intellectual life which regulationists have made concerns the conceptualisation of recent social and economic change through the categories of 'Fordism' and 'post-Fordism'. Fordism has been used to designate the regime of accumulation which, arguably, became the prevailing one in the USA and spread throughout Europe, beginning in the inter-war period and culminating in the decades after the Second World War. Getting to grips with the strengths and limitations of these notions reveals much about the efficacy of regulationist analysis, though it is important to realise that many usages of these terms stem from outside this perspective.

Returning to the ideal typical regulationist account of the Fordist regime of accumulation, it is clear that one of the most important dimensions of this analysis concerns the explanatory linkages posited by regulationists between mass production and consumption (Aglietta, 1979). Also significant is the proposed interpretation of the interconnections between the new forms of social provision, changing cultural styles (for instance, the impact of the growth of the 'mass media' as well as other newly available commodities like package holidays after 1950) and key macroeconomic developments. Commentators from this perspective have pointed to the role of expanded welfare systems in supporting the rising living standards which underpinned the increase in consumption levels (Tickell and Peck, 1995, pp. 361–3). Equally this application of 'Fordism' illustrates an important aspect of the MSR. This is the realm where the social product is divided up, where 'norms' of distribution (that is, the values that determine which social groups get how much of the total social product) are affirmed and contested. It is also the sphere where crucial national differences are established, and the specific terms of the social compromises at the heart of these Fordist regimes – between capital and labour, for instance – are determined. Thus politics and social values cannot be simply 'read off' from the prevailing regime: if so, how can we account for the very different social structures, patterns and changes which these states experienced?

But despite this commitment to understanding the 'differentia specifica' of the social structures of particular states (or 'national Fordisms' (Tickell and Peck, 1995, p. 362)), some critics wonder about the validity of applying this theory of socioeconomic development, on several grounds. First, its utility as a historical descriptor of a mass of nationally specific policy and social changes is questionable (Clarke, 1986). Whether the application of this broad macroeconomic label adds to our understanding of the history of, for example, France in the postwar period is debatable (Noel, 1987). Fordist-looking economic enterprises co-existed throughout these years with local centres of more specialised production, whilst mass consumption was always riddled with niche marketing practices and more differentiated norms. A deeper methodological question about the validity of interpreting economic behaviour through the lens of macroeconomic descriptive categories underlies this kind of example. Moreover Fordism is offered not just as a description but also as an explanation of the social and economic crises experienced by a cluster of Western industrialised states. Here too its validity is questionable according to rival historians who focus on causal processes neglected by regulationists: for instance, the role of exogenous economic factors in generating the crisis of the 1970s, and as the oil price crises and more competitive international trading environment; the apparently autonomous impact of non-economic factors upon the pattern of economic development in the 1980s; and the degree of social and institutional continuity between the 1970s and later years (Hirst and Zeitlin, 1990; Ruccio, 1989). In all these areas, the explanatory status of Fordism needs further elaboration. Questions have been posed too about the validity of applying this theory beyond these particular cases (Perrons, 1986). Analysts like Lipietz have tried to conceptualise Fordism in a way that might take account of the international division of labour and the complexity of trade and financial flows between different parts of the world, talking of 'peripheral Fordism' to characterise trends in manufacturing in a number of developing countries in the 1980s, at the moment when the industrialised world was allegedly shifting to post-Fordist types of manufacture (Lipietz, 1987a). Above all, regulationists face the problem of reconciling the ideal type of Fordism with the overwhelming amount of 'exceptional' characteristics of states to which it is applied.

It is important to realise though that the mere existence of non-Fordist economic organisations does not invalidate this analytical approach per se; as different regulationists have argued, their intepretation involves an argument about the cutting edges of economic development – the leading sectors which may become paradigmatic for other success-seeking enterprises. Whether a single 'logic' can be ascribed to the Fordist system of accumulation is doubted even by proponents of this approach (Jenson, 1989; Lipietz, 1987b). In the case of one of the most successful economies of the last decade, Japan, the application of the notion of Fordism has generated mixed results. If regulation theory is to have any explanatory value, it needs to interpret plausibly how and why the Japanese economy has moved into the top rank of nations in the last fifteen years. Yet, in the terms of this theory, Japan's combination of rigid social codes and hierarchies with traditionally 'flexible' economic sectors, which sometimes employ mass production techniques, is hard to convey in regulationist language (Peck and Miyamachi, 1994).

But the real purchase of regulationist analysis comes with its analysis of the demise of these Fordist accumulation regimes. These ideas about social change and economic crisis were developed in the shadow of the political and economic instability of the 1970s in western Europe, and became meaningful in the crisis-ridden atmosphere of the later years of that decade and the early 1980s. These apparently disparate fiscal, economic and social problems should, regulationists argued, be regarded as the symptoms of the faltering of the prevailing regime of accumulation, which could no longer be legitimated and reproduced by the mechanisms and institutions which comprised its accompanying regulatory mode. Thus the declining profitability of these years was immediately manifested in ruptures within the various regulatory institutions and cultures (Lipietz, 1987b, p. 19). The upshot of this analysis was that the crises experienced by these states were impossible for the prevailing system to resolve. Here the regulationist case looks stronger. Many intellectuals agree that the dynamics of crisis and reconstruction appear to have generated sufficient institutional and cultural changes to suggest that the prevailing social paradigm has disappeared. Yet regulationists have proved unable to agree about how best to characterise the newly emerging patterns of social organisation and economic development.

Life after Henry: Post-Fordism or the Road to Nowhere?

Fordism has thus entered the lexicon of social scientific analysis of recent economic history. Connected with the popularisation of this term has been the propensity to talk of the transition to a post-Fordist socioeconomic system, though regulationists are merely one source of the dissemination of this rather ambiguous concept and have, in fact, proved formidable critics of many contemporary usages of this notion. Post-Fordism has commonly been deployed by commentators who have little relation to regulationist thinking and has become a fairly controversial and perhaps rather abused term. It has undoubtedly offered the most important conduit for the transmission of regulationist ideas, yet, in the process of being disseminated beyond this intellectual milieu, this idea has taken on some very different connotations (Tickell and Peck, 1995). Some of these can be briefly illustrated. For a number of pundits, the idea of organising a post-Fordist economic regime in effect came to mean the adoption of a stable medium-term economic strategy in the risk-ridden conditions of the 1980s. Certain social-democratic parties for a while adopted the language of post-Fordism as a means of discussing the construction of an alternative development trajectory. And, finally, intellectuals of the left have seized upon post-Fordism as a general description of some of the social changes which have reshaped nearly all industrialised states since the 1970s. In Britain, this idea was popularised by the 'new left' intellectuals associated with the journal *Marxism Today*, which for a brief period adopted post-Fordism as a way of characterising the 'new times' into which the economy had moved (Hall and Jacques, 1990).

A common weakness dogged these appropriations of this concept. Built into many usages of post-Fordism is the assumption that what comes after the ideal type of Fordism must be its opposite (Graham, 1992). Thus post-Fordism has been characterised as the necessary shift towards smaller-scale production units, economies of scope, the spread of flexible working methods and relationships within firms, as well as the diffusion of new trust relationships between firms in areas characterised by economic success. One can find echoes of the reservations expressed above about the notion of Fordism in criticisms of these versions of post-Fordism. According to Mike Rustin, the apparent cogency and explanatory power of the model of post-Fordism conceals 'serious problems in determining its scope of application'. In particular:

> it is far from clear how much of the emerging economic system fits this new pattern of technology and organisation, and how much still operates either in old 'mass production' modes, or by still more technologically backward methods dependent on unskilled labour, such as those found in most of the (expanding) hotel and catering trades. (Rustin, 1989, p. 59)

He points to the problem of characterising the changes of the 1980s in terms of the emergence of a single new production paradigm, preferring to talk of a 'plethora of co-existing and competing systems, whose ultimate relative weight . . . is impossible to predict' (Rustin, 1989, p. 59).

In the context of regulationist research, such criticisms are telling. Adam Tickell and Jamie Peck go so far as to suggest that regulationists should not deploy this concept given the absence of any substantive demonstration that a stable and coherent new mode of regulation, which approximates to the post-Fordist model, has come into being (Tickell and Peck, 1995). Arguing that some commentators were too hasty in delineating neo-liberalism as the next paradigmatic mode of regulation, they assert that it is far from clear whether a coherent mode has come into being which satisfies the central criteria of regulationist research of being generalizable and reproducible.

Interestingly there is no consensus amongst regulationists about how best to comprehend the paradigmatic shift which industrialised societies have experienced. For theoretical reasons, some wish to 'retain a vision of the future as the product of contestation, of many possibilities and unforeseeable outcomes' (Amin, 1994, p. 19). Nor is there agreement about what political forms can best be said to characterise the newly emerging paradigm. The question of which political forms and structures are most appropriate for the newly emerging RA has been handled differently by writers in this tradition. Jessop is relatively pessimistic in his account of the ideal typical Schumpeterian workfare state arising from the 'hollowing out of the national state in an emerging context of a simultaneously internationalised and regionalised post-Fordist accumulation regime' (Jessop,

1993, p. 28). The state, he suggests, will increasingly work 'to promote . . . organisational and market innovation, in open economies' and 'to subordinate social policy to the needs of labour market flexibility and/ or the constraints of international competition' (ibid., p. 28). Others are more optimistic, connecting the development of economic diversification and localised networking with new political possibilities, involving the decentralisation of political power and new forms of social partnership (Lipietz, 1994; Mayer, 1991). In fact Jessop is one of the few avowed regulationists to specify what a distinctively post-Fordist mode of social regulation looks like. Significantly, however, he agrees with Peck and Tickell that neo-liberalism cannot be ascribed the paradigmatic regulatory mode of post-Fordism, citing its inability to sustain the stable medium-term reproduction of the economic growth spurt it initially released.

A further complication in these discussions of the emergent social paradigm after Fordism stems from the tendency to confuse arguments about post-Fordism with a related, but separate, category: flexible specialisation. While there are certain similarities between the ideal type of post-Fordist production offered by writers like Jessop and the flexible specialisation model, the latter has emerged from a rather different theoretical project (Hirst and Zeitlin, 1990). Flexible specialisation is associated with the work of American sociologists Michael Piore and Charles Sabel (Piore and Sabel, 1984). They argue that the rough equilibrium which had been sustained since the mid-nineteenth century between the two prevailing modes of production – mass and craft-based systems – broke down in the 1970s. This occurred because a number of core markets within Western capitalism were disrupted whilst rising prices and spiralling inflation combined powerfully with the development of niche consumer tastes to weaken the existent paradigm of mass production and its corollary – collective forms of consumption. This engendered a dramatic changeover from one mode of production to smaller-scale forms of manufacture which harked back to the craft cultures of pre-industrial Europe. A number of regions whose industrial prowess was based on these kinds of production methods were highlighted as exemplars of this new production paradigm, for instance the so-called 'Third Italy', Silicon Valley in California or the Baden-Würtemberg region in Germany. These industrial districts are said to possess 'organisational structures drawing on decentralised management, worker participation, polyvalence, skills and active labour-management co-operation' (Amin, 1994, p. 22; Sabel, 1989). Critics, meanwhile, point to problems affecting these and other supposedly 'post-Fordist' regions, as well as the rather idealised representation of them in these literatures. More generally, this perspective depends on two ideal-type production regimes to which few regional or sectoral economies actually correspond.

Whilst the features of flexible specialisation are often elaborated in connection with regulation theory, the relationship between the two is contingent (Hirst and Zeitlin, 1990). But the concepts of regulation and flexibility have not only entered the lexicon of social scientists at about the same time, they have become irretrievably interlinked in the minds of many. Certainly different regulationists have deployed the language of 'flexibility' – in terms of labour markets or regional economic development – in their accounts of the emerging societal paradigm after Fordism. The geographer David Harvey has synthesized these theoretical approaches, arguing that the 1980s can be characterised as a period in which a new regime of 'flexible' accumulation was organised in a number of industrialised states (Harvey, 1989; Schoenberger, 1988).

But if 'post-Fordism' remains a rather open category, currently interpreted in a plethora of different ways, 'flexibility' remains an even more problematic term. Not only is it tainted by the highly euphemistic usage to which it has been put by corporate managers seeking to 'rationalise' or 'slim down' their workforces, or by government ministers justifying the closing of uncompetitive industrial concerns, but it remains a rather woolly concept mingling very different normative and analytical connotations. Both advocates and analysts of post-Fordism and flexible specialisation have received criticism on this score. Several of these weaknesses will be reviewed below, but it is worth noting the nature of some of the principal criticisms which these thinkers have received. For some, post-Fordism smacks too much of an overly enthusiastic embrace of new technological and economic developments which may actually have rather regressive consequences such as exacerbating distinctions between a privileged 'core' labour force and a deskilled pool of casual workers. Others point to the analytical weakness of an approach which conceives of social change in such an epochal fashion, abandoning more familiar conceptual traditions organised around class or ideology, for example. As Amin observes, the critique of the regulation literature for its failure to transcend weaker analytical versions of classical Marxism has been repeated by those hostile to post-Fordism:

Critics of the post-Fordist literature . . . tend to reject the debate for its functionalist or systemic theorisation of the historical process, preferring instead an approach which stresses the non path-dependent, contextual and open nature of change in class societies . . . Reliance on sharp distinctions between phases has been criticized for falling prey, in its worst applications, to a logic of binary contrasts between say, rigid or collective 'old times' and flexible or individualistic 'new times'. (Amin, 1994, p. 3)

Problems with Regulation Theory

Stressing their Marxist heritage, David Ruccio points to the language of simple historical succession which still prevails amongst regulationist researchers, which 'means that the history of capitalist development is constructed on the basis of a notion of functional prerequisites in which the activities of agents are said to conform – either through coercion or persuasion – to the necessities of accumulation' (Ruccio, 1989, p. 37).

Amin likewise synthesises the views of different commentators when he observes that 'the regulation approach ends up ascribing to history a stylistic, functionalist and logical coherence which it rarely possesses' (Amin, 1994, p. 11). Whilst this criticism may be over-general in scope, it is true that regulationist analysis remains caught between a desire to couch capitalist development in the form of a 'universal' logic of accumulation, on the one hand, and its sense of the contradictory and uneven character of socioeconomic change on the other. This tension is most apparent in the work of those seeking to deploy this paradigm to interpret a wide range of social and cultural phenomena. Whilst some commentators are convinced that this approach has avoided the problem of economism (Elam, 1994), others see a more indirect kind lurking beneath the work of these analysts. Yet it is clear that regulationists are committed to the belief that the processes of regulation necessarily involve human subjects and subjectivities, and that these different phenomena can be understood in a more integral fashion. Regulationists, therefore, vehemently oppose the charge of functionalism. Mostly they do so through an underspecified theory of interactive causation and in other cases by developing a commitment to the discursive character of the objects of regulation. As Jessop puts it: 'it is in and through grievance (or regulation) that the elementary objects of their attention are transformed through complex articulation into specific moments within a given mode of governance (or regulation)' (Jessop, 1995, p. 326).

Unfortunately many regulationist analysts assume rather than demonstrate how the connections between individual identities and values and larger structural changes work. As we have seen, these theoretical problems are thrown into relief when regulationists try to throw light on complex patterns of social and political change. This accusation has been supplemented more recently by the suggestion that the core tenets of regulation theory are meaningful only in the context of the recent histories of a small group of industrialised nation-states (Ruccio, 1989). Here the universalist pretensions of these theoretical claims have been particularised by critics who see them as emerging from specific temporal and spatial locations. Even in terms of Western states, it is suggested, it is no longer accurate to aggregate economic behaviour to the level of the national economy, making the idea of regimes of accumulation organised at the national level largely redundant. This poses a great challenge to regulationist research: to what extent are the central categories of this school premised upon the experiences and histories of the industrialised states on which they are based? Some regulationists have always been sensitive to the international dimensions of economic change and crisis. Lipietz has been especially forthright in considering transnational linkages and the implications for developing nations of the demands generated by Western Fordism. His most recent work reveals his commitment to a new kind of global settlement, given his sense of the limitations facing regulatory powers at the nation-state level (Lipietz, 1986b; 1987a). Others, however, are less sure that extrapolating these concepts to very different locations, such as the East Asian Tigers or Japan, is the most fruitful approach (Sum, 1996).

Conclusions

The regulationist approach has proved illuminating when applied to a number of themes in contemporary political economy. In the most general sense, its devotees' commitment to understanding the nature and processes of regulation is a useful antidote to the assumptions underlying some brands of mainstream economics. Regulationists have forcefully pointed to the social and cultural conditions which make markets and 'rational' economic behaviour possible. This approach can, for instance, be used to dissect the limitations of neo-liberal political strategies which neglect the construction of a regulatory institutional framework in civil society. More positively there may be connections between these ideas and recent debates about the co-existence of different models of capitalism – Rhenish, Confucian and Anglo-American, for example. Arguments about the respective merits of each have come to the fore in intellectual and political discourse (Hutton, 1995) and might benefit from consideration of the kinds of analysis of macroeconomic variables and conditions proposed by regulationists. In this sense the regulationist paradigm has proved sensitive to some of the key trends in the political economy emerging out of the 1980s through its proponents' willingness to ignore the artificial barriers still maintained between different social scientific disciplines.

Yet some difficult questions about the explanatory power and descriptive precision of the central categories of regulationist thinking remain. Its more sophisticated proponents have undoubtedly shown themselves aware of the limitations observed here, and have set out to address them. This suggests that in certain respects this theoretical paradigm is still in its developmental stage. But it may well be that this kind of theory lends itself to some crude and misleading interpretations which serve to discredit the wider research programme. At the very least, regulationists need to devote more energy to specifying the causal claims on which their interpretations rest. Indeed this may represent a theoretical paradigm which can be enhanced by intermingling it with other approaches, for instance discourse or governance theory.

Regulation theory therefore offers one possible path down which neo-Marxist analysis may continue to move. Yet, for all the quasi-Marxist vocabulary deployed by these researchers, this paradigm appears to be developing in ways that are taking it further from the orbit of classical Marxism. Regulationists are increasingly sensitive to the complexity and contingency of social identity, for example, and have drawn from sources outside Marxism to elaborate their ideas (Jenson, 1989). In certain respects, though, the origins of this body of thought remain crucial to its development. Regulationists are committed to understanding accumulation drives as central to contemporary socioeconomic change, and have contributed significantly to the reformulation, if not the rescue, of the Marxist interpretation of capitalist development.

Acknowledgements

I am indebted to the following for their advice, criticisms and patience: Ellen Andersen, Andrew Gamble, Bob Jessop and Ngai-Ling Sum. Ian Parker helped me with sources and ideas, Neil Kenny with translation problems, and I have benefited greatly from my discussions with the first two generations of students on the Graduate Programme in Political Economy at Sheffield University.

4

Marxism and Postmodernity

GLYN DALY

In certain respects the so-called 'postmodern' condition is easy to characterise. Essentially it refers to the break-up of the Cold War landscapes and to the gradual dissolution of those globalising ideologies which underpinned them. Now what is tending to replace these ideologies is not the affirmation of some new universalistic idea but rather an increasing diversification of particularistic identities and political demands constituted around new sites of antagonism: gender, sexual, environmental, ethnic, cultural and so on. Thus, according to Lyotard, the new spirit of the age is marked by a deep suspicion of 'metanarrativity': that is to say, a suspicion of all those attempts to establish a unified language of truth to which we could refer the diversity and richness of human culture and historical potential. In paradoxical terms we might say that what current developments are tending to bring about is an end of 'endisms' – i.e. all those grand narratives proclaiming some sort of end (such as Bell's 'end of ideology' and Fukuyama's 'end of history') – and increasingly the historical and provisional character of all social order and identity.

For many writers these developments signal a deep-seated crisis of modernity and essentialist universalism. The promise of modernity – born out of the Enlightenment – was to replace God with an ultimate conception of Man and Reason. There was a basic aspiration to rational mastery over the real (the 'out there') and to establish a fully objective perspective which would correspond to the way the world actually is. In this manner, modernity sought to establish the rational foundations for the good society on the basis of a philosophical system of unbroken continuity from metaphysics to objectivity and the social order.

Postmodern thought, by contrast, may be characterised as a developing tradition which has simply given up this kind of aspiration. It has given up all those analytic (modernist) traditions which, from

61

the referent to the phenomenon to the sign, have sought to establish some kind of direct access to a pre-given objective reality; or to what Derrida calls a 'metaphysics of presence'. In the terms of Putnam (1981) and Rorty (1991), postmodern thought sees the attempt to replace God with our own God's-eye point of view – an ultimate vantage point from which to adjudicate in all matters of truth, history, human nature and so on – as a rationalist vanity which inhibits our understanding of reality.

By various twists and turns a postmodern sensibility has gradually developed which takes for granted the impossibility of penetrating to a world of objectivity beyond the 'grammar' of our cultural and historical rules of encounter; beyond the discourses which we inhabit. In simple terms, there has been a decisive shift away from objectivism – the belief that objectivity can be conceptually mastered in a universal and neutral manner – towards a fundamental emphasis on contextuality. Thus there can be no objectivity (a final picture) – in Kuhnian terms there can be no paradigm-free encounter with the world – because objects do not speak for themselves. On the contrary, the meaning of any object wholly depends upon how we encounter it in particular discursive contexts. As Derrida puts it, 'there are only contexts without any absolute centre of anchorage' (1988, p. 12). And a condition of any context is that it is always (ultimately) prone to historical transformation. Using Gramscian terminology, we are constantly involved in wars of position and interpretation in respect to any representation of reality and objectivity. In this regard, a crucial assertion of the postmodern perspective is that 'society' and the 'self' are centreless networks of historical/contextual identification which can never be finally completed or represented.

What theoretical and political consequences flow from the postmodern perspective and, in particular, how do they affect on the body of Marxist thought? The general response from Marxist writers has tended to be negative and even rejectionist in character. Writers like Geras (1987, 1988), Callinicos (1989), Eagleton (1991) and Norris (1990, 1992, 1993) see in this perspective only a reactionary threat to Marxism and, indeed, to the entire radical tradition. Their central concern is that if we give up the attempt to provide rational objective foundations on which to base political judgement then we cannot develop any project of emancipation and that we fall into randomness and relativism where 'anything goes'.[1]

For Laclau and Mouffe, on the other hand, there exists no inherent incompatibility between Marxist themes and a postmodern approach.

Indeed they argue that it is only by moving to a postmodern position that it becomes possible to reactivate the emancipatory potential of Marxism beyond the epistemic constraints of its totalising tendencies. In this regard these authors have been concerned to develop a postmodern Marxism (or, more formally a 'postmarxist' perspective) as part of a broader project of radical democracy. For this to happen, they argue that Marxism must be placed within a wider history of intellectual–political development which grows out of the Enlightenment. In other words, it should be considered as a limited emancipatory discourse rather than the totalising horizon of emancipation as such. Thus, far from postmarxism constituting any abandonment of Marxism, on the contrary it marks a reinscription of Marxist thought in a way which acknowledges both its contribution and its limitations in respect of the ongoing development of the emancipatory imagination. To this effect, Laclau and Mouffe assert that socialism is integral to, but not totalising of, an open-ended project of emancipation which will continue to develop in new and unanticipated ways.

Three points are especially worth making here. First, it is simply nonsensical to speak about a politics *of* post-modernity. If postmodern thought affirms the *lack* of an ultimate foundation – if it affirms the lack of an algorithm for determining decisions – then the political consequences of this are wholly indeterminate; in Derrida's terms, they are radically undecidable. Everything depends, therefore, on the ability of concrete social forces politically to constitute their definition(s) of reality in a historical context of possibilities. In a social formation, any 'foundation' or 'ground' is always the result of hegemonic struggle which, because it is partial and incomplete, is always vulnerable to alternative hegemonic interventions.[2] And if the processes of grounding are undecidable – if they are a historical matter of political encounter – this clearly does not rule out the possibility of developing a radical postmodern tradition. Indeed Laclau and Mouffe argue that it is absolutely crucial to move to a postmodern position in order to liberate the potential of democracy from any metaphysical attempts to establish a final closure. This is precisely what Laclau and Mouffe mean by a radical democracy: that is, a democracy which inscribes within itself, as a positive feature of its political culture, the impossibility of democracy (as an ultimate model) and is always open to the subversive possibilities of a democracy to come (Derrida, 1994).

The second point is that Marxism is not a unified body of thought which one is obliged to stand or fall with. Laclau and Mouffe (1985) demonstrate that Marxism never presented a coherent and transcendental perspective but was, from the very beginning, marked by an original ambiguity in respect of two entirely different (and contradictory) conceptions of historical development. Whereas certain texts stressed an active and creative involvement of specific classes in concrete struggle, and thus there was an emphasis on the primacy of the political, other texts tended to see politics as merely the effect of an underlying structural process: an unfolding contradiction between the forces and relations of production.[3] In this way, Laclau and Mouffe have identified an irresolvable dualism in Marx between a logic of contingency (in which there is a more open-ended conception of historical struggle) and what they call a logic of historical necessity in which the emphasis is on teleological determinism. The crucial point here is that, while these two logics certainly co-exist in Marxist texts, they cannot logically be combined; the one, ultimately, negates the other. But the tension between these two logics is also creative. In fact, the subsequent history of Marxist intellectual development may be seen in terms of the playing out of this tension in various directions. Thus with the thinkers of the Second International we see how the logic of historical necessity receives its fullest expression in terms of a very mechanistic account of the inevitable collapse of capitalism; an orthodoxy which underpinned a policy of political inaction in the face of European Fascism.

From Kautsky to Lenin, and later with Gramsci and Althusser, on the other hand, there is a progressive emphasis on the historical effectivity and constitutive nature of politics, ideology and hegemony which increasingly compromises the themes of necessity and inevitability. Thus what we tend to see in the development of Marxist thought is what Mouffe (1993) would call a gradual 'return of the political': that is a process whereby politics comes to be seen less as a secondary effect or epiphenomenon of an objective movement of history and more (especially with Gramsci) as the very terrain for constituting identity and objectivity as such. To this effect, Laclau and Mouffe have radicalised the emphasis on the constitutive nature of politics and hegemony – beyond any pre-given agency or historical task – and have affirmed that nothing can be identified outside the constitutive process itself and that all identity, order and objectivity must be considered as fully discursive: that is, as phenomena which are wholly the result of articulatory and political (power) practices and which are ultimately prone to other articulatory practices. In short, everything depends upon the political attempts to establish some kind of discursive context with which to make sense of the world.

So there is a sense in which Marxism was always already 'post-modern'. Indeed Marx may be considered to be also the first postmarxist precisely because he begins to postulate (albeit in a limited way) a secularisation of, and constitutive role for, politics and the logic of contingency, as with the notion that history is made and depends upon forms of political struggle, against which the more deterministic themes cannot be sustained. Thus Marxism cannot be counterposed to postmodern thought in any absolutist sense. On the contrary, the tensions between the modern and the postmodern are played out *within* the body of Marxist thought in such a way that we see a progressive undermining of its metaphysical and aprioristic categories/themes.

The third point concerns the role of metanarratives and the possibility of developing universalistic discourses of emancipation – like Marxism – within a postmodernist perspective. According to Laclau, it is not a question of abandoning the metanarrative but of critiquing its ontological (or essentialist) status (1988, p. 23). To replace the metanarrative with an unqualified conception of atomised narratives would simply be an inversion on the same terrain of necessity: either we have a necessary unity or a necessary dissolution-ism (that is, a new 'endism' with no scope for universalistic forms of activity). In this sense both universalism and particularism are equally essentialist.

What Laclau and Mouffe demonstrate is that it is possible to cut through this exclusivist alternative and to construct a 'metanarrativity' (or universalist-type politics) which is perfectly compatible with a postmodern perspective provided it is based upon political argumenta-tion rather than epistemic foundation. Indeed their conception of radical democracy, as based upon the continual amplification of the Enlightenment values of freedom and equality without final comple-tion, precisely constitutes a metanarrativity which is postmodern in character.

Two consequences flow from this. First, that any universalistic project is always going to be historically bound as some sort of context – it is always ultimately 'provincial' in character – and therefore can always be challenged by alternative projects. To put it paradoxically, the very impossibility of universalism is the condition of possibility for a politics of universalism in which different conceptions compete with each other. Second, and relatedly, any universalist project, including that of radical democracy, is always going to be a hegemonic or power construction which actively seeks to exclude or repress its alternatives.

It is in this sense that Laclau and Mouffe have argued that power and antagonism cannot be eliminated and that, in consequence, we are permanently in exile from any utopian stasis. But there is nothing negative or regrettable about this. While their position is certainly anti-utopian it is not dystopian. Power and antagonism have an essentially constitutive role to play. Thus the very possibility of democracy or tolerance is one which actively depends upon repressing or excluding what is anti-democratic and intolerable (in a historical context). And precisely because of its power/hegemonic character there is always the possibility of a future, more progressive, transformation.

With these three points in mind, the themes of postmodern thought and those of Marxism may be articulated together. There are two main elements in this articulation. The first is that while Laclau and Mouffe fully endorse an anti-foundationalist perspective, they also combine this with an insistence on the ineradicable nature of power and antagonism (something which is far more present in the Marxist tradition and, in particular, the Gramscian notion of hegemony). The second is that while the postmodern perspective does not have any necessary political consequences, Laclau and Mouffe demonstrate how it provides the opportunity (but no more than that) to develop a much richer and deeper approach to democracy than Marxism or, indeed, liberalism. And, in this respect, the concern has been to reinscribe socialist discourse within an ongoing project of emancipation.

The following discussion will examine the development of postmodern tendencies within Marxist thought. It will then move to a consideration of Laclau and Mouffe's conception of the discursive nature of reality. Finally it will address the historicisation of Marxism within what Laclau and Mouffe have called the 'democratic revolution' (1985, p. 152).

Deconstruction within Marxism: from Economism to Hegemony

The logic of deconstruction[4] unfolds in Marxism as a progressive movement away from objectivism and aprioristic categories such as 'class' and 'economic base'. That is to say, we see an increasing emphasis placed upon the contingent and constitutive effects of political and hegemonic practices and a steady downgrading of the mechanistic themes of causality and teleological determinism. And it is in this respect that we see a playing out of the tensions between modernist and postmodernist tendencies in Marxist thought.

As one of the (modernist) traditions which grows out of the Enlightenment, classical Marxism believed it had attained intellectual mastery over the real through an analysis of what it saw as the logical and objective mechanisms of the economic space. Thus the economy could be analysed as a fully autonomous (extradiscursive) realm in which universal developmental laws could be identified. In this way, Marxism aspired to be an objective science which had discovered the very anatomy of history and social reality. Or, as Rudolf Hilferding put it, 'History' itself could be considered 'that best of all Marxists' (1940).

The modernity of Marxism, therefore, was rooted in economism. But this was by no means restricted to Marxism. In a similar vein, liberalism – which also grows out of the Enlightenment – stressed the objective and autonomous character of the economic space and likewise attempted to ground its emancipatory discourse on its laws and mechanisms.

In both cases, then, emancipation was seen to fully depend upon a specific economic milieu: liberalism – the consumer/possessive individual in the free market; Marxism – the producer/worker within the socialisation of the means of production. Both liberalism and Marxism, therefore, may be regarded as versions of economistic modernities where perhaps the overarching paradigm is characteristically Newtonian (that it is possible to discover objective principles of cause and effect). Thus the critique of economism must be extended to both classical Marxism and classical liberalism.

In the classical Marxism of the Second International there exists two main forms of economism which have been variously combined: epiphenomenalism and class reductionism. The former presents the superstructures as playing no active part in the historical process and simply reflecting the economic base. For this reason, the Second International saw little or no scope for political or ideological activity of any kind: everything depended on the objective movement of the economy. This led to the situation where, in inter-war Germany, socialists tended to abandon the ideological terrain, regarding the themes of liberal democracy as simply 'bourgeois', and thereby gave free rein to Fascism. Now while this crude epiphenomenalism has been generally abandoned, it is also clear that the sophisticated versions of Marxist analysis do not escape the basic problem of epiphenomenalism. Thus while in Althusser and Poulantzas there is a conception of the 'relative autonomy of the state' this is immediately contradicted by an insistence on the determination in the last instance by the economy: whether we are talking about the first or the last instance does not matter, there is a basic division in which the economic can be identified in an independent manner as having an ultimately causal role.[5]

Class reductionism, on the other hand, presented a conception of social and political identity purely in terms of the position occupied in the relations of production. There were two main aspects to this. First, workers were seen to have an objective interest in socialism which would form the basis of their solidarity – the inexorable movement of the class in itself to the class for itself. Second, all political struggle under capitalism would eventually be resolved into a fundamental antagonism between workers and capitalists.

Both types of economism have been subjected to what might be called a postmodern thaw in which the emphasis has increasingly shifted from aprioristic determinism to the contextual and pragmatic issues of actual political engagement. Thus, for example, Kautsky was to observe that towards the end of the nineteenth century the working class was not only becoming less homogenous, it also revealed a far greater predisposition towards social democracy and trade unionism which were quite compatible with (even supportive of) the continuing existence of capitalism. For these reasons – and despite all his economistic leanings – Kautsky began to affirm a crucial mediating role for socialist intellectuals in order actively to stimulate a revolutionary class consciousness (rather than simply await its emergence). These tentative movements towards a political pragmatism – that is, a process whereby the logic of the contingent increasingly supplements, or 'fills in' for, the failure of the logic of determinism and automaticity – are, of course, considerably widened with Lenin, the vanguardist party which would be responsible not only for establishing broader class alliances (that is, peasants and workers) but also for developing a revolutionary strategy which abandoned teleological stageism in favour of a developmental socialism: a socialism which would bring about the modernisation and technological advances which were being denied by capitalist imperialism.

However in each of these cases there is only a partial move away from economism. In Kautsky the role of intellectual is restricted to explaining the objective (preconstituted) character of class identity, while in Lenin the possibility of political or vanguardist activity can only take place under the determinate conditions of economic crisis (see Laclau and Mouffe, 1985).

It is not until Gramsci that the economy itself is submitted to contextual forms of analysis which reveal its articulatory (discursive) nature. Indeed in Gramsci there is a complete recasting of Marxist economic categories which effectively deconstructs their aprioristic and objectivist status. The most important advance here is Gramsci's affirmation of the material character of hegemony and ideology. Thus ideology is no longer seen as a secondary effect, as something which expresses something which is already there (at the level of the economic base), but instead becomes the 'organic cement' for constituting an entire complex of political and cultural practices with economic and institutional arrangements in a 'historical bloc'. This is crucial because if the economy cannot be identified independently of the superstructures which it is supposed to effect then it loses its causal–objectivist status. Thus in Gramsci's notion of historical bloc the classical distinction between base and superstructure is dissolved. The economy is not separated from politics, ideology or culture but is articulated with these phenomena in a characteristically relational (and therefore non-causal) manner. In Gramsci, then, there is a decisive move away from a transcendental conception of 'mode of production' to a context-based (and we would say postmodern) conception of historical bloc in which the very dimensioning and functioning of the economic space must also be considered as part of an entire historical construction.

The consequences of this argument can hardly be exaggerated. If we cling to the notion of a universal mode of production, as the underlying reality of all capitalist social formations, it becomes impossible to distinguish between different types of capitalism (for example liberal democracy and Fascism). Following on from the *Communist Manifesto*, capitalism would be regarded as a simple model which would be universally reproduced. But if we take up the Gramscian argument of the contextual character of capitalist construction then nothing automatically follows from the productive mode and we cannot predict whether it will be articulated as a liberal, social democratic or fascist construction. In other words, a radical undecidability has been introduced whose resolution will depend upon the outcome of concrete forces in political struggle. And this will have crucial consequences for the construction of the economic space and the types of practices carried out.[6]

Thus there exists no increasing conformity to a pre-given model of capitalism, but rather unstable forms of politically contested and subvertible historical blocs. It is in this sense that Laclau states: 'There is therefore no "capitalism", but rather different forms of capitalist relations which form part of highly diverse structural complexes' (1990, p. 26). And if the economy does not stand outside history – if it is submitted to the contingent logics of contextual construction – then it must also be regarded as a fundamentally discursive construction.[7]

Gramsci carries out a similar deconstructive operation in respect of the category of 'class' such that nothing automatically follows from the position occupied at the level of productive relations. Class identity is not given in advance (thereby negating any notion of 'false consciousness') and there is no guarantee that workers will eventually grow into revolutionary socialists. In fact Gramsci's experience in Italy was quite the opposite: an extensive fascist mobilisation of the popular classes. For Gramsci, the particular orientation of a class wholly depends upon the forms of 'political, intellectual and moral leadership': in short, hegemonic constitution. Again the concept of class is stripped of its transcendental aprioristic status and is placed back in history as a formation which can only take shape through contextual hegemonic practices. Indeed Gramsci is concerned to drop the notion of class in favour of what he calls 'collective wills' in which a complexity of historical ideological elements (with no natural or pre-given class belonging) are involved in their hegemonic constitution.

Nevertheless, despite the ground-breaking advances of Gramsci in developing a context-based approach, there remains in his thought a residual economism (Laclau and Mouffe, 1985, p. 69). Thus even though Gramsci presents a thoroughly relational/articulatory view of class identity he assumes that it is *only* fundamental classes which are capable of hegemonic practice. In other words, classes – because they are classes – are bestowed a privileged and predetermined role as the exclusive agents of hegemony. Once again, politics is seen to have a transcendental source, the relations of production, which fixes the identity of the players in advance and (economistically) determines that hegemonic struggle is always going to be a zero-sum game between the main classes (ibid.).

Laclau and Mouffe are concerned to break definitively with this last residue of economistic orthodoxy. They argue that it is simply impossible to predetermine the identity of a political actor independently of the processes of hegemonic constitution themselves. There is not therefore an identity on the one hand, which can be identified in a universalist and objective manner, which subsequently engages in hegemonic activity. Rather the distinction identity/hegemony is dissolved and, radicalising the Gramscian argument, hegemony itself becomes the very terrain for constituting identity as such: 'The logic of hegemony, as a logic of articulation and contingency, has come to determine the very identity of the hegemonic subjects' (ibid, p. 85).

Two consequences flow from this. First, political/hegemonic activity does not possess an ultimate source of determination – the sphere of production – but is, in principle, extended to all aspects of human engagement. Second, it is impossible to predict who the political actors are going to be independently of a historical context of hegemonic practices. Thus in certain instances it may very well be that ecological, feminist or gay/lesbian liberation movements constitute the most radical forms of hegemonic struggle against an existing set of power structures. The particular orientation of the workers, then, will wholly depend upon the articulatory forms of identification which are established with such movements and their struggles. In this respect, we could summarise the Laclau–Mouffe perspective by saying that there is no such thing as identity, only hegemonic (and therefore incomplete and vulnerable) forms of identification which never reach a point of ultimate closure or completion. In this respect, class loses its aprioristic status as providing an objective basis for unification or revolutionary transformation and we are fully in the realm of historical and hegemonic possibility: a discursive realm.

Let us conclude this section. The tensions between the modern and the postmodern are played out within Marxism insofar as there is a steady movement away from the transcendental to the contextual. In particular, we see how the crisis of economic determinism led to an increasing emphasis on hegemony as a logic of contingency and articulation. Thus what begins in Marx as an irresolvable dualism – between necessity and contingency (with the latter increasingly supplanting the former) – matures in Gramsci with a perspective in which economic categories themselves are submitted to contextual analysis and are seen to make sense only, in relational terms, as part of a characteristic ensemble of institutional and ideological practices. Radicalising the arguments of Gramsci, Laclau and Mouffe deconstructs the apriori status of all economic categories (including class) – that is, place them back in history – and demonstrate that hegemony itself is the terrain for the (undecidable) constitution of all identity and, indeed, all order.

By fully developing the logic of deconstruction, Laclau and Mouffe affirm that there are no hard-edged immutable truths or objectivities at the level of the economy or anywhere else. Nothing can be identified, in a positivistic way, independently of all context or systems of belief and, in consequence, there can be no 'extradiscursive'. In short, everything depends, finally, upon wars of interpretation; everything depends upon discourse and the political possibilities of subversion by other discourses.

Discourse and Politics

There are two central and related assertions in the perspective of Laclau and Mouffe: (i) that 'every object is constituted as an object of discourse' (1985, p. 107); and (ii) that 'antagonism is the limit of all objectivity' (ibid., p. 125; Laclau, 1990, p. 17). We will examine each of these.

The insistence on the discursive nature of reality and objectivity often meets with the 'commonsense' objection that there is a physically existing world which imposes real limitations on what we can do independently of any discourse. However discourse theory does not deny the existence of a physical world – it is fully realist in this sense – indeed it takes it for granted. What discourse theory argues, however, is that we can only have access to that world through historical discourses. As Rorty argues, the world is certainly out there but the truth about the world is not (1989, p. 5). Thus the world does not manifest a pre-existing set of truths which simply need to be discovered. On the contrary, the world can only be described within certain contexts of historical encounter. There exists no 'skyhook' which could lift us out of all history and context and allow us to describe the world, once and for all, as it actually is. In contrast to the idealism of modernity (in both its liberal and Marxist variants), there exists no possibility of absolute intellectual mastery over the real world which would finally settle all wars of interpretation.

Discourse theory, therefore, simply accepts (in materialist fashion) that there is always going to be a gap between the world of objects and the way we interpret that world – a gap through which the ontological possibility of politics emerges. No discourse can establish an absolute closure, or totally eliminate the gap, otherwise there would be a perfect overlap between object and discourse: that is, a final description, or transparent objectivity, which would make redundant the notion of discourse.

This does not mean that everything is in a constant state of flux. What it means is that, in principle, every object is ultimately vulnerable to alternative forms of articulation. To this effect, no transcendental appeal to the 'inherent properties' of an object can be made independently of discursive context.[8]

Thus while we are constantly bumping into the real world, like Dr Johnson kicking a stone this world always has to be interpreted, and it cannot be interpreted beyond interpretative paradigms themselves. The same also applies to the idea of physical limits: that is, something which is seen to resist all manner of 'discoursing'. The point is that the very idea of a limit is always going to be a matter of historical encounter. A limit can only be a limit *in relation* to some kind of endeavour. A mountain, for example, represents a different kind of limit in the age of air travel than it did previously (in the age of Star Trek it will be different again). Just as the limits encountered by nineteenth century science have been transcended or redefined in the twentieth century the same provisionality must also apply to our current understanding of physical limits against the possibility of future paradigmatic shifts.

Against this perspective Norris insists that we must ultimately have something hard-edged, something which stands outside the wheeling and dealing of 'postmodern sophisticates' and against which we can measure the validity of what we do and to which we can hold our understanding of reality accountable. For Norris, this 'extra-discursive' comes in the shape of 'factual truths' and 'determinate standards' (1992, p. 110).

Now the question which immediately arises is which 'determinate standards' are these and how could they be formulated? Again a standard can only be invoked in relation to a set of cultural and historical practices which make sense of that standard and the way it should be applied.[9] But, in that case, a standard is never totally determinate but amounts to something more like an 'institutional norm', which is to agree with Foucault that knowledge (and facts) cannot be separated from questions of social power.

But more generally we could ask how would it be possible to have a fact independently of any discourse or system of belief? Before any kind of fact gathering can take place we are already faced with the prior question of 'What do you want to know?' And the answer to this question can only be given within the context of a system of belief which will privilege certain types of fact gathering over others. An anti-semite, for example, might think it important to gather the facts about the number of Jews participating in the financial sector; that is, he already 'knows' something about the world: Jews are not 'us' and they are conspirators. A feminist, on the other hand, will want to examine the facts concerning gender discrimination, and so on and so forth.

Facts cannot be separated from systems of belief. On the contrary, they are what make fact gathering possible in the first place. Nor is this simply restricted to the 'fuzzy' issues of ethics or social science. Kuhn, (1970) for example, has shown how all scientific endeavour, as a condition of its possibility, takes place within a certain discursive formation or what he calls a 'paradigm'. Such paradigms (involving all kinds of social, cultural and normative assumptions) will determine the priorities of scientific enterprise, the allocation of funds and resources, and so on. And here again, just as in Gramsci's notion of hegemony, we should emphasise the material character of discourse in which the very configuration of institutions and their practices and objectives take place. And in this sense there is nothing 'playful' about discourses; they involve the very process of ordering in which global strategies, affecting the lives of millions, are formulated and implemented.

A second point, implicit in Norris, is the question of whether facts 'speak for themselves'. If we take the fact concerning the age of the Earth through carbon dating and the analysis of dinosaur fossils then this clearly demonstrates that there was life before Adam and Eve and contradicts the account in the Bible according to which the universe was created only 5000 years ago. However Christian fundamentalists will happily agree with all these facts, but they argue that all this 'evidence' has already been put in place by God in order to test our faith (which, if one believes in an all-powerful being, could be a distinct possibility). Thus, far from having a transforming effect, the mere repetition of the fact of the Earth's age actually begins to function in favour of their belief (for example, 'Are we up to the test which God has presented to us?').

Similarly when unemployment figures reach a certain threshold does this indicate the imminent collapse of capitalism, the immorality of inflation control, or is it seen as a regrettable but necessary sacrifice in the long-term optimisation of the economy? None of these perspectives can be derived from the facts alone. Facts do not speak for themselves but always have to be given a significatory value.

Now the familiar objection is made that if there is no factual objectivity – if everything is constituted as an object of discourse – then this can only lead to a relativist irrationalism in which objects can be constructed in as many ways as there are conceivable discourses: 'If there can be no meta-language to measure the "fit" between my language and the object, what is to stop me from constructing the object any way I want?' (Eagleton, 1991, p. 205). The answer to this question is that, *in principle*, nothing stops a person from constructing an object the way they want to except, of course, other people constructing the object in a different manner. Thus what prevents arbitrary whim and caprice is not a cosmic (paradigm-free) metalanguage but rather the human structures of power and repression which identify the nature of objectivity in a historical way. In other words, objectivity is always going to be a political power construction which actively excludes other alternatives. This is precisely what Laclau and Mouffe mean when they argue that antagonism is the limit of objectivity. Once again, it is a question of wars of interpretation in which the (provisional) outcome will depend upon the capacity of certain types of interpretation to constitute objectivity hegemonically through the repression of alternatives.

In this regard, Laclau and Mouffe show how objectivity must be carved out as a historical field of intelligibility through logics of exclusion and antagonism which in providing the sense of 'limits', are constitutive and affirming of that objectivity: a 'not that' in order for a 'this'. This argument is crucial in turning foundationalism on its head: objectivity cannot be identified positivistically (as an 'extra-discursive') but is shown to grow out of negativity and antagonism as its anti-foundationalist 'foundations'.

It is on this basis that Laclau and Mouffe advance their central theory of 'the political' as that which enables the constitution of objectivity (as a hegemonic construction) and at the same time prevents objectivity from achieving a final closure – from becoming a paradigm-less objectivity. And in this respect the political does not have a particular location, nor can it be reduced to an epiphenomenon: 'The political is not an internal moment of the social but, on the contrary, that which shows the impossibility of establishing the social as an objective order' (Laclau, 1990, p. 160).

A fully integrated society is therefore impossible precisely because it is founded on acts of exclusion – a 'them' in order for a 'we' – which always present the possibility of antagonistic eruption within, and political challenge to, a social order. Moreover it is at the point of such challenge and antagonism that the undecidable and subvertible character of all objectivity and identity is revealed (Laclau and Mouffe, 1985, p. 127). Thus, for example, it is at the point of feminist challenge that the traditional discourses on 'womanhood' are revealed as artificial power constructs.[10] So the question of objectivity and identity – its failure and undecidable recomposition – is always going to be a political matter in which present certainties are essentially vulnerable to future subversion.

In an interesting Marxist engagement with the Laclau–Mouffe perspective, Jessop (1990) has taken up many of the insights of discourse theory in an attempt to develop an anti-essentialist 'strategic relational' approach to the study of the state. However Jessop maintains that there are intractable problems of a substantive and metatheoretical character which can only 'be resolved by articulating discourse analysis with realist accounts of extra-discursive mechanisms' (ibid., p. 302). Jessop quite rightly points out that discourse theory has tended to be negligent in its consideration of concrete institutional arrangements (but see Daly, 1993, Torfing, 1996). However we will argue that it is not consequently legitimate to assume, as Jessop does, that: (i) there is an inherent problem which, in principle, prevents concrete analyses; and, much less, (ii) that it is a problem which can in any way be solved by reintroducing a vague and mystical notion of the extradiscursive. In what follows we will examine the metatheoretical objections of Jessop and insist that institutions (like any other form of identity) must be considered as fully discursive phenomena.

Against a discursive perspective, Jessop argues that:

> a strategic–relational approach would distinguish two levels of ontological analysis: 'ontology in general' and 'particular ontologies'. The first involves a transcendental, philosophical enquiry into what the real world must be like in order for knowledge to be possible (cf. Bhaskar, 1989). The second comprises various ontologies consistent with a defensible ontology in general. (1990, p. 295)

However, this amounts to little more than a restatement of the classical objectivist perspective: that behind all historico-discursive interpretations there is the possibility of what Rorty calls a skyhook view of the world (the way things really are). And as Jessop does not specify what the 'ontology in general' actually comprises, or provide any examples, this can only appear as a dogmatic assertion. But let us examine the statement more closely. If there is a multiplicity of 'various ontologies' then where is the point where such a multiplicity could be resolved into a unicity or a general ontology about the nature of the real world? Which claims to a general ontology would we accept? Even to speak of a general ontology (beyond the abstract) means that we have to place it within some conceptual scheme which makes sense of its claims – and then we are right back to Kuhn's paradigms and discursive contexts.

Jessop's second main criticism concerns what he calls a 'chain of action' in which he argues that 'the meaning of an action can usefully be distinguished from its experiential aspect'. In terms of any action then, Jessop argues that:

> we can say that its 'meaning' depends on how an actor constructs its significance from among available meanings (which, as discourse analysts often note, are typically 'in surplus') in terms of her own hermeneutic system. Conversely 'experience' involves a reflexive relation to the impact of the natural and social world beyond and outside the meaning system of the agents in question. Accordingly meaning and experience comprise two distinct moments of the same chain of action and recursively condition each other. (Jessop, 1990, p. 299)

The first point is that if meaning and experience are in a relation of recursivity then they cannot be separated; in which case the claim that experience is possible beyond and outside meaning is an incoherent one. But what exactly would an experience beyond a meaning system be? How would the experience be experienced? An experience must be given some kind of significatory value if it is to be intelligible. Even to call an experience 'meaningless' – for example in trying to explain away a sexual experience – is to affix to it a significatory value within a discursive context.

When we move to the level of the concrete analysis of institutions exactly the same argument applies. That is to say, institutions cannot be identified outside history or all discursive context. The institution of the monarchy provides a good example. If the monarchy belonged to the 'extradiscursive' – if it possessed a transcendental identity which was not prone to any articulatory logic – then presumably we would still believe that it embodied the divine authority of God. However it is clear that the monarchy has been massively reconfigured in respect of a whole range of political, social and cultural developments. And this reconfiguration can only be understood by placing the monarchy within the realm of historico-articulatory practices; within the realm of discourse.

All institutions, in this respect, must be regarded as fully discursive phenomena (with no extradiscursive, or metaphysical, bits to them). Thus whether we are talking about Parliament or the oracle of Ancient

Greece we can only make sense of these institutions – their authority, function, rituals, architecture and so on – in terms of the historical discourses in which they were constituted. In this way, the affirmation of the discursive character of such phenomena returns the Gramscian insight that institutions can always be subverted and reconfigured, beyond their original intention, through hegemonic practices.

Postmodernity and the Democratic Revolution: Putting Marxism Back into History

Another central criticism by Jessop is that, in focusing on discursive articulation, Laclau and Mouffe 'ignore the various unintended, unanticipated aspects of the social order' (Jessop, 1990, p. 298). Now this would be a valid criticism of all those attempts which try to establish an ultimate closure for objectivity and meaning and thereby prevent further modification. But it has no purchase on the Laclau–Mouffe perspective which argues precisely the opposite: that there is no possibility of any identity or objectivity establishing a final closure and that, in consequence, there is always the possibility (indeed an essential possibility) of contingent political disruption and subversion. This point is absolutely crucial for an understanding of postmarxism. It is precisely because there is no ultimate mastery over the real, and because we are always within the horizon of discursive instability and contextual vulnerability, that we can intelligibly formulate a conception of the contingent effects of the unintended and the unanticipated. By contrast, if we cling to the idea of an extradiscursive – something which is transcendentally stable – then the latter becomes strictly unthinkable.

It is on these grounds, moreover, that it becomes possible to see Marxism as a limited political project in the history of emancipatory discourses which continues to unfold in unintended and unanticipated ways. Thus, by putting Marxism back into history, socialist demands may be construed as integral to the ongoing development of a postmodern emancipatory project.

In this respect, Laclau and Mouffe identify Marxism as just one paradigmatic development (albeit a fundamental one) within a much broader set of historical movements, stemming from the Enlightenment, which they refer to as the 'democratic revolution'. This democratic revolution may be understood in terms of a symbolic chronology of major conjunctural shifts (1789, 1848 and 1968) in which the discourse of emancipation has been progressively enlarged to include more and more aspects of social relations. Thus what crucially develops in the French Revolution is the radical secularisation of the principle of equality: the assertion of equality before the law (instead of the restrictive pre-modern conception of equality before God which justified, and stabilised, all kinds of earthly inequalities) as a new institutional norm around which to constitute hegemonically the social order. With the popular mobilisations in Europe, and the publication of the Communist Manifesto, on the other hand, there is a further extension of the principle of equality to the realm of the economy in which the demands for workers' rights are increasingly taken up. And in the present conjuncture, which may be symbolically associated with all the political mobilisations around 1968 (civil rights, feminism, peace, ecology, gay/lesbian movements and so on), we have seen how the demands for equality and emancipation have been taken up in more and more areas of social and cultural life.[11]

This, of course, does not mean that everything since the Enlightenment has been uniformly democratic or that there is a new teleological process of historical transformation. Quite the opposite. What it reveals is an ongoing process of dislocation in which more and more antagonisms, points of challenge and resistant identities have been generated precisely through a widening of the discourses of emancipation and equality. In other words, it chimes with de Tocqueville's intuition that the democratic 'revolution' is not simply a moment but develops as an ongoing logic of dislocation in which the experience of equality in certain areas (such as the law) leads to wider egalitarian demands in other areas. In this sense we can say that there has been a heightening of the moment of the political which has a tendency to disrupt the constitution of the social as a stable order. And thus modernity unleashes precisely the force it cannot control: a widening democratic/emancipatory imagination which constantly exceeds all those attempts to impose a metaphysical closure, such as the reduction of democracy to a question of how we produce (classical Marxism) or how we consume (classical liberalism). A postmodern radical tradition, therefore, grows out of modernity as an ongoing process of hybridisation in taking up the themes of equality and liberty in an indeterminate number of ways.

Thus Marxism is not separate from the dislocatory developments of the democratic imagination but is, in fact, internal to it. To this effect, it becomes possible to combine (hegemonically) Marxist discourse with a set of other emancipatory discourses – feminism, ecologism, anti-racism and so on – which do not naturally or spontaneously converge. So Marxism must be de-divinised, lest it too becomes an opiate hindering critical enquiry and a wider radical politics, and regarded historically with all the limitations that would be inevitable in the labour of two men living in the Victorian age.

A postmodern and universal radical tradition, which includes within it a socialist dimension, is perfectly feasible provided (i) there are no privileged historical identities which can be pre-specified outside the process of a radical hegemonic constitution; and (ii) there is no pre-given emancipatory task which would establish a final epoch. The universalism, or 'metanarrative', of radical democracy – freedom and equality for all – cannot be grounded in philosophy (as a final determination) but only through the processes of hegemony and political argumentation. This means, again following the Gramscian insight, that power and antagonisms can never be eliminated and there will always be the possibility of new forms of challenge and political protest. No universalism, therefore, is ever going to be completely integrationist (in the sense that it simply includes everybody, or tolerates everything). Rather it will always be a power construction which establishes exclusivist (historical) frontiers between its 'we' and its 'them'. And if it is a power construction, the contents of the 'we' can always be modified by new resistant identities, taking up the principles of liberty and equality, in unanticipated and unintended ways. Paradoxically, it is the recognition of the impossibility of democracy, as such, which becomes the first principle of the democratic encounter. It is an encounter which, on the basis of hegemonic practices, keeps alive the promise of a democracy to come.

But here perhaps the analysis of democracy has been too one-sided. That is to say, in focusing on democracy as a logic of subversion the analysis of the concrete institutional forms which would embody the principles of a radical and plural democracy has tended to remain underdeveloped. As Laclau and Mouffe point out, while the liberal institutions and mechanisms of democratic representation – separation of powers, elections, universal law and so on – are certainly important, they are also limited and even constraining of democratic advance. Moreover liberal democracies have historically evolved with nation-states whose traditional 'constituencies' have been national and regional; an institutional arrangement which in an era of increasingly diverse (and mobile) political identities is less and less appropriate. Such problems are further compounded when we look at the major reconfigurations taking place between the local, national and international levels of political interaction.

In this respect, Laclau and Mouffe (1985, p. 185) affirm the need for an increasing multiplication of the spaces of democratic representation/empowerment which respond to the widening diversity. And here the various debates around decentralisation and 'associative democracy' (see Hirst, 1994) can make a positive contribution to establishing those institutional forms which would be capable of sustaining a radical democratic culture which would be both flexible and responsive to new democratic demands and political dissent.

Conclusion

In this chapter we have seen how postmodern tendencies have emerged within Marxism in terms of a progressive movement away from economism and objectivism towards a greater emphasis on context, politics and hegemony. By fully engaging with these tendencies, Laclau and Mouffe have demonstrated the possibility of developing the democratic imagination beyond the epistemic and metaphysical constraints of Marxist theory.

Nevertheless it is also important to underline the fundamental contribution which Marxism makes to the continuing development of postmodern thought. In particular – and especially with Gramsci – there is a compelling insistence on the ineradicable nature of power. Indeed, if Derrida shows that there are only contexts, Laclau and Mouffe, drawing on the Marxist tradition, may be said to provide a crucial theory of the politics of the context. Thus contextualisation, as an act of delimitation, is always a hegemonic/power process of excluding alternatives. Objectivity and society, therefore, can never be (geometrically) defined, only maintained through provisional frontiers which can always be challenged and displaced.

In this regard, Laclau and Mouffe demonstrate that the postmodern era is not characterised by increasing integration or the triumphalism of global capitalism. On the contrary, the historical expansion of emancipatory discourses (especially post-1968), combined with the critical Marxist identification of the increasing dislocatory effects of capitalism, reveals a proliferation of the sites of antagonism which present new challenges to the social order and which go way beyond traditional questions of how we produce or consume.

The issue of universalist emancipation similarly persists. There are two aspects here. As we have seen, the Marxist universalist aspiration can certainly be articulated with postmodern themes. This requires, however, that a postmodern project of universalist emancipation must inscribe within it the principles of impossibility and incompletion. Such a project will only be 'grounded', therefore, as the result of political enthusiasm and hegemonic effort, not philosophical meditation.

The second aspect concerns the reinscription of Marxist discourse within an (ongoing) history of emancipation whereby socialist demands could be made integral to a radical universalistic emancipation – freedom and equality for all – rather than totalising of the emancipatory imagination itself.

A final point concerns the essentially hegemonic character of Laclau and Mouffe's conception of a radical and plural democracy as a certain type of 'regime'. Thus pluralism in the project of radical democracy does not simply refer to difference: it is not a project which, for example, can tolerate Fascism, racism and so on simply on the grounds of difference. Rather pluralism, if it is to remain compatible with a universalist type of emancipation, must always pass through a 'grammar' of political engagement which sustains the principles of democratic constitution against its other. Which is to say that radical–plural democracy, like any other political project, is always going to be a power construct but which, unlike other political projects, is one which actively conjures with its own transformation and negativity.

However what has not been so well developed in Laclau and Mouffe is a conception of the practical forms of institutionality which would be capable of sustaining the grammar, or power system, of radical democracy. This imbalance needs to be redressed in analysing democracy not only as a logic of subversion but also as a logic of embodiment. This would be an embodiment capable of sustaining pluralistic forms of representation/empowerment but which would also be open to further modification: and the promise of a renewable democracy.

Notes

1. For an extended discussion of these points – particularly in relation to the objections of Geras and Eagleton – see Daly (1994).

2. For example, the definitions of 'human nature' or 'citizen' are not given as transcendental objectivities but are always open to challenge and political reconstitution.

3. An example of the former is the Marx and Engels (1845/6); of the latter, Marx (1859).

4. Derridean deconstruction has nothing to do with taking things apart. One of the best expositions of this perspective may be found in Staten (1985). The central argument is that the identity of 'X' can only be given *in relation* to a conception of 'not-X'. In other words, the very possibility of X actually *requires* its not-X: for example, a 'not us' in order for an 'us'. Now this is crucial because it means that no identity can be given positivistically as a 'metaphysics of presence'. On the contrary, every identity is penetrated by a basic negativity which in providing the sense of a limit (a not-X) is at the same time *affirming* of that identity. Thus all positivity and objectivity may be said to grow out of negativity. Indeed every identity may be said to exist in an ultimate state of deconstruction – and through which the very possibility of politics emerges.

   This brings about a decisive movement away from the object to a consideration of the context. This is because if all identity is penetrated by a basic negativity then identity can never establish an absolute closure or become a full positivity. The question of identity and the (relative) stability it establishes with its outside (or not-identity) becomes a fully historical and contextual one. For example, the idea of 'womanhood' (and its relation to what was considered 'not feminine') is radically different now to what it was in the nineteenth century. Thus the possibility of politicising traditional notions of 'woman', and the sub-sequent displacement of its frontiers of exclusion/affirmation, comes about because of a primal irresolvability between positivity and negativ-ity: that is, the condition of deconstruction – a condition of possibility *and* impossibility for all identity.

5. For an elaboration of this argument see Laclau and Mouffe (1987) in their reply to Geras (1987).

6. For example, the identification of a 'Jewish conspiracy' became part of the economic diagnosis of Germany under Nazism. This in turn led to the creation of enormous state bureaucracies to oversee the dispossession of the Jews and to carry out the redistribution of their wealth.

7. See Daly (1991).

8. For example, the 'inherent properties' of mercury and gold were under-stood differently by alchemists than by the scientists of today. No doubt these properties will again appear differently in future science.

9. We only have to look at the various standards of 'intelligence', 'hygiene', 'morality' and so on to appreciate the ambiguities here.

10. And this evidently does not mean that feminism is, by contrast, authentic or comes any closer to what womanhood *really* is. Feminism too is an artificial power construct which has to be constituted and defended, in its own terms, through language, policies, institutional arrangements and so on.

11. Again the point should be emphasised that this refers to a *symbolic* chronology of thematic developments. Thus we see the unfolding of the

moments of 1789, 1848 and 1968 – in microcosm – in the evolution of feminist discourse. Whereas first it was a question of securing votes for women in the legal domain, later there is an extension of the demands for equality in the workplace, while more recently we see the articulation of a whole range of sociocultural and sexual rights.

5

Marxism and New Right Theory

ANDREW GAMBLE

One of the greatest challenges Marxism has faced in recent years has come from the New Right. The validity of the term, 'New Right', has been much questioned, since there is not a single doctrine or movement to which it refers. In this chapter we will not be dealing with all the various doctrines and ideas which have been associated with the New Right, but with two particular strands, the neo-liberal, particularly its Austrian variant, and the neo-conservative. Although they differ in important respects (most notably in their evaluation of liberalism) they share a common approach to Marxism, arguing that, despite its pretensions to be scientific, it misunderstands key aspects of the nature of human societies and the modern world. This misunderstanding is so profound that any attempt to realise Marxist goals is bound to fail, and this is why, according to Austrian and neo-conservative thinkers, Marxism has been associated with totalitarian forms of government, despite its stated aims of building free, democratic and egalitarian societies. Marxism stands condemned not only for its normative shortcomings but because it is bad social science.

The criticisms made by contemporary Austrians and neo-conservatives are not new. Both draw on long traditions of critical analysis of Marxism which go back to the last decades of the nineteenth century. One of these strands is the conservative anti-enlightenment tradition, which helped to shape several social science disciplines, most notably sociology. Although no longer the favourite academic discipline of conservatives, sociology developed originally as a critique of the theoretical claims and methodology of Marxism on the one side and of economic liberalism on the other. The analysis of the impact of modernity in the form of secularisation, rationalisation and bureaucratisation emphasised the continuing importance of the institutions through which identity, community, status and authority were created and sustained for understanding social behaviour. Parts of this tradition have been revived and continued by the neo-conservative strand of the New Right.

The Austrian critique of Marxism also goes back to the nineteenth century, and took firm shape in the early decades of the twentieth century. Carl Menger continued the critical rationalist tradition of Mandeville, David Hume and Adam Smith which put the emphasis on the unplanned evolution of certain key institutions which were not designed or planned or foreseen but which had emerged gradually as a result of trial and error and therefore represented the accumulated wisdom of human social experience. These institutions, which include law, language and the market, were essential for the co-ordination of modern societies and the creation and maintenance of a social order. Marxism was criticised for failing to understand the importance of these institutions and for imagining that new institutions could be designed without any regard to the accumulated wisdom that resided within institutions. The Austrians were not conservatives, however, but liberals because they regarded the full development of these institutions in the modern world not only as necessary for the survival of modern societies but also as a sign of progress.

The conservative and the liberal critiques of Marxism could not prevent the establishment of a communist state in Russia in 1917 or the emergence of Marxism in its various forms as one of the leading intellectual doctrines of the twentieth century, with a profound influence on all branches of social science. Marxism was never dominant in the academy, but it was always a serious presence and, at certain times, its influence expanded and liberalism and conservatism were placed on the defensive. In the last twenty years, however, both the conservative and the liberal critique of Marxism have been revived and restated with new cogency, spurred on by the weakening and then collapse of Soviet communism which many on the New Right hailed as empirical confirmation of the validity of their theoretical critique.

There is a strong normative aspect in the Austrian and neo-conservative rejection of Marxism, as there is in libertarianism. Marxism is condemned as inherently totalitarian and as inimical to key values such as freedom and justice. However what gives this critique a particular edge is that it is grounded in particular claims about how the world works. It is the intellectual errors in the theory of Marxism which make it totalitarian whenever there have been attempts to put it into practice.

There is nothing new in this charge. Marxism has always been under sustained intellectual and practical assault ever since it first appeared as a doctrine and as a political practice. Most of the specific arguments currently used against Marxism are also not new. Marxism no longer appears as resilient as it used to be, however. The version of Marxism which has been dominant in the twentieth century, Marxism–Leninism, has disintegrated with the disintegration of the Soviet Union.

Marxism was always a much more diverse tradition, however, than Marxism–Leninism. The tendency to lump all forms of Marxism together and suggest that there is a single 'essential' Marxism to which all forms of Marxism can be reduced is common among even sophisticated critics of Marxism (Kolakowski, 1978) and seriously underplays the genuine pluralism of the Marxist tradition. Marxism can no more be reduced to a single doctrine than can the New Right. This pluralism has always existed, and has become more, not less, pronounced in the last fifty years.

Much of the criticism of Marxism is directed at a composite Marxist position, rather than acknowledging the variations and diversity of Marxist thought. This chapter will first set out the substance of the criticisms which come from the Austrian liberal and the neo-conservative strands of the New Right. The historical roots of these lines of criticisms, and the way in which they have been used in New Right discourses, will be briefly traced. The chapter will then go on to consider the Marxist responses to these criticisms and to the changing intellectual and political challenges of the post-communist era.

New Right Critique I : Austrian School

The Austrian critique of Marxism focuses on the claim made by Marxists that there is a stage of social development beyond capitalism, which will have as one of its key features alternative institutional arrangements to the market and private property for co-ordinating economic behaviour. The belief that it will be possible in the communist society of the future to do without personal private property, money, commodities and markets appears in several key passages in Marx (Marx and Engels, 1968a, 1935). He qualified it by arguing that human societies would first have to pass through a stage of socialism in which many features of markets, commodities and private property would remain. This socialist society would be run on the principle from each according to their ability to each according to their work. In the communist society which would emerge out of socialism, however, distribution would no longer be based on market principles but on the principle of from each according to their ability to each according to their need.

Austrians regard this Marxist belief in the possibility of a world without markets, without money and without personal property as a Utopia fraught with danger. They criticised Marx for not being willing to discuss in detail how a socialist or a communist society would be organised. Marx argued that it was senseless to provide blueprints in the manner of the utopian socialists. Socialism would be built pragmatically and democratically and the problems could not be foreseen in advance. The Austrians regarded this as an evasion. It must be possible, they argued, for the principles underlying alternative systems of allocation and distribution to be identified in advance so that they could be subjected to critical scrutiny. What evidence, they asked, was there that a modern industrial society, relying on complex patterns of division of labour and exchange which were global in scope, could continue to achieve its present levels of output and standard of living if it abandoned markets and money (Mises, 1936; Hayek, 1935)?

Austrians predict that any attempt to suppress markets not only leads to economic collapse, but also undermines other parts of the inherited social and institutional capital of society – notably moral codes and legal rules. Both of these are essential supports for markets and are, in turn, sustained by the kind of behaviour which participation in markets encourages. The destruction of the spontaneous orders of morals, law and markets makes despotic government inevitable, because coercion becomes the only means for holding society together.

Marx's careless utopianism, therefore, is for Austrians the weakest point of his whole system and also has an effect upon Marxist thinking about capitalism. Because Marxists believe without argument that an economy without markets and money is possible in an advanced industrial society, they are biased against markets, competition, individualism and private property in actually existing capitalist societies, and in favour of state ownership and state regulation, indeed anything that supports planned rather than unplanned economic outcomes. Such has been the intellectual prestige of Marxism in the socialist movement that these assumptions have influenced all forms of socialism. They help account for the preference that twentieth century socialists have had for planning over markets, regulation over competition and central intervention over mutual adjustment. The guided market economy is a long way from the centrally planned economy (which was nowhere realised completely, least of all in the Soviet Union). But the belief that there does exist an alternative to capitalism as a form of socioeconomic organisation has been powerfully sustained both by Marxism and by the existence of the Soviet Union through the twentieth century.

If one single thread unites the different figures in the Austrian school it is rejection of these Marxist claims. Many of the principal figures in the Austrian school such as Eugen von Böhm-Bawerk, Ludwig von Mises and F.A. Hayek saw Marxism as the principal intellectual adversary of liberalism. Böhm-Bawerk wrote a famous attack on Marx, *Karl Marx and the Close of his System*, in which he tried to show that there was a radical inconsistency between Volumes I and III of *Capital*. But the most important attack on Marxism came from Mises in an article published in 1920 in which he argued that rational economic calculation would be impossible in a socialist commonwealth which had nationalised all the means of production, distribution and exchange (Mises, in Hayek, 1935). Without private property and prices formed through competitive exchange, there was no means of ensuring that resources were allocated efficiently between alternative uses.

The article by Mises began a great controversy which lasted two decades, although it was conducted not with the Marxists, who mostly ignored him, but with socialist economists who used neo-classical economic models to demonstrate that, under certain assumptions, rational economic calculation was possible under socialism (Gamble, 1996). Many who reflected on the debate, including Joseph Schumpeter, concluded that Mises and Hayek were simply wrong in the claims that they made (Schumpeter, 1950). Socialism might not be desirable but it was not impossible. A planned economy could apply the same rational criteria in allocating resources as a market economy, and the results might even be superior.

In the 1930s the debate eventually petered out. The war economies of the 1940s gave a great boost to planning and collectivist solutions throughout the world and the survival of the Soviet Union added prestige to the Soviet model. If a planned economy could not allocate resources in a rational manner, how had the Soviet Union won through against Germany? The waste and inefficiency represented by the poverty and unemployment in many capitalist economies in the

1930s were contrasted with the opportunities which planning provided to achieve full employment of resources and a growing economy.

But although the debate was stilled in the 1940s and 1950s it did not go away and it was revived in the 1980s. The growing crisis of the economies of the Soviet bloc and the new ideological strength of economic liberalism was a spur for rediscovering and redeploying the arguments which Hayek and others had made (Lavoie, 1985). The focus was once more upon the Marxist claim that there was an alternative to capitalism, a different way of organising an economy under conditions of advanced technology and an advanced division of labour. The Austrians retorted firstly that this had never been established theoretically, and secondly that in practice there was mounting evidence of deep economic malaise in the Soviet bloc which they argued confirmed their prediction that socialism could not be made to work, and could not deliver the kind of economic performance enjoyed by countries with free market economic institutions.

The heart of the Austrian critique focuses on competition and on knowledge. Unless there is competition and competitive exchange between economic agents there is no means by which prices reflecting the aggregate of the subjective valuations which each individual places on a good can be formed. If there are no prices there is no means of signalling to other economic agents what they should consume or produce. The result will be a mismatch between what consumers want and what is available, and therefore a misallocation of resources. Critics of Mises, such as Oscar Lange, disputed this. If all property was owned by the state, a Central Planning Board could be established which could set prices and adjust them according to supply and demand, thus ensuring all the requirements for economic rationality and giving appropriate signals to economic agents (Lange and Taylor, 1938).

The Austrian response to this argument came from Hayek. He argued that a Central Planning Board could not set prices in a rational manner because it could never command sufficient knowledge to take the right decisions. In a market economy knowledge was dispersed and fragmented and it was the competitive process itself which drew together all this dispersed knowledge in the form of prices which were then constantly adjusted as a result of further information coming from the decisions made by individual agents (Hayek, 1937).

Hayek's point was that only a decentralised market system could operate a price system which was sensitive to dispersed knowledge and individual preferences. Any attempt to supplant this spontaneous order with a central plan would produce waste, inefficiency and, ultimately, a breakdown of the economic system. In a modern economy with specialised division of labour and large-scale impersonal production and exchange, only the market order which had evolved through trial and error as a mechanism for co-ordinating society was capable of ensuring both predictability and progress. Marxism was a delusion. Its conception of the future socialist society in whose name it asked its followers to struggle was incapable of being realised. Any attempt to realise it would lead to the despotism and, sooner or later, the economic collapse so evident in the Soviet Union.

The strength of the Austrian critique is that it confronts Marxism on its own ground, how capitalism works as an economic system and how it reproduces itself. It does not make use of the abstract models of neo-classical economics. It accepts that markets and competition are never perfect, that there will always be uncertainty and frictions, booms and slumps, unemployment and bankruptcies. Making allowance for the language used and the different normative judgements, Lavoie points out the similarities between Marx's and the Austrian view of capitalism as a dynamic process of capital accumulation in which competition or rivalry between firms is the motor which drives firms towards searching out new ways to make profits or face extinction (Lavoie, 1985). The key difference between the Austrian and the Marxist view of capitalism is that the Marxists believed there was a way of organising an industrial society without rivalry and competitive accumulation, while the Austrians think that it is a permanent feature of modern economic life. They argue that there is no scientific basis for seeking to transcend it. Marxism has a realistic analysis of how capitalism works, but a utopian view of how it can be replaced.

This Austrian critique has its roots in the rejection of the labour theory of value which Marx took from classical political economy in favour of a subjectivist theory of value, the marginal utility theory. The labour theory of value gave Marx the means of formulating his theory of modes of production. He argued that a distinct mode of production underpinned every social formation in human history. They had certain elements in common but they also differed in crucial respects, notably in the social relations which organised the extraction and distribution of surplus labour. The conception of different historical modes of production provided the possibility of imagining a future mode of production beyond capitalism.

The Austrians rejected these arguments as historicist, because they suggested there was an end-state to which societies were moving and made the 'truth' of statements about the world relative to the particular contexts in which they were produced. The Austrians were Kantian and universalist in arguing that there were certain concepts, among them the concept of marginal utility, which were applicable at all times and in all places. They rejected the idea that costs were in any sense objective and could be measured. Costs were subjective and depended exclusively on the valuation and the trade-offs established by each individual in relation to particular goods and activities. Viewed in this way, economic behaviour was an aspect of human behaviour, and something which human beings had always done. They had always been obliged to decide a rank order between their different preferences and then choose the most efficient means to realise them.

New Right Critique II: Neo-conservatism

The neo-conservative critique of Marxism has a different emphasis from the Austrian school, although there are important points of convergence. Conservatives agree with the Austrian emphasis on the traditional and accumulated wisdom contained in institutions and, like the Austrians, are critical of the rationalist faith in planning which characterises Marxism. The key neo-conservative objection to Marxism, however, is one that the Austrians cannot make, because it might apply equally well as an objection to Austrian liberalism. It is that Marxism is a liberal doctrine and shares the same vices as liberalism. Although it presents itself as a critique of liberalism and promises to go beyond liberalism, in the eyes of neo-conservatives it has similar roots in those Enlightenment discourses which elevate reason above tradition and subscribe to a heroic view of human beings taking control of their societies and reshaping them, free from traditional and conventional restraints (Scruton, 1980).

The objection of the neo-conservatives to Marxism is that it misunderstands the essential elements of human societies, in particular what constitutes human identity. While the methodological criticism of Marxism by neo-liberals is that it is not reductionist enough because some of its key concepts like class are not disaggregated to the level of individual intentions and preferences, the methodological criticism of Marxism by neo-conservatives is that it is much too reductionist. By privileging the economic in its explanations of social outcomes, there is a tendency, even in the most sophisticated Marxist analyses, to discount other levels of social reality, in particular the social relationships and beliefs which make possible order and identity. For neo-conservatives the preservation of culture is the most important political task. Marxism, like other Enlightenment doctrines, is careless of culture and therefore cannot understand some of the deepest forces in modern life, such as religion and nationalism. For neo-conservatives the forces which bind societies together are not in the end economic. In its neglect of the true bases of social order and in its pursuit of a socialist Utopia, Marxism in practice become totalitarian, because it must seek to overcome all cultural obstacles to the creation of a new human nature and new human beings required by the socialist society. Since egalitarianism is contrary to the fundamental nature of human beings, attempts to achieve an egalitarian society can only end in disaster.

This critique of Marxism as inherently totalitarian is shared by the Austrian school. For the Austrians, however, it is Marxism's disregard of economic realities that leads to totalitarianism. Co-ordinating an economy with a specialised division of labour requires private property and markets. For neo-conservatives it is Marxism's disregard of human nature, the deep need individuals have for family, ethnic and national bonds, which produces totalitarianism. Human societies cannot endure if the individuals composing them do not accept the obligations of being members of a society, including adherence to its rules. The reason why individuals accept such obligations is that they are socialised into particular identities, which they accept without question. These identities define who they are and how they should act.

Marxism and liberalism destroy the basis of social order by encouraging the spread of instrumental rationality in the pursuit of either individual or class goals. Individualism is the great disorder of modern times which neo-conservatives wish to combat, because it means that individuals become detached from social obligations and group networks. Throwing off the constraints of convention, individuals begin experimenting with new ways of life, and come to reject all obligations to families, groups and networks. Marxists, in contrast, have stressed the importance of collective associations such as class in binding individuals together and providing them with common purposes and common identities. But for neo-conservatives class identities are artificial. Classes are utilitarian associations whose goals are economic. If they exhibit solidarity, it is because they are rooted in particular communities and groups. The idea of a universal class, spanning whole countries and continents, is anathema to neo-conservatives, a delusion that can never be realised.

Classes, like individuals, pursue their goals in an instrumentally rational manner. For neo-conservatives this means that advocates of class politics are prepared to sacrifice any other value, convention or set of rules which stands in the way. The pluralism and diversity of society becomes submerged in a confrontation between classes. Marxists, it is argued, conceive of class struggle as a zero-sum game in which whatever one class gains is always at the expense of the other. Such a conception leads to an instrumental view of the institutions and organisations of the state and civil society. They exist to serve class interests. The state, for example, becomes an instrument in the hands of the capitalist class used to preserve the capitalist order and to overcome opposition.

Neo-conservatives were aware that crude instrumentalist theories of the state had been abandoned in the various strands of western Marxism. The concept of the relative autonomy of the state had allowed Marxists to develop pluralist accounts of the interaction between political and economic power. But neo-conservatives continued to argue that the essence of the Marxist doctrine was unchanged. Ultimately class was the determinant of what happened in society and in politics. No other institution or organisation had the same importance (Kirk, 1982).

The neo-conservatives challenge the accuracy of the Marxist analysis of modern society by disputing this centrality which it gives to class. For neo-conservatives the proletariat does not exist. There are a myriad of groups with different statuses, different identities and different aims. The aggregation of all these groups into the proletariat with a common identity and common interests, and the capacity to act as a single agent in pursuit of these interests, is regarded as a fiction and a dangerous fiction because of its practical implications. All other social forms become expendable.

Marxism is also criticised for its blindness to the importance of ethnic solidarities as the basis of political identity. Class is again at the root of this, but so too is the idea of universalism and the transcending of local particularities and connections in the creation of the cosmopolis, the world city. The Marxist argument that workers have no country and therefore have an interest in acting together in international solidarity is dismissed by neo-conservatives as a delusion, contradicted by all the available evidence.

Neo-conservatives put a strong emphasis upon nation and national sovereignty. But they are hostile to nationalism as a doctrine, particularly where it is used to justify national self-determination. For neo-conservatives, nations exist, they do not have to be created. They have emerged over very long periods and are a crucial component of every individual's identity. But neo-conservatives are generally wary about arguing that nationalism is the only source of legitimacy in the modern world, and that therefore state boundaries must be coterminous with national boundaries. They regard that kind of nationalist doctrine as another legacy of the Enlightenment, a rationalist discourse which substitutes ideological constructions for social realities (Letwin, 1992).

The Marxist Response: Markets and Planning

The intellectual challenge of the New Right penetrates to the heart of Marxism by questioning its claim that it offers a scientific account of the world. Both Austrians and neo-conservatives regard it instead as an ideological doctrine which rests on deeply flawed assumptions about the nature of social reality and social organisation. Its critique of social reality is grounded in a utopian rather than a feasible view of human possibilities and is incapable of realisation. The proof of this is taken to be the fate of the attempt to establish communist states in the twentieth century. Far from ushering in more democratic, egalitarian and materially abundant societies, they created totalitarian despotisms and grossly inefficient economies, which eventually collapsed.

The Austrian and neo-conservative critiques are different but both focus on the adequacy of Marxist accounts of how social order is established and sustained. The challenge to contemporary Marxism is to show why a Marxist view of social order is not utopian. Is an economy organised on other than capitalist lines a practical possibility? And can a political order be legitimate which is not rooted in ethnic and kinship identities?

The Marxist response to these two questions has taken a long time to emerge. In the 1930s Marxists took little notice of the economic calculation debate. This was fought out between Austrian economists on one side and socialist economists on the other, employing standard neo-classical tools of analysis, which both Austrians and Marxists rejected (Lavoie, 1985). When they considered the matter at all, Marxist economists, like Maurice Dobb, believed that the problems of organising a socialist economy were being solved practically by the experiment taking place in the Soviet Union, and took the standard Marxist line that because this was a new stage of human economic development there was no prior theoretical knowledge which could help in drawing up a blueprint (Dobb, 1937).

This position had a better rationale than Mises would allow. Marx had adopted it from Hegel, who had argued that a way of life could only be fully comprehended when it was past – the owl of Minerva only spread its wings with the coming of dusk (Avineri, 1968). Marx had argued strongly against the blueprints for new societies offered by the utopian socialists, because he believed that it was impossible to design and impose new institutions and relationships which were not organically rooted and grew out of the old society. He claimed his socialism to be scientific because he thought that it was possible to show that the future society was maturing within the old society. Marx's position was an anti-utopian position in this important sense. The few passages of speculation (in *The German Ideology* and in *Capital* itself) about future society do not flow from the main body of his work, which sets out to lay bare the laws of motion of capitalist society. Any hope of transcending capitalist society for Marx has to be based on the identification of trends within capitalism. Only capitalism creates the possibility of socialism.

The objection by Mises to the unwillingness of Marxist economists to state precisely the kind of institutions and organisation which would be necessary for a socialised economy which had abolished private property and markets misses the point. Marx believed that it was possible to demonstrate that capitalism was creating the basis for socialised property and global interdependence, in which the need for both private property and wage labour would disappear as the world economy approached automation of production processes and the expulsion of living labour from it (Nicolaus, 1968). Marx's concept of the falling rate of profit (always much misunderstood) was a way of seeking to capture theoretically the dynamism and the fragility of the capitalist mode of production: the competitive pressure that would push out the bounds of capitalism until the whole world had been incorporated into a single economy and organised within the same social relationships, but which would in the process increase the costs of maintaining capital accumulation in the next phase of reproduction (Harvey, 1982).

There has always been a tendency within Marxism, starting with Marx himself, to disregard the implications of the Marxist theory of capital accumulation and Marx's famous injunction that no social order ever perishes before all the social forces for which there is room in it have developed. If Marx's theory is taken seriously, capitalism would seem assured of several more centuries of development. Marxist theory itself suggests therefore that there is no practical alternative to capitalism until that point is reached. What Marxists have often done, however, is to forget the logical implications of their own theory and concentrate on every short-term crisis of capitalism as heralding the beginning of its demise. The political urge to see capitalism replaced has often overwhelmed the sternly realist analysis implied by Marx's own method of the material conditions under which a replacement might be possible.

This urge was never stronger than in the 1930s, stimulated by the evident disarray of the global capitalist economy following the Great Depression, the collapse of the gold standard and the slide into competing trading and military blocs. This contrasted with the apparent stability and progress of the Soviet Union, the world's first workers' state, which appeared immune to the ills of capitalism. The belief that a centrally planned economy would prove in the long run both more productive and less wasteful than capitalism was widely held, even among many political opponents of communism. Such views were still widespread in the 1950s, despite the reconstruction of the capitalist global economy and the new evidence of capitalist vitality and dynamism.

The charge of totalitarianism was also for a long time parried, partly by a deliberate refusal to consider the evidence about the nature of communist regimes, and partly by the argument that, if these regimes were not fully democratic, the explanation lay in the backwardness of their economies and the pressures of capitalist encirclement. Another argument widely used in the 1930s was that the world was facing a straight choice between fascism and communism and that the democratic forms of capitalism would be discarded in favour of fascist forms once there was any serious democratic challenge to the rights of capitalist property (Strachey, 1932).

By the 1970s and 1980s these arguments had become hollow, and almost everywhere abandoned. The revival of Marxism as a mode of intellectual enquiry and critical analysis in the 1960s in western Europe and the USA was based on a fundamental questioning of the Soviet experience. Western Marxism, as it came to be known, was highly critical of Stalinism and utterly rejected the Soviet Union as a model of either socialist economy or socialist democracy (Anderson, 1976). The diverse intellectual traditions stemming from Trotsky, Gramsci, the Frankfurt school, Sartre, Althusser and the British New Left created new kinds of Marxist discourse which broke decisively with the sterile orthodoxy of Marxism–Leninism and pinpointed with great accuracy the faults of the Soviet Union (Kenny, 1995).

The renewed intellectual onslaught of the New Right rarely discriminated between Marxism as a form of critical social analysis and Marxism–Leninism, the sterile doctrine of state communism. Although Marxists had analysed both the sclerosis and the despotism of the Soviet system, their response to the New Right critique tended to be defensive, because the communist states were the only example of states which claimed to be guided by Marxist principles. The argument that the principles had been wrongly applied, or not applied at all, was always a weak one, when no evidence of an actual alternative to Soviet communism existed anywhere. Marxism could be dismissed as utopian, believing in a form of society which had never existed and could never exist. Marxists might dissociate themselves from Soviet Communism, but if they did so on what did they base their faith that an alternative to capitalism existed? The collapse of communism discredited more than the dogmas of Marxism–Leninism. It also discredited Marxism.

Nevertheless Marxism does have the intellectual resources to respond to the New Right critique, although this has not often taken the form of a direct reply, but rather a fundamental critical reassessment of the Marxist tradition itself, in the course of which many key aspects of it have been abandoned or modified. Many Marxists no longer define themselves as Marxists, or even as post-Marxists. A separate Marxist intellectual tradition may not continue. However many of the concepts and insights of Marxists will live on.

One of the problems in assessing the Marxist response to the New Right critique is that so many of the New Right criticisms are really criticisms of Marxism–Leninism and have already been anticipated by Marxists in their reassessment of the Marxist tradition and of Marx himself. The teleological aspects of Marxism have been abandoned. Most Marxists no longer profess faith in any kind of inevitable progression to a higher stage of civilisation beyond capitalism and no longer believe in the efficacy of central planning. These aspects of Marxism have been shown to be dispensable rather than essential parts of a Marxist approach.

Freed from some of these shackles, Marxists have been able to rediscover Marxism as a form of critical analysis, concerned with examining what is actually happening in capitalism rather than with the possibilities of realising a utopian alternative. One of the signs of this has been a fundamental rethink on the economy and the nature of economic organisation, in the course of which Marxists have recognised the importance of both markets and entrepreneurship (Blackburn, 1991). Does this amount to accepting the New Right critique? Only to the extent that it involves abandoning what was always indefensible in terms of Marx's own method – a utopian vision of how a communist society might be organised.

The feasibility of socialism or any other alternative to capitalism becomes a matter of detailed social investigation of capitalism as it actually is, and of the potentialities for change which exist within it. Capitalist development is marked more by evolution than by revolution. Marxist political economy can accept all this and still offer a more complex account of contemporary capitalism than the Austrian school, whose analyses are frequently marred by partisan preference for the free market (Hodgson, 1988; Elson, 1988). The great strength of a Marxist approach is its focus on the capitalist mode of production and how it reproduces itself. It can therefore provide a dispassionate analysis of the evolutionary trends in capitalism which have produced both the global market-place and the extended state. With the renewed recognition of the importance of the global economy, a Marxist approach is particularly appropriate for mapping and analysing the interconnections between the global, the national and the local (Cox, 1987). Austrian analysis is deeply flawed because it has its own utopian vision of what capitalism should be like and treats the growth of the state as pathological (Gamble, 1996).

In responding to the New Right critique of the possibility of socialism, Marxists have no need to defend comprehensive central planning as a method of allocating resources except in very special circumstances, and they are on strong ground in declining to endorse the Austrian metanarrative about the inherent superiority of market exchange. The Austrian argument can be turned back on itself. The state too is a spontaneous order and its role in securing the reproduction of capitalism and maintaining the conditions for profitable accumulation is central to an understanding of contemporary capitalism. Marxism can learn from the Austrian critique and emerge the stronger for it. John Roemer has reopened the debate on the feasibility of socialism and a new literature is emerging around the concept of an egalitarian market economy (Roemer, 1994; Pollin, 1996; Gamble and Kelly, 1996).

The Marxist Response: Democracy and Identity

The Marxist response to the neo-conservative critique centres on the issue of whether the Marxist concept of class is adequate for understanding problems of agency, legitimacy and order in modern political systems, whose structure is very different from the ones with which Marx was familiar. He was writing, for example, before the establishment of mass democracy and the rise of the extended state.

One of the consequences of the revival of a critical Marxist tradition separate from Marxism–Leninism has been a re-evaluation of the Marxist concept of class and specifically the notion of the proletariat as an agency of change. The simplified picture of class struggle popularised in the Communist Manifesto has been strongly criticised and several Marxists have pointed out that there is a disjunction between the conception of political agency deriving from the Manifesto (written when Marx was 30 and before he had commenced his detailed analysis of capitalism) and his mature analysis contained in the *Grundrisse* and *Capital* (Nicolaus, 1968).

One consequence of this reassessment has been the rejection by Marxists of the economic reductionism implied by simplified class analysis and the exploration of the complex process of the formation of identities and agency. In this reassessment the concept of democracy as a space which is not reducible to class interest, but has its own specific autonomy and character, has been central (Hall, 1988). In responding to the charge that a Marxist understanding of politics is inherently totalitarian, Marxists have emphasised the link between socialism and democracy. Only a socialism that is fully democratic can be socialist (Miliband, 1977). Totalitarian and despotic forms of rule are therefore not simply deformations of socialism but not socialism at all. The cruder economism in some forms of Trotskyism which argued that the Soviet Union remained socialist even though power had been transferred to a bureaucratic elite is rejected in terms of a definition of socialism which makes political criteria, such as the democratic forms of the regime, an essential condition.

Using democracy in this way allows Marxists to argue that any process of social transformation and any regime that is established as a result of it will only move society in a socialist direction if the process has been democratic. Against the charge that any attempt to implement socialism leads to serfdom or the creation of a totalitarian society, Marxists have responded by making the link between socialism and democracy indissoluble. Without democracy there can be no socialism. If socialism can only be implemented through consent then the possibilities of imposition through some Jacobin conspiracy which results in despotism disappears. Instead the focus moves to the institutional conditions for new forms of decentralised democracy (Hirst, 1994).

Are socialism and democracy, however, compatible? Austrians and neo-conservatives argue that although a democracy might vote for a socialist programme it can only be implemented by suppressing democratic institutions. Either the party will be forced to abandon socialism or it will be forced to abandon democracy. Some Marxists also have pointed to the dilemma of socialist parties operating in mass democracies. The consequences of pushing ahead with a socialist programme may create such hardship, dislocation and opposition that if the regime remains democratic the socialist party will be voted out (Przeworski, 1985).

One Marxist response to this has been to analyse the obstacles in the way of assembling a democratic majority for fundamental social change. The stream of work inspired by Gramsci has moved far away from the unitary view of class and identity characteristic of some forms of Marxism–Leninism, stressing instead plurality, contingency, the absence of guarantees and the creativity and openness of democratic politics (Laclau and Mouffe, 1985). The nurturing and development of new forms of political agency and political argument utilising the extremely diverse identities and interests of a complex civil society are emphasised in place of the imposition of a single identity and purpose derived from class (Rustin, 1985; Butler, 1995). Such arguments need careful handling. Pushed too far they could suggest that class withers away or disappears entirely. In any Marxist analysis class must remain a fundamental concept, since it focuses attention directly on the relationships of power and inequality which are at the heart of a capitalist social and economic order. But its connection with agency needs to be reassessed, as well as its relationship to other forms of inequality and injustice in capitalist societies (Fraser, 1995).

The strength of the critical Marxist response to the neo-conservative critique is that it registers the importance of identities and interests other than class, at the same time not losing sight of the interaction between these identities and the class structure of capitalism. Neoconservatives often write as though class and power do not exist. They are right to criticise the teleology and essentialism of much Marxist writing on class and identity, but their bias towards making culture their key explanatory variable sacrifices the insights of Marxism into the wider social and class context in which identities and agencies are formed in contemporary societies.

One neo-conservative retort to this would be that Marxists only overcome the problems inherent in Marxism by ceasing to be Marxists. A politics of plurality and difference, they would argue, would either be a sham or would produce conservative and not radical outcomes. They dispute that a socialist programme is feasible which does not involve a move towards totalitarianism. A considerable literature has grown up analysing whether a democratic socialist programme can ever win popular assent (Przeworski, 1985). If such a programme cannot be implemented without causing economic chaos then, either it will be abandoned in the face of electoral unpopularity, or it will be imposed by non-democratic means. Nothing within Marxism can provide a guarantee that this problem can be overcome. The neo-conservative challenge, however, is not only to socialist but to all forms of liberal politics, and to the possibility of democracy being more than an empty shell. The retreat to ethnic and tribal solidarities as the only basis for legitimacy in the modern world is unappealing, and carries with it its own dangers. What is needed is the building of a democracy that addresses the problems of an extended market and the extended state, and therefore operates at local, national and international levels (Held, 1992; 1996).

Conclusion

Marxism is a critical analysis of social reality. It also has to be self-critical. The most promising response to the Austrian and neo-conservative critique has been the further purging of the utopian elements in Marxism, such as the abandonment of the notion that there is some unproblematic alternative way of managing the contemporary modern economy without markets and prices. The traditional opposition between co-ordination by markets and co-ordination by bureaucracy is increasingly seen as false, hard though it is for either side of the argument to rid themselves of it. But there is a growing recognition that Marxism does not have to be chained by these false antinomies that have structured so much of twentieth century debate.

Marxists disagree profoundly with the Austrian argument that markets are spontaneous orders which will produce benign results if they are left alone. All markets are socially constructed and involve mechanisms of both exit and voice. The balance between these is not something which is automatically given, but something which can only be explored through trial and error. The modern global capitalist economy continues to evolve in ways which can be understood through the Marxist concepts of mode of production and capital accumulation. It is characterised by profound frictions and conflicts, inequalities of power and wealth, market and state failures, problems of co-operation and co-ordination, which threaten not just its own survival but the survival of the human species itself.

In its engagement with Austrian and neo-conservative critiques Marxism has much to learn and to absorb. The revival of critical Marxism has meant the abandonment of many of the statist and centralist assumptions inherent in much classical Marxism. Its approach to social change has become pluralist and experimental. Dogma and fundamentalism are more often found these days among the New Right than among Marxists. Marxists accordingly have no reason to be defensive. There are no automatic guarantees of a socialist future. But that is liberating for both social analysis and political action. As a method and theoretical perspective Marxism still has much to contribute to the development of a non-doctrinal, critical social science.

6

Marxism as Social Science: celebration or nonchalance?

Tony Tant

Perhaps the longest-standing dispute between Marxism's proponents and detractors is that as to whether its theoretical and analytical bases are 'scientific'. Within this question two major positions present themselves. The 'traditional' orientation, accepting the superiority of the scientific over the non-scientific, has thus turned upon establishing or refuting the scientific status of Marxism. Hence opponents, following for example Durkheim's differentiation between science and ideology,[1] have sought to establish it as mere ideology. Popper's characterisation of Marxism as one among many 'pseudo-sciences' epitomizes this general position (see e.g. Popper, 1963, 1980), as Althusser's proposition of the 'epistemological break' in Marx (see Althusser, 1969), can be seen as a Marxist response. A second, more recent approach has however questioned the very idea of science's superiority to other forms of knowledge, thereby putting a radically different emphasis upon the question of its relationship to Marxism. The plethora of contemporary 'postmodernist' writings would for example relegate the question of scientific status to one little short of irrelevance.

Both these orientations demand proper consideration of the meaning(s) of 'science'. This chapter will therefore begin by considering science's emergence and development. This will establish that there are alternative conceptions of science spawning alternative traditions of scientific methodology – 'empiricist'/'positivist', 'formal idealistic', 'practical materialist', 'critical rationalist', 'inductivist', 'falsification-ist' and 'realist'[2] – which vary in their criteria by which the scientific and non-scientific are differentiated. It will be seen that Marxism is able to be embraced by some – particularly the practical materialist and realist conceptions – but is excluded by other scientific models. The foundations for a Marxist response to this whole question will then be laid by examining the methodological and purposive foundations of Marx's writings against these alternative conceptions of science and the critique of the privileging of science over other modes of knowledge. Finally some recent developments in scientific theory will be considered, their implications for the relationship between natural and social science reviewed, and conclusions will be drawn from all of the foregoing.

Science: its Origins, Rise and Triumph

The original meaning of 'science', from the French, is simply 'knowledge' (Roskin *et al.*, 1988, p. 12). Subsequently, as will be seen, the *means* by which such 'knowledge' is accumulated becomes crucial in regard to whether it is deemed 'scientific'. However, from a modern perspective, Nagel's suggestion that science aims to provide systematic and responsibly supported explanations 'controllable by factual evidence', seems as uncontroversial as his view that its purpose 'is the organisation and classification of knowledge on the basis of explanatory principles' (see Beardsley, 1974, p. 46). By comparison, the claims of Bernal (1969), that ideas of science and scientific method influenced beliefs at least back to classical Greek times, and of Malinowski (1982, p. 86), that scientific knowledge is common to even the most primitive peoples, seem far less plausible. Yet they demand closer examination.

For Bernal, science is so old, has undergone so many changes and is so linked at every point with other social activities, that any attempted definition can 'only express more or less inadequately one of the aspects, often a minor one, that it has had at some period of its growth'. No lesser figure than Einstein is cited in support of this view:

> Science . . . in the making, science as an end to be pursued, is as subjective and psychologically conditioned as any other branch of human endeavour – so much so, that the question 'what is the purpose and meaning of science?' receives quite different answers at different times and from different sorts of people. (Einstein, quoted in Bernal, 1969, p. 30)

Indeed perhaps the most important aspect of science is its being something 'in the making'. Long before it could be considered as an institution, or to have evolved a distinct method, its origins can be seen in the tradition of knowledge passed down through generations (see Bernal, 1969, p. 31), with its true history commencing 'when men and women learn to dispense with mythology, and attempt to obtain a rational understanding of nature' (Woods and Grant, 1995, p. 38). The development of philosophy played a leading role in accomplishing this transition, and certainly in this sense science can be traced back to the classical Greeks. Nevertheless a bitter and protracted war with religion needed to be won before further progress could be made; the Renaissance period seeing Galileo, for example, forced to compromise his views during the Inquisition.

The formalisation of the distinctiveness of science, and its emergence as an institution, can be traced to the subsequent period seeing a reaction against ignorance, mysticism and superstition, and the development of the best intellectual inheritance of the Renaissance: the Enlightenment. Prior to the end of the seventeenth century then, most Europeans believed they lived in a divinely created finite cosmos, with the Earth at its centre. With the encouragement of the Church they saw themselves as at the mercy of supernatural forces, continually menaced by Satan and his allies. Not until the Newtonian revolution did educated Europeans come to accept their location on a tiny planet in elliptical orbit around the sun and within an infinite universe, and the menaces lying within the natural world, control of which now lay within their grasp (see Easlea, 1980, p. 1).

Science did not destroy but merely modified religious discourse. Rather than omnipresent, God was now author of an ordered, systematic machine, the universe, the workings of which were mechanically set in perfect balance, and thereby open to scientific discovery. Coincidental to these changed perceptions of God and the universe was the widespread theological doctrine of 'predestination' (individual salvation as immutably predetermined). The simple association of these ideas saw human beings, as the planets in space, pushed in a set pattern of movement, their ultimate fate sealed. Nevertheless progressively scientists were making 'causal' discoveries revealing the mechanisms pushing humanity and the universe towards their appointed destiny. Science thereby initially came to incorporate the assumption that wherever causes could be found for actions, they were unavoidable; causes were irresistible, compelling. Thus from Renaissance to Enlightenment, the transition from Christian mediaeval to scientific means of understanding nature and the social world saw 'causal explicability' and 'causal inevitability' fused in a mechanistic, materialistic conception of the universe.

Scientific Method: Sources of Dispute

The above philosophical orientation was epitomised in England by Francis Bacon (1561–1626). For Bacon, deriving theories from facts collected through organised observation was the scientific means to improvements in human conditions. Reinforcing this apparent empiricist orientation he condemned the rationalists' belief that reason and logic alone were sufficient to acquire true knowledge: rationalists were 'like spiders spinning ideas out of the recesses of their mind'. Yet he also opposed 'brute empirics' holding true knowledge to be obtainable via human sense experience alone. They were 'like ants, aimlessly collecting data', whereas 'bees provide the proper model for scientific procedure':

> Order is the secret – the amassing of data on natural history, storing it, and interpreting it judiciously according to definite canons (Urmson and Ree, 1991, p. 39).

The attempt to construct a 'science of society' in this spirit is subsequently exemplified by: Hobbes' (1588–1679) mechanistic materialist understanding of actions in human and natural life, explainable with geometric precision; Locke's (1632–1704) empiricist opposition to rationalism (particularly the conception of 'innate' human ideas); and the empiricism of Hume (1711–76) and others following Locke. Such a conception of social science was thus inevitably dominated 'by the example of the physical sciences', and:

> by an appeal to those who, it was thought, had established firmly the character and universal scope of scientific enquiry – Bacon, the propounder of scientific method, and Newton, its brilliant exponent (Lively and Reeve, eds, 1989, p. 184).

Of the relationship between this scientific spirit of the seventeenth century and the *human* sciences, Sartori (1974) writes:

> All sciences are measured by a reigning science which constitutes their archetype: here science means exact science, science in the physicalist sense. In the broad sense, the 'unity of science' refers to the minimum common denominator in whatever scientific discourse: here science stands for science in general. In this second case we can recognise a plurality of sciences and of scientific methods ranging across a variety of intermediate cases (Sartori, 1974, p. 134).

We are thus counselled to reject any conception of science as constituting a single method of pursuing knowledge about the nature of humankind and society, and indeed, such an absolute conception is belied by the whole history of science with its continual development of a multiplicity of new methods.

In fact a sometimes latent, sometimes manifest struggle between a formal and idealistic tendency, and a practical, materialist one, has characterised science since its dawn. The idealist side emphasises 'order', aristocracy and established religion; its object to explain things as they are and the impious impossibility of changing their essentials. This view affected profoundly the development of science, particularly in astronomy and physics, and remains influential today. Science *as an institution* can therefore be seen as markedly conservative. Hence the materialist view, because of its revolutionary implications rather than its practical nature, did not for centuries find much support in literature circles and rarely formed part of official philosophy. Thus at every historical stage the formal idealist side propounded the illusory nature of current sources of discontent and justified the status quo, whilst materialist philosophy propounded the necessity of change and demanded judgements based upon practical testing (see Bernal, 1969, pp. 53–4).

However once the Industrial Revolution was underway science became in practice materialist, if its political and religious conservatism ensured a continued role for idealism. But whether natural or social, with science perceived as the rational pursuit of verifiable knowledge, suitable criteria to judge what is 'rational', and *how* to verify knowledge, continued to be disputed. Frazer for example (in Wilson, 1981), represents the opposite 'positivist' pole to Sartori (above), by embracing the physical or natural sciences as providing an appropriate methodology for the human sciences; setting out such criteria around approximation to the coherence and predictive power of natural science.

Nineteenth and twentieth century positivism followed in the track of eighteenth century empiricism, holding explanatory and predictive knowledge to be gained through studying phenomena via systematic observation and experimentation, from which theories – general statements expressing the regular relationships found to exist in the world – are constructed. Thus 'objective' observational and experimental testing is the only source of sure and certain knowledge; there are no necessary connections in nature, only regularities, successions of phenomena amenable to systematic representation in universal laws of scientific theory. It follows that any attempt to go beyond this representation plunges into unverifiable metaphysics and/or religion (see Keat and Urry, 1982, pp. 4–5).

Yet against this, the distinction made by Marx between 'appearance' and 'reality' is undeniably important beyond its critical utility against entrenched belief systems. From at least as far back as Copernican science and Descartes' philosophy it had been realised that despite the domination of human consciousness by sense experience – making it difficult for us to accept the point – 'there is no necessary correspondence between sense-experience and reality' (see e.g. Bhaskar, 1975). Indeed, the inadequacy of attending only to appearance can be said to have been systematically articulated as early as Aristotle. Concomitant is the view that it is as essential to go beyond 'common sense' as it is inevitable that conclusions thereby reached might be incongruous with accepted belief. By the nineteenth century Marx had refined the distinction between appearance and reality, holding the 'real' causal relations to lie beneath the surface 'appearance', the general proposition which has come to be known as 'realism' within the philosophy of science:

> to explain phenomena is not merely to show there are instances of well-established regularities. Instead we must discover the necessary connections between phenomena, by acquiring knowledge of the underlying structures and mechanisms at work. It is only by doing this that we get beyond the 'mere appearance' of things, to their natures and essences (Keat and Urry, 1982 p. 5).

Further, for the realist there is an important difference between explanation and prediction, with 'explanation' pursued as the primary objective. Thus a scientific theory is a description of structures and mechanisms which causally generate the observable phenomena. Marxism's congruence with the scientific realist and practical materialist conceptions of science (as well as that between dialectics and Kuhnian scientific paradigms) will be demonstrated in depth subsequently. It might be mentioned here however that positivistic science shares with classical Marxism a view of the world as predictable and manipulable, and a conception of science as a rational and objective enterprise, the purpose of which is to provide true explanatory and predictive knowledge of nature. Indeed, regardless of the varying orientations, the rise of science was accompanied by the belief that through it humankind could improve society and social conditions; a matter influential in maintaining its status.

Changing Expectations, Continued Esteem

Science's high status derives from popular belief that it and its methods are somehow special (see, for example, Chalmers, 1982). The naming of a claim or piece of research 'scientific' thus implies special merit or reliability, and conversely, as in relation to Marxism, to deny scientific status devalues that so denied. Maslow (1970, p. 8) points out, however, that science 'is only one means of access to knowledge of natural, social and psychological reality', and Chalmers (1982, p. xvi) considers science's high esteem to be undeserved, since: 'there is just no method that enables scientific theories to be proven true or even probably true'. Feyerabend (1975), goes further, arguing that no feature of science renders it intrinsically superior to other branches of knowledge. Thus of Lakatos (see, for example, Lakatos, 1974), Feyerabend writes:

> having finished his 'reconstruction' of modern science, he turns it against other fields as *if it had already been established* that modern science is superior . . . However, there is not a shred of an argument of this kind. 'Rational reconstructions' take 'basic scientific wisdom' *for granted*, they do not *show* that it is better . . . (p. 205, italics in original).

Hence 'critical rationalists' and defenders of Lakatos have examined science in great detail, whilst in relation to Marxism (or astrology, or other traditional heresies), 'the most superficial examination and most shoddy arguments are deemed sufficient' (Feyerabend, in Howson, 1976, p. 315).

Feyerabend in fact denies that there *ever can be* a decisive argument favouring science over other forms of knowledge, and therefore knowledge should not be 'imprisoned' within the bounds of rationalist models, bolstering Western modes of thinking and representing 'the truth' (see Docherty, 1993, p. 35). Thus a proper comparison of science with other forms of knowledge would necessitate investigation of the nature, aims and methods of each form (see Chalmers, 1982, p. 140). Indeed, reinforcing the view of Sartori (1974) considered earlier, Feyerabend too shows the extent to which

> the false assumption that there is a universal scientific method to which all forms of knowledge should conform plays a detrimental role in our society here and now, especially in the light of the fact that the version of the scientific method usually appealed to is some

crude empiricist or inductivist one (Feyerabend, cited in Chalmers, 1982, p. 141).

We have already rehearsed the realist critique of empiricist/positivist scientific models and vice-versa. Realists cannot *prove* to the satisfaction of empiricists/positivists that there *is* a reality separate from our ability to experience it, nor can empiricists/positivists satisfy realists that there is *not*. Each merely *operates as if* its position is 'true', and is critical of the 'knowledge' derived from the other. Marxism is congruent with the realist model, but *incongruent* with aspects of empiricism/positivism. Similarly, 'inductivist' models, again holding scientific knowledge as derived from the secure foundation of observation statements via inductive reasoning, thereby also exclude Marxism from science. But again, such a position is vulnerable to a realist critique, to criticisms of inductive (as opposed to *deductive*) reasoning, and in relation to the assumption that the *observer* of such crucial observations has no preconceptions, expectations or biases. Rather, *theory precedes observation*; observations and experiments serving to test or perfect a theory (see, for example, Chalmers, pp. 32–3).

'Falsificationists' however freely admit that observation is guided by and presupposes theory. Further, following Popper, they grant the employment of speculative and tentative conjectures in the attempt to overcome previous theories' problems, and given that failure to withstand rigorous observational and experimental testing *eliminates* a theory, they grant the superiority of current theories over their predecessors. Nevertheless, falsificationists would not claim that truth or even probable truth could ever thereby be established. Science thus progresses by trial and error; by conjectures and refutations (see Chalmers, pp. 38–45), rather in the manner proposed by Kuhn (1970), as will be taken up subsequently. But it is crucial to emphasize that inherent in the above is that observation statements forming the basis by which the merit of a scientific theory is to be assessed *are fallible*. Popper himself emphasises this point with a striking metaphor:

> Science does not rest upon solid bedrock. The bold structure of its theories rises, as it were above a swamp. It is like a building erected on piles. The piles are driven down from above into the swamp, but not down to any natural or 'given' base; and if we stop driving the piles deeper, it is not because we have reached firm ground. We simply stop when we are satisfied that the piles are firm enough to carry the structure, at least for the time being (Popper, cited in Chalmers, 1982, p. 63).

But if a given enterprise is deemed good or poor, science or 'pseudo-science' upon *fallible* only tentatively acceptable bases, then *any claim or conclusion thereby arrived at* – including that of falsificationist epistemological superiority – must also be tentative and fallible. Hence we see another example of a scientific model merely favouring certain modes of operation following its quite subjective rejection of others (see, for example, Chalmers, p. 63).

From Lineal Pursuit of 'Truth', to Dialectical Progress to 'Pragmatic Usefulness'

The early twentieth century saw positive or natural science championed as the *only* adequate means of analysing the world. Hence it marginalised all other forms of knowledge by claiming a monopoly on objective truth. The demand that only what is immediately observable can count in contributing to genuine knowledge eliminated religion, metaphysical philosophy, and analytical realism as viable approaches. Yet, as Kingdom (1991) writes:

> As the 'hard' sciences press further into the unknown, they encounter less rather than more precision in the phenomena they observe. Hence they are forced to construct 'uncertainty principles' and 'chaos theories' resembling the uncertainties that have long confronted the social scientist (p. 16).

Indeed 'recent advances of the theories of chaos and complexity show that an increasing number of scientists are moving in the direction of dialectical thinking' (Woods and Grant, 1995, p. 26). Dialectics will be taken up subsequently, for now let us remain with the contemporary widespread agreement that the social and natural sciences have more similarities than was previously recognised: 'Both have problems with objectivity, competing perspectives and replication' (Lawson, 1986, p. 38). The movement towards this recognition can perhaps be said to begin with Kuhn (see, for example, Chalmers, p. 77).

Beginning his academic career as a physicist, on turning his attention to the history of science, Kuhn found traditional accounts to be incongruous with historical evidence. He thus came to propose, in 1962, a specific characterisation of the procedures through which scientific models of explanation change through history, arguing that science has thrown up succeeding 'paradigms'[3] through which the world has been satisfactorily explained. Given the expansion of scientific research and increasingly exacting methods of testing, each paradigm eventually comes to produce less satisfactory, less predictable results. At this juncture a revolutionary phase constituting the search for a new paradigm is instigated, culminating with its discovery. Thus science moves from 'normal' to 'revolutionary' and back to normal phases of activity, the shifting between paradigms constituting 'the structure of scientific revolutions'.

Kuhn's book had enormous influence, accomplishing a 'paradigm shift' itself in the philosophy of knowledge 'away from a model which proclaimed the availability of "truth" towards one which proclaims instead the much more modest "pragmatic usefulness"' (Docherty, 1993, p. 36). Beyond the germane point that, in practice, science *fails to live up to* its ideological representation of itself, Kuhn shows that for long periods science works upon false assumptions. For example, the Newtonian paradigm did not ***become** false* when succeeded by that of Einstein. Einstein proved Newton *had **always** been false* This both poses the question as to whether the Newtonian revolution can in fact have been *non*-'scientific', and leads to the inescapable conclusion that great progress can be made in accumulating valuable knowledge via such false or 'non-scientific' theories – a point to which we will return in relation to Marxism.

Following Kuhn, there has been greater flexibility in defining science. Maslow, for example (1970, p. 8), extends the point made earlier regarding observers' preconceptions and so on, arguing that science *in general* is not and cannot be objective and independent of human values:

> Science is a human creation, rather than an autonomous, non human, or per se 'thing' with intrinsic rules of its own. Its origins are in human motives, its goals are human goals . . . Its laws, organization, and articulations rest not only on the nature of the reality that it discovers, but also on the nature of the human nature that does the discovering (Maslow, ibid, p. 1).

Indeed, science 'is itself a value system' (ibid, p. 6). This echoes Bernal's earlier point that *as an institution*, science embodies a *conservative* value system. In this regard Barnes (1982) points out that it is scientists who decide what is a scientific field and what is a pseudo-scientific one, and what is properly scientific argument and what is not. Clearly 'such decisions relate to issues of great moment, concerning which expert is to be believed, which institutions are given credibility, where cognitive authority is to lie' (Barnes, 1982, p. 90).

Thus the crucial 'boundary' between the scientific and non-scientific – and the 'appropriate' social status of each – derives from mere 'convention', generated within a socially conservative atmosphere (ibid, p. 93).

A reluctance among scientists in general to embrace radical or revolutionary modes of thinking – except when the current orthodoxy is found wanting – is thus unsurprising. But increasingly, current orthodoxies *have* been found wanting, and thereby, as already indicated and will be further demonstrated, the claim to scientific status of dialectical method is strengthened. Being central to the methodology of Marx and Engels, dialectics will shortly be taken up, and its relevance to modern scientific theory elaborated. To conclude this section we need only point out that the 'orthodox' modern societal perception of Marxism's non-scientific status derives not just from the generally *conservative location* within which that judgement has been made and passed down, but also from the fact that we are, as Kuhn implies, still too easily persuaded that science *is* what its 'ideology' represents it to be.

Marx, Materialism and Scientific Method

As indicated, Marx lies within a tradition including Descartes, Rousseau, Kant and Hegel before him: that holding the task of social science to be to penetrate observation and experience to identify underlying causal relationships governing society. Thus Marx penetrates the appearance of bourgeois society as free individuals entering voluntary agreements exchanging labour time for wages, and unmasks the reality of exploitation and alienation, exposing their causes. Moreover, *the processes which generate* the appearance or misperceptions are also discovered and explained. But for Marx, *mere recognition* of, for example, the existing separation between 'material life' and 'species life' (the individual as worker and as citizen), is not enough, *action* in 'material life' is necessary to mend it.[4] Indeed the unity of theory and action, 'praxis', held the *point* of this scientific project to be to attain progressive *change*. The congruency between Marxism and realist and practical materialist scientific models is thus apparent.

There is therefore a necessary relationship in Marx's work between critique and science; as Gouldner (1980, p. 79) puts it, *philosophy* was insufficient to *know* the world, *science* insufficient to *criticize* it. Marx employs the materialist scientific analytical approach to expose the progress of humankind and society as inextricably bound together; the transformation of the human environment, through the labour process, directly related to society's transformation through internal conflict between opposing factions. Humankind and society together move towards ever higher stages of societal organisation, but in the higher *societal* stages achieved, *human* existence becomes increasingly 'alienated'.

For Marx, throughout history humanity develops and expands its potential, human 'powers', through the satisfaction of human (primarily biological) 'needs'. Reiterating the point of departure from the Hegelians, and specifically Feuerbach, Marx focuses upon the human individual not just as a seeing and knowing *subject*, but as social *actor*; engaged in productive material life. Ultimately communist society will allow human potential to be realised to the full, facilitating the emergence of 'generic man'. History therefore charts the development of practical human action, combining mind and body (theory and action): 'praxis'. This indeed creates humankind's 'natural' environment; as powers develop in satisfying needs, those needs change, resulting in the modification of nature and further changes in human activity. Hence the dynamics of history as they apply to the human actor are seen in the scientific principle of dialectics: the emergence (thesis), development (antithesis working within and against the thesis), and satisfaction (synthesis) of human needs, to subsequently re-emerge in modified form (synthesis as new thesis), to continue the process. Engels defined dialectics as 'the most general laws of motion of nature, society, and human thought':

> Dialectics . . . sets out from the axiom that everything is in a constant state of change and flux. . . . Dialectics explains that change and motion involve contradiction and can only take place through contradictions. So instead of a smooth, uninterrupted line of progress, we have a line which is interrupted by sudden and explosive periods in which slow, accumulated changes (quantitative change) undergoes a rapid acceleration, in which quantity is transformed into quality. (Woods and Grant, 1995, p. 15 and 43)[5]

More will be said of dialectics and science subsequently, but first their operation at the level of societal change, and the links between the individual and societal levels, must be outlined. Here we might reiterate that human development, tied to the productive process, is accomplished through co-operative human social action; such relations between actors in this labour process being termed 'social relations of production'. Since cooperation is primarily aimed at production (to satisfy needs), it is limited by the level of development of productive forces and nature of its social organisation. At a certain stage, says Marx, that nature of social organisation has to be transformed in order to facilitate further development of the productive forces. Such transformations constitute the manner by which society itself is transformed.

The continued mastery of nature by co-operative human actors increases their interdependence within the social relations of production. In this sense economic relations are human creations, *but not consciously so*, writes Marx:

> In the social production which men carry on they enter into definite relations that are indispensable and *independent of their will* (Marx, 1859, cited in Aron, 1979, p. 119, my emphasis).

An important component of historical progress is therefore the movement towards the coming to consciousness of the nature of economic relations and, thereby, of the divergence between appearance and reality, and things as they are and as they could be. Such recognitions also encompass further revelations: that the appearance of class society as 'natural' and legitimate is socially constructed; that the *appearance* of legitimacy is a bulwark in the defence of the status quo. Hence the scientific study of history unites knowing and criticizing the world, and thereby facilitates the movement towards human appropriation of collective control – *changing* the material reality.

As humankind and societal productive forces develop together, new forms of the division of labour emerge, thus changing the relationship between the human actor and the means of production. Hence new 'social' and 'technical' relations of production arise, the latter referring to relations in the labour process between humans and machines. So the development both of the means of production and of organised labour around the productive process constitutes development of the productive forces, the ultimate productive force being labour itself, since a machine cannot be productive until utilized.

Marx analyses successive historical stages as forms of the division of labour relating to different levels of development of the productive forces, the division of labour being only truly such after a division of material and mental labour appears, and a system featuring class relations – between slaves and citizens – emerges. Thus Marx's view of class struggle as the 'motor' of history becomes formalised within a systematic analytical approach seeing the surface appearance of society explained via the operation of the underlying – economic – causal relations.

Owing to the nature of the division of labour under capitalism human powers are markedly *unevenly* developed, with much human capacity entirely untapped. Work is unfulfilling; the inner creative human potential unrealized. Divorced from the product of labour, from an end, work becomes merely a means, the worker does not live to work, but must work to live: 'the work of the proletarian has lost all individual character, and consequently, all charm for the workman. He becomes an appendage of the machine' (Marx and Engels, *Manifesto of the Communist Party*, cited in Feuer, 1984, p. 55). Thus for history to attain its ultimate goal, for the proletariat to emancipate itself and all humanity, capitalism and its distortion of the human essence must be transcended.

Alienation is concerned both with the 'essence' of humanity (in the unity of humankind and nature) and with the 'distortion' of human labour under capitalist production. Scientifically, it refers to an *objective* state with identified underlying causes, what can be *observed* are its *consequences* in individuals' states of mind. In this passage from *The Economic and Philosophical Manuscripts* (1844), elements of the objective condition are combined with subjective indications of its existence – *feelings* of alienation:

> the work is *external* to the worker, it is not a part of his nature, consequently he does not fulfil himself in his work, but denies himself, has a feeling of misery, not of well-being, does not develop freely a physical and mental energy, but is physically exhausted and mentally debased. The worker therefore feels himself at home only during his leisure, whereas at work he feels homeless. His work is not voluntary but imposed, *forced labour*. It is not the satisfaction of a need, but only a *means* for satisfying other needs. Its alien character is clearly shown by the fact that as soon as there is no physical or other compulsion it is avoided like the plague. Finally, the alienated character of work for the worker appears in the fact that it is not his work, but work for somebody else, that in work he does not belong to himself but to another person (Marx, cited in Bottomore and Rubel (eds), 1978, pp. 177–8, emphases are in original).

Thus the individual's *sense-experience* of alienation is in 'surface' consciousness, *feelings* understood philosophically in terms of the negation of the human essence, but *explained* 'scientifically' via *the underlying causal relations* which produce the objective condition of alienation.

The other aspect of alienation relates to the distorted form of labour arising out of capitalist production. Whereas the natural unity of humankind and nature derives from what Marx termed production for 'use-values', in capitalist society this becomes the production of 'exchange-values'. Thus the capitalist mode of production is that in which the product takes the form of a commodity, or is produced directly for exchange (see, for example, 'Commodities: Use-value and Exchange Value', from Marx, *Capital*, Vol. 1, in McLellan, 1985, pp. 421–35). Hence, rather than serving to fulfil *human* needs, production 'for the market' fulfills the needs of *Capital*.

Thus dialectical method in the identification of contradictions, the analysis of their causes and the means of their resolution, is clearly evident alongside the scientific realist and practical materialist approaches. Nowhere is this more so than in Marx's analysis of historical progress to the contemporary 'bourgeois' era from earlier epochs. Each is characterised by class struggle, but each mode of production also represents a *thesis*, within which works its *antithesis* – forces not just in opposition to the existing mode of production, but whose triumph would usher in a new, higher mode of production. As intimated earlier, the conflict between thesis and antithesis is resolved only when the following occurs:

> At a certain stage of their development the material forces of production in society come into conflict with the existing relations of production . . . From forms of development of the forces of production these relations turn into their fetters. Then comes the period of social revolution (from Marx, 1859, cited in Feuer, 1984, p. 84).

The ultimate outcome of a successful revolution sees the *synthesis* of the best of the old order and the new, but revolutions do not happen because revolutionaries *want* them to.

As alienation is analysed both objectively and subjectively – scientifically explaining both the appearance and the (underlying) causal reality – so too is the means of its transcendence. The objective conditions for revolution are indicated above, but a successful revolution requires the correspondence between these and necessary *subjective* conditions: the 'revolutionary class' must move from the objectively identifiable position of a 'class *in* itself' to subjective *recognition of itself as a class with its own class interests*; in other words it must become 'a class *for* itself' *acting* in its own class interests. Given the proletarian class interest in the abolition of the distinction between capital and labour, for the first time the victory of this revolutionary class serves to abolish class itself:

> the proletariat . . . cannot attain its emancipation from the sway of the exploiting and ruling class – the bourgeoisie – without, at the same time, and once and for all, emancipating society at large from all exploitation, oppression, class distinctions and class struggles (Marx and Engels, 'Preface' to the 1888 English edition of the *Manifesto of the Communist Party*, cited in Feuer, 1984, p. 46).

From 'Early' to 'Mature' Marx

In later works, Marx moves from social and political philosophy, to contemporary empirical research and analysis in sociology and political economy. He applies the theoretical and analytical bases previously outlined to provide both objective description and explanation of the underlying causal realities, and to account for the subjective 'surface' understandings of involved social actors, and hence the level of appearance. Marx's *The Eighteenth Brumaire of Louis Bonaparte* (1852) marks this analytical transition.

The Eighteenth Brumaire analyses a society *in transition* (France 1848–52), and if in retrospect (as in the *Manifesto* for example) the transition from one mode of production to another can appear uncomplicated, *during* such a transition elements of more than one mode of production can be identified, and therefore the class picture can appear ambiguous and even contradictory. In considering the nature of the class struggle Marx analyses the *motivations* for agents' actions as *surface* differences (within individual consciousnesses) relating to the *appearance* of things. But support for different forms of monarchy and republicanism produce real effects in the material world; implicitly granting a certain autonomy of the political and ideological. Nevertheless the *underlying* different forms of property and property relations bound up with and/or represented by these surface differences are, for Marx, the crucial factor in the analysis. Thus the ultimate effect of Louis Bonaparte's rule is the state's facilitating the economic development which makes possible bourgeois political rule, at which time Bonaparte is cast aside. But if the move from the abstract to the empirical is epitomised sociologically with *The Eighteenth Brumaire*, given his emphasis upon the centrality of underlying economic relations, Marx's 'moving on' inevitably culminates with *Capital* (1867).

Marx asserts that *Capital* is a work of science, and explains that his object is the study of 'the natural laws of capitalist production . . . these tendencies working with iron necessity towards inevitable results' (*Capital*, Vol. 1, cited in McLellan, 1985, p. 416); the nineteenth century conception of the unity of causal explicability and causal inevitability is plainly in evidence. Following from his work in *The Eighteenth Brumaire*, *Capital* stresses the 'needs' of the structure above human needs, emphasises alienated labour above human alienation, with both downgraded by the focus upon the means of capitalist appropriation from the proletariat: surplus value. 'Surplus value' emerges from the idea that, in creating commodities for the market, labour creates the exchange-value of those commodities, but receives only a small part of that value created, the difference equalling the capitalists' profit. But beyond this demonstration of exploitation, Marx's concern with conditions appertaining to 'the working day', and thereby the effects of 'the English factory acts' and so on, leads him to write, for example:

> in its blind unrestrainable passion, its werewolf hunger for surplus labour, Capital oversteps not only the moral, but even the merely physical maximum bounds of the working day . . . Capital cares nothing for the length of life of labour power. All that concerns it is simply and solely the maximum of labour power that can be rendered fluent in a working day . . . Hence Capital is reckless of the health or length of life of the labourer (Marx, *Capital*, Vol. 1, cited in Feuer, 1984, pp. 188–9, 192).

It is clear from the above that capital is *the cause* of these *effects* on the individual worker; capit*al* is the prime mover rather than capital*ists*. Indeed, for Marx *humanity as a whole – even the capitalist –* is alienated and debased in being compelled to serve the interests of capital. Capital is the 'autocrat' over all society. This is quite consistent with Marx's concerns in earlier works. To take alienation for example, in relation to religion, Marx shows how humans come to attribute to God qualities the essence of which are human. The more the 'greater glories of God' are celebrated the more humanity, by comparison, becomes debased; humans thus become subordinated to God, alienated in religion, and thereby dominated. So with politics, the state is a human creation within which humans become alienated; the state comes to dominate them, they serve the state instead of seeing it as created to serve their needs. So with law, so with morality, and *so with* *capital*. It is also consistent in that the scientific realist, practical materialist and dialectical approaches are clear within *Capital*, as in other works by Marx and Engels.

Marxism and Modern Science

Whilst the value of empirical observation and research within scientific enterprise is disputed, the *need* for (as opposed to the *derivation of*) scientific theory – to 'put phenomena into systems' (Sayer, 1979, p. 115) – is not. Given that the less constancy found in the qualities of the subjects for study, the less reliable will be the theories appertaining to them, the traditional greater acceptance of natural rather than social scientific theories as genuinely 'scientific' derived largely from natural science's subject matter being seemingly constant in a way that social phenomena could never be; the greater *inconstancy* found by the 'hard' sciences more recently has certainly made theoretical precision much less possible. This indicates both the closer congruence than previously thought between natural and social science, and that between dialectical method and theories of chaos and complexity. The similarity indicated earlier between Kuhn's theory of scientific advance and Woods and Grant's outline of dialectics (see note 5) is striking, and other examples abound.

One scientific illustration of dialectical qualitative from quantitative change is provided by water at boiling point. If we take water as the thesis, the presence of heat, its antithesis, will first produce quantitative changes, progressively more bubbles appearing on the water's surface:

> As the temperature nears boiling point, the increase in heat does not immediately cause the water molecules to fly apart. Until it reaches boiling point, the water keeps its volume. It remains water because of the attraction of the molecules for each other. However, the steady change in temperature has the effect of increasing the motion of the molecules. The volume between the atoms is gradually increased, to the point where the force of attraction is insufficient to hold the molecules together. At precisely 1000°C, any increase in heat energy will cause the molecules to fly apart, producing steam (Woods and Grant, 1995, p. 49)

Steam, the qualitative change produced out of the contradiction between thesis and antithesis, *synthesises* qualities from both.

The nature and mechanics of dialectical transition from quantitative to qualitative change seems virtually identical to that which science calls 'phase transitions'; the manner by which solid changes to liquid, or liquid to vapour, non-magnet to magnet or conductor to super-conductor (see Woods and Grant, 1995, p. 53):

> [P]hase transitions involve a kind of macroscopic behaviour that seems hard to predict by looking at the microscopic details. When a solid is heated its molecules vibrate with the added energy. They push outward against their bonds and force the substance to expand. The more heat, the more expansion. Yet at a certain temperature and pressure, the change becomes sudden and discontinuous. A rope has been stretching; now it breaks. Crystalline form dissolves, and the molecules slide away from one another. They obey fluid laws that could not have been inferred from any aspect of the solid. The average atomic energy has barely changed, but the material – now a liquid, or a magnet, or a superconductor – has entered a new realm (Gleick, 1988, p. 127)

Woods and Grant (1995) offer similar examples in abundance, but there is space here for only one – particularly apposite – further example of dialectics/phase transition.

The genetic difference between humans and chimpanzees is less than 2 per cent; *quantitatively* then there is little to separate the two. However:

> Recent research with bonobo chimpanzees has proven beyond doubt that the primates closest to humans are capable of a level of mental activity similar in some respects to that of a human child [Yet] . . . Despite all the efforts of the experimenters, captive bonobos have not been able to speak or fashion a stone tool remotely similar to the simplest implements created by early hominids. The two percent genetic difference between humans and chimpanzees marks the *qualitative leap* from the animal to the human. (Woods and Grant, 1995, p. 31, my emphasis)

Moreover, modern scientific discoveries in the field of paleontology 'show that hominid apes appeared in Africa far earlier than previously thought, and that they had brains no bigger than those of a modern chimpanzee. That is to say that *the development of the brain came after the production of tools, and as a result of it.*' (see Woods and Grant, 1995, p. 33, my emphasis)

This is striking evidence of praxis and historical materialism: mental development following from the manual tasks necessarily undertaken in order to overcome environmental challenges.

The congruence between dialectical analysis and both Kuhnian 'paradigm shifts' and the 'phase transitions' of chaos theory is thus as clear as Marxism's incompatibility with theories derived from empiricist bases.

However, having considered scientific *theory*, it is broadly agreed that science must employ an appropriate *method* of study towards an appropriate *purpose*. Taking the methodological question first – how might we best *know* and understand, the world – dialectical method and scientific realism hold that the (observable) *appearance* of things (and our experience of them) must be penetrated to identify underlying causal relations; including what *causes* things to *appear* to us the way they do. We may thereby penetrate *mis*-perception, *mis*-understanding, and avoid being *misled* by associations derived from observation alone. This quotation from *Capital* highlights this:

> A Negro is a Negro. He only becomes a slave in certain relations. A cotton-spinning jenny is a machine for spinning cotton. It becomes *capital* only in certain relations. Torn from these relationships it is no more capital than gold in itself is *money* or sugar the price of sugar (Marx, cited in Sayer, 1979, p. 145).

However, we have also seen that for Marx, 'the point' of properly *knowing* the world, is to *change* it. Is this congruent with the purpose of science? Well, the 'orthodox' view of the purpose of science is its furtherance of technology, the 'official' purpose of which is to improve human conditions; hence the purpose of *science* may be said to be to improve the way in which we humans experience the world. Thus, it would seem that the Marxist project is perfectly consistent with the purposive requirements of science. But given this need to change the world (and the critique from 'hostile' scientific models), the charge that Marxism is unscientific *because of the failure of its predictions* requires consideration.

Since prediction on 'irrational' bases (for example, tarot cards), has no scientific basis, any claim to predictive power by science must be founded upon the discovery of antecedent *causes* of those events predicted. Hence, in fact, science has always been more about *prognoses* than *predictions*. Meteorological 'forecasts' provide an instructive example. These are generated from systematically gathered empirical evidence analysed within a framework of known causal relations. It is thus the *method* which assigns meteorology the status of science, even despite its forecasts – or prognoses – often proving inaccurate. We are thus returned to the methodological question already dealt with, and to the contemporary recognition of the similarity between natural and social science following from the increasing uncertainties found by the so-called 'hard' sciences; there is now less talk of immutable scientific 'laws' than scientifically identified – but not necessarily invariable – 'trends' and 'probabilities'.

Sadly, Marx's 'predictions' are far better known than their bases. As shown, Marx identified both objective and subjective conditions as necessary for the proletarian revolution; each aspect constituting a necessary but not sufficient condition, the conjunction of the two being required. Marx certainly *expected* and thus 'predicted' such a conjunction – *on the basis of known contemporary trends and their measured and indicated effects.* His *prognosis* for capitalism – his prediction of the proletarian revolution – was however faulted by subsequent *changed behaviour* of the capitalist state and so on, which inhibited the development of the *subjective* requirement for revolution. The absence of mass proletarian class consciousness has therefore become a major concern of modern Marxism, which explains its primary focus upon the hegemonic nature of the capitalist state.

Conclusion

The only certainty in relation to the question of Marxism's scientific status is that it can never *be* certified one way or another, whilst there exist incompatible 'models' of science competing for dominance and legitimacy. That said, it is my view, on the basis of the foregoing consideration, that Marxism's claim is as good as that of other disciplines generally *accepted* as scientific, and that the latest scientific developments have only strengthened that claim. This conclusion is somewhat ironic however, in the light of the intensifying contemporary questioning of such scientific status itself. A more apposite conclusion might then be that, as with, for example, Newtonian theory, Marxism's validity should not be seen to rest upon whether it is or is not scientific or indeed 'true', but rather, upon its practical usefulness in increasing our store of knowledge and aiding progressive social change. If Marxism's theoretical and analytical bases are unable to facilitate meaningful and fulfilling human progress and development, any 'success' elsewhere would surely be meaningless.

1. Durkheim, in *The Rules of Sociological Method* (1895), held that whilst (social) science employed the study of (social) facts constituting 'a constant standard which is always to hand for the observer, and which leaves no room for subjective impressions or personal observations', the 'ideological method' employed 'the use of notions to govern the collation of facts rather than deriving notions from them' (quoted in McLellan, 1986, p. 36).
2. This is very much a generalized, indicative rather than specific, exhaustive list, but is sufficient for present purposes.
3. 'Universally recognised scientific achievements that for a time provide model problems and solutions to a community of practitioners' (Kuhn, 1970, p. viii).
4. 'philosophers have only interpreted the world, in various ways; the point, however, is to change it' (Marx, *Theses on Feuerbach*, 1845).
5. We might note at this point the similarity between this exposition of dialectics and Kuhn's exposition of how scientific progress is made.

PART TWO

SUBSTANTIVE ISSUES

7

Marxism and Social Class

JIM JOHNSTON AND DAVID P. DOLOWITZ

The aim of this chapter is to examine the development of the concept of 'class', within the Marxist theoretical tradition. First, we establish the centrality of this concept within the original writings of Marx. Second, we address some of Weber's key criticisms of classical Marxist theory and discuss his alternative class schema. Finally, we analyse the manner in which modern Marxists have responded to both Weber's initial critique and the changes in class composition which have occurred, particularly since the Second World War. In doing so we aim to illustrate the continuing utility of a Marxist approach to the study of social class.

The Dualistic Nature of Marxist Theory

In examining the concept of social class, it is necessary to explore the dualism which exists within Marxist theory; essentially there is both a voluntarist element and a determinist element within Marx's works. On the one hand, he views socialism as developing inevitably as a result of the internal contradictions of capitalism. Consequently, he aims to explain the objective conditions which act as the motor-engine of historical change. For this purpose, Marx conducted an exhaustive empirical study of nineteenth century European capitalism in an attempt to uncover the 'laws of history' which were guiding humanity on an inexorable odyssey towards an inevitable revolutionary moment on the cusp of a brave new socialist world. It is this enormous empirical investigation which forms the bulk of *Capital*.

A deterministic reading of Marx's writings necessarily understates the role of social classes within Marxist philosophy. Therefore, in emphasizing the centrality of the concept of social class to Marx we are rejecting a vulgar reductionist interpretation of his work. One of the enduring criticisms of Marxist theory is that it denies the influence of conscious human agency in history. If this were the case, the role of social classes would become largely insignificant within a schema which emphasised the determinacy of structural factors. For example, if the collapse of the capitalist economic system of production is inevitable, owing to its inherent, internal contradictions, the need for a revolutionary class to overthrow it is negated. The role of both capitalist and wage-labourer alike is reduced to that of a passive onlooker as history unfolds before them.

However Marx does not expect socialism simply to evolve from the ashes of capitalism, but advocates a violent revolution to overthrow it. Marxism becomes the theoretical motivation for such a revolution. This creates a paradox: if capitalism is creating the conditions for its own downfall, why the need for a revolution? Marx answers this by arguing, as in 'The Eighteenth Brumaire of Louis Bonaparte', that it is men who make history: 'Men make their own history, but not spontaneously, under conditions they have chosen for themselves; rather on terms immediately existing, given and handed down to them' (Kamenka, 1983, p. 287).

Additionally, in *The Holy Family*, Marx writes: 'History does nothing; it "does not possess immense riches," it "does *not* fight battles." It is *men*, real, living men, who do all this, who possess things and fight battles History is *nothing* but the activity of men in the pursuit of their ends' (Bottomore and Rubel, 1956; rpt, 1990 p. 78). Despite the contradictions which may exist within any given society, it is only through the conscious actions of men that they become apparent. It is this voluntarist element and, in particular, the emphasis on the need for a revolutionary movement to overthrow capitalism which accords the concept of social class a central role within Marx's theory of history.

Historical Materialism

This material interpretation of history, commonly referred to as historical materialism, is most clearly set out in *The German Ideology* (1968a). Marx views history in terms of the development of a succession of *modes of production*. He identifies a mode of production as a combination of the productive forces (machinery, tools, technology and so on) and the relations of production (principally those between the owners and non-owners of private property) which exist in any society. This position is also summarised in a well known passage in Marx (1859) in which he refers to historical materialism as 'the guiding principle of my studies'.

Within this passage Marx identifies four main factors which constitute the basis of his material interpretation of history. First, the sum total of the relations of production constitute the real basis of society. Second, as the forces of production continue to develop, the existing relations of production become obsolete and hinder further development, thus precipitating a period of social revolution. Third, it is necessary for the forces of production to develop as fully as possible under the existing relations of production before the old social order collapses. Finally, the Asiatic, ancient, feudal and capitalist modes of production are progressive epochs in the economic formation of society.

From this passage it also becomes clear that historical change is the consequence of two interrelated factors. First, the primary driving force of history is the technological development of the forces of production. The basis of all societies is the machinery, tools, technology and so on which is available for employment within the productive process. It is the level of the development of these productive forces which determines the immediate relations of production in any society.

The relations of production include both property relations and the division of labour. Property relations constitute the legal arrangements guaranteeing the ownership of both the forces of production and the subsequent products of labour. The social division of labour is determined, not by differences in the type of production which individuals are engaged in, but by their relationship to the means of production. As we will discuss below, it is the social division of labour which leads to the formation of social classes. For example, those who are manually involved in the production of material commodities are differentiated from other functions such as management, administration or intellectual work.

The Origins of Social Classes

Within Marxist theory the starting-point of human history is Man's struggle with nature to meet his immediate material means of subsistence: 'The first premise of all human history is, of course, the existence of living human individuals. The first historical act of these individuals distinguishing them from animals is not that they think, but that they begin to produce their means of subsistence' (Marx and Engels, 1969, vol. 1, p. 20). The fundamental basis of all societies is economic: how we produce our basic material means of subsistence. In contrast to the metaphysical and idealist philosophy of Hegel, within which history is the product of the progress of human thought or reason, Marx argues that any study of historical change should begin with the real, practical activities of Man. Societies are formed out of the necessity of co-operating on a social level in order to produce a minimal level of subsistence:

> In production, men not only act on nature but also on one another. They produce only by cooperating in a certain way and mutually exchanging their activities. In order to produce, they enter into definite connections and relations with one another and only within these social connections and relations does their action on nature, does production, take place. (Ibid., p. 89)

From this passage we can also establish that Marx views the productive process as involving a definite set of social relations. It is here that Marx radically distances himself from the liberal individualism of philosophers such as Locke and Bentham. Whereas the latter view social and economic change in terms of the actions of individual actors, Marx emphasises the communal nature of the production process. Societies emerge from the co-operation of a number of individuals seeking to meet a basic level of subsistence.

However the social organisation of production leads to the creation of a division of labour. Put simply, this entails each individual specializing in a particular area of the production process; for example, one individual may excel at hunting while another may develop skill as a tool maker. Crucially the increasingly sophisticated nature of this process means that the level of output is raised to such a point that a surplus is created beyond the bare minimum required to meet a basic level of subsistence. Marx argues that it is this development which leads to the emergence of social classes. As soon as any society is able to produce more material goods than the bare minimum needed to survive, classes emerge. Primarily a minority class emerges which is able to seize the surplus, thus freeing it from the immediate productive process and allowing it to strengthen its dominance, over both society in general and the producer class in particular.

Marx views history as a process of successive stages of class domination. In every society and every stage in the evolution of that society there exists a dominant class which although being in a minority is able to exploit a subordinate, majority, class. The ruling class is able to appropriate the economic surplus created by the productive class (slaves, feudal serfs, wage-labourers). It is this ability to appropriate an economic surplus which forms the basis of the wealth and the private property of the ruling class.

However, as the basis of the ruling class's wealth is the exploitation of a subordinate class, all class societies are inevitably antagonistic. Although class relationships are necessarily interdependent in the sense that each class relies on the other for its material wealth, it is an unequal relationship. It would initially appear that the wage-labourer is free both to choose for which capitalist he wishes to work and to negotiate the price of his labour. However, as the capitalist can survive much longer from the luxury of his own private property than the labourer can on his wages, the capitalist's need to create more surplus value is not as great as the worker's need to earn a wage. Consequently the capitalist can refuse to employ workers seeking too high a wage and find other labourers prepared to work for a lower rate. Therefore social inequality stems from the owners of production exploiting the non-owners. It is impossible to reconcile the antagonistic nature of class relations within the existing mode of production in which those relations were formed.

Because of the inherently unstable nature of class relations and the continual development of the forces of production, society exists within a constant state of flux. Social change is driven by two interrelated antagonistic relationships. First, there is a conflict between the relations of production and the forces of production. As the machinery and technology employed in the production process evolve and develop, the existing relations of production inevitably become obsolete. For example, the invention of the steam engine facilitated mass production within factories and led to the development of industrial towns which necessitated the end of the feudal system. Consequently a class struggle ensued between the aristocracy, whose political and cultural dominance was ensured by the feudal economic system, and the nascent capitalist class. This conflict is realised primarily at a political and social level. As such, objective economic conditions are realised subjectively in the political struggle between the conflicting classes.

What Constitutes a Social Class?

Despite the centrality of the concept of class within the overall Marxist schema, it is astonishing that no exact definition of class exists anywhere in the writings of Marx. However, from some of the references to 'class' in key passages within his work, it is possible to establish general criteria for a Marxist theory of social class. First, it is clear that an individual's class position is not simply determined by his/her employment. Second, class relations are social in character as opposed to involving a purely economic relationship. Third, Marx makes a clear distinction between an objective class position and a subjective class position: between a 'class in itself' and a 'class for itself'. Fourth, although his primary view of class relations is dichotomous, within Marx's later writings there is a growing awareness of the development of intermediate strata.

The Inadequacy of an Employment-based Definition of Social Class

As has been well-documented within the literature, the manuscript of the third volume of *Capital* breaks off at the moment when Marx was about to answer the question: 'What constitutes a class?' However, before the manuscript ends, he makes it clear that class should not be identified with either source of income or location within the division of labour:

> What makes wage-laborers, capitalists and landlords constitute the three great social classes? ... At first glance – the identity of revenues and sources of revenue ... However, from this standpoint, physicians and officials, e.g., would also constitute two classes, for they belong to two distinct social groups, the members of each of these groups receiving their revenue from one and the same source. (Tucker, 1978, pp. 441–2)

Consequently, Marx argues that it would initially appear that class is determined by sources of income. However, on this basis, doctors, officials and many other income groups would constitute separate classes. This criterion is rejected as being insufficient.

Instead Marx argues that class relationships are social relationships rather than purely economic relations. As such, class is not simply a reflection of a specific economic system. Similar production techniques have existed within different class societies; for example, non-mechanical farming techniques have been employed in slave, feudal and early capitalist societies. What distinguishes the slave from the serf, from the farm labourer is not the production methods which they utilised, but their relationship with the dominant class. The slave was coerced into producing; the serf subsisted on his produce, while the surplus was expropriated by the feudal lord; and the farm-labourer received a wage which was less than the total value of the product which he created.

Rather than being defined by income group, class position is determined by an individual's position in the organisation and relations of production. Classes are an aspect of the relations of production. Consequently an individual's class position is determined by his/her specific relationship to the means of production. This allows us to differentiate between self-employed workers and wage-labourers. An electrician employed directly by a large building company becomes a member of a different class from a self-employed electrician who is contracted by the same firm.

Although Marx recognises that there are other classes, the fundamental division is that between exploiter and exploited. In particular, two primary classes emerge: the owners and the non-owners of private property. Within the capitalist mode of production, the bourgeoisie derive their class position from their ownership of the means of production. In direct contrast, the proletariat owns no means of production. The relationship between these two classes is necessarily conflictual, in the sense that each class can gain materially only at the other's expense. Most obviously any increase in wages achieved by the proletariat results in a decrease in profits for the capitalist. Consequently all class societies are characterised by the antagonistic relationship between the dominant owners of production and a subordinate class of non-owners. As we discuss below, Marx argues that it is only through a process of conflict that individuals become aware of their common class identity.

The nature of class conflict is intrinsically linked to the mode of production existing in any society. In pre-capitalist societies, class relations are much more personalised, whereas in capitalist society they are governed by the workings of the market. In feudal society there are closer individual ties between the dominant and subordinate classes. The serf is tied to an individual master and must pay tithes directly to him. In contrast, the wage-labourer has no definite ties with an individual capitalist, but is dependent on the workings of the market as a whole. Additionally the serf retains a degree of autonomy in that he possesses a large level of control over his means of production. It is only through the emergence of the capitalist economic system that the exploitative nature of the relations of production becomes explicit and universalised. Bourgeois society

> has pitilessly torn asunder the motley feudal ties that bound man to his 'natural superiors', and has left no other nexus between man and man than naked self-interest, than callous 'cash payment' In one word, for exploitation veiled by religious and political illusions, it has substituted naked, shameless, direct, brutal exploitation. (Kamenka, 1983, p. 206)

It is the economic development of capitalism which creates the conditions for the development of a class with the potential to realise its own revolutionary role. The development of large-scale industry leads to the concentration of the proletariat in densely populated urban centres where they can collectively realise the injustice of their economic position. In contrast to earlier social groups such as feudal serfs and peasants who lived in isolated communities, the working class are brought together by the nature of the capitalist system.

A 'Class in Itself' or a 'Class for Itself'?

In addition to its economic character Marx also introduces a psychological and sociological criterion to his concept of class. He makes a distinction between a class which exists objectively (*Klasse an sich*) and a class in which its members have become fully conscious of their common interests (*Klasse für sich*). At times Marx distinguishes between the two types of class by referring to the objective class as forming only a 'stratum'. The class-in-itself, exists objectively in the sense that a number of individuals share a common structural position in relation to the means of production. In particular, there are owners of property and non-owners of property. However, in order to become a class-for-itself, it is necessary for individuals sharing a common objective position to recognise their common interests and their common class opponent. Only when a class has become aware of its common position and common enemy can it be said to exist as a truly viable social class: 'the separate individuals form a class only insofar as they have to carry on a common battle against another class; otherwise they are on hostile terms with each other as competitors' (Marx and Engels, 1969, Vol. 1, p. 65). That is, unless the two principal classes recognise their respective interests vis-à-vis each other, they will sink into a self-defeating intra-class conflict.

Therefore it is only through a process of conflict that individuals become aware of their common class identity. This point can be illustrated by Marx's comments on the nineteenth century French peasantry in 'The Eighteenth Brumaire of Louis Bonaparte':

> In so far as millions of families live under economic conditions which divide their way of life, their interests and their cultural level from those of other classes, and foster hostility towards them, they form a single class. In so far as a purely local connection only exists among the smallholders and the identity of their interests fosters no community spirit, no national association and no political organization among them, they do not form a class. (Kamenka, 1983, p. 312)

From the above quotation it becomes clear that class is not simply an economic concept. Although the peasants occupy a similar position in relation to the means of production, this is not sufficient for them to form a class. It is necessary for them, first, to realise that they hold similar interests and, second, to realise these interests can be advanced through collective political action against a common class enemy. Thus it is necessary for a class to form a political organisation which will advance its collective interests. Therefore it is at the superstructural level that class conflict is realised. Class antagonisms manifest themselves in terms of a political, social, cultural and ideological struggle. For example, the state becomes a principal stage on which the class struggle is fought out (see Chapter 10 of this book).

Intermediate Classes

The revolutionary nature of much of Marx's writings and, in particular, his emphasis on the need for the proletariat to overthrow capitalism through revolutionary means necessitates an emphasis on a dichotomous view of social class. Although at an empirical level Marx recognises the existence of a number of marginal classes within capitalist society, at a theoretical level he continues to emphasise the polarisation of classes into an increasingly capitalist class and an expanding proletariat. The ranks of the proletariat are swollen by petty capitalists, independent artisans, peasantry and other strata from outmoded productive forces or relations of production. This is a position which is most famously depicted in *The Communist Manifesto:* 'the epoch of the bourgeoisie possesses . . . this distinctive feature: it has simplified the class antagonisms. Society as a whole is more and more splitting up into two great hostile camps, into two great classes directly facing each other – bourgeoisie and proletariat' (Kamenka, 1983, p. 204).

However, as Giddens argues, 'the dichotomous class conception appears in Marx's writings as a theoretical construct' (1971; rpt, 1991, p. 38). Essentially the Marxist theory of social class is based on an ideal type which would only emerge from the real social world in the final stages of capitalism. In reality, all societies within the Marxist schema are more complex than is immediately suggested by a dichotomous model. It was clear to Marx from much of his empirical work on the development of nineteenth century capitalism that the intermediate stratum was in fact increasing in size. Indeed, he makes this point explicitly in a comment on Ricardo in the manuscript of 'Theories of Surplus Value':

> What [Ricardo] forgets to mention is the continual increase in the numbers of the middle classes . . . situated midway between the workers on one side and the capitalists on the other, who rest with all their weight upon the working class and at the same time increase the social security and power of the upper ten thousand. (Bottomore, 1973; rpt, 1979, p. 23)

Similarly the degree to which a class exists as a homogenous entity varies throughout history; for example, within 'The Class Struggles in France' (1850), Marx recognises the divisions between industrial and financial capital. However, despite this awareness of the heterogeneity of classes at an empirical level, it is arguable that at a theoretical level a dichotomous model of class relations remains dominant. In particular, Marx's prediction of the inevitability of a proletarian revolution and the emergence of a socialist society is heavily dependent on the polarisation of classes.

From the above we have established that Marx prioritises the existing economic conditions in analysing the character of all societies. In particular, social inequality is determined by the exploitative relationship between the owners of production and the non-owners of production. Although this exploitation has historically taken different forms, the social, political and ideological power of the dominant class is directly related to their ownership of the means of production.

The Weberian Critique: Class, Status and Power

In contrast, Max Weber argues that economic wealth is only one of a number of factors which influence social inequality. Whereas Marx argues that social relations are determined by an individual's relation to the means of production, Weber argues that, in addition to social class, an individual's 'status' and 'power' have a direct bearing on their position within the social hierarchy.

Class

Weber also views class in economic terms and accepts Marx's view that the major class divisions are those between the owners of production and the non-owners of production. However he departs from Marxism on the degree of homogeneity within the propertyless class. Weber argues that the propertyless class can be distinguished by their relative market situation. This leads to a greater emphasis on employment in identifying an individual's class position than exists within the Marxist model.

For Weber, an individual's class position is determined by their 'market situation'. Individuals are grouped together on the basis of a similar position in a market economy. Although Weber agrees with Marx on the centrality of property-ownership to an individual's class position, he also identifies other factors which influence an individual's market position. In particular, he emphasises a number of important differences in the market situation of the propertyless groups in society. A clear distinction is made between occupational groups such as managers and professionals, whose skills and experience are a useful resource in bargaining for higher levels of remuneration and relatively unskilled workers who lack similar resources. This observation led Weber to formulate the following class schema: (i) the propertied upper class, (ii) the propertyless white-collar workers, (iii) the petty bourgeoisie, and (iv) the manual working class. Therefore Weber argues that factors other than ownership or non-ownership of the means of production are significant in the formation of classes. Class is determined by an individual's market position which is primarily dependent on skills and qualifications.

Weber also rejects Marx's theory on the polarisation of the classes and the inevitability of a working class revolution. In particular, Weber argues that the white-collar middle class will grow in size as capitalism develops. The expansion of the capitalist economic system and the increasing size of the modern state both lead to a growth in bureaucratic administration. Consequently there is a huge growth in the number of managerial and white-collar workers. Additionally he argues that there is no reason to believe that a similar class background is a sufficient basis for the formation of a revolutionary struggle. There is no guarantee that a group of individuals sharing a similar class position will develop a collective awareness of their communal interests or that they will respond to their circumstances through collective action.

Status

Whereas class refers to the unequal distribution of economic relations, status refers to the unequal distribution of 'social honour'. Those who share the same class position will not necessarily share the same status. Weber argues that the factors determining individual status are multi-dimensional; for example, gender, income, educational attainment and ethnic background may all contribute to an individual's status in society. Crucially, and in contrast to economic classes who are not always aware of their collective interests, status groups are continuously aware of their commonality.

Status groups continually identify with a collective interest and continually seek to reproduce themselves through educational achievement in order to demonstrate their exclusiveness. In developing the concept of status groups, Weber is clearly attempting to provide an alternative to a Marxist analysis of economic class. He argues that, whereas economic classes are simply an aggregate of individuals within the market, status groups represent an integrated whole which is continually aware of a common identity and willing to act politically to uphold communal interests.

Power

The final factor which Weber identifies as influential in determining social stratification is power. In contrast to Marx, Weber argues that economic advantage is not the only basis of power within society. Through his analysis of a number of historical societies, Weber sought to demonstrate that various factors other than the ownership of the means of production were influential in forming power structures.[1]

Therefore, in developing his analysis of social inequality, Weber argues that we need a much more complex model of societal relations than the dichotomous model provided by classical Marxism. In particular, he rejects a narrowly economistic explanation of social inequality within capitalist society. He argues that Marxism prioritises economic relations within society so that all other relational forms are to some extent influenced by the ownership of property. Consequently Marxists have difficulty in explaining inequalities which are not related to class, for example, age, gender and race.

The Increasingly Complex Organisation of Modern Capitalism

Weber's powerful critique of the classical Marxist position has been strengthened by the *actual* development of modern capitalism. In particular, the development of joint-stock companies, the subsequent separation of ownership and the management of capitalism and a concomitant explosion in the number of intermediate occupations has resulted in an apparent diffusion of social class rather than the polarisation predicted by Marx. The emergence of joint-stock companies resulted in the multiple ownership of the means of production. This plurality of ownership, allied to the complexity of the production process, made it impossible for the owners of capital to participate directly in the day-to-day running of individual firms. Consequently there has been a rapid expansion of the technical division of labour and a huge increase in the number of intermediate occupations.

In response to developments within the structure of capitalist organisation and Weberian critiques of the classical Marxist analysis of social class, modern Marxist writers have become increasingly concerned with the class positions of intermediate occupations such as engineers, technicians, professionals, experts, managers, administrators, teachers and bureaucrats. The key question neo-Marxists are trying to address is whether these workers have a class interest distinct from that of the 'old' working class. It is necessary to discover the class interest of these intermediate occupations because only then will a viable socialist project emerge. If the class interests of these intermediate occupations are different from those of the old working class, a mechanism for linking the interests of white collar workers and the proletariat must be found.[2] As the American neo-Marxist, Erik Olin Wright argues:

classes are not merely analytical abstractions in Marxist theory; they are real social forces and they have real consequences. It matters a great deal for our understanding of class struggle and social change exactly how classes are conceptualised and which categories of social positions are placed in which classes. Above all, it matters for developing a viable socialist politics how narrow or broad the working class is seen to be and how its relationship to other classes is understood. (Wright, 1978, p. 30–1)

With the decline of liberal capitalism and the rise of monopoly capitalism during the twentieth century, there emerged a new stratum of intermediate occupations, lying between the manual worker and the capitalist. These occupations emerged as capitalist firms were transformed from simple organisations, under the control of a single owner, to complex associations of individuals and functions within the context of 'scientific organisation'. In this process, work was split into a number of different 'technical divisions', each performing different tasks under distinct section managers.[3] As Wright argues:

As the scale of capital-accumulating units expanded in the course of the concentration and centralisation of capital, it became impossible for the capitalist to participate directly in all aspects of decision-making . . . it became particularly imperative to develop a responsible managerial hierarchy to conduct the day-to-day operations of capitalist productions. (Wright, 1976, p. 30)

This development was accelerated by the emergence and expansion of the joint-stock company, in which 'ownership' has been taken out of the hands of a single individual and distributed to numerous stock holders. As ownership has shifted, managers have taken on the role once played by the capitalist under the nineteenth century's system of private capitalism. As Carchedi noted, if we are to understand the place of managers in the social structure,

we must start by examining how the production process has changed in shifting from private capitalism to monopoly capitalism. On this level, the manager, rather than the capitalist rentier, is the central figure, he, rather than the capitalist rentier, is the non-labourer, the non-producer, the exploiter. (Carchedi, 1975, p. 48)

This process has been exaggerated with the expansion of share ownership throughout the later decades of the twentieth century. With the spread of share ownership, each 'owner' has less overall power, which increases the autonomy of managers in the day-to-day operations of business. Consequently a major problem which has to be addressed by neo-Marxists is where to locate this managerial stratum within their class schema.

The Neo-Marxist Response

The fundamental structural changes within the capitalist economic system since the time of Marx's writings has led many neo-Marxists to reappraise the simplistic dichotomous class schema which exists within classical Marxism. Within the existing literature we can identify four typical responses to the increasing number of intermediate strata. First, contemporary Marxists such as Harry Braverman (1974) simply relocate these intermediate positions within either the bourgeoisie or proletariat, therefore retaining a dichotomous schema.[4] Second, Poulantzas (1975) argues that the emerging intermediate strata form a 'new' petty bourgeoisie which is ideologically linked to the 'old' petty bourgeoisie. Third, Barbara and John Ehrenreich (1979) identify the emergence of a 'new class'. Finally, the most theoretically developed analysis places the intermediate positions within contradictory locations which contain elements of the petty bourgeoisie, proletariat and bourgeoisie (Wright, 1985).[5]

A Defence of the Classical Position

There remain some Marxists who continue to utilise a dichotomous class schema. For such authors, the main criterion in identifying an individual's class position remains the ownership or non-ownership of the means of production. As the vast majority of the emerging intermediate stratum remain dependent on a wage they are located within the ranks of the proletariat: 'at most, professional and managerial wage-earners constitute a privileged stratum of the proletariat, but their existence or expansion does not require any modification of the basic class map of capitalism' (Wright, 1985, p. 38). While managers and professionals act as agents of capital, performing the work of *control and surveillance* they are viewed as working class because they do not own their means of production. Consequently they must sell their labour in order to survive and remain exploited in the same way as manual workers.

Owing to the impact of the technological revolution within modern capitalism, Braverman argues: 'I cannot accept the arbitrary conception of a "new working class" that has been developed by some writers during the past decade' (1974, p. 25). For example, with the rise of Taylorism and scientific management, office work, once a privileged position, has been reduced to little more than manual labour:

> The traditional distinctions between 'manual' and 'white-collar' labour, which are so thoughtlessly and widely used in the literature on this subject, represent echoes of a past situation which has virtually ceased to have meaning in the modern world of work. And with the rapid progress of mechanisation in offices it becomes all the more important to grasp this. (Ibid., pp. 325–6)

Central to Braverman's analysis is his rejection of the distinction between the mental and manual divide used by other modern Marxists to develop the idea of a 'new' petty bourgeoisie. Rather Braverman argues that, through the implementation of scientific management techniques, the 'functions of thought and planning became concentrated in an ever smaller group . . . and for the mass of those employed . . . the office became just as much a site of manual labour as the factory floor' (ibid., p. 316).

Therefore, according to Braverman, all members of the intermediate strata, with the exception of the most senior executives who have stock options and portfolios, are located within the ranks of the working class: 'For these employees . . . their fundamental condition of subordination as so much hired labour, increasingly makes itself felt . . . particularly . . . technicians, engineers . . . and the multiplying ranks of supervisors, foremen and petty managers (ibid., p. 407).

The Petty Bourgeoisie

Within the neo-Marxist literature, a second class schema emphasises the emergence of a 'new' petty bourgeoisie. Drawing upon Marx's distinction between productive and unproductive labour, neo-Marxists such as Poulantzas argue that the intermediate strata form a different class from the bourgeoisie and the proletariat. This class grouping is characterised, firstly, by their ' "ownership" of skills or "human capital" which places them in a social relation with capital akin to that of the traditional petty bourgeoisie' (Wright, 1985, p. 39). Secondly, as their labour is largely unproductive they are viewed as living off the surplus value produced by workers. Poulantzas excludes unproductive wage-earners from the working class because they are 'not directly exploited in the form of the dominant capitalist relations of exploitation, the creation of surplus value' (1975, p. 221).

Poulantzas views the basis of class inequality not only in terms of economic exploitation but also as a consequence of political and ideological domination. The use of political criteria is crucial for his analysis because at the economic level Poulantzas admits that managers and supervisors are exploited in the same manner as productive workers. Moreover he recognises that, by virtue of their role in co-ordinating and integrating the labour process, they are themselves productive labour. However, within the social division of labour, as opposed to the technical division of labour, managers and supervisors politically dominate the working class as their primary role is the 'extraction of surplus-value from the workers' (ibid., p. 228). On this basis they must be excluded from the working class.

At the same time, the intermediate strata are able to dominate the working class at an ideological level. For Poulantzas, the basis of this domination is the division between mental and manual labour. He argues that the intermediate strata are able to differentiate themselves from productive labour through their privileged access to 'secret knowledge': 'We could thus say that every form of work that takes the form of knowledge from which the direct producers are excluded, falls on the mental labour side of the capitalist production process' (ibid., p. 238). Through this ideological separation of mental and manual labour, the intermediate strata are able to strengthen their domination over the working class. However, at the same time they remain both ideologically and politically subordinate within the wider class system.

As a result, Poulantzas argues that, because of their occupation of both dominant and subordinate positions within the social relations of production, the intermediate strata closely resemble the traditional petty bourgeoisie:

> The structural determination of the new petty bourgeoisie in the social division of labour has certain effects on the ideology of its agents, which directly influences its class position, . . . these ideological effects . . . exhibit a remarkable affinity to those which the specific class determination of the traditional petty bourgeoisie . . . thus justifying their attribution to one and the same class. (Ibid., p. 287).

Although having different political and economic interests, the petty bourgeoisie and intermediate strata can be located at a similar structural position within a Marxist class schema.

The New Class

Barbara and John Ehrenreich (1979) identify the emergence of a 'new class' which is characterised by its control over cultural production. They argue that the new class is distinctive in terms of a common 'position within the social relations of *reproduction*' (Wright, 1985, p. 41; emphasis in original), rather than within the social relations of production. The Ehrenreichs define this class as 'consisting of those salaried mental workers who do not own their means of production and whose major functions in the social division of labour may be described broadly as the reproduction of capitalist culture and capitalist class relations' (1979, p. 12). The key to this 'professional–managerial class' (PMC) is that it has developed specialised professional associations with their own ideology, recruitment and training structures. These characteristics differentiate it from either the capitalist or working classes. However, the Ehrenreichs are careful to point out that the role of the new class in the process of reproduction

> may be more or less explicit, as with workers who are directly concerned with social control or with the production and propagation of ideology . . . Or it may be hidden within the process of production, as in the case with the middle-level administrators and managers, engineers, and other technical workers whose functions . . . are essentially determined by the need to preserve capitalist relations of production. (Ibid.)[6]

Consequently this class cannot be treated as a 'separable sociological entity'. Rather it must be seen as a 'derivative class' whose existence presupposes

> that the social surplus has developed to a point sufficient to sustain the PMC in addition to the bourgeoisie, for the PMC is essentially non-productive; and . . . that the relationship between the bourgeoisie and the proletariat has developed to the point that a class specialising in the reproduction of capitalist class relationships becomes a necessity to the capitalist class. (Ibid., p. 14)

Additionally the Ehrenreichs argue that the new class is distinct from the petty bourgeoisie:

> The interdependent yet antagonistic relationship between the working class and the PMC also leads us to insist that the PMC is a class totally distinct from the petty bourgeoisie. The classical petty

bourgeoisie lies outside the polarity of labour and capital . . . The PMC, by contrast, is employed by capital *and* it manages, controls, has authority over labour . . . The classical petty bourgeoisie is irrelevant to the process of capital accumulation and to the process of reproducing capitalist social relations. The PMC, by contrast, is essential to both. (Ibid., pp. 17–18)

Therefore the main function of this class is the *reproduction* of the social conditions which facilitate continued capital accumulation.

Contradictory Positions

In contrast to the polarisation, petty bourgeoisie and new class approaches, a fourth group of modern Marxists analyse intermediate occupations in terms of ambiguous or contradictory locations. The two chief proponents of this view are Eric Olin Wright and Guglielmo Carchedi. While using different terminology and having slightly different analytical frameworks they both see the emergence of monopoly capitalism as creating the basis of contradictory or ambiguous class locations:[7] 'Instead of regarding all positions as located uniquely within particular classes and thus having a coherent class character in their own right, we should see some positions as possibly having a multiple class character; they may be in more than one class simultaneously' (Wright, 1985, p. 43).

Underlying this analysis is the tendency of monopoly capital, in the form of joint stock companies, to separate economic ownership from legal, judicial ownership. Consequently the actual day-to-day control over businesses has shifted from the judicial owners (stock holders) to professional managers. Specifically, legal ownership is the title to physical objects and financial securities, such as machines, stock and shares. Economic ownership, on the other hand, refers to the effective control over capital in the production process. Consequently, given the separation of ownership and control, 'legal ownership may allow people to participate in effective control, but it is not, in itself, a *sufficient* condition for this control' (Scott, 1996, p. 176; emphasis in original).

Wright advances his argument by distinguishing between control over the physical means of production, control over labour power or authority, and control over investments. He argues that the first two categories refer to *possession*, or control over the day-to-day operations of production, while the third pertains to *ownership*. On the basis of this categorisation of control, Wright develops a 'contradictory' class schema which is shown in Figure 7.1. As we will see below, there are a number of other class distinctions, based upon the amount of authority or freedom of action which different actors possess within this schema. As Wright argues, the

> contradictory quality of a particular location within class relations is a variable rather than all-or-nothing characteristic. Certain positions can be thought of as occupying a contradictory location around the boundary of the proletariat; others as occupying a contradictory location around the boundary of the bourgeoisie. (Wright, 1985, pp. 75–7)

Wright identifies three class positions: basic; contradictory locations between the proletariat and bourgeoisie; and contradictory locations between the petty bourgeoisie and other classes. As we can see from Figure 7.1, the basic class positions reflect the dichotomous model prevalent within classical Marxism: the polarisation between the bourgeoisie and the proletariat.

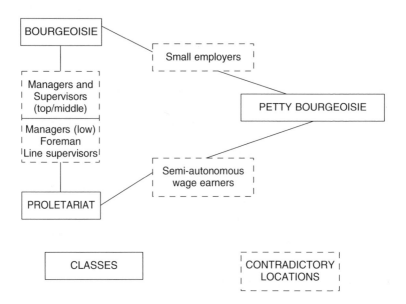

Source: Wright 1985, p. 48.
FIGURE 7.1   *A 'contradictory' class schema*

Wright's emphasis on the contradictory nature of class leads him to develop a hierarchical class model in which an individual's class location is dependent on the extent of control which they have within the production process. Within this model, the occupational positions closest to the proletariat are low-level managers, foremen and line supervisors. As Wright argues:

> The contradictory location closest to the working class is that of foremen and line supervisors. Foremen typically have little real control over the physical means of production, and while they do exercise control over labour power, this frequently does not extend much beyond being the formal transmission belt for orders from above. (Wright, 1978, p. 77)

In contrast, senior management are located around the margins of the bourgeoisie. However they are denied full membership of the ruling class by the limited extent of their property ownership. Nevertheless Wright acknowledges that some senior managers and chief executives tend to form an alliance with the ruling class as a result of the rewards of their position and their ownership of stock options. Finally, as we would expect, the contradictory position of middle management and technocrats is the most acute. While they have some control within the productive process, they have little or no power over appropriation.

Wright identifies two further contradictory positions. First, semi-autonomous employees who fall between the petty bourgeoisie and the proletariat and are identifiable by the fact that, while they have considerable control over the direction of their work, they do not own or control their means of production, the work of others, or even money capital. Second, Wright identifies small employers who fall between the petty bourgeoisie and the ruling class. Wright argues that small employers are identifiable by the fact that they own and use their own means of production yet at the same time they employ workers.[8]

The significance of these contradictory class locations is emphasised by Wright who argues:

> They are not contradictory simply because they cannot be neatly pigeon-holed in any of the basic classes. The issue is not typological aesthetics. Rather they are contradictory locations because they simultaneously share the relational characteristics of two distinct classes. As a result, they share class interests with two different

classes but have interests identical to neither. It is in this sense that they can be viewed as being objectively torn between class locations. (Wright, 1980, p. 331)

Conclusion

The increasingly complex character of advanced capitalism has led many neo-Marxists to re-examine the classical dichotomous model of class relations. As we have seen, a major problem facing modern Marxism has been the expansion of intermediary occupations and the concomitant absence of any polarisation between the two dominant classes. However, in continuing to emphasise the primacy of class relations in explaining who has power within a capitalist society, it can be argued that many neo-Marxists continue to understate the influence of other structural and sociological cleavages. In particular, there has been a failure fully to respond to the Weberian critique of Marxist class analysis.

While we would argue that social class remains a powerful factor in studying power relations within a capitalist society, it is also necessary to account for other social variables such as gender, race and religion, which cross-cut class cleavages, but ultimately have a direct bearing on who has power. Consequently the continued theoretical efficacy of a Marxist class analysis of contemporary capitalist societies is dependent on an ability to incorporate these variables into its model of power.

Notes

1. For example, in his study of Chinese society, Weber emphasises the powerful influence of the literati. He argues that power is not based on economic wealth, but on the social prestige associated with a high level of education. The Chinese literati were able to legitimise their dominance through a cultural process in which educational attainment was viewed as a prerequisite for positions of power.
2. While not discussed within this chapter, it should be noted that, in addition to attempting to classify the middle class, many modern Marxists have also begun to address the position of individuals falling outside the basic class system of industrial societies: 'transitional classes'. These classes exist because the emergence of capitalism does not eliminate all the previous relations of production. For example, Marx discussed the class location of landowners within Chapter 52 of *Capital*. Modern Marxists are also interested in analysing 'transitional classes' as they

may form the basis of new classes. See for example, Scott (1996); Wright (1985).

3. Carchedi (1975, pp. 1–87) argues that this process has led to the development of the 'collective worker'. Although many individuals do not perform manual work, all workers are viewed as contributing to the 'surplus value creating process'. Thus, regardless of occupation, all workers operating within the capitalist mode of production are seen as part of the collective worker.

4. See also Loren (1977), Freedman (1975), Cutler *et al.*, (1977) and Becker (1973; 1974).

5. This approach emerged primarily as a criticism of Poulantzas' petty bourgeoisie model. In particular, the conceptualisation of the working class within a dichotomy based productive and unproductive labour is viewed as being extremely arbitrary. For example, within modern capitalism all service and retail workers produce surplus value for capitalists even if not in commodity form. It is also questionable why managers who do not possess any capital should be located within a different class from the proletariat.

6. See also Gouldner (1979); Ehrenreich and Ehrenreich (1971); Bourdieu (1979).

7. Carchedi refers to the intermediate classes as the 'new middle class' and views their position as 'ambiguous' rather than contradictory. Additionally, unlike Wright, Carchedi places legal owners (stock holders) outside class relations as he argues that they have no role within the production process. See Carchedi (1975, 1977); Wright (1980).

8. A major difficulty with this dichotomy, as Wright acknowledges, is that there is no way of determining a formal distinction between a small employer and a small capitalist.

9. While Wright has recently returned to this model it should be noted that he also developed another class model based upon the exploitation of different assets. In this model Wright develops twelve class positions based upon the assets controlled. The owners of the means of production exploit property assets while non-owners exploit organisational assets and/or skill/credential assets. Thus he developed three owning and six non-owning classes (Wright, 1985, ch. 3).

8

Marxism and the State

COLIN HAY

At a time when Marxism is in retreat across the globe following the implosion and disintegration of 'actually existing socialism' (see, for instance, Aronson, 1995; McCarney, 1990; cf. Callinicos, 1991; Magnus and Cullenberg, 1995) and in an era in which the inexorable tide of globalisation is seemingly laying waste the nation-state (for an emblematic account see Dunn, 1994), it is tempting to conclude that: (i) *Marxist* state theory is an anachronism; (ii) *contemporary* Marxist state theory is an oxymoron; and (iii) a review of developments in the Marxist theory of the state is an exercise in flogging a dead horse. The central aim of this chapter is to suggest otherwise. Indeed the 'rectifying revolutions' of 1989 in Eastern Europe provide a long-overdue opportunity for Marxism – and hence the Marxist theory of the state – to liberate itself from what has too often passed in its name (namely the tyranny, autarky and oppression of 'actually existing socialism'). Reinvigorated in this way, Marxist state theory can provide a powerful critical and analytical tool in the interpretation and interrogation of 'actually existing capitalism'. In so doing it can contribute to our understanding of processes as seemingly diverse and as far from the gaze of Marxist orthodoxy as the reproduction of patriarchal relations in contemporary societies (see, for instance, Jenson, 1992) and the political economy of global environmental degradation (see, for instance, Hay, 1994a; O'Connor, 1991; Pepper, 1993).

Our analysis proceeds in three stages. In the first section we consider why it is that Marxists require a theory of the state and how Marxists have conceptualised this focus of their attention. We then trace the development of the Marxist theory of the state through the work of the founding fathers, its reformulation by Lenin and Gramsci, and the revival of interest in Marxist state theory in the postwar period. Finally we consider current developments in the Marxist theory of the state before asking why do *we* need a *Marxist* theory of the state *today*?

Marxism and the State: Flogging a Dead Horse?

> The modern state is . . . an amorphous complex of agencies with ill-defined boundaries performing a variety of not very distinctive functions. (Schmitter, 1985: p. 33)

It might seem somewhat strange, if not downright defeatist, to begin a chapter on the Marxist theory of the state with this comment. Yet in one sense it provides a particularly appropriate starting point. For, as has been remarked elsewhere, 'there is no more arduous task in the theory of the state than defining this notoriously illusive and rapidly moving target' (Hay, 1996a, p. 2). We begin then with perhaps the second most neglected question in the study of the state – what is it? – before moving on to the first – why do we need a theory of it anyway? In fact, as we shall see, although the definitions offered by Marxists are often implicit rather than explicit, and although their justifications for a concern with the state are often somewhat cryptic, it is to their credit that theorists within this tradition have not been short of answers.

What is the State?

A moment's foray into the now substantial annals of Marxist state theory will reveal that whilst Marxists may well rely *implicitly* upon certain conceptions and understandings of the state, they are notoriously bad at consigning these to the page. This makes it somewhat difficult to identify any analytically precise Marxist definition of the state as an object of inquiry, let alone one that is commonly agreed upon. Immersion in the archives, however, eventually yields certain family resemblances in the assumptions which inform Marxist conceptions of the state. These can be crystallised into a number of somewhat different formulations. Here we concentrate on four (for a more detailed discussion, see Hay, 1997).

The State as the Repressive Arm of the Bourgeoisie According to Martin Carnoy: 'it is the notion of the [capitalist] state as the repressive apparatus of the bourgeoisie that is the distinctly Marxist characteristic of the state' (Carnoy, 1984, p. 50). This somewhat one-dimensional conception of state power (the state as the expression of the repressive might of the ruling class) is most closely associated with Lenin's *The State and Revolution* (1917 [1968]), but is also appealed to in the work of Engels (see, for instance, 1844 [1975] pp. 205–7; 1884 [1978] p. 340; cf. van den Berg, 1988, pp. 30–1). Its distinctive brand of functionalism (the attempt to explain something by appeal to its consequences) is well summarised by Hal Draper: 'The state . . . comes into existence insofar as the institutions needed to carry out the common functions of society require, for their continued maintenance, the separation of the power of forcible coercion from the general body of society' (Draper, 1977, p. 50).

The State as an Instrument of the Ruling Class   The 'instrumentalist' position as it has become known (see below) provides perhaps the most prevalent conception of the state within Marxist theory. It is most often accorded the status of *the* Marxist theory of the state, despite the fact that instrumentalism itself spans a wide diversity of positions expressing rather divergent *theories* of the state. In its most crudely stated form it implies that the state is 'an instrument in the hands of the ruling class for enforcing and guaranteeing the stability of the class structure itself' (Sweezy, 1942, p. 243). Within this distinctive school, 'the functioning of the state is understood in terms of the instrumental exercise of power by people in strategic positions, either directly through the manipulation of state policies or indirectly through the exercise of pressure on the state' (Gold, Lo and Wright, 1975a, p. 34). Accordingly, the 'influence theorists', as Offe terms them (1974, p. 32), have concerned themselves with the analyses of (i) the patterns and networks of personal and social ties between individuals occupying positions of economic power in so-called 'power structure research' studies (Domhoff, 1967; 1970; 1980; Mintz and Schwartz, 1985; for a review, see Barrow, 1993, pp. 13–24); (ii) the social connections between those holding positions of economic power and the state elite (Domhoff, 1979, 1990; Miliband, 1969; for a review see Barrow, 1993, pp. 24–41); and (iii) the social processes moulding the ideological commitments of the state and social elite (Miliband, 1969).

The State as an Ideal Collective Capitalist   The conception of the state as an ideal collective capitalist has its origins in Engels' frequently cited (though incidental) remark in *Anti-Dühring*, that 'the modern state, no matter what its form, is essentially a capitalist machine, the state of the capitalists, the ideal personification of the total national capital' (1878 [1947] p. 338). Advocates of this conception of the state point to the fact that capital is neither self-reproducing nor capable on its own of securing the conditions of its own reproduction. For the very continuity of the capitalist social formation is dependent upon certain interventions being made which, though in the general interest of capital collectively, are not in the individual interest of any particular capital (Hirsch, 1978, p. 66). An external, and at least *relatively* autonomous, body or institutional ensemble is thus called upon to intervene on behalf of capital in its long-term general interests (as opposed to the conflicting short-term interests of individual capitals). This body is the state – the 'ideal collective capitalist' (Altvater, 1973; Offe, 1974, p. 40).[1]

The State as a Factor of Cohesion within the Social Formation
Though most clearly associated with the work of Nicos Poulantzas, whose phrase it is, the notion of the state as a 'factor of cohesion' can be traced (as indeed it is by Poulantzas) to another incidental and (characteristically) underdeveloped comment by Engels in *The Origin of the Family, Private Property and the State*:

> in order that . . . classes with conflicting economic interests, shall not consume themselves and society in fruitless struggle, it became necessary to have a power seemingly standing above society that would moderate the conflict and keep it within the bounds of 'order'; and this power, arisen out of society but placing itself above it and alienating itself more and more from it, is the state (Engels, 1884 [1978] pp. 205–6; see also Bukharin, 1921 [1926]).

Within this conception, the state is understood in terms of its effects and is defined in terms of its role in maintaining 'the unity and cohesion of a social formation by concentrating and sanctioning class domination' (Poulantzas, 1975, pp. 24–5; see also 1973, pp. 44–56, esp. 44, Gramsci, 1971b, p. 244; Jessop, 1985, 61, 177). We return to the problems of this conception below.

As the above discussion demonstrates, the state has meant (and continues to mean) many things to many Marxists.

Why do Marxists Need a Theory of the State?

Had Little Red Riding-Hood, having escaped the clutches of the wolf in the forest, found herself confronted by a Marxist state theorist, it is not at all clear that her new adversary would have had much of an answer to her inquisitive 'what big books you write'. A particularly quick-witted Gramscian might well have replied: 'all the better to help *us* understand the conditions conducive to socialist transformation'.[2] Yet even this begs more questions that it answers. How precisely does a Marxist theory of the state advance the cause of progressive social transformation? The point is that Marxist state theorists – unlike, say, their feminist counterparts (compare Allen, 1990, with Brown, 1992; Connell, 1990; MacKinnon, 1982; 1983, 1985) – have rarely been called upon to offer any such justification for their theoretical endeavours and choices. There is, for instance, no explicit answer to the question 'why do *Marxists* need a theory of the state?' (far less, 'why does anyone else need a *Marxist* theory of the state?') within the voluminous Marxist literature on the state. Having said that, however, such answers are not difficult to construct.

Here, for once, we can usefully follow the so-called German 'state-derivationists'. For although their work is in many respects deeply problematic (see Barrow, 1993, pp. 94–5; Jessop, 1982, pp. 78–101), it did succeed in highlighting the centrality of the state to the process of capitalist reproduction. The derivationists, as the label would imply, sought to *derive* the form and function of the capitalist state from the requirements of the capitalist mode of production. For our purposes we are not concerned to demonstrate, as they were, that the state must by some inexorable inner logic necessarily satisfy such functional requirements, but merely that it is indeed implicated in processes crucial to the reproduction of capitalist relations. Thus, although their perspective can never *explain* the form and/or (dys)function of the capitalist state, as its advocates believed, it can nonetheless provide us with an exceedingly useful heuristic. For insofar as capitalist social relations *are* reproduced (and it does not take much insight to see that in the societies we inhabit they are), such functions must indeed be performed by some institution, apparatus, or combination thereof. It is not a particularly large step to suggest that many (if not all) of these institutions are either state apparatuses themselves or are heavily regulated by the state. The state thus emerges as a nodal point in the network of power relations that characterises contemporary capitalist societies and, hence, a key focus of Marxist attention. It is not surprising then that Ralph Miliband is led to conclude that: 'in the politics of Marxism there is no institution which is nearly as important as the state' (1977, p. 66).

So how, precisely, is the capitalist state implicated in the expanded reproduction of capital? Or, to put it another way, what are the functions that must be performed by the state *if* capitalist social relations are to be reproduced? Numerous aspects of this role can be identified. Taken together they provide ample evidence of the need for a distinctively Marxist theory of the state within Marxist theory more generally.

Firstly we might point to the fact that capital is fragmented into a large number of competitive units, yet crucially relies on certain generic conditions being satisfied if surplus value is to be extracted from labour and profit secured (Altvater 1973). Picture a hypothetical capitalist economy unregulated by the state (the archetypal free market) and comprised inevitably of a multitude of competing capitals. Such an economy is inherently crisis-prone. For no individual capital competing for its very survival will sacrifice its own interest in the general interest. Contradictions or 'steering problems' inevitably arise within such an unregulated economy, yet can never be resolved. Accordingly they will accumulate until they eventually threaten the very stability of capitalism itself, precipitating a fully-fledged crisis of the mode of production. A capitalist economy without regulation, despite the now pervasive rhetoric of the free-marketeers, is inherently unstable (Aglietta, 1979; Habermas, 1975, pp. 24–31; Hay, 1996a, ch. 5; Jänicke, 1990, p. 8; Offe, 1975).

Now enter the state – as a more or less 'ideal collective capitalist'. Altvater argues that this state must necessarily intervene within the capitalist economy to secure conditions conducive to continuing capitalist accumulation, thereby performing what he calls a 'general maintenance function' (Altvater, 1973; Jessop, 1982, pp. 90–1). This comprises (i) the provision of general infrastructure: 'the material conditions that are necessary to all business activities but that cannot be produced directly [*and profitably*] by individual private businesses' (Barrow, 1993, p. 80); (ii) the capacity to defend militarily a national economic space regulated by the state and to preserve an administrative boundary within which the state is sovereign; (iii) the provision of a legal system that establishes and enforces the right to possession of private property and which outlaws practices (such as insider-dealing) potentially damaging to the accumulation of capital within the national economy; and (iv) the intervention of the state to regulate and/or ameliorate class struggle and the inevitable conflict between capital and labour.

Such interventions establish what Jürgen Habermas terms the 'logic of crisis displacement'. By this he means that fundamental crises originating (as 'steering problems') within the economy (and which previously would have rung the death-knell of capitalism itself) now become the responsibility of the state as the supreme regulator of the economy. Crises are thus *displaced* from the economy (which does *not* have the internal capacity to resolve them) to the state (which *may*, or *may not*). If the state as currently constituted cannot resolve such a crisis, then in the first instance it is the particular form of the capitalist state that is called into question, not the very stability of the capitalist mode of production itself.[3]

The implications of this for a Marxist theory of the state are profound. For the state is revealed, once again, as playing a crucial role in safeguarding the circuit of capital. If we want to understand the operation of the capitalist mode of production we cannot afford to dispense with a theory of the state. Moreover Habermas' argument suggests that, if we wish to develop a theory of capitalist crisis (an understandably high priority within Marxist theory), then it is to the state that we must turn initially. For economic crises, at least within contemporary capitalism, are likely to become manifest as crises of economic regulation and hence crises of the state. In summary, if we wish to develop insights into the 'normal' functioning of the capitalist mode of production, and into the transformation of capitalism in and through moments of crisis, we require a dynamic theory of the capitalist state. It is to the resources we have at our disposal in developing such a theory that we turn in the next section.

The Genealogy of the State in Marxist Theory

No aspect of Marxist theory has been so greatly blurred, distorted or befogged as this, (Lefebvre, 1972, p. 123).

Marx and Engels: Horses for Courses

In 1977, in the first (and probably still the best) systematic and comprehensive review of Marxist theories of the state, Bob Jessop noted that it was a 'truism' that Marx and Engels developed no consistent, single or unified theory of the state (1977, p. 353). By 1982 (in his book *The Capitalist State*) this truism had become a 'commonplace' and it is now so often remarked upon that it is perhaps one of the few truly undisputed 'social scientific facts' (see, for instance, van den Berg, 1988, p. 14; Bertramsen, Thomsen and Torfing, 1990, p. 38; Carnoy, 1984, p. 45; Dunleavy and O'Leary, 1987, p. 203; Finegold and Skocpol, 1995, p. 175; Miliband, 1965; Poulantzas, 1978, p. 20; Wolfe, 1974, p. 131; cf. Draper, 1977). *There is no (single) Marxian, far less Marxist, theory of the state*. This might be considered something of a devastating blow for a chapter on the Marxist theory of the state. Indeed reviewing Marxist state theory might be considered not merely an exercise in flogging a dead horse, but one that first required the altogether more macabre practice of exhuming and assembling a dismembered corpse limb by limb. Moreover, given the great variety of concerns that animated Marx and Engels' work (to say nothing of Marxism more generally), it is not at all clear that all the limbs belong to the same corpse. For, as Jessop notes, 'Marx and Engels adopted different approaches and arguments according to the problems with which they were concerned' (1982, p. 28). Nonetheless a clear development of Marx and Engels' ideas on the state can be traced.

The Early Marx   The *Critique of Hegel's Doctrine of the State* (1843a [1975]) contains Marx's first extended reflections on the state. Though a sustained and at times polemical critique of Hegel, it is still couched within a fundamentally Hegelian framework. In Hegel's almost mystical idealism the separation between the state and civil society – between the universal and the particular – finds its resolution in the state. The latter is understood, not as an ideal collective capitalist but as an *ideal collective citizen* capable of expressing the general and communal interest of all its subjects. Marx regards this as pure mystification. Thus, although he accepts Hegel's distinction between state and civil society, sharing his understanding of the latter as 'the sphere of economic life in which the individual's relations with others are governed by selfish needs and individual interests' (ibid., p. 59), Marx denies that the state can indeed act in the universal interest. For insofar as state power is thoroughly implicated in the protection of property rights, the state actually functions to reproduce 'the war of each against all' in civil society. The solution lies in what Marx terms 'true democracy', 'the first true unity of the particular and the universal' (ibid., p. 88). The interpretation of this concept in the early Marx is highly contentious. The Althusserian structuralists wish to dismiss these early formulations as unredeemably Hegelian, and as separated by a radical 'epistemological break' from his 'mature' and 'scientific' later writings (Althusser, 1969, pp. 32–4, 62–4, 249). In complete contrast, Shlomo Avineri detects in the concept of 'true democracy' what would later be termed 'communism'. Accordingly, he argues:

> the decisive transition in Marx's intellectual development was not from radical democracy to communism, any more than it was from idealism to materialism . . . The *Critique* contains ample material to show that Marx envisages in 1843 a society based on the abolition of private property and on the disappearance of the state. Briefly, the *Communist Manifesto* is immanent in the *Critique*. (Avineri, 1968, p. 34; see also Colletti, 1972, pp. 41–2)

This latter reading is perhaps reinforced by Marx's essay *On the Jewish Question* (1843b [1975]). Here he distinguishes between political emancipation – associated with formal (and constitutionally codified) democracy – and real human emancipation (or 'true democracy'). While the former represents a significant advance it is but one step on the road to full human emancipation. The latter can only be realised by the transcending of bourgeois society to usher in a qualitatively new social order (Miliband, 1965, pp. 281–2). In his *Introduction* (1844 [1975]) to the *Critique*, Marx eventually identifies the proletariat as the agents of this transformation, laying the basis for a class theory of the state in his later writings.

Marx Mark Two: The 'Mature' Works 'like Henry Higgins who, through his work changed the object of his studies into something other than what it was, the purpose of the Marxist theory of the state is not just to understand the capitalist state but to aid in its destruction' (Wolfe, 1974, p. 131). In the *German Ideology*, Marx and Engels come closest to formulating a systematic theory of the state as a class state. They assert famously that the state is 'nothing more than the form of organisation which the bourgeoisie necessarily adopt both for internal and external purposes, for the mutual guarantee of their property and interest' (1845/6 [1964] p. 59), a conception echoed in the *Communist Manifesto* (1848 [1967] p. 82). This broadly instrumentalist framework (which conceives of the state as an instrument in the hands of the ruling class) is identified by Miliband as Marx and Engels' 'primary' view of the state (1965, p. 283; see also Sanderson, 1963). Yet it is not their only formulation, nor does it remain unqualified. Indeed as Marx notes in 'The Class Struggles in France' (1850 [1978]) and 'The Eighteenth Brumaire of Louis Bonaparte' (1852 [1979]) it is often not the ruling class so much as fractions of the ruling class which control the state apparatus. This is particularly so in the case of the most advanced capitalist societies of the time, England and France. Furthermore the personnel of the state often belong to an entirely different class to that of the ruling class. Such comments are a reflection of a modified and qualified, but nonetheless still essentially instrumentalist, conception of the state. The state is granted a certain degree of autonomy from the ruling class, but it remains *their* instrument – ultimately those who pay the piper call the tune.

At times, however, and particularly in their more historical writings, Marx and Engels' qualified instrumentalism gives way to a more structuralist position. Thus in 'The Eighteenth Brumaire' and again in 'The Civil War in France' (1871 [1986]), Marx grants the state a far more independent role than that previously assigned to it in, say, *The German Ideology*. This 'secondary' view of the state as Miliband describes it (1977, pp. 284–5), is restated by Engels in *The Origin of the Family, Private Property and the State* (1884 [1978]). Thus, although Louis Bonaparte is seen by Marx as 'representing' (or at least claiming to represent) the smallholding peasants, neither he nor the state is a genuine expression of their interests. As Miliband explains, 'for Marx, the Bonapartist State, however independent it may have been *politically* from any given class remains, and cannot in a class society but remain, the protector of an economically and socially dominant class' (ibid., p. 285, original emphasis). The very structure and function of the (capitalist) state would appear to guarantee (or at least powerfully select for) the reproduction of capitalist social relations. This impression is confirmed in 'The Civil War in France'. Here Marx categorically states that the apparatus of the capitalist state cannot be appropriated for progressive ends and that the revolutionary project of the proletariat must be to smash this repressive bourgeois institution. In so doing:

> Marx implies that the state is a system of political domination whose effectiveness is to be found in its institutional structure as much as in the social categories, fractions or classes that control it . . . the analysis of the inherent bias of the system of political representation and state intervention is logically prior to an examination of the social forces that manage to wield state power. (Jessop, 1978, p. 62; see also Jessop, 1982, p. 27).

Given the sheer scope and diversity of the positions briefly outlined above, it is not surprising that Alan Wolfe is led to conclude, 'to study the state from a Marxist perspective means not the application of an already developed theory to existing circumstances, but the creation of that very theory, based on some all too cryptic beginnings in Marx himself. Hence the excitement of the project, but hence also its ambiguity' (1974, p. 131). In the next section we embark on a roller-coaster ride through this exciting yet ambiguous world.

The Ambiguity and the Excitement: Marxism and the State After Marx

Lenin and Gramsci   Lenin's writings on the state can trace a strong lineage to the Marx of 'The Civil War in France'. In *The State and Revolution* (1917 [1968]), regarded by Lucio Colletti as 'by far and away his greatest contribution to political theory' (1972: 224), Lenin draws out the implications of Marx's writings on the Paris Commune for revolutionary strategy. The state, he argues, is 'an organ of class *rule*, an organ for the *oppression* of one class by another' (1917 [1968], p. 266, original emphasis). Since the state is simply and unequivocally the repressive apparatus of the bourgeoisie, it cannot be used to advance the cause of socialist transformation. Moreover, as a coercive institution, it must be confronted by force. Hence, 'the liberation of the oppressed class is impossible not only without a violent revolution, but also without the destruction of the apparatus of state power' (ibid.). As Colletti again observes:

> The basic theme of *The State and Revolution* – the one that indelibly inscribes itself on the memory, and immediately comes to mind when one thinks of the work – is the theme of revolution as a *destructive* and *violent* act . . . The essential point of the revolution, the *destruction* it cannot forgo is . . . the destruction of the bourgeois state as a power *separate* from and *counterposed* to the masses, and its replacement by a power of a new type. (1972, pp. 219–20, original emphasis)

Lenin's narrow definition of the state as an essentially coercive apparatus is reflected in his vision of revolution as a violent act in which the repressive might of the state is pitched against the massed ranks of the proletariat. Its consequences, of historical proportions, are all too apparent. Thankfully they may now be viewed with the benefit of some degree of hindsight. In contrast, Gramsci's more inclusive definition of the state leads him in a somewhat different direction.

Gramsci's distinctiveness and enduring significance lies in his attempt to incorporate human subjectivity as a dynamic agent within the Marxist philosophy of history (Femia, 1981, p. 1; see also Taylor,

1995, p. 252). His work thus marks a clear break with the economism and crude reductionism that had come to characterise the Marxist tradition since the death of Marx. The central question that he poses, and with which contemporary Marxist theorists continue to grapple, is this: what gives capital the capacity to reproduce and reassert its dominance over time despite its inherent contradictions? His search for an answer leads him to define a new concept (or, more accurately, to redefine an old concept) – that of *hegemony*; and to extend the Marxist definition of the state to include all those institutions and practices through which the ruling class succeeds in maintaining the consensual subordination of those over whom it rules (Gramsci, 1971b, pp. 244, 262). The key to Gramsci's theoretical toolbox is the concept of hegemony. With this he demonstrated that a dominant class, in order to maintain its supremacy, must succeed in presenting its own moral, political and cultural values as societal norms thereby constructing an ideologically engendered *common sense*. Yet, as Miliband observes, hegemony is not merely about instilling the values of the ruling class within civil society. Increasingly,

> it must also be taken to mean the capacity of the ruling classes to persuade subordinate ones that, whatever they may think of the social order, and however much they may be alienated from it, there is no alternative to it. Hegemony depends not so much on consent as on resignation. (Miliband, 1994, p. 11)

For Gramsci then the obstacles to class consciousness are far greater than Lenin envisaged (and, it might well be argued, have become far greater since the time of Gramsci). While there is football on TV, the revolution is likely to be postponed indefinitely. As Gramsci's biographer, Giuseppe Fiori, comments:

> the [capitalist] system's real strength does not lie in the violence of the ruling class or the coercive power of its state, but in the acceptance by the ruled of a 'conception of the world' which belongs to the rulers. The philosophy of the ruling class passes through a whole tissue of complex vulgarisations to emerge as 'common sense': that is, the philosophy of the masses, who accept the morality, the customs, the institutionalised behaviour of the society they live in. (Fiori, 1970, p. 238)

Gramsci's central contribution is to insist that the power of the capitalist class resides not so much in the repressive apparatus of the state as an instrument of the bourgeoisie – however ruthless and efficient that might be[4] – but in its ability to influence and shape the perceptions of the subordinate classes, convincing them either of the legitimacy of the system itself or of the futility of resistance. This leads him to a highly significant observation and one for which he is rightly famous:

> In the East the state was everything, civil society was primordial and gelatinous; in the West, there was a proper relation between state and civil society, and when the state trembled a sturdy structure of civil society was at once revealed. The state was only an outer ditch, behind which there stood a powerful system of fortresses and earthworks. (Gramsci, 1971, p. 238)

The implications of this for socialist strategy are highly significant, and Gramsci was not slow to point them out. Whereas in the East (Russia) where civil society was 'primordial and gelatinous' a *war of manoeuvre* – a 'frontal assault' on the state – was indeed appropriate, in the West such a strategy was doomed to failure. For in societies like his own the strength of the bourgeoisie lay not in the coercive resources that it could muster, but in its ability to legitimate its domination within civil society, thereby securing passive acquiescence. Thus before the proletariat could challenge the state it would first have to wage a successful *war of position* – a 'battle for the hearts and minds' within civil society. As Carnoy notes: '*consciousness itself* becomes the source of power for the proletariat in laying siege to the state and the means of production, just as lack of proletarian consciousness is the principal reason that the bourgeoisie remains in the dominant position' (1984, p. 88). Gramsci had indeed succeeded in reinserting human subjectivity as a dynamic agent within the Marxist philosophy of history.

Structuralism, Instrumentalism and the Miliband–Poulantzas Debate
If the historical significance (however unfortunate) of Lenin's writings on the state, and the theoretical and strategic prescience of Gramsci's work, should guarantee them both a place in any discussion of the Marxist theory of the state, the same cannot be said of the (in)famous Miliband–Poulantzas debate (Poulantzas, 1969, 1976; Miliband, 1969; 1970; 1973; Laclau, 1975). Indeed its importance lies neither in the quality of the theoretical exchange nor thankfully in its historical significance, but rather in the problems it reveals in Marxist conceptions of the state and in its symbolic status as a point of departure for many contemporary developments. The debate sees neither protagonist at his brilliant theoretical best. Yet it does well display the

extremes to which Marxist state theorists seem, on occasions, inexorably drawn.

It takes the form of a dense theoretical exchange, initially polite but increasingly ill-tempered, about the source of power within contemporary capitalist societies and the relationship between the ruling class and the state apparatus in the determination of the content of state policy. Is the modern state a state in capitalist society or a capitalist state, and what difference does it make anyway?

Poulantzas' opening salvo (1969) takes the form of a detailed textual critique of Miliband's path-breaking *The State in Capitalist Society* (1969). Poulantzas notes the absence (excepting the work of Gramsci) of a systematic attempt to formulate a Marxist theory of the state and praises Miliband for his attempts to fill this theoretical vacuum as well as his devastating critique of the bourgeois mythology of the state. However, after the spoonful of sugar comes the medicine. In seeking to expose the dominant bourgeois ideology of the neutrality and independence of the state, Miliband is unwittingly drawn onto the terrain of his adversaries (1969, pp. 241–2). His reflections thus remains tarnished by the residue of bourgeois assumptions about the state – principally that power resides not in the state apparatus itself but in the *personnel* of the state. He thereby fails to grasp what Poulantzas sees as the objective structural reality of social classes and the state. Instead Miliband entertains the bourgeois mythology of the free-willed active agent. Accordingly he focuses on *class* in terms of intersubjective relationships instead of objective structural locations within the relations of production, and on the *state* in terms of the interpersonal alliances, connections and networks of the state 'elite' (ibid., p. 242) instead of the structure, form and function of this (capitalist) institution.

This point lies at the heart of the debate. Yet from here on it degenerates into a somewhat crude and polarised struggle between *instrumentalism* (Poulantzas' caricature of Miliband's position) and *structuralism* (Miliband's caricature of Poulantzas' position). Ironically, in the debate itself (though not in their more thoughtful work), both protagonists come close to living up to the crude parodies they present of one another.

Instrumentalism, as we have seen, tends to view the state as a neutral instrument to be manipulated and steered in the interests of the dominant class or ruling 'elite' (the term Miliband deploys). Its basic thesis is that the modern state serves the interests of the bourgeoisie in a capitalist society because it is dominated by that class. Such a perspective asserts the causal primacy of *agency* (the conscious actions of individuals or social forces) over *structure*. In the determination of state policy, the personnel of the state are thus accorded primacy over the state's form and function (as a capitalist apparatus). As Kenneth Finegold and Theda Skocpol note:

> An instrument has no will of its own and thus is capable of action only as the extension of the will of some conscious actor. To understand the state as an instrument of the capitalist class is to say that state action originates in the conscious and purposive efforts of capitalists as a class. (Finegold and Skocpol, 1995, p. 176)

Instrumentalism (as expressed in the work of Domhoff and the early Miliband) may thus be regarded as *agency*- or *personnel*-centred, and as expressing a simple view of the relationship between the state apparatus and the ruling class: the ruling class is an instrument of the state apparatus (see Table 8.1). The instrumentalist thesis can be summarised in terms of its answers to three questions (see Box 8.1)

An instrumentalist theory of the state is thus a theory of *the state in capitalist society* (the title of Miliband's book) as opposed to a theory of the capitalist state. For if the state in a capitalist society is indeed

---

Box 8.1

Q: *What is the nature of the class that rules?*
A: The capitalist class rules and is defined by its ownership and control of the means of production.

Q: *What are the mechanisms that tie this class to the state?*
A: Socialisation, interpersonal connections, and networks. The capitalist class uses the state as an instrument to dominate the rest of society.

Q: *What is the concrete relationship between state policies and ruling class interests?*
A: State policies further the general interests of the capitalist class in maintaining their domination of society.

Source: Questions from Gold, Lo and Wright, 1975a, p. 32; answers adapted from Barrow, 1993, p. 16.

---

capitalist it is only contingently so. That the state is engaged in the reproduction of capitalist social and economic relations is not in any sense guaranteed. Rather such a situation can arise only by virtue of the dominance of a capitalist 'ruling elite' within capitalist society and its personal ties to the members of the state apparatus.

In marked contrast, a *structuralist* position (such as that outlined by the state derivationists and by the Poulantzas of 'the debate') asserts the causal priority of structures over agents and their intentions. Agents are conceived of as the 'bearers' (or *Träger*) of objective structures over which they can exercise minimal influence. Within such a framework, the capitalist state is viewed as a structural system with form and function determined largely independently of the aspirations, motivations and intentions of political actors or members of the dominant class. It is a theory of the *capitalist state*. A structuralist account, as the term would imply, is *structure-* or *state*-centred. It also expresses a simple view of the relationship between the state apparatus and the ruling-class: the former acts in the long-term collective interest of the latter (see Table 8.1).

The Miliband–Poulantzas debate did not advance the cause of Marxist theory very far. However, in pointing to the limitations of both structure-centred and agency-centred accounts (see also Hay, 1995a), it has provided a point of departure for many recent developments in state theory. It is to the two most fruitful attempts to exorcise the ghost of the Miliband–Poulantzas debate that we now briefly turn.

Beyond Structuralism v. Instrumentalism: Block and Jessop Before considering the 'state of the art' in the Marxist theory of the state, it is important first to note that Miliband and Poulantzas were not to

TABLE 8.1 *Beyond structuralism vs. instrumentalism*

	Personnel-centred (Agency-centred)	State-centred (Structure-centred)
Simple view of the relationship between the state apparatus and the ruling class	Instrumentalism (Domhoff, early Miliband)	Structuralism (early Poulantzas, state derivationists)
Dialectical view of the relationship between the state apparatus and the ruling class	The state as custodian of capital (later Miliband, Block)	Strategic-relational approach (Jessop, later Poulantzas)

remain resolute and intractable in defence of the positions to which they were drawn in the heat of the theoretical exchange. Indeed both moved towards more dialectical conceptions of the relationship between structure and agency in their later work, locating political actors as strategic subjects within complex and densely structured state apparatuses. Thus Miliband, in an exercise of apparent contrition, concedes, 'the notion of the state as an "instrument" . . . tends to obscure what has come to be seen as a crucial property of the state, namely its *relative autonomy* from the "ruling class" and from civil society at large' (1977, p. 74). He emphasises the need for a considera-tion of 'the character of [the state's] leading personnel, the pressures exercised by the economically dominant-class, *and* the structural constraints imposed by the mode of production' (ibid., pp. 73–4; see also Miliband, 1994, pp. 17–18). Such observations are more system-atically developed in the work of Fred Block (1987a, 1987b).

Block's concern is to demonstrate how, despite the division of labour between 'state managers' and the capitalist class, the state tends to act in the long term collective interest of capital. He begins by noting that the capitalist class, far from actively sponsoring major reforms in its long-term interest, often provides the most vociferous opposition to such measures. The capitalist class must then be regarded as simply incapable of acting in its own long-term collective interest. Yet at the same time

> ruling class members who devote substantial energy to policy formation become atypical of their class, since they are forced to look at the world from the perspective of state-managers. They are quite likely to diverge ideologically from politically unengaged ruling-class opinion. (Block, 1987a, p. 57)

This provides the basis for an answer to Block's conundrum. State managers may in fact have interests far closer to the long-term collective interest of capital than capital itself (see also Marsh, 1995b, p. 275). Here Block points to the relationship of 'dependency' between state managers on the one hand, and the performance of the capitalist economy on the other. As Carnoy explains, such dependency exists since:

> economic activity produces state revenues and because public support for a regime will decline unless accumulation continues to take place. State managers willingly do what they know they must to facilitate capital accumulation. Given that the level of economic

activity is largely determined by private investment decisions, such managers are particularly sensitive to overall 'business confidence'. (Carnoy, 1984, p. 218)

The state becomes the *custodian* of the general interest of capital. Block manages to reconcile within a single account a sensitivity to the intentions, interests and strategies of state personnel (and their relative independence from the ruling class) with an analysis of the structural context within which these strategies are operationalised and played out. His work displays a complex and *dialectical* view of the relationship between the state apparatus and the ruling class which escapes both the intentionalism and indeterminacy of instrumentalist accounts and the functionalism and determinism of structuralist formulations. In its overarching concern with state managers as utility-maximising rational subjects (Taylor, 1995, p. 264), it is nonetheless *personnel-* or *agency*-centred (see Table 8.1).

Though it represents a considerable advance on its more instrumentalist forebears, Block's work is still ultimately somewhat frustrating. For as Finegold and Skocpol point out (1995, p. 98), he remains ambiguous as to whether capitalist reforms initiated by state managers – and the subject of political pressure from both working and ruling classes alike – will *always* prove functional for capital in the last instance (for evidence of this ambiguity compare Block, 1987a, p. 62, with 1987a, p. 66). If so, then Block's gestural nod to the independent interests of state managers in promoting economic growth is scarcely sufficient to account for such an exact (and convenient) functional fit. If not, then how precisely is it that dysfunctional outcomes that might prove threatening to capitalist stability are avoided whilst those less damaging of the system (and, one might have thought, easier to avoid) are allowed to develop? Either way, Block seems to fall back on a residual functionalism which is not so very different from that associated with the notion of the state as an 'ideal collective capitalist'. His achievement should not, however, be underemphasised. Yet it surely lies more in his *recognition* of the need to specify the mechanisms ensuring that the actions of state personnel do not, by and large, jeopardise continued capital accumulation, than in the particular mechanisms that he proceeds to specify.

If Block's conception of the state as *custodian of capital* is the dialectical heir to the legacy of instrumentalism, then Bob Jessop's *strategic–relational approach* is the dialectical heir to the structuralist inheritance (see in particular Jessop, 1990; for commentaries, see

Barrow, 1993, pp. 153–6; Bonefeld, 1993; Hay, 1994b; 1995b, pp. 199–202; Mahon, 1991; Painter, 1995, pp. 63–6; Taylor, 1995, pp. 259–63). More convincingly than any other Marxist theorist past or present, he succeeds in transcending the artificial dualism of structure and agency by moving towards a truly dialectical understanding of their inter-relationship. Structure and agency logically entail one another, hence there can be no analysis of action which is not itself also an analysis of structure. All social and political change occurs through strategic interaction as strategies collide with and impinge upon the structured terrain of the strategic context within which they are formulated. Their effects (however unintentional, however unanticipated) are to transform (however partially) the context within which future strategies are formulated and deployed.

Such a formulation has highly significant implications for the theory of the (capitalist) state. Jessop follows the later Poulantzas in conceiving of the state as a strategic site traversed by class struggles and as 'a specific institutional ensemble with multiple boundaries, no institutional fixity and no pre-given formal or substantive unity' (Jessop, 1990, p. 267; Poulantzas, 1978b). The state is a dynamic and constantly unfolding system. Its specific form at a given moment in time in a particular national setting represents a 'crystallisation of past strategies' which privileges certain strategies and actors over others. As such, 'the state is located within a complex *dialectic of structures and strategies*' (ibid., p. 129, emphasis added). This introduces the important notion that the state, and the institutions which comprise it, are *strategically selective.* The structures and modus operandi of the state 'are more open to some types of political strategy than others' (ibid., p. 260). The state presents an uneven playing field whose complex contours favour certain strategies (and hence certain actors) over others.

Within such a perspective there can be no guarantee that the state (and governments wielding state power) will act in the general interest of capital (whatever that might be). Indeed, insofar as the function of the capitalist state can be regarded as the expanded reproduction of capital, the specific form of the capitalist state at a particular stage in its historical development is always likely to problematise and eventually compromise this function. The state thus evolves through a series of political and economic crises as the pre-existing mode of intervention of the state within civil society and the economy proves increasingly dysfunctional. The outcome of such crises, however, and the struggles that they engender cannot be predicted in advance. For if we are to apply the strategic–relational approach, they are contingent upon the balance of class (and other) forces, the nature of the crisis itself and (we might add) popular *perceptions* of the nature of the crisis (Hay, 1996b, 1996c) – in short, on the strategically selective context and the strategies mobilised within this context.

Jessop's approach then, despite its concern with state structures and their strategic selectivity (see Table 8.1), and despite its structuralist pedigree, eschews all forms of functionalism, reductionism and determinism. The strategic–relational approach offers no guarantees, – either of the ongoing reproduction of the capitalist system or of its impending demise (though, given the strategic selectivity of the current context, the odds on the latter would appear remote). It is, in short, a statement of the contingency and indeterminacy of social and political change (1990, pp. 12–13). The casualty in all of this is the *definitive* (and very illusive) Marxist theory of the state. As Jessop himself notes, there can be no general or fully determinate theory of the capitalist state, only theoretically informed accounts of capitalist states in their institutional, historical and strategic specificity (Jessop, 1982, pp. 211–13, 258–9; 1990, p. 44).

We would appear to have come full circle. We end where we began, with a paradox: there is no Marxist theory of the state – there couldn't be.

Conclusions

Why do *we* need a *Marxist* approach to the state *today*? For in a world which is seemingly either globalised or globalising and in which Marxism as a political project is defunct, it is tempting to dismiss Marxist attempts to theorise the state as anachronistic and of purely historical interest – if that. With the nation-state on the wane do we really need a theory of the state anyway? And even if we think we do, with Marxism in retreat why a *Marxist* theory of the state?

The first objection can be dealt with fairly swiftly. Yes, the current phase of capitalist accumulation is qualitatively and quantitatively different from all previous stages – both in terms of the international mobility of capital and in the truly global nature of the social, political and environmental pathologies with which it is associated. Yet it would be dangerous to conclude either (i) that this threatens to precipitate the end of the nation-state or (ii) that, even if it did, we could afford to dispense with the theory of the state. For whilst national communities, states and governments still provide the primary focus of political socialisation, mobilisation, identification and representation, the nation-state is firmly here to stay. Moreover, while this remains so, the sort of concerted inter-state response necessary to deal with global ecological crisis is likely to be thwarted and hijacked by more parochial national interests and considerations. Hence the very form of the state itself (its national character) may militate against a genuinely global response to a genuinely global crisis. The *national* form of the state may problematise its *global* function. Environmentalism may concern itself with global problems, but environmentalists require a theory of the state (Hay, 1994b, p. 218; 1996d). Furthermore, as Jessop notes, the internationalisation of capital has rendered (more) porous the boundaries of formerly closed national economies, but it has not lessened the significance of national differences or indeed national *states* in the regulation of capitalist accumulation. The form of the state may have changed, and it may have been subject to a 'tendential hollowing-out' as many of its previous functions and responsibilities have been displaced upwards, downwards and outwards, but its distinctively national character remains (Jessop 1994a, 1994b, 1995; Hay and Jessop, 1995). Thus the process of globalisation (more accurately, the processes that *interact* to produce a tendential globalisation) merely demonstrate the continuing centrality of the state to the dynamics of capitalist accumulation.

Yet it is one thing to demonstrate the continuing need for a theory of the state in the abstract; it is another thing altogether to claim this as justification for a distinctively *Marxist* approach to the study of the state. The proof of this particular pudding must be in the eating and it should be recalled that there are a great variety of different flavours – and an even greater variety of different tastes. Nonetheless two general arguments for a sophisticated Marxist conception of the state (such as that formulated by Jessop) can be offered: one substantive, the other methodological.

For the first we can return to the above example. Environmental crisis has its origins in an industrial growth imperative. This might suggest the relevance of a theory of *the state in industrial society* to the political economy of ecology. Yet a moment's further reflection reveals that the growth imperative that characterises modern societies – and is thus responsible for the environmental degradation we witness – is a *capitalist* growth imperative, sustained and regulated by the institutions of a capitalist state. Environmentalists then need, not merely a theory of the state, but a theory of the *capitalist* state. As such a theory, Marxism clearly has much to offer.

The second reason is somewhat more esoteric, and relates to the methodological sophistication of modern Marxist approaches to the state. Though characterised for much of its history by the seemingly intractable dispute between structural functionalism on the one hand and instrumentalism on the other, considerable methodological advances have been made in Marxist state theory in recent years. In this respect modern Marxist state theory has much to offer to Marxists and non-Marxists alike. For as authors like Anthony Giddens (1984) and Nicos Mouzelis (1991; 1995) have noted, the dualism of structure and agency (of which the structuralism–instrumentalism battle is merely a reflection) is not only a problem within Marxism but has characterised social and political science since its inception. In the strategic-relational approach it has been transcended in a simple yet sophisticated manner. Though not all will share the analytical, critical and political concerns that animate contemporary Marxist theory, few can help but benefit from the methodological insights it offers.

Jessop's central achievement has been to take Marxist state theory beyond the fatuous question *is the modern state a capitalist state or a state in capitalist society?* If his work receives the attention it deserves, feminists need not duplicate the errors and deviations of Marxist theory by asking themselves: *is the contemporary state essentially patriarchal or merely a state in a patriarchal society?* Modern Marxist theory will probably never get the chance to follow Henry Higgins in transforming the object of its study. But those who might can surely learn a thing or two from its deviations . . .

Notes

1. As Offe notes, 'it is not without good reason that Engels . . . calls the state the "ideal" collective capitalist; for the state as a "real" collective would clearly be a logical impossibility . . . firstly because the state apparatus is not itself a "capitalist" . . . and secondly because the concept of the collective capitalist is itself nonsensical in that competition . . . is essential for the movement of capital' (1974, p. 31).
2. To which an equally sharp Little Red Riding-Hood might be tempted to retort, 'My, what big words you use.' To that there is probably no suitable response.
3. Here we might think of the crisis of the 1970s in Britain. Though precipitated to some extent by economic factors (such as the exhaustion

of the postwar 'Fordist' mode of economonic growth), as the subsequent Thatcherite restructuring demonstrates, this was a crisis of the British state, not of British capitalism per se (see Hay, 1996a, chs 5 & 6).

4. Languishing in a cell in one of Mussolini's prisons, Gramsci was only too well aware of the ruthless efficiency of the state's coercive arm.

9

Marxism and the Welfare State

Chris Pierson

The relationship between Marxism and the welfare state is complex. Since there is not one 'true' Marxism but many and since the experience of the welfare state under advanced capitalism has proved to be quite diverse, we should hardly expect to find a single and wholly consistent Marxist explanation of welfare state development. And so it proves. Some Marxists have seen the welfare state principally as a controlling agency of the ruling capitalist class. Others have seen it as the 'Trojan Horse' within which socialist principles can be carried into the very heartlands of capitalism. Again some Marxists have argued that the welfare state provides the indispensable underpinning for a market-based social and economic order, whilst others have seen it as incompatible with the long-run integrity of a capitalist economy. A number of Marxist and neo-Marxist commentators have managed to affirm all of these principles more or less simultaneously! At the same time, both Marxism and the welfare state have a history. It is clear that the welfare state as an object of Marxists' inquiry has changed through time and so (often in response to these changes) has the intellectual apparatus with which they have sought to explain it. In this chapter, we try to make sense of this diversity of Marxist explanations and consider whether Marxism can still tell us anything useful about welfare states.

Marx and the Welfare State

It is natural enough to begin our consideration of Marxism and the welfare state with Marx. In doing so, two general comments are in

175

order. First, what passes for Marxism is something quite other than a simple *résumé* of Marx's thought. Marxism definitely came *after* Marx and what became identified as 'orthodox' Marxism was in effect a quite selective codification of certain key elements in his mature account of capitalist development. Within a decade of its launch (in the German SPD's Erfurt Programme of 1891) this 'official' reading of Marx was under sustained challenge, as it has been ever since. In this context, we need to recognise both that Marx's intellectual heritage was far from unambiguous (especially where the welfare state is concerned) and that the unity of Marxist thought (whatever official Communist Parties were to come to say) was comparatively fleeting. The greatest insights of Marxism (on the welfare state as in other areas) have come quite as much from dissenters and revisionists as from the orthodox tradition. Secondly, Marx did not live to see anything more than the first primitive stirrings of welfare state activity and it is hardly surprising that he had very little to say about states and welfare. Nonetheless it has to be observed that the emergence of welfare states within capitalism is, at first sight, a rather surprising development in terms of classical Marxism. It is certainly possible to reconstruct an account, consistent with some of the things that Marx said about the state, which 'explains' the emergence of state welfare provision under capitalism. It is, however, difficult to represent this as the *main* line in Marx's own thinking about the capitalist state which he clearly saw as a much more straightforwardly repressive apparatus.

Indeed Marx's core critique of capitalism suggests that it is generally incompatible with state-secured forms of welfare. This critique is built upon three insights that Marx 'borrowed' from the classical political economy of Adam Smith and David Ricardo: first, capitalism is an economic system based upon the production and exchange of privately owned commodities within an unconstrained market; secondly, the value of any commodity is an expression of the amount of human labour power expended upon its production. Upon these premises, Marx develops an account of capitalism as a necessarily exploitative and class-based system, one in which unpaid labour is extracted from the sellers of labour power by the owners of capital under the form of a 'free and equal exchange' in the market-place. Such market exchanges do not, however, optimize individual (and thus social) welfare. Rather, the radically unequal exchange (the extraction of surplus value) that is masked by a formally 'free and equal' market in commodities means that capitalist economic organization only secures the welfare of the capitalists (as individuals and as a numerically declining class), while prescribing diswelfare for the great majority of the exploited working class. The third element that Marx derives from classical political economy is the claim that capitalism is a dynamic system in which the competitive search for profit and responses to the long-term tendency for the rate of profit to fall lead to the intensification of exploitation and the heightening of class conflict. It is a system chronically prone to periodic crises (of overproduction). While such crises do not straight-forwardly occasion the economic collapse of capitalism, they do determine a cyclical intensification of the contradictions that are to lead to its eventual demise. As a part of this process, capitalism in its historically 'declining' phase comes to be ever less efficient and less equitable in delivering individual and collective social welfare. According to Marx, this radical inequality of welfare outcomes is endemic to capitalism and *not open to redress by an interventionist state.*

In summary, the state under capitalism might intervene in the reproduction of social relations, however in Marx's view it could not (i) intervene in such a way as to undermine the logic of the capitalist market economy or (ii) act against the long-term interests of the capitalist class. Whatever institutional form the state under capitalism might take (and even under the governance of social democratic forces), it remained in essence a capitalist state. For Marx, securing the real welfare of the broad working population and articulating their real needs were simply incompatible with the structure of a capitalist economy. Real welfare for the majority of the population could only begin with a revolutionary transition to socialism.

Twentieth-century Marxism and the Welfare State

Until the Second World War, mainstream classical Marxists saw little reason to amend Marx's rather stark judgement about the impossibility of securing the welfare of the working class under capitalism. Although it was during the interwar years that many formative welfare states emerged, provision was seen to be minimal and in the 1930s rising unemployment and falling benefits were seen to express the dominance of the (crisis) logic of capital over the wishful thinking of those who argued for gradual change through parliamentary means. By contrast, in the golden years of social democratic success after 1945, it was those reformist social democrats who had embraced the welfare state as a major agency of gradual social(ist) change who lost patience with Marxism. Orthodox Marxism, with its outdated appeal to the class war and revolutionary change, belonged to a bygone era of working class poverty, mass unemployment and class privilege. Meanwhile the Marxist left, demoralized by the experience of the Hungarian uprising, the (limited) exposure of Stalinism and the seemingly uninterrupted growth of the postwar economy, increasingly directed its attention towards alienation and the cultural consequences of capitalism. Herbert Marcuse's *One-Dimensional Man* (1972) depicted organized capitalism as a system of *total administration* in which the working class was lost as the revolutionary agent of social change. Even opposition was now co-opted within an all-embracing system of structured irrationality (of which the welfare state was an important component). The provision of welfare to the working class became not an avenue for their gradual advance towards socialism – as the non-Marxist left and Austro-Marxists (see p. 184 of this chapter) had envisaged – but the means by which workers were controlled, demoralized and deradicalized.

By the end of the 1960s, however, and more especially under the impact of the events loosely and graphically associated with 1968, the image of unproblematic postwar social democratic consensus began to crack. A period of uninterrupted political and industrial unrest also saw a reemergence of academic interest in Marxist and other radical/socialist thinking. It is from this period that we can date the real emergence or possibly revival of Marxist interest in the welfare state.

Neo-Marxist Analysis of the Welfare State

Although others, most notably the Italian inter-war Marxist leader Antonio Gramsci, might lay claim to initiating Marxist study of the welfare state, the origins of this renaissance are widely seen to reside in the lively debate that developed in the late 1960s between two distinguished Marxist theoreticians: Ralph Miliband and Nicos Poulantzas (Miliband, 1969; Poulantzas, 1973; Poulantzas, 1978b). Although it now seems as if rather less divided these two antagonists than was apparent at the time, their exchanges did encourage a number of important amendments to classical Marxist thinking on the capitalist state. Three suppositions were of especial importance to the Marxist debate on the welfare state. First, there was the claim that the state enjoys *relative autonomy* from the capitalist class. The state is not simply the instrument of the ruling class and its capacity to act in the general interests of the capitalist class may require it to be partially independent of the individual representatives of capital. Secondly, the state articulates the general systemic needs of capital accumulation – and this may include paying an *economic* price to secure the *political* compliance of non-ruling class interests. Thirdly, the state is not a seamless whole; it is, as Poulantzas had it, 'constituted–divided' by the same divisions that characterize capitalist society more generally.

These theoretical developments opened up a new terrain on which questions about the welfare state could be engaged. In fact, the revival of Marxist interest in the welfare state has taken a wide variety of forms. This chapter considers five such approaches, discussed under the labels social control, Marxism–feminism, power resources, crisis of the welfare state and post-crisis developments.

The Welfare State as Social Control

At least one important strand in Marxist opinion has continued to regard the welfare state as predominantly an instrument for the social control of the working class, acting in the long-term interests of capital accumulation. This is the view that remains closest to the classical Marxism of Marx, Engels and Lenin. Ginsburg (1979, p. 2) is characteristic in arguing that, under capitalism, 'the functioning and management of state welfare remains part of a *capitalist* state which is fundamentally concerned with the maintenance and reproduction of capitalist social relations'. Above all else, the welfare state is involved in securing the production and reproduction of labour power under capitalist forms. The benefits of the welfare state to the working class are not generally denied, but they are seen to be largely the adventi- tious by- product of securing the interests of capital. Here there is an echo of Marx's own comment (1973, p. 348) on an earlier series of reforms, the Factory Acts, which, while a gain for the working classes thus protected, arose from the 'same necessity as forced the manuring of English fields with guano' – that is, the need to preserve from total exhaustion the sole source of surplus value.

This broad thesis about the role of the welfare state in the reproduction of capitalism is reinforced by a number of more specific claims about the operation of social policy. Thus, for example, social provision under the welfare state is seen characteristically to be geared to the requirements of capital and not to the real needs of the working population. It is argued that many welfare policies were originated not by socialists or social democrats but by conservative or liberal elites, whose intention was to manage/regulate capitalism and to discipline its workforce not to mitigate the social hardship of the working class. Again the funding of welfare state measures has often been regressive and/or associated with an extension of the tax base. At best, welfare state spending has been redistributive within the working class or across the life cycle of the average worker. A number of Marxist critics have also argued that the compulsory state administration of welfare deprives the working class of the management of its own welfare, yielding to the state and its agents wide-ranging and discretionary powers to interfere in the everyday lives of its individual citizens.

In its most vulgar and conspiratorial form, the 'social control' thesis is unsustainable. The welfare state was not the cunningly preconceived master plan of the ruling capitalist class through which the workers were duped into paying for their own exploitation and subjection. Nonetheless, and in the face of the no less fantastic account of traditional social democrats in which the welfare state expresses society's general and benign interest in the well-being of all its citizens, there is plenty of evidence to suggest that many agencies of the welfare state have been agencies of social control. Welfare states have never been straightforward expressions of 'social citizenship'. To a greater or lesser extent (and internationally there has indeed been great variation), welfare states have always been regulative, coercive and oriented towards the imperatives of the labour market. There is plenty of evidence of conservative elites (from the innovating Bismarck on) using social policy as an anti-socialist measure. It is also true that welfare states do much more to redistribute resources across individuals' life cycles (between their working and non-working years), rather than from rich to poor. Indeed there is even evidence that in some programmes resources are transferred *upwards* from poor to rich (see Hills, 1994). There is also a marked continuity with pre-welfare states in the management of the able-bodied poor and in the policing of the labour market. All of this persuades Piven and Cloward (1971), for example, to describe the defining purpose of the American welfare state as 'regulating the poor'. 'Social control' is not the whole story of the welfare state, but it is an important part of it.

Marxism–Feminism and the welfare state

Marxist–feminists are also centrally concerned with questions of the welfare state as an agency of social control, but they have been much more focused upon the dynamics of the long-term reproduction of capitalism (beyond the market and the labour contract) and with the specific consequences of these arrangements for women. Their analyses begin from the recognition that, left to themselves, markets are unable to secure the circumstances for the long-term reproduction of capitalism. Particularly within advanced capitalism, the state must intervene within the economy and society to guarantee conditions for sustained capital accumulation. It is in this context that the development of the welfare state must be understood. The welfare state describes all those state interventions which are required to ensure the production and reproduction of labour power in forms which will sustain capitalism's profitability. However, given the (ideological) imperatives of maintaining the family, in which labour power is reproduced, as a 'private' sphere, the state typically intervenes 'not directly but through its support for a specific form of household: the family household dependent largely upon a male wage and upon female domestic servicing' (McIntosh, 1978, pp. 255–6). Thus the profitability of capitalism is sustained not just through the state-sanctioned oppression of labour under the wage contract but also through the oppression of women within the state-supported form of the 'dependent-woman family' (Weir, 1974). Thus the welfare state has to be explained simultaneously in terms of *patriarchy* (the systemic oppression of women by men) and *capitalism* (the systemic oppression of labour by capital).

The state-sponsored family form is promoted through a range of taxation and benefit provisions (differential arrangements for men and women, and for single and married women) and omissions (the absence of statutory nursery places or collective cooking/laundry facilities). It secures the interests of capital in three main ways. First, it lowers the costs of the reproduction of labour power. A major determinant of the wage costs of capital is the reproduction (on a day-to-day and generation-to-generation basis) of labour power. These costs are substantially cut where they can be displaced upon either the state (public education, public health care), or upon women's unpaid domestic labour, (cooking, washing, childcare, care of dependent relatives). Second, it provides employers with a 'latent reserve army of labour'. Married women are a source of potential cheap labour (given the prioritization of the male 'family wage'), to be drawn into employment in times of labour scarcity and to be redeployed towards their 'natural' role in the home when jobs are scarce. Third, where 'caring'/reproduction services are performed within the waged sector of the economy, the definition of such employment as 'women's work' enables it to be provided at comparatively low cost.

In recent years, a number of important qualifications have been appended to this position. First, it has been suggested that such accounts tend to underestimate the specific impact of *patriarchy*. It is argued that greater weight must be given to the way in which the welfare state serves the interests of (especially white and skilled) working class *men*. Some commentators suggest that the welfare state has an *economic* cost for capital (in privileging male wages) but that this is outweighed by the *political* benefits of the gender division of interests within the general category of wage labour which it sustains (Barrett, 1980, p. 230). Secondly, greater attention has been directed towards the *ideological* construction of women's subordination under welfare state capitalism. The capacity of the welfare state to organize the interests of capital in the ways indicated relies upon pre-existing forms of oppression of women by men which the state is able to shape and exploit but not to create. Thus more weight is given to the deep-seated ideology of men and women's 'natural' roles, which are seen to be crucial in underpinning the structures of patriarchal capitalism. Thirdly, there has been a re-evaluation of the nature of women's work in the welfare state. Women do not function straightforwardly as a reserve army of labour. In fact the dependent-female, male-waged household is increasingly untypical within modern economies, while labour markets are heavily sex-segregated, so that expanding women's employment does not typically mean supplementing or replacing a male workforce. Finally, it is argued that, while the expansion of the welfare state has often meant the replacement of womens' unpaid labour in the home by womens' underpaid 'caring' work in the public sector, state provision of such services can represent a *strengthening* of women's position. It does, for example, embody the recognition of a public responsibility for those forms of care which were previously defined as exclusively a private (and woman's) responsibility. It has afforded an avenue of (otherwise blocked) career mobility for some women. It has offered (albeit very limited) childcare provision and healthcare services. These are not to be exhaustively understood as securing the long-term interests of capital, but rather as forms of provision which constitute a 'second-best' for both women *and* capital.

There are certainly weaknesses in this Marxist–feminist approach. The male breadwinner/dependent woman family is increasingly atypical of the complex patterns of gendered employment (and unemployment) in modern capitalist economies. Similarly the structure of these economies (particularly the increase in female labour force participation rates) mean that the story of women functioning as a 'reserve army of labour' is too simple. Sheila Shaver (1989, pp. 91–3) is probably right to argue that the Marxist–feminist paradigm on welfare has tended to lapse into functionalist modes of explanation and that, in general, 'Marxism's categories were too little questioned, and feminism's too superficially applied'. Furthermore Marxist–feminists are not the only ones to have drawn attention to the patriarchal character of the welfare state.

Nonetheless exposing the gendered character of capitalist welfare states has probably been the single most important analytical development of the past twenty years. In this context, Marxism–feminism involves two major advances: first, it discloses the fact that the experience of the welfare state is *systematically* different for men and women and, secondly, it stresses that a proper understanding of the functioning of the public apparatus of welfare requires us to consider its relation not only to the economy but also to the 'private' world of family and non-institutional welfare provision. Once these conceptual spaces are opened up, a whole new world of welfare comes into view. The welfare state is largely provided for, and by, women. Because they are poorer than men, live longer than them and generally have less access to market-provided services, women are much more reliant on welfare state provision. Women are much more vulnerable to poverty, not least because state support for single-parent families and lone pensioners (both of which categories are predominantly female) are insufficient. In welfare states in which retirement income is dependent upon lifetime earnings, women (with lower average earnings than men and with careers characteristically interrupted by extended periods of childcare), have substantially lower pension incomes. At the same time, women's unpaid domestic labour – both in the social reproduction of the workforce and in caring for unwaged dependents – subsidises those economic costs which would have otherwise to be met by capital, through the direct provision of services, increased taxation or an increase in workers' wages. The echoing silence in traditional accounts of the welfare state, which the feminists have effectively broken, is that the majority of welfare is provided not by the state but within the family, and largely through the unpaid labour of women. Anyone who takes the Marxist–feminist position seriously (as they should) will see the welfare state in a quite different way.

The Power Resources Model of the Welfare State

Although advocates of the social control and Marxist–feminist approaches have generally been hostile to the welfare state (as essentially an element in the non-market reproduction of capitalism), not all Marxists have been so sceptical and those who favour the power resources model have been broadly sympathetic to what the welfare state (under certain well-specified and favourable circumstances) can be expected to deliver. Their confidence turns upon what for Marxists is a rather unusual faith in the possibilities opened up by the winning of mass suffrage in parliamentary democratic institutions. Marx did not live into the age of mass parliamentary democracies. For the first generation of Marxists (active in the period after 1890), however, the status of parliamentary democracy under a newly mass (male) suffrage became a bitterly contentious issue. In the aftermath of the First World War and the Russian Revolution, a deep division arose between those who believed socialism could now be realised through gradualist and parliamentary tactics (the social democrats) and those who followed Lenin in judging that parliamentary institutions did nothing to change the essential nature of what remained a *capitalist* state (the Marxist–Leninists). Given his status in the communist movement, it is unsurprising that Lenin's scepticism came to define the prevailing Marxist view of parliamentary democracy. But there was always a secondary school of Marxist thought which held that Marx was correct about the nature of capitalism, the inevitability of class struggle and the need for revolutionary change, but believed that, under universal suffrage, parliamentary institutions could be the medium for processing this class-based politics. Such a radical social democratic position is best represented in the epoch of 'classical' Marxism by the Austro-Marxists and the leader of the German SPD, Karl Kautsky.

The power resources model can be read as a contemporary variant of this distinctively *Marxist* social democracy. At its heart lies a perceived division within the advanced capitalist societies between the exercise of economic and of political power, often presented as a contrast between markets and politics. In the *economic* sphere, the decisive power resource is control over capital assets, the mechanism for its exercise is the (wage labour) contract and its principal beneficiary the capitalist class. However, in the *political* sphere, power flows from the strength of numbers, mobilized through the democratic process and tends to favour 'numerically large collectivities', especially the organized working class. Institutionalized power struggles under advanced capitalism are best understood as a struggle between the logic of the market and the logic of politics. The more successful are the forces of the organized working class, the more entrenched and institutionalised will the welfare state become and the more marginalised will be the principle of allocation through the market.

Generally the inception of welfare state policies is seen to follow upon the universalization of the franchise, itself seen as a victory for the organized working class. Initially social policy may represent an attempt to pre-empt political reform or else to disorganize or demobilize the organized working class. But under wise and far-sighted social democratic governance, welfare state policies can be used both to counteract the dominance of capital that market relationships entail and to reinforce the effective solidarity of organized labour. Where social democratic governments become more or less permanently entrenched in office (and this is an essential precondition) an effective balance or at least stalemate may be established between the political powers of social democracy and the economic powers of capital. Under these circumstances, some sort of working compromise between capital and labour is likely to emerge, characteristically under the rubric of the welfare state. But the left social democrats insist that, however longstanding, such a compromise is in essence temporary. Indeed, if the social democrats govern wisely and make the right strategic choices, it is argued that the (Marxian) logic of continuing capitalist development will increasingly tilt the balance of power in favour of organized labour and against private capital. Thus it is suggested that continuing capitalist development will tend to produce an expanding and homogeneous broad working class. Social democratic governments that mobilize this constituency and promote its internal solidarity can undermine the effectiveness of traditional market disciplines and further entrench their own political power. At a certain point in the strengthening of the powers of organized labour, conditions of balance/stalemate with capital no longer apply. At this point, it is possible for the social democratic movement to advance beyond the 'political' welfare state, with its indirect (Keynesian) influence upon the management of the economy, and to engage directly the traditional socialist issue of socialization of the economy.

The greatest strength of the power resources model is that it has something positive and *programmatic* to say about the welfare state. Given Marx's own contempt for those who only thought about the world instead of changing it, the advocacy of a clear political strategy for moving through the welfare state towards socialism may seem, at least upon these grounds, to have good Marxist credentials. And advocates of this position do well to show that left incumbency (that is, the capacity of parties of the left to win and maintain political office) *does* make a difference. But there are also problems with the model. First, while the more naive evolutionism of traditional social democracy is rejected, elements of a Marxist evolutionism persist. Presumptions about the uniformity of workers' interests, the necessary growth in the proportion of the working class and the weakening of the powers of capitalism in the face of the collective action of the workers underpin several of the strategic claims in the 'power resources' model. However there are good grounds for doubting that these presumptions about a majoritarian working class with unified interests are true (see Przeworski, 1985) It may also be that the political focus of the 'power resources' model is too narrow. Middle class support has been crucial to the pattern of welfare state development, particularly in the postwar period, and at strategic times in the historical emergence of the European welfare states, the attitudes of the rural classes have also been a decisive element. Similarly parties other than the social democrats (especially the confessional parties of continental Europe) have also played an important historical role in the expansion of the welfare state and their position has not always been one of seeking to minimise levels of social expenditure. This suggests that any understanding of the class politics of the welfare state must be one that considers the positions of a number of classes (not just capital and labour) and of a number of parties (not just the social democrats), and that the decisive element in the success of the social democratic welfare state project may lie in the capacity of the working class and social democratic parties to forge long-term, majoritarian alliances in support of its decommodifying form of social policy. But the most important objection to the power resources model is that, even upon the most favourable terrain, it does not any longer appear to be working. Critics have always objected that the model tells a peculiarly Scandinavian, perhaps even just a Swedish, story. Now it is argued that, even here, the virtuous cycle of social democratic incumbency, incremental growth of social citizenship and mobilisation in the direction of socialism has been broken.

Neo-Marxism and 'The Contradictions of the Welfare State'

Undoubtedly the most influential of all Marx-derived accounts of welfare in recent years has been that literature which focuses upon the 'contradictions of the welfare state'. This perspective draws upon the third innovation to have arisen from the Miliband–Poulantzas exchanges, developing the idea of contradiction and struggles existing *within* the (welfarist) form of the capitalist state. It first gained prominence in the 1970s, when its account of contradictions within the welfare state seemed to chime with the lived experience of crisis in the postwar social democratic order. Indeed it is difficult to isolate a *general* statement of this (neo-)Marxist view from the specific context of perceived *crisis* in the welfare state out of which it arose. This is most clearly the case with James O'Connor's (1973) path-breaking work on *The Fiscal Crisis of the State* but it is also true of the best-known statement of this position in the work of the German social theorist Claus Offe (1984).

Offe follows Marx in arguing that capitalism is innately crisis-prone. However this tendency does not now manifest itself predominantly as an economic crisis. In fact the welfare state emerges as an institutional form for averting economic crisis by managing the social and political consequences of the privately regulated capitalist economy. It is a form of systemic crisis management and, for twenty-five years following the end of the Second World War, a remarkably successful one. But in the long run this process of reconciliation through the welfare state proves unstable, as the welfare state is subject to a crisis logic of its own. The success of the capitalist economy based upon private ownership is indispensable to the long-term viability of the welfare state, both because it is the ultimate source of that state's fiscal viability (through taxation and borrowing) and because consequently it is the basis of mass loyalty and legitimacy for the state (through the funding of welfare services, the securing of 'full employment' and so on). The key problem for the crisis management strategy of the welfare state is that, in practice, 'the dynamics of capitalist development seem to exhibit a constant tendency to paralyse the commodity form of value', and thus to imperil the state's primary source of revenues (Offe, 1984, p. 122).

Unregulated, it is suggested by Offe, the development of the capitalist economy tends systematically to exclude elements of labour power and capital from productive exchange (through the under-employment of labour or the underutilization of capital). The state cannot itself generally restore effective and profitable commodity exchange by intervening directly in the accumulation process, as this would both undermine the normative basis of the private-exchange capitalist economy and engender the risk of an (anti-nationalization) capital investment strike. Since the state is prevented from intervening directly in the economy, it has to proceed indirectly, through essentially Keynesian means, to re-establish the conditions under which capital and labour will be drawn *into profitable* commodity exchange, through regulations and financial incentives (corporate tax concessions, special development areas, interest-free industrial loans, subsidizing energy costs), public infrastructural investment (training and retraining, recruitment services, subsidized transport facilities) and the sponsoring of neo-corporatist arrangements (between trades unions and employers). Offe calls this strategy 'administrative recommodification'. The intention is to promote the fuller utilization or *commodification* of both capital and labour through indirect, administrative means. Its vitiating weakness is that, in practice, it promotes a process of *decommodification*: that is, it undermines the circumstances for the fuller utilization of capital and labour. Thus the strategies which are supposed to encourage *more* effective commodity exchange in fact place ever greater areas of social life *outside* the commodity form and *outside* the sphere of market exchange. The principal (and rather cumbersome) contradiction of the welfare state is that strategies of recommodification effect a widespread process of decommodification (Offe, 1984).

This is an elegant argument and, has already been indicated, probably the single most influential neo-Marxist account of recent developments in the welfare state. It certainly gave powerful theoretical expression to the problems of state management in the 1970s, when public indebtedness and the tension between welfare state expenditures and economic growth seemed to be at their peak. But, in the end, it is an account with problems of its own. Part of the difficulty springs from an overburdened usage of the ideas of 'contradiction' and 'crisis'. 'Contradictions' were seen, following Marx, as endemic to the capitalist mode of production. In the long run, they were likely to trigger episodes of 'crisis' in which the reproduction of the existing order would itself be imperilled. But, if the terms 'contra-diction' and 'crisis' are applied to the circumstances of the 1970s, it must be with a recognition that they cannot carry the full weight of expectation (of resolution through the transition to a new and distinct mode of production) which classical Marxism would imply. The advanced capitalist societies and their welfare states certainly faced an acute challenge in the 1970s (and beyond). The 'old order' (established after 1945) could not go on as before. But, in practice, the problems were resolved or (more properly) contained not by a revolutionary transformation but through a much messier and incre-mental reordering of the political economy. What we had in the wake of this restructuring was meaner benefits, tighter budgets, firmer labour market disciplines and mass unemployment, but still within a framework we would recognise as a 'welfare state'.

There is certainly a problem for the state when the costs of funding its legitimating activities start to undermine the processes of accumula-tion from which all its revenue is finally derived. But the idea of a *contradiction* between accumulation and legitimation functions proves to be too simple. In fact, the greatest source of a state's legitimacy is its capacity to generate (or at least to be lucky enough to officiate over) successful accumulation. Economic growth may not benefit every-body, but, if it benefits enough of the right people, the state may find that accumulation and legitimation coincide. Under these circum-stances, the function of the welfare state may be to manage and control those elements of the population who are excluded from this accumulation–legitimation coalition. Certainly there were important changes after the hiatus of the 1970s. Welfare states after 1980 were significantly meaner. They were more explicitly subservient to the needs of the economy, in terms both of a more coercive labour market and of a much 'flatter' funding structure. But in most cases they were not very much smaller, continuing (for the time being) to deliver the same sorts of services within a (reconstructed) public sector. With hindsight, though the pressures upon welfare state structures were (and are) real enough, they were not resolved in the climactic way that this (neo-)Marxist literature of the 1970s had suggested. In the face of O'Connor's (1973, p. 221) belief that 'the only lasting solution to the crisis is socialism', if there was a decisive political change in this period it was a shift *rightwards*. This brought a severe attenuation in many elements of the postwar regime, but it did not generally see a wholesale dismantling of welfare state structures.

'Post-Crisis' Accounts of the Welfare State

It is to explaining these new or 'reconstructed' welfare state regimes, emerging from the 'crisis' of the 1970s and 1980s, that the attention of contemporary neo-Marxists has increasingly turned. Their (diverse) efforts are well represented by the leading British Marxist theoretician, Bob Jessop. Jessop (1988, 1994b) seeks to make sense of these recent developments in the welfare state in terms of a broad process of restructuring in the global capitalist political economy. His assessment is made in terms of a large-scale process of change in the general configuration of contemporary capitalism, often characterised (and, with some severe qualifications, by Jessop himself) as a transition from Fordism to post-Fordism. In summary, his analysis theorises a transition from the *Keynesian welfare state* or KWS (corresponding to a Fordist regime of accumulation) towards a *Schumpeterian work-fare state* or SWS (in line with the requirements of a post-Fordist regime).

Very broadly, Fordism is taken to describe the characteristic regime of capital accumulation (or 'mode of regulation') that prevailed in the advanced capitalist societies between the end of the Second World War and the turn of the 1970s. This was a period of unprecedented and sustained economic growth, based upon the dominance of mass production and mass consumption and massified, semi-skilled labour. It saw an enhanced status for the collective bargaining of wages and conditions (increasingly upon a national basis) and a correspondingly increased role for both large-scale capital and organised labour. At the international level, it was built upon a commitment to 'free markets' and stable exchange rates, both under American leadership. Domestically it was secured around Keynesian economic policies to promote economic growth and a more or less 'institutional' welfare state.

In what is by now a familiar story, the early 1970s are seen to have heralded a crisis for this Fordist regime and to have seen the first moves towards restoring the conditions for successful capital accumulation through a new and distinctively 'post-Fordist' order. The watchword of the post-Fordist age was *flexibility*. There was to be greater flexibility in production (involving constantly updated technologies, techniques and product lines), greater flexibility in the workforce (multi-skilling), 'flexible' labour markets and 'flexible' wages), deinstitutionalization of labour market management (with a drastically reduced role for trade unions and collective bargaining), greater permeability of national borders, greater diversity of financial instruments, floating exchange rates and so on. At the same time, the primarily *domestic* orientations of both economy and economic policy making which characterised the Fordist epoch were giving way to a heightened process of economic internationalisation or even *globalisation*, disempowering governments as agents of domestic macroeconomic management but also giving them a greatly strengthened interest in international competitiveness.

As the transition from Fordism to post-Fordism progresses, so Jessop anticipates a further move from Keynesian welfare state regimes towards what he calls a *Schumpeterian workfare state*, more consistent with the needs of the new accumulation regime. This new arrangement is *Schumpeterian*, in Jessop's terms, because it is oriented around the imperative of *permanent innovation* which the Austrian economist Joseph Schumpeter saw as a distinctive characteristic of the capitalist mode of production. It is a *workfare* state not so much because it will be characterised by the 'working for benefits' strategy that US 'workfare' provision has mandated, but more generally because it will encourage welfare arrangements which are quite explicitly oriented around labour market discipline in an economy exposed to fierce international competition.

The 'distinctive objectives in economic and social production' of the Schumpeterian workfare state are these:

> [1] to promote product, process, organisational and market innovation in open economies in order to strengthen as far as possible the structural competitiveness of the national economy by intervening on the supply side; and [2] to subordinate social policy to the needs of labour market flexibility and/or to the constraints of international competition.

In this sense it marks a clear break with the KWS as domestic full employment is deprioritised in favour of international competitiveness and redistributive welfare rights take second place to a productivist reordering of social policy (Jessop, 1994b, p. 24).

Jessop is careful not to suggest that the SWS has everywhere simply swept aside the old KWS regimes. He does argue, however, that 'that there are good grounds for believing that there really is a widespread tendential shift in Europe and "Europe abroad" from the sort of Keynesian welfare state regimes associated with Atlantic Fordism to the dominance of the sort of Schumpeterian workfare state regimes found in the paradigmatically post-Fordist economies of East Asia and successful regions in the other growth poles' (Jessop, 1994b, p. 36).

He seems to suggest that future struggles will be over the form the SWS takes, not over whether this is the kind of state regime under which we will find ourselves living.

A stormy debate still rages around the claims that the world is now 'post-Fordist' and its economy 'globalised' (see Burrows and Loader, 1994; Stubbs and Underhill, 1994). All we can usefully say here is that those who have advocated this new terminology have registered some real and deep-seated changes in the structures of the international political economy but that, at the same time, they have been tempted to underestimate the aspect of *continuity* with pre-existing institutional orders. The same comment might apply in miniature to Jessop's account of a transition from the Keynesian welfare state to the Schumpeterian workfare state. First, few pre-reform welfare states ever really approximated the KWS ideal type. As we have already seen, welfare states were always concerned with policing of the labour market and containing costs, even if these concerns were to some extent masked by more favourable domestic economic circumstances. Most awkwardly for Marxist and neo-Marxist explanations, much welfare state spending both before and after the move to post-Fordism seems rather remotely connected with controlling labour markets. In the case of retirement pensions, for example, it is considerations of cost and demographic change rather than labour market discipline which have driven the process of policy reform. At the same time, the 'welfare into workfare' perspective is rather unhelpful. As Jessop makes clear, his analogous use of 'workfare' refers to state *intentions* rather than *institutions*, but it is still rather misleading. First, Jessop is not suggesting that the SWS is actually characterised by the introduction of workfare arrangements; secondly, 'real' workfare is certainly concerned with labour market discipline, but not necessarily so as to improve the international competitiveness of the economy; thirdly, the broad workfare remit (labour market discipline to facilitate international competitiveness) is only *one* very important aspect of social policy. Across the welfare state more broadly conceived, sheer *cost* is still as important a consideration as international competitiveness.

Talk of a shift from Keynesian welfare state to Schumpeterian workfare state may be justifiable as a provocative thesis, but its use to underpin a generalised expectation that welfare state arrangements will tend to converge towards an East Asian model is misleading. Keynesian welfare states were always quite diverse and so, should they come to pass, will be the Schumpeterian workfare states.

Conclusion

In the face of its many critics, it is important that we give due weight to Marxism's distinctive contribution and, as has been frequently pointed out, there is a certain irony in the way that Marxists and neo-liberals found themselves in seeming agreement about the instability of the postwar welfarist form of capitalism. Certainly neo-liberal analyses have good claim to have been the more *influential* because they have done more, in however modified a form, to drive the actual policy agenda of advanced capitalist states. But Marxism does not just deserve a share of the credit as a junior partner in recasting the way we think about the welfare state. For neo-liberals and neo-Marxists actually saw the contradictions of welfare capitalism rather differently and, while both had major weaknesses (and strengths), these were not always the same. At its simplest, the neo-liberals were strongest on the ways in which states usurped markets and in which 'too much democracy' and dominant coalitions of producers' interests threatened the integrity and effectiveness of market institutions (sometimes independently defended in terms of their capacity to maximise individual freedom). Neo-Marxists, by contrast, were much stronger on the ways in which the difficulties of welfarist social democracy reflected the deep-seated contradictions of a *capitalist* society. Of course, these proved not to be contradictions of capitalism in the strong and teleological sense of classical Marxism (that is, as tendencies which could only be resolved by revolutionary transition to a new mode of economic organization). They were contradictions in the weaker, but still important, sense of irresoluble tensions in the underlying structure of the political economy which need to be continuously managed and policed. The neo-liberals' celebration of the market made it extremely difficult for them to identify these underlying weaknesses. By contrast, neo-Marxist accounts have been able to make a much more critical and realistic appraisal of the claimed qualities of markets in relation to the welfare state. This becomes increasingly important as reforms informed by neo-liberal ideas (especially the restructuring of the public service in line with the expectations of public choice theory) fail to deliver all of the gains which its architects had envisaged. In these circumstances, a focus upon the welfare state within a perspective which is sceptical about the universal and grandiose claims made for markets is of considerable value.

Finally, however, there is an unresolved problem. Neo-Marxist approaches to the welfare state have tended either (i) to be informed by an unsustainable evolutionary account of the (long delayed) transition from capitalism to socialism or else, (ii), rejecting this Marxian evolutionism, to be left without any plausible account of a political alternative to neo-liberalism. The marriage between theory and practice to which Marx aspired proves to be an unhappy one. The strengths of Marxist analysis of the welfare state have generally been critical ones. Its programmatic ambitions look much less plausible. 'Marxism without socialism' is a strange destination for a critical social theory but it may prove to be the terminus for Marxism's account of the welfare state.

10

Marxism and Culture

CHARLIE MCMAHON

Marxism (as a theoretical approach) has, from the outset, been concerned to develop a materialist account of the interrelations between the cultural dimension of social existence and other aspects and conditions of human practice. Debate in this particular area has centred around the manner in which these relations are portrayed. Thus, in the Marxist paradigm, questions arise as to whether the cultural features of social life should be interpreted as a determined superstructure or, often in the conviction that Marxism itself will be enriched, are better represented as themselves having a determining effect upon the nature and course of social development.

Although these different emphases have often coexisted, this chapter will trace the development of the latter out of the former. As such, the chapter is divided into four sections. The first section examines the dialectical materialist contribution in this area (largely formulated by Engels and Plekhanov), where culture is viewed as determined by socioeconomic factors. The second section focuses on the formalist and humanist responses to dialectical materialism in which ideas, knowledge, language, ideology and consciousness are given a greater degree of autonomy and significance for societal existence. The third section subsequently considers the contributions of structuralism, poststructuralism and postmodernism in the area of social and cultural theory. This is crucial since, for many, these contributions have provided insights which have initiated 'a move away from Marxist thinking in cultural studies', accompanied by 'a more widespread feeling that Marxism is no longer relevant to current social conditions' (Giddens, 1994, p. 10). The final substantive section then offers a critique of the views of poststructuralists and postmodernists arguing that a distinct Marxist approach to the role of culture is both possible and essential.

By highlighting the gaps and occlusions of alternative accounts of the relationship between culture and society, this chapter will argue for the continuing relevance of Marxist theory for the comprehension of the fundamental condition of social being: a condition which provides the raw material for cultural practices.

Dialectical Materialism

'Base' and 'Superstructure'

When considering the place and significance given culture within Marxist theory, Marx's observation that 'it is not consciousness which determines existence but social existence which determines consciousness' could serve as a point of departure. It is this general formulation which, most often, provides the basic frame of reference in discussions of the way literature, art, literary theory, ideology and consciousness are treated in the Marxist tradition. When combined with certain other formulations – drawn invariably from *The German Ideology* (1845) – the above quotation forms a component part of what has become known as the 'base–superstructure' model. It is this model, and the picture of unidirectional causality it is seen to propose, which has served as the definitive statement of the classical Marxist view of how cultural phenomena are to be considered.

Although the standard compendium of the writings of Marx and Engels on literature and art runs to some 500 pages, no developed theory emerges from them' (Mulhern, 1992, p. 3; see also Nelson and Grossberg, 1989, p. 6, Bennett, 1979, p. 100; Lifshitz, 1970, p. 10). Perhaps unsurprisingly, then, most critical and evaluative accounts of the Marxist treatment of culture concentrate upon the 'base–superstructure' model which is chosen as paradigmatic and it is to this model which we now turn.

Classical Perspectives: Dialectical Materialism

Given the fragmentary nature of Marx and Engels' writings on literature and art, it seems surprising that Marxism was ever able to develop a coherent standpoint in regard to literary and artistic activities; yet, for a time it did. Plekhanov and Mehring were amongst the first Marxists who 'thought it necessary to supplement Marx's thought by extending it to areas of knowledge which go beyond social and economic questions' (Lukács, 1983, p. 86). Indeed Lukács argues that 'Mehring introduced Kantian aesthetics into Marx', while Plekhanov developed 'a positivist one'.

Plekhanov's contribution was much more influential, helping to consolidate what he called 'dialectical materialism' as the philosophy of Marxism (Plekhanov, 1961, p. 447). His work, like that of Labriola, Mehring and Kautsky, was strongly influenced by Engels' later works, especially *Anti-Dühring* (1878) and *Ludwig Feuerbach and the End of Classical German Philosophy* (1888). In his 1888 text, Engels speaks of the positive results which followed from 'doing away with' the 'ideological perversion' of the Hegelian system, for example when 'we comprehend the concepts in our heads as images of real things'. Hence, when extracted from its idealist shell, materialist dialectics became 'the science of the general laws of motion, both of the external world and of human thought – two sets of laws which are identical in substance'. In this way, 'the dialectic of concepts became merely the conscious reflex of the real world' (Engels, 1888, in Marx and Engels, 1968, p. 619). Engels' characterization of consciousness as purely reflexive, which stemmed from his concern to subsume idealism into materialism, remains a characteristic of this entire tradition. What Engels had sketched was a reflectionist theory of knowledge, that is, one where consciousness plays a purely passive or contemplative role, picturing or mirroring a more objective reality, which is seen to exist externally and independently of the cognizing subject. Thus there is a parallelism or correspondence between reality and our knowledge of it. If Hegel's 'idealist' philosophy depicted the material world as a product of mind, then Engels' 'materialism' can be seen as a direct inversion of this: mind was a product or an instance of the material world.

Unsurprisingly, then, in its treatment of cultural phenomena, this perspective develops a criticism based upon mimesis, which regards literature and art as imitating life, and a corresponding set of aesthetic criteria which stressed the truth or accuracy of this representation. Thus Plekhanov praised Mehring's work on Lessing for tracing what he termed the 'social equivalent' of Lessing's work; Mehring had 'translated Lessing from the language of literature to the language of society' (Mehring, 1938, pp. 10–14).

Contrary to what Lukács had suggested, then, rather than going beyond social and economic questions, any particular writer or artist had only translated social and economic questions into literary and artistic ones and the task of the Marxist critic consisted in decoding these facts back to their more substantial reality (Eagleton, 1976, p. 23; Lukács, 1962, p. 54).

In his *Fundamental Problems of Marxism*, Plekhanov introduces a series of mediations between the economic base and the cultural superstructure, from 'the state of the productive forces' to 'the mentality of men' and the various ideologies which 'reflect that mentality', in the attempt to temper the determinism of the model. However Plekhanov's mediations do little to alter the determinism and reductionism which had become the characteristic feature of the materialist monism which his own works and Engels' had done much to establish.

On the other hand, Plekhanov had helped to develop a kind of Marxist cultural criticism, to the extent that cultural products were directly related to their determining social and economic contexts. At the same time, however, a gap remained between this explanatory level and 'a level of judgement or prescription of what constituted a successful artistic work from the Marxist point of view' (Laing, 1978, p. 16). In a passage which typically occludes the role of consciousness as actively organising, and being indissolubly linked to, practice, Plekhanov states that 'people had to make their history unconsciously, so long as the motive forces of historical development worked independently of their consciousness' (1961, p. 479). This fact, however, did not prevent a certain type of artistic creation from exposing precisely these 'motive forces' of historical development, whether its author were aware of it or not.

In a letter to Margaret Harkness of April 1888, Engels speaks of the 'triumph of realism' over Balzac's 'own class sympathies and political prejudices'; Balzac 'saw both the necessity for the downfall of his favourite nobles' and the emergence of 'the real men of the future' (in Craig, 1975, p. 271). Lukács extended these comments of Engels into a fully fledged aesthetic theory. Thus 'Scott too, like so many great realists, such as Balzac and Tolstoy, became a great realist despite his own political and social views' (Lukács, 1962, p. 54). These arguments were to have a powerful influence on the codification of Marxist aesthetic values in the aftermath of the Russian Revolution.

The Seeds of a New Era: Formalism and Humanism

The Formalists were a group of literary theorists (Jackobson, Shklovsky, Tomashevsky and Tynyanov) who held that literary texts should be analysed with reference to their formal properties alone – to style, form and technique – and, thus, without reference to their substantive content. Moreover, as they saw it, this task necessarily entailed 'the exclusion of all mimetic (that is to say, realist) representations of the world' (Jefferson, in Jefferson and Robey, 1986, p. 26; see also Belsey, 1980; Bennett, 1979; Erlich, 1981; Seldon, 1985). Trotsky was particularly critical of the Formalists whom he saw as 'exponents of an idealist philosophy', one 'whose greatest genius was Kant' and, for whom, 'in the beginning was the Word'. For Marxists, on the other hand, 'in the beginning was the deed. The word followed as its phonetic shadow' (cited in Craig, 1975, p. 379).

Although formalism was undermined in Russia by the Stalinist pressures of the 1920s, its perspective survived in the work of the Prague Linguistic Circle (1926–39), of which Jackobson was a founder member. Basing their work on Saussure's model of structural linguistics, the Prague Formalists argued that literature was a construct: a signification of reality rather than a reflection of it. It is the practice of literary criticism upon texts which organizes them into the literary and the nonliterary, rather than any inherent property in texts themselves, which can only be divined by some form of spiritual empathy (Bennett, 1979). Rather than reflecting reality in some way, literature, and language more generally, bestows forms of conceptual organization upon it. For this reason, the Formalists eschewed the classical ideal that art should disguise its own constructedness: should seek to conceal its own process of artistic production.

This is a formulation which Barthes later used to identify the specifically ideological, or what he terms mythical, function of language: that is, that, as myth, it perpetuates the illusion that it is merely the reflection of what exists, rather than a particular, or interested, interpretation of what exists. In other words, it conceals the fact of its constuctedness, purporting to hold a mirror up to reality. We shall return to this aspect below.

While the debates on cultural matters in the Soviet Union culminated in the banalities of socialist realism, the years from 1917 to 1945 also witnessed the emergence of a critical humanist Marxism, which would provide an interpretative canon for Marx almost as influential as that of Engels himself. In the works of Lukács, Korsch and Gramsci, the principal emphases of the dialectical materialist tradition are dramatically reversed. This Western, critical, humanist Marxism was critical of the dialectical materialist tradition's positivistic blurring not only of the distinction between natural and social science, but of science and technology themselves. It was humanist in the sense that it stressed the ontological differences between humanity and the rest of nature, focusing on the subject as a site of 'consciousness' and insisting that human cultural products were not amenable to the reductive analyses of science.

Adorno, Horkheimer and the Frankfurt school, Marcuse, Benjamin, Sartre and Goldmann should also be included in this tradition. This emphasis upon 'philosophy' over 'science', and dialectics over materialism, meant that consciousness and culture were treated as more than the mere effect of a somehow more substantial reality. On the other hand, if the dialectical materialist tradition had tended to reduce the subject to the object of knowledge, then this critical humanism – rather in the manner of the hermeneutic tradition – tended to reduce science to its positivistic misrepresentation and, in this way, reduce the object to the subject of knowledge.

This is clearly evident in the central thesis of Lukács' 1923 *History and Class Consciousness* (Lukács, 1971), arguably the founding text of the entire Western Marxist tradition. For Lukács, the culture of commodity-capitalist society was reified, it was a culture in which subjective human properties had been transformed into the properties of things – commodities, which ruled the producers instead of being ruled by them. He takes Marx's exposition of 'commodity fetishism' as his point of departure, viewing it as ' the central structural problem of capitalist society in all its aspects' (Lukács, 1971, p. 83). The solution to this central structural problem lay, for Lukács, in the activity of consciousness, more specifically in the consciousness of the proletariat who, as 'the identical subject–object of history', possessed the exclusive ability to overcome this reification. That is to say, as owners of the commodity labour-power, the proletariat were *themselves* commodities: objects. As possessors of consciousness they were, at the same time, subjects. Hence, when speaking of this unique consciousness of the proletariat and its transformative power, Lukács writes: 'since consciousness here is not the knowledge of an opposed object, but the selfconsciousness of the object, the act of consciousness overthrows the objective form its object' (1971, p. 178).

However, whereas Marx had described the process of objectification as an essential human property, and as 'an eternal nature-imposed necessity, without which there would be no material exchange between man and Nature, and therefore no life', Lukács, following Hegel, uses the term alienation to include *every* type of objectification (Marx, 1983, p. 50; Lukács, 1971 pp. xxiii). The result is that, 'when the identical subject–object transcends alienation, it must also transcend objectification at the same time'. In other words, since for Marx the perennial process of objectification only *becomes* alienation in definite historical circumstances, Lukács subsumes the ontological ground of reified consciousness (the value relation between the producers) in this consciousness itself. As a result, in overcoming the latter, the very same act of consciousness simultaneously overcomes the former. Consequently, whereas for Marx commodity fetishism is not primarily a phenomenon of social consciousness but of *social being* – that is, is ontological – to Lukács the epistemological dimension of social existence tends to subsume the ontological one. Here, as a consequence of its eschewal of science, Marxism is less the scientifically correct comprehension of an object (the capitalist system of production) and more the expression of a subject, 'the ideological expression of the proletariat' (Lukács, 1971 p. 113; Marx, 1981, p. 101).

As suggested, this is a consequence of this tradition's rejection of Marxian political economy and its purely negative view of scientific method. This is a view which later, given the failure of proletarian revolution and the rise of Fascism and the culture industry (that is, the commodification of culture), produced, in the hands of the Frankfurt theorists, a pessimism reminiscent of Max Weber.

We could say that Lukács seeks to straddle the dualism of the base–superstructure model with the identical subject–object of history. However the antirealist note he strikes in seeking to accomplish this remains a feature of this entire tradition, resounding in culturalism and its centring of the lived experience of a class-subject.

Post-Formalism

As a founder member of the critical humanist tradition, Lukács, as has been suggested, was deeply influenced by Hegel. On the other hand, his aesthetic theory, or what he termed 'the erection of a systematic aesthetics on the foundation of dialectical materialism', is just that: a disowning of Hegel coupled with the provision of a sophisticated legitimation for much of socialist realism's antimodernism and its glorification of nineteenth century Russian and European realism (Lukács, 1971, p. xxxvii).

In his literary theory, Lukács largely follows Plekhanov, seeing the rise and fall of the great literary genres as intimately connected with the struggles and conflicts between classes. Thus, when the bourgeoisie is a revolutionary class, it provides the progressive ground for the great realist novels of Balzac and Stendhal. After the revolutions of

1848, however, this class enters its reactionary period, thereby ensuring the beginnings of the deterioration of modern European literature (Lukács, 1962, 1972). Realism declines into naturalism (Flaubert, Zola) and into modernism (Joyce, Proust, Kafka, Beckett), literary forms which recorded only the surface appearance of social reality, whereas the great realists had penetrated beneath surface appearances to disclose the social totality in all of its movements and contradictions (Metzaros, 1980, ch.7).

For some, this is Lukács at his dogmatic worst, 'incapable of understanding contemporary literature and assessing its aesthetic validity' (Laurenson and Swingewood, 1971, p. 57). Similar views were expressed in the works of Bloch, Brecht and Adorno in a series of written debates in the 1930s which challenged Lukács's slavish adherence to Stalinism and his dismissal of literary modernisn as only the decadent product of late capitalism (Bloch *et al.*, 1977; Benjamin, 1973; Forgacs, 1986; Jameson, 1971; Laing, 1978).

Neither Lukács' more philosophical theories nor his literary analysis have much to do with language; that is to say, he depicts reified consciousness as being *automatically* appropriated by both the bourgeoisie and the prerevolutionary proletariat while, on the other side, he conceives of the literary genre as a linguistically faithful representation of the ebb and flow of the class struggle. However, as Eagleton (1991) remarks, 'Human subjects figure here as the mere passive recipients of certain objective effects, the dupes of a social structure given spontaneously to their consciousness'. To Eagleton, capitalism, as a particular and historically evolved organization of social existence, provides the ontological ground upon which various and conflictual ideologies go to work; from this point of view Lukács' treatment is seen to close off the question of 'what human agents *make* of these material mechanisms, of how they discursively construct and interpret them in accordance with particular interests and beliefs' (Eagleton, 1991, p. 88). In other words, Lukács ignores ideological contestation, an area with which much of Gramsci's work is concerned, or the class struggle in language, an idea which became the focus of the Bakhtin Circle, a group of Russian post-Formalist theorists (Volosinov, Bakhtin and Medvedev). To Volosinov, the ruling class 'strives to impart a supra-class, eternal character to the ideological sign, to extinguish or drive inwards the struggle between social value judgments which occurs in it, to make the sign uniaccentual (*sic*)', but this result is by no means guaranteed, and must be continually renewed and renegotiated (Volosinov, cited in Morris, 1994, p. 55).

For Volosinov, this continual renegotiation occurs because 'the ideological sign' (or 'word'; see Morris, 1994, p. 252) is 'mutable', 'multiaccentual' and 'Janus-faced'. As such, it can look to the right or to the left, depending upon which social class or group has provisionally achieved 'mastery in discourse'; that is, 'has established an achieved system of equivalence between its own particular meanings and reality'. It followed then, that the meaning of the ideological sign was not predetermined by the structure of reality itself, but was 'conditional on the work of signification being successfully conducted through the social practice of meaning production'. Hence this meaning was not the result of a functional reproduction of the world in language, but 'of a social struggle' a struggle for 'mastery in discourse – over which kind of social accenting is to prevail and win credibility' (Hall, 1985, pp. 43–4).

The work of the Bakhtin Circle in the late 1920s and 1930s cast serious doubts on the dialectical materialist account. For Volosinov, social existence is not reflected in the ideological sign, but refracted in it (that is, bent from a straight line). In other words, language was not conceived of as reflecting a pre-existing meaning, but was active in the process of *making things mean*, playing an active role in the construction of social reality – rather than being its mere passive reflection. Of course, this is not to say that reality has no inherent meaning, only that language is not its unmediated reflection.

While Formalism and post-Formalism shared the view that meaning was the product of certain shared systems of signification, what kept the Bakhtin Circle within the Marxist tradition was its location of the source of meaning in the generating process of class struggle. It was thus critical of what it saw as the 'abstract objectivism' of the Saussurean model of language and its location of the source of meaning in an abstract system of rules (*langue*) which, rather like a Durkheimian social fact, were external to and constraining in the production of meaning by social agents (*parole*). Similarly, in its notion of the 'arbitrary' nature of language (that there was no necessary or isomorphic resemblance between signifiers and the object-world), the Saussurean model seemed to assume a special kind of discontinuity between language and reality: it appeared to substitute for the really existing objectworld the 'mental' or purely 'conceptual event' which was the 'signified' (Hodge and Kress, 1988). Thus what signifiers signify are not *real* objects, events and processes, but the mental image or concept associated with signifiers – what they spark-off, as it were, when seen or heard. Individual signifiers, the sounds made by a speaker or the marks on a page, are thus able to function as signs, not because of any correspondence with real objects, but because of the sets of *differences* that exist between them. Thus the signifier 'hot' is able to work as part of a sign because it *differs* from 'hit', 'hog', 'hot', 'lot', and so on; in other words, signifiers gain their specificity and meaning from what they are *not* (Saussure, in Lane, 1970; Seldon, 1985, p. 22). Language is *self-referring* and does not mirror any anterior reality.

This emphasis upon *deference*, as well as much else, will be retained and mutated by that theoretical tradition in cultural theory which emerged in the 1960s and came to be known as structuralism. Structuralist thought and the rival tradition of culturalism were twin tendencies which – coming to be aligned around the concepts of ideology and culture, respectively – in their oppositions, and in the absence of any major rivals, became highly influential, not only within Marxism, but in cultural theory more generally.

Structuralism

French structuralism developed Saussure's model of language into a fully fledged scientific enterprise. The name of this new science was semiology and its object of study 'the life of signs at the heart of social life' (Lévi-Strauss, 1967, p. 16; Coward and Ellis, 1977). This science aimed to go beneath the surface events of language (*parole*) in order to investigate the deep structures of concealed signifying systems (*langue*). Lévi-Strauss was thus able to argue that it was not the particular utterances of speakers which was the object of analysis, but the classificatory systems which underlay these and from which they are produced as a series of variant transformations (Hall, 1985, p. 37).

Saussure was to be joined by Freud (Lacan) and Marx (Althusser) in the creation of a new scientific trinity, whose varying emphases on determining properties of structures were to be combined in the attempt to oust forms of voluntarism and humanism, represented in France by the existentialism of Sartre and the phenomenology of Merleu-Ponty. In direct contrast to the phenomenological centring of subjective experience, the structuralists sought in their various ways to establish that individuals were defined by structures beyond their control and that these were the producers, not the products, of subjective experience.

Thus, while Lacan explored the unconscious structures of language and Lévi-Strauss sought to map the contours of a 'universal cultural grammar', Barthes saw semiology as a 'science of forms' which could account for any system of signs. 'A particular text, the giving of a gift or a particular meal, could, within this schema, be treated as a sort of "utterance", that is, an example of "parole", beneath which lay a complete structure or "grammar". It is this pre-existing structure (or "langue") which allows utterances to be made; we are the subjects, not the authors, of cultural processes' (Barthes, 1967; 1973).

At the same time, ideology – or myth as Barthes terms it – was seen to operate by disguising the fact that language *constructs* reality in particular ways, passing itself off as only a replication or reflection of what exists. In this way myth was seen to naturalize sociohistorical existence by eclipsing the conditions of its own process of production. Barthes speaks of 'the very principle of myth' as that 'which trans-forms history into nature' (1973, p. 129). Hence, in sharp contrast to Lukács and the dialectical materialist tradition, Barthes sees literary realism as exemplary of this deception (perpetuating the illusion that language mirrors reality) a reality which is thereby taken for granted as natural and transparently available to our descriptions of it (Belsey, 1980; Eagleton, 1983; Harland, 1987; Hawkes, 1977; Jefferson and Robey, 1986).

Since ideological texts are indeed constructions, they are amenable to critique: what the surface narrative conceals can be disclosed by conducting what Althusser termed 'a symptomatic reading', that is, reading for silences or absences, which can point up the ideological perspective of the work in reference to what it attempts to emasculate, such as the contradictory nature of social reality (Althusser, 1969, p. 254). While Althusser applied a 'symptomatic reading' to Marx himself, Macherey utilized the concept more generally, where it involved 'superimposing a coherent theoretical framework (Marxist theory) on the gaps and silences of a given writer's texts' (Larrain, 1989, p. 181; see also Althusser and Balibar, 1970; Macherey, 1978, p. 87).

In his work on ideology, Althusser, influenced by Lacan, adapted the quintessentially structuralist view that language speaks us. To Althusser, like Lacan, the subject of ideology is a symbolically constructed one, and it is precisely the construction of the subject which is the key mechanism of ideology: 'all ideology has the function (which defines it) of "constituting" concrete individuals as subjects' (Althusser, 1985, p. 81). Thus ideology does not operate explicitly but implicitly, in the unconscious categories through which social conditions are represented and lived. Ideological representations 'have nothing to do with "consciousness" . . . it is above all as *structures* that they impose on the vast majority of men' (Althusser, 1969, p. 233).

In rejecting the reductionism of the base–superstructure model, Althusser seeks to emphasize the *functioning* of ideology in the process of social reproduction, rather than the manner in which it is *determined*. He sees the social formation as a complex whole, constituted by a network of autonomous 'practices' – economic, political, ideological – none of which is reducible to a single or 'master' contradiction (as in Hegel), and which 'expresses' itself at the levels of politics and ideology. Instead Althusser argues: 'change occurs not from the working out of one essential contradiction, but when the contradictions which are unique to the ideological level . . . overlap and combine with those which are unique to the economic and political levels . . . thus where contradiction is overdetermined' (Althusser, 1985, p. 65).

Despite his reworking of the base–superstructure model and the emphasis upon autonomous practices, Althusser's work contains the general structuralist tendency to hypostatize or 'reify' the symbolic order, that is where individuals are only the 'bearers' of, and are constrained by, certain ideological meanings. In effect, the social formation is a process without a subject (Benton, 1984; Callinicos, 1976; Geras, 1977; Larrain, 1983, 1989).

As Eagleton remarks, structuralism is an inheritor of the belief that 'reality, and our experience of it, are discontinuous with each other' (1983, p. 108). Having said that, however, structuralism does not conduct its critique of reflection in order to distinguish appearance from any underlying ontological essence since, as we have seen, it brackets off the real object as simply not available to us. If one of its positive moments was that it referred surface to depth, at the same time, this depth was ideal – was an essentially cognitive or epistemological one. Structuralism thus tends to a reduced view of the subject as well as to the ontological ground upon which subjects generate their meanings, or 'go to work on', and which is not reducible to these meanings. 'Structuralism,' according to Bennett, 'rests upon the anthropological conception of "man the communicator"', with the result that the study of culture is entered exclusively through the problematic of the exchange of messages' (1979, p. 71), rather than through the exchange of *things* (commodity values), what Marx termed the 'allsided mediation', which forms the ontological ground of meaning production (Marx, 1981, p. 156). Moreover, since for structuralism reality, as it exists 'in itself', as it were, is not available to us, there exist no criteria for distinguishing a more or less correct representation of this reality from a more or less 'incorrect' one, or, rather, in this perspective, what is considered incorrect is the belief that language can refer to something beyond itself – to an extralinguistic reality. Structuralism thus refuses to identify that function of linguistic consciousness when it is employed (for example, by Marx himself) in the attempt to represent in thought those essential relations which are seen to generate surface appearances, causing them to appear as they do (Marx, 1981, pp. 100–8). In sum, if language and ideology speak us then the subject here is just as disempowered as in the strongest form of Marxist determinism.

Culturalism

Being both Marxist, or Marx-influenced, structuralism and cultural-ism shared one or two features. Each insisted on a radical break with the terms of the base–superstructure model, ascribing to the super-structure of cultural and idealizational phenomena an effectivity and constitutive primacy which were absent in the earlier model (Harland, 1987).

Again one of the principal accomplishments of structuralism and its Formalist heritage was its radical demystification of the category of literature, where this had been conceived of as an ontologically privileged form of discourse. The consideration and treatment of a certain finite body of texts as literature – as opposed to other forms of socioverbal intercourse – 'is not a response to a property that is internal to them, but a signification that is bestowed upon them from without by the practice of criticism' (Bennett, 1979, p. 10; see also Eagleton, 1983, ch.1).

To some extent, culturalism shared in this 'secularization' of the purely 'literary', representing as it did a break, not only from a reductionist and mechanistic Marxism, but also from the academic discipline of literary theory which, in the hands of the Leavisites, was both conservative and unashamedly elitist, treating culture exclusively in the manner of Matthew Arnold as 'the best that has been thought or said' (Mulhern, 1981).

A group of seminal texts (Hoggart, *The Uses of Literacy*, 1957; Williams, *Culture And Society*, 1958, *The Long Revolution*, 1961; E. P. Thompson, *The Making of the English Working Class*, 1963 which appeared in the late 1950s and early 1960s signalled the emergence of 'culturalism'. In the same period, that branch of phenomenological sociology was emerging in the USA which had as its primary concern the problem of how social actors make sense of their world – in particular those labelled deviant and/or inhabiting a subculture. Parallel developments were also taking place with the arrival of the newer forms of popular politics: CND, the early New Left, student movements, black power, countercultures and women's liberation. According to Johnson, 'these trends tended to focus in their different ways on the 'inwardness' of experience and the 'apprehension' of the world, usually in opposition to a sociology, a Marxism (or a world) that has been seen as oppressive, mechanical, reductive or deterministic' (1979, p. 50).

In keeping with these sentiments, culturalism embraced a radically different set of emphases with regard to the construction of the subject than that envisaged by Althusser and Lacan. In foregrounding culture as lived experience, culturalism set itself the task of examining the everyday and the ordinary, in the attempt to understand the attitude of the working class to popular culture, rather than simply condemning it as low culture in the manner of the Leavisites. In the process, the concept of culture was expanded far beyond the narrow range of literary and artistic pursuits the concept had in traditional academic discourse. One of Williams' earliest definitions of culture was as 'a whole way of life', where what was understood in relation to this totality was described as 'the words and sequences which particular men and women have used in trying to give meaning to their experience' (1958, pp. 15–16). Almost from its inception, then, culturalism had as its primary concern the subjective experience of social actors and the understanding (*verstehen*) of this experience.

This principal focus would also be used to counter what culturalism saw as the denial of selfactivity in the structuralist (particularly the Althusserian) account of ideology. Culturalism's more inclusive concept of culture included a stronger sense of the power of human agency, as against the reduction of this power to the determining properties of structures. In direct contrast to structuralism, culturalism 'tends to read structures in terms of how they are 'lived' and 'experienced' . . . the experiential pull of this paradigm and the emphasis on the creative and on historical agency constitute the two key elements in the humanism of the position outlined' (Hall, 1981, p. 26). In rejecting the determinism of the dialectical materialist tradition as well as the deep structures of structuralism for their coercive reductionist properties, culturalism rejects any allusion to the presence of an underlying generative system, prioritizing instead the particular utterances of speakers.

It is not surprising, then, that with the publication of the works of Lukács and Gramsci in English in the 1960s, culturalism embraced those tendencies in Western Marxism which offered related ways of accounting for the 'relative autonomy' of cultural phenomena, while also welcoming the stress on the philosophical – as opposed to the scientific, – reading of Marx. Culturalism thus tends to be an inheritor of the hermeneutic conviction that the recognition of the essentiality conceptual nature of social existence rules out its scientific comprehension. While owing more to Weber than to Durkheim, culturalism nevertheless shares with structuralism the tendency to a reduced view, not only of political economic relations, but of what Marx termed the 'scientifically correct' method of political economy and its disclosure of the salience of social–ontological categories over their forms of appearance – forms of appearance which social actors go to work on, and, in this way, mould their lived experience. It thus belongs 'to that family of sociologies which seek to grasp social phenomena in their own terms, in their forms of appearance in the world. The problem with such sociologies is that they abandon the ground of determination or explanation which does not show up in the experience of actors' (Johnson, 1979, p. 65).

In other words, the culturalist conviction that what is most 'real' is what is 'experienced' leaves out of account the fact that the conceptions of social actors may conceal or obscure the true nature of the activities with which they are implicated. Not only are there social–ontological events and processes which take place behind men's backs, there are also aspects of the commodity-form of the product of labour which are simply not available to the experience of social actors. Thus, 'turn and examine a single commodity, by itself, as we will, yet insofar as it remains an object of *value* it seems impossible to grasp it' (Marx, 1983, p. 54).

That is to say, as a value, it is only possible to grasp it by means of the application of the theoretical method of political economy, or by the utilisation of what Marx termed 'the method of abstraction', that is, by a process of production of knowledge which goes beyond the immediately experiential in order to disclose the real nature of value, thus explaining why the product of labour appears – or is experienced – in precisely this form (Marx, 1981, pp. 100–6; 1983, p. 19). Again, however, theoretical abstraction is shunned by culturalism, depicted by Thompson as taking us further away from reality rather than closer to it (1978, pp. 32–3). If the oppositions of structuralism and culturalism can be portrayed as contemporary variations on the theme of structure versus agency, the contribution of cultural studies can be seen as the self-conscious attempt to synthesize – via the work of Gramsci – what it sees as the theoretical gains of both of these traditions. Amongst these, the mutual rejection of the base–super-structure model, combined with the centring of autonomous practices (in both Williams and Althusser), allows for the possibility of this synthesis, its first and most enabling result being its emphasis upon culture and ideology as sites of domination and resistance.

In accordance with Williams' dictum that 'culture is ordinary', the focus of cultural studies has been on everyday life or the structures and practices in and through which modern society constructs and circu-lates its meanings and values (Brantlinger, 1990; Hall, 1992; Turner, 1990; Nelson *et al.*, 1992). In particular, work at the Birmingham Centre for Contemporary Cultural Studies, under the stewardship of Stuart Hall, did much to ensure that 'what was once regarded as a rather marginal, even eccentric, preoccupation, the field of cultural studies has now moved to the centre of the social sciences and humanities' (Giddens, *et al.*, 1994, p. 1). According to Hall 'the dominant paradigm in cultural studies conceptualizes culture as interwoven with *all* social practices; and these practices, in turn, as common forms of human activity . . . sensuous human practice' (1981, p. 25).

Cultural studies has accomplished much that is valuable for Marxist theory in its attempt to provide an emancipatory critique of the ways in which relations of domination are institutionalized through linguis-tic usage – developing themes from Marxism and feminism, psycho-analysis, poststructuralism and postmodernism – in the attempt to unearth the processes by which culture forms its subjects. At the same time, and in keeping with the gaps and omissions of its twin theoretical legacies, it tends to reject as outmoded any attempt to disclose the fact that reality *itself* may possess an inherent meaning. We have suggested how Marx attends precisely to this disclosure, attempting to explain why things appear as they do through the investigation of their social–ontological ground. The main anxiety of cultural studies seems not to be over the provision of an explanation of things in this sense, but to avoid being reductive about them. In terms of social scientific explanation, it is difficult to see how the theoretical orientation of cultural studies can take us much further beyond Weber's tendency to view society in terms of the values of its members. However, as we have been at pains to show, these values, significant as they may be, do not *exhaust* the subject matter of social scientific inquiry.

Poststructuralism and Postmodernism

In the 1970s the basic structuralist claim to develop a 'science of signs' by uncovering hidden structures behind surface meanings was being seriously challenged by what has become known as poststructuralism (represented by the *Tel Quel* group around Derrida and Kristeva and the later Barthes; Foucault; Deleuze and Guattari). The principal target of the poststructuralists was the surface–depth (*parole/langue*) distinction which lay at the heart of the structuralist programme. Indeed it was this fundamental duality and the mapping of the interrelationships between its terms – through detailed observational and objective analyses – which provided structuralism with its claim to a scientific rationale. Poststructuralism retained the Saussurean principle that it is language which is fundamental and that, far from language reflecting some preexisting meaning, meaning was an effect produced by it. Again, following Saussure, poststructuralism was particularly keen to emphasize that there was no necessary connection between signifier and signified and that words got their meanings from their relations with each other – from the differences that exist between them – and not by referencing some extralinguistic reality. As Saussure had put it: 'A linguistic system is a system of differences of sound combined with a series of differences of ideas' (in Seldon, 1985, p. 72).

At the same time, poststructuralism was critical of the surface–depth distinction at the core of the structuralist project, as well as of the attempt to build a science (whose aim was objectivity and truth) on its basis. As Jackson remarks of the emergence of poststructuralism, 'The main thing that is new about this phase is that the central intention to provide large scale formal systems in the human sciences has been given up: is seen indeed as an aggressive and oppressive intention and one that ought to be subverted. This is a change so radical that it must be described as the collapse of structuralism rather than as a development of it'. (1991, p. 115).

With regard to the dualism of structuralism, poststructuralism countered this by cancelling one side of the duplex, thereby giving primacy and sole dominance to the one that remained. As Harland (1987) puts it, poststructuralists 'invert our ordinary base-superstructure models until what we used to think of as superstructural actually takes precedence over what we used to think of as basic'. This one-sidedness – where cultural and ideational phenomena are accorded priority – is also common to postmodernism (Lyotard, Baudrillard), so that this giving precedence to superstructures represents what Foucault calls an *episteme*, that is, an underlying framework of assumptions and approach, characteristic of much of contemporary social and cultural theory. Consequently, 'Even when Derrida refutes Lévi-Strauss or Baudrillard declares war on Foucault, the hostilities are still conducted over a common ground' (Harland, 1987, pp. 1–2).

This common ground finds its expression in these writers where signifiers lord it over signifieds, surface over depth, subject over object, form over content, appearance over essence, particular over universal and consumption over production. Here it is the very predilection, which poststructuralists and postmodernists see as characteristic of Western thought, to treat language as subservient to some referent that lies outside it which they are most concerned to deconstruct; that is, to show that signifieds, depth, content, essence and so on are no more than elements of particular systems of meaning, rather than indicators of what props these up from the outside. Thus, poststructuralism develops, and postmodernism refines, the thesis that 'objects should be considered not as external to a realm of discourse, which seeks to appropriate them, but as wholly internal to such discourses, constituted by them through and through'. (Eagleton, 1991, p. 203). Moreover, for this position, 'there is no given order in reality at all . . . just ineffable chaos' (Eagleton, *ibid*). In a similar vein, the post-Marxists Hindess and Hirst (1977, pp. 216–17) and Laclau and Mouffe (1985, p. 107) argue that everything in society is discursively constructed and that every object is an object of discourse; that is, in keeping with this entire tradition, they subsume the real in the signified or conceptual real.

To be more precise, the contention that nothing exists outside of discourse (Foucault) or of 'language games' (Lyotard), carries with it the conviction that nothing has any significance for societal existence unless and until it has been inscribed with 'meaning'. The enrolment of what exists into a 'frame of meaning' or 'discursive formation' also marks its baptism as a distinctly social object – only thenceforth can it have any efficacy for us. It is this aspect that Laclau and Mouffe are referring to when they state that 'we assume that there is a strict equation between the social and the discursive' (1990, p. 101).

Here, then, social objects and entities, as well as their relations and connections, are discursively produced, that is, they have no given or inherent meanings or relations. What they are – any essential meanings, connections or identities they may be said to possess – is no part of them as objects, but is entirely the product of the discursive formations in which they are caught up. So, whereas for Marx 'all science would be superfluous if the outward appearance and the essence of things directly coincided' (1984, p. 817), for postmodernists one reason why science has been declared redundant in their anti-Enlightenment critique is precisely that essence and appearance do indeed coincide. Thus, for example, with his concepts of 'simulacra' and the 'hyperreal', Baudrillard's theory of commodity culture removes all distinctions between objects and their representations (Baudrillard, 1988). Here, as elsewhere, it is the surface appearance of things which is effective for social existence, not some latent or hidden essence or structure, as claimed by, for example, Marxism.

It is clear that there are elements in this case which are enabling for a Marxist theory of culture, in particular the extent to which it serves as a corrective to forms of determinism and reductionism, such as a mimetic or reflectionist theory of meaning production. As Eagleton remarks, the 'kernel of truth' in the postmodernist case consists in the fact that "signifiers" are always *active* in respect of what they signify' and that ' discourse goes to work on the real situation in transformative ways' (1991, p. 208).

At the same time, what must also be seen as foundational for a Marxist theory of culture is the conviction that there are indeed essential processes and structures which, although they may not be observable at the level of surface appearances, have a real causal efficacy for contemporary social existence and its cultural forms. These essential relations mean something for societal existence (in the sense that they *matter* for it) *whatever* meanings we may ascribe to them. So, for example, when, discussing the formation of money and the 'value' of commodities, Marx writes, 'Value, therefore, does not stalk about with a label describing what it is' (1983, p. 67), he does not mean that what it 'is' is entirely determined by the place it occupies in this or that discursive formation. On the contrary, Marx continues, 'it is value which converts every product into a social hieroglyphic. Later on, we try to decipher the hieroglyphic, to get behind the secret of our own social products, for to stamp an object of utility as a value, is just as much a social product as language' (1983, p. 67).

A number of points arise from this which are of significance here. For one thing, the ontological properties of capitalist social existence, which are made manifest in the product of labour assuming the form of a commodity, are active in *engendering* discourses (such as that of 'political economy'), that is, the form in which reality appears is the preexisting material *referent* of discursive practices, not the 'signified' of them. For another, when Marx says that the 'value' of the product of labour is as much a social product as language, he is referring to the fact that *we* are its authors – although we may not be aware of this in the same way that we may be aware that we are the authors of our linguistic practices and sign systems. In other words, Marx is saying that value is neither the quality nor property of a thing, an object, that is money; as he says, so far, no chemist ever discovered value either in a pearl or a diamond' (1983, p. 47). Rather, value is a social production relation between people expressed or objectified in a thing. It is how the different kinds of commodity producers stand in relation to one another – the social production relations between them and, thus, between their products – which causes the necessity for exchange and, with that, causes the products of labour to appear as values – commodity values.

Marx discloses the 'secret' of value by showing that the quality of having value is essentially a structural or social–relational property of the product of labour, not essentially a natural or discursive quality. The 'categories' of Marx's political economy do not express relationships between people and things, but between people themselves. Of course this is not to argue that the production and reproduction of commodities is not dependent upon the meanings which the agents who reproduce it have, only that it is not reducible to these meanings. Value is 'just as much' a social product as language, but this is not to say that it is identical with it.

At the same time, Marx seeks to unveil why a humanly produced or sociological objectivity *appears* as a naturally given one, that is as a property of the object itself; why the personal relationship is concealed by the objectified form (see Marx, 1983, ch. 1, Sect. 4; 1984, ch. 48; Rubin, 1983, pt 1; Rosdolsky, 1980, pt 2). This requires the disclosure of those essential ontological relations which generate surface appearances, thus explaining why phenomena should appear as they do. Unlike these phenomenal forms, however, essential relations may not be transparent to direct experience, only being identified and revealed through the application of what Marx termed 'the scientifically correct method' (1981, p. 101). In distinguishing essence from appearance, Marx demarcates the terrain upon which the cultural practices of meaning making go to work. Thus, in the discourse of 'political economy', Petty, Smith, Ricardo, Say, Bailey, Bastiat *et al.* construct varying and different meanings around these forms of appearance;

but, by itself, this does not alter their essential identity, or the manner in which their social determination takes place. As E. H. Carr remarks: 'It does not follow that because a mountain appears to take on different shapes from different angles of vision that it either has no shape at all or an infinity of different shapes' (1992, p. 27).

Postmodernism's insistence upon the irreducibility of these different angles of vision, coupled with its rejection of the critical concept of 'ideology' – and its replacement by the more neutral 'discourse' – are direct consequences of its refusal of the essence/appearance distinction. Similarly this refusal means that here there can be no level of social reality which could possibly act as a foundation from which to assess these different angles of vision for their accuracy, explanatory power, scientific acumen, partisanship and so on. Having a theoretical purchase upon essential relations allows Marx to judge the aforementioned contributions in the area of political economy in precisely these terms.

As well as its relativism, there are other issues arising from postmodernism's collapsing of essence into appearance, such as its emasculation of contradiction, which cannot be gone into here. However, at a more general level, one can agree with Eagleton when he says that no critique of poststructuralism and postmodernism 'could be negative enough. Its grosser political and philosophical absurdities, which have managed to turn the heads of a whole younger generation of potentially valuable militants now arrogantly confident that they have reconstructed a Marxism many of them have not even encountered, merit the most implacable opposition' (1986, p. 93).

Here this opposition has consisted in the attempt to argue that the point of departure for any adequate understanding of culture must include reference to those engendered 'forms of appearance' which form the raw material upon which practices of meaning making are forced to 'go to work'. While, as we have seen, meaning 'shapes' – that is, it does not passively 'reflect' – it is also, and irrevocably, 'shaped' in a society where the *exchange relation is the universal relation* between people; that is, 'when the aim of labour is not a particular product standing in a particular relation to the particular needs of the individual, but *money*, wealth in its general form, then the individual's industriousness knows no bounds, it is indifferent to its particularity, and it takes on every form which serves the purpose; it is ingenious in the creation of new objects for a social need' (Marx, 1981, p. 284).

This 'industriousness' and 'ingenuity', whose teleological aim is wealth in the abstract (money), forms that ongoing dynamic of capitalist societies which is the ontological *referent* of the cultural practice of bringing phenomena into meaning.

Conclusion

This chapter welcomes the renewed emphases upon agency and culture (long submerged in positivistic and Stalinized Marxism) as essential to an adequate Marxist theory of culture. At the same time, it also wants to argue for the continuing validity of Marx's analysis of capitalism for the comprehension of the cultural practices of social classes. Much of the time this analysis is either entirely ignored or simply assimilated into the base–superstructure model, which is then presented as the definitive statement of the Marxist treatment of culture. Indeed, in a great deal of contemporary cultural theory, this model is presented as the paradigmatic example of how not to assess the validity of cultural practices. But what is presented as the unidirectional causality of this model bears little resemblance to Marx's disclosure of capitalist society as 'a rich totality of many determinations and relations'. In the same way, the theoretical results of *The German Ideology* 1845 do not always coincide with those of the *Grundrisse* 1858 and the causal features ascribed to the economic base are by no means identical with the conclusions produced through the application of what Marx termed his 'dialectic method' to the analysis of capitalist society. What this analysis does is to disclose the inner dynamic of a society where 'a definite social relation between men . . . assumes the fantastic form of a relation between things' (Marx, 1983, p. 77). This ontological ground of capitalism, as well as its theorization, is basic in the sense of *fundamental* for a proper understanding of cultural phenomena, not in the sense of unproblematically determining it.

11

Marxism and Nationalism

TREVOR PURVIS[1]

Palestine, Bosnia, Chiappas, Kwazulu, Kashmir, Kurdistan, Quebec, Chechenya, Khanesatake, Ulster . . . the list is daunting. In an era when the forces of 'globalization' have led some to consign the nation-state to the dustbin of history, struggles over national identity and the drive for national self-determination abound. The recent upsurge in nationalist struggles around the globe has been met by a flurry of activity in social theory, with nationalism and the theoretical status of 'the nation' at the centre of much debate. For Marxism, however, 'the national question' has long been a point of theoretical weakness. Nairn's assessment that 'The theory of nationalism represents Marxism's great historical failure' is a familiar lament (1981, p. 329; cf. Poulantzas, 1978b; Anderson, 1991; Laclau, in Nimni, 1991). It is not, however, that Marxists ignored the national question, but early Marxist reflections on these issues were hardly of a kind, and were plagued by theoretical problems.

After a significant hiatus Marxists are again thinking about the national question, endeavouring to overcome the inadequacies of the classics. These interventions mark a genuine attempt to take the nation seriously as a relatively autonomous dimension of the social world, and constitute a significant point of intersection between Marxist and non-Marxist social science. This chapter explores the treatment the national question received in the classic texts of Marxism, how the inadequacies of those treatments led to their marginalization in the burgeoning recent literature on the subject, and how some recent Marxist interventions help to resolve those inadequacies. Ultimately the chapter offers some thoughts on where issues related to the nation and nationalism might fit into the future of Marxist social theory.

Classical Marxism and the 'National Question'

Marx himself had little of a theoretically rigorous nature to say regarding the nation and nationalism; what he did say was marked by deep contradictions and inconsistencies. We might put these failings down to the fact that Engels 'generally acted as the pair's spokesman on national questions' (Fernbach, 1973, p. 50). But a more important source of these problems lay in Marx's dedication to proletarian internationalism and his focus on the increasingly global character of capitalist social relations. The *Communist Manifesto's* suggestion that 'working men have no country' (Marx and Engels, 1848, p. 235) sets the tone which would dominate Marx's consideration of these issues. For Marx, the internationalization of capitalism implied a corresponding internationalization of the interests of the proletariat, whose collective interests would explode the borders of the modern nation-state. Marx tended to treat the nation, like the state, as a transitory form of association, one whose importance would diminish in the face of the dynamism and constant revolutionizing force of capitalism – one that, in the terms of the *Manifesto*, would become antiquated before it could ossify.

Marx's scattered comments on the issue evince a rather naive optimism that the nation-state was being rendered archaic by the expansion of capitalist social relations: the force that had given rise to it in the first place. This optimism was nevertheless tempered by a simultaneous recognition that, whilst they 'had no country', 'the struggle of the proletariat with the bourgeoisie is at first a national struggle. The proletariat of each country must . . . first of all settle matters with its own bourgeoisie' (Marx and Engels, 1848, p. 230). This tension between the nation-smashing force of capitalism and the continuing influence of chauvinistic bourgeois nationalism remained seriously under-theorized in Marx's work.

Where Marx did turn his attention to the 'national question' – particularly vis-à-vis Polish and Irish nationalism – we find the outlines of a general strategic approach to the politics of national liberation which would influence subsequent formulations, particularly Lenin's. For Marx, the economic dimensions of national oppression strengthen the 'ideological hegemony of the bourgeoisie over workers in the oppressor nation' (Lowy, 1976, p. 83). So long as the seeds of division immanent in bourgeois nationalism continued to infect and divide proletarians, revolutionary internationalism would falter. 'A people which subjugates another people forges its own chains' (Marx, 1870 [1974a], p. 118). It was only through the liberation of oppressed nations that bourgeois domination in both oppressed and oppressor nations could be smashed, and the seeds of proletarian internationalism effectively sown. The problem with this formulation lay in its predetermination of viable nations: whilst Marx supported some national liberation movements (particularly Irish, Polish and eventually Indian), his formulation betrayed a form of 'great-nation chauvinism', in that no theoretical account was offered as to why *these*, as opposed to other national minorities, should merit special treatment (Fernbach, 1973, p. 51).[2] Such considerations were left to Engels.

While still surprisingly underdeveloped, Engels' reflections on the national question represent perhaps the most contentious of all Marxist commentaries on the subject. The problems stem from his appropriation of Hegel's notion of 'peoples without history'.

> Hegel distinguished between world-historical peoples, who were culturally developed and capable of building a strong state, thus contributing to the progress of world history, and peoples without history, who were spiritually weak and unable to build a strong state, thus having no civilizing mission to carry out in history. The latter had to submit to the former. (Larrain, 1994, p. 20).

This teleological conception of the viability of nations and national movements, lifted virtually intact from Hegel, became the cornerstone of Engels' treatment of the national question.

This ill-conceived adoption of the theory of non-historic nations arose out of an effort to come to grips with the failures of the revolutions of 1848–9 in central Europe. This formulation offered a post hoc rationale for the apparent tenacity of the 'minor' nationalisms – specifically pan-Slavic nationalism – that had been instrumental in undermining the revolutionary impetus of that great historic moment. Engels portrays these nations as too small, inconsequential and archaic to be anything but an ideological springboard for reaction and counterrevolution.[3] The emergence of nationalistic impulses among the minor Slav peoples was thus put down to counterrevolutionary agitation sown by Tsarist Russia (which Marx and Engels considered the heart of counterrevolution in Europe). These 'non-historic' peoples were regarded as crude relics of the past, destined to fade into obscurity before the march of history and the expansion of the great 'historic nations' of central Europe (Germany, Hungary, Poland and Italy). Their apparent vitality was thus put down to the influence of greater – and reactionary – 'historic' nations. As dubious and ill-conceived as these formulations were, Engels neither developed them further nor repudiated them. Indeed, as late as 1866, they would resurface in discussions of Polish national liberation (see Engels, 1852; 1866). While the concept of non-historic nations was largely rejected in subsequent Marxist reflections on the national question,[4] as we will see, it has re-emerged as a central point of contention in at least one important re-evaluation of Marxist reflections on the national question.

By the turn of the century it had become increasingly apparent that the nation-state was not the transitory phenomenon Marx had envisaged. Although many continued to hold that the importance of the nation would fade under socialism, the turmoil leading up to the First World War and the Russian Revolution spurred a recognition that any project for the transition to international socialism must contemplate, at some level, the powerful mediating force of the nation. Confronted by this challenge, the national question was taken up by some of the central figures within Marxism, most importantly, Luxemburg, Lenin, Stalin, Bauer and Gramsci.[5]

Luxemburg's contribution was shaped by her opposition to calls for Polish independence, particularly insofar as these were driven by the notion of the 'right of nations to self-determination'. Hers marked one side of an emerging theoretical debate within Marxism (see, for example, Kolakowski, 1978, pp. 88–94; Nimni, 1991, pp. 50–7, 80–2). For her, national self-determination, conceived as an inherent right of peoples, was a bourgeois myth: 'a metaphysical cliche of the type of the "rights of man" and "rights of the citizen"' (Luxemburg, 1976, p. 111). Luxemburg argued that historical materialism had repudiated such mythical 'eternal truths', showing their content to be the product of material social conditions, and hence subject to change across historical epochs. Historical evidence suggested that the rhetoric of the 'right of nations to self-determination' merely obscured the fact that capitalism's global expansion 'condemns all small nations to political impotence' (Luxemburg, 1976, pp. 129–30). If socialism's primary aim was the eradication of economic/class oppression, then dedication to an inherent right of national self-determination was illusory, for only those national liberation movements whose programme contemplated the eradication of class oppression could be supported by socialists. To mask the *class* nature of this struggle behind a rhetoric of *nation* was only a 'mystifying paraphrase of the class position' (Luxemburg, 1976, p. 149). Ultimately, however, her steadfast insistence on the primacy of class as the touchstone of socialist politics has led some to dismiss Luxemburg as essentialist, reductionist and determinist (Laclau and Mouffe, 1985; Nimni, 1991).

Often in direct opposition to Luxemburg, Lenin addressed the problem of the nation at the tactical level. In the tumultuous political environment leading up to the Russian Revolution, Lenin was acutely aware that a successful revolution would have to incorporate the claims to self-determination emanating from the many sub-nationalities that comprised the Russian Empire. Thus his dedication to the right of nations to self-determination was inscribed within a (pragmatic) revolutionary strategy demanding that the national claims of the proletarians of small nations be taken seriously. Self-determination of hitherto oppressed nations was a crucial dimension of political democracy, irreducible to economic, cultural or psychologistic explanations or solutions. But though the national question posed immediate strategic/tactical-level problems, Lenin nonetheless envisaged the withering of national differences under socialism:

> Just as mankind can achieve the abolition of classes only by passing through the transition period of the dictatorship of the oppressed class, so mankind can achieve the inevitable merging of nations only by passing through the transition period of complete liberation of all the oppressed nations. (Lenin, 1916, p. 6).

Nations were regarded as transient social forms whose importance would fade, albeit over a longer time frame than Marx or Engels might have anticipated. Ultimately the importance of Lenin's contribution to thinking about these issues lies in his break with Marx and Engels on the measure of strategic importance and, in turn the theoretical pride of place he granted the national question.

Stalin's support for national self-determination is also worthy of note, but not because of its influence on the resolution of the Soviet nationalities question; rather his represents the most schematic and objectivist Marxist formulation of the problem of the nation. For Stalin:

> A nation is a historically evolved, stable community of language, territory, economic life, and psychological make-up manifested in a community of culture . . . [None of these] . . . characteristics is by itself sufficient to define a nation. On the other hand, it is sufficient for a single one . . . to be absent and the nation ceases to be a nation (Stalin, 1913, pp. 8–9).

With these objective criteria in place Stalin sought to purge the concept of the nation of its many 'mystical, intangible and supernatural' connotations. From our vantage point at the end of the twentieth century, such efforts at rooting the concept of the nation in the regular articulation of a constellation of supposedly objective criteria seems nothing short of intellectual and political hubris, sweeping aside all claims to nationhood which fail to meet the criteria of the theoretician. Alternative claims to nation are rejected by definitional fiat, whilst the qualities of the nation are given a profoundly positivist hue, as though they were 'out there', self-evident, and readily recognizable.

At a strategic level, both Lenin and Stalin thought that promotion of the right to self-determination of the numerous Russian-subjugated ethnic nationalities might further undermine an already tenuous Empire, whilst promising fresh ground for proletarian internationalism. They were also concerned with the increasingly important matter of how to hold together transnational socialist alliances. But while moving away from the economism of the Second International, this perspective remained class reductionist: instrumental for the mobilization of revolutionary forces, the importance of nationalities would nonetheless wither under communism. Moreover both regarded national self-determination as primarily an issue of the right to establish sovereign statehood. This conception is seriously flawed, for it assumes precisely what needs to be problematized: how is the apparent 'unity' of the people nation constituted (institutionally, territorially, ethnically, linguistically, politically and so on)? The assumption of a necessary relationship between a relatively homogeneous 'nation' and the organization of some relatively self-evident political space tends to obscure more than it explains.[6]

The complex ethnic, linguistic, religious and geographical make-up of the Habsburg Empire set similar practical and theoretical problems for the Austro-Marxists, but their response was significantly different from that of the Soviets. The differences arose largely out of Austro-Marxism's critical engagement with neo-Kantian philosophy, and the challenges thereby posed to monocausal reductionism in sociological and philosophical explanation. Whilst other Austro-Marxists would make significant contributions to debates on the national question.[7] Otto Bauer's contribution would be the most important.

In contrast to the Leninist approach to 'self-determination', Bauer was anxious to secure the conditions for the cultural autonomy of the many national minorities within the Austro-Hungarian Empire, while avoiding the politically divisive and territorially complex 'solution' of granting each nationality an independent state of its own. The demographic complexity of the Empire rendered the prospect of such a statist option eminently unappealing if social and political solidarity were ever to be realised and/or sustained. Hence Bauer strove to develop a non-reductionist approach to the concepts of nation and nationalism, and only here do we find, among the 'classic' texts, a systematic effort to problematize the nation as a social force irreducible to any of its conjuncturally specific elements.

Bauer rejected approaches (like Stalin's) which reduce the nation to any one or necessary combination of its oft-presumed elements: territory, mores, religion, language, customs and so on. Instead he stressed their combinatory contingency, one which is spatially and historically determined, and whose precise constituent elements cannot be presupposed. He also rejected and moved beyond the approaches which reduce nations to 'the nationalities principle' (that is, the statist focus which suggests every nation should have its own state, and every state its own nation). He pointed, rather, to the often antagonistic relationship between states and nations, stressing the ways those elements commonly associated with the constitution of nations have combined in concrete historical cases, and the array of factors which might alter their place in the constitution of future nations. This is a particularly valuable insight, as it highlights the mutability of nation as an overdetermined combinatory which can only be understood in terms of its conjunctural specificity and effectivity.

Finally, he explicitly rejected the metaphysical and psychologistic theories of nation which were emerging in bourgeois social theory at the time (Bauer, 1978a, pp. 103–9).[8] Nations are constituted by social agents in their day-to-day communal activities, while being irreducible to those agents' perceptions of their national belonging. National character is neither innately given, nor does it reside in the conscious subjectivity of individuals (that is, in the 'will to nation'). It is, rather, the expression of national existence. Thus, crucially, nations are never static, but always *in process*. Of the classic Marxist interventions, then, Bauer more than any other provided the foundations for a tenable theoretically informed Marxist account of the nation, one which problematizes its presumed unity, composition and relationship to the state.

Bauer's work has been variously received. Roundly criticized by many of his Marxist contemporaries, his efforts to decouple nation and class and to refute the myth of the essential promiscuity of nations and states were sharply criticized by some as inimical to Marxism, and as lapsing into idealism and voluntarism. His detractors would even challenge his Marxist credentials.[9] Recently, though, some have argued that his thoroughgoing anti-reductionism marks the principal strength of Bauer's contribution (Nimni, 1991, p. 194). His greatest contribution may lie, however, in his conception of nations as fluid and conjuncturally determined social formations. While not without its problems – for instance, while critical of the statism of other Marxist approaches, he fails to address why the sub-nationalities of the Habsburg Empire should forgo state autonomy and accept the dominance of the Austro-Hungarian state – Bauer's work nonetheless marks a watershed in Marxist thinking on the national question.

Antonio Gramsci is another classical Marxist thinker deserving mention here, albeit not so much in terms of a formulation of the national question per se. Like Marx and Engels, Gramsci never confronted the question systematically. He was, however, far more aware of the nation's importance for revolutionary socialism, and his contributions to social and political theory help us to supersede some of the difficulties encountered in much of the early literature in this area. His development of the concept of hegemony provides Marxism specifically, and social and political theory more generally, with valuable insights for understanding the condensation and articulation of social elements in an analysis sensitive to conjunctural specificity, all within a framework fundamentally opposed to economism and class reductionism. For Gramsci *nations are hegemonic projects*: 'It is in the concept of hegemony that those exigencies which are national in character are knotted together' (Gramsci, 1971b, p. 241). Hegemony is secured through intellectual and moral leadership and is mediated through various institutions. Moreover, constituted through leadership and direction, hegemony is to be contrasted with forms of coercive domination more readily associated with the repressive apparatuses of the state.

Whilst Gramsci does not develop a general theory of the nation, this contrast between hegemony and coercive domination, and his theorization of the 'historic bloc' as typically in a state of 'unstable equilibrium', mark useful points of departure for thinking through the mechanisms whereby nations, as *hegemonic projects*, are secured, reproduced and contested. In highlighting the articulation of domination/hegemony, leadership/consent and violence/coercion, Gramsci opens space for a concept of nations as hegemonic projects with violence/coercion deployed to police the sociocultural 'boundaries' and the discursive 'space' occupied by particular conceptions of nation, and for understanding the counterhegemonic potential inherent in the articulation of alternative claims to nationhood. Conceiving of nations as hegemonic projects highlights the fluidity, mutability and contestability of the nation and its constituents. As a hegemonic project, the nation partially occludes alternative ways of seeing and thinking the world and imagining community, subsuming them beneath the exigencies of a 'greater' national interest. But these exigencies are constituted and reproduced through networks of social power which vary across time and space. The deep horizontal comradeship implied by national identity does not appear uncontested, but is, rather, always subject to resistance (indeed is, in a dialectical sense, constituted by this resistance) and alternative claims are disciplined and coerced in various ways. It is through the constitutions of nations in parallel, competing and complementary discourses that we can see the politics of nation played out.

Critical Appraisal of the Classics: a Cool Reception

Given the many problems attending much of the early Marxist discussion of these issues, it is perhaps not surprising that early Marxist treatments of the 'national question' have been largely bypassed in recent theoretical debates. In his classic text *Theories of Nationalism*, Anthony Smith pushes through Marxism in a matter of a few short pages (1971, pp. 72–80). For him, Marxism's 'great nation' thesis and its crude 'conflict-theory' foundations yield few substantive theoretical insights. At other points in these debates, when Marxism is considered, it is often as an historical datum, equated with the experience of the Soviet Union. The manifest chauvinism in Russian domination of the Soviet experience is cited as putting paid to Lenin's professed belief in the right of nations to self-determination (Hutchinson, 1994). In turn, early Marxist contributions to these issues are rejected as having been invalidated by historical experience. For John Breuilly, Marxism's difficulties in this area arise from its tendencies to regard national struggles as either a direct product of the class struggle or as a response to imperialist expansion (1993, pp. 407–14) Again Marxism is by passed rather perfunctorily. Still other contributors to these debates tend to reduce Marxism to a crude caricature. Here it is rejected in light of its perceived broader inherent inadequacies, with early Marxist treatments of the national question given no consideration at all. Thus, for Gellner (1983), Marxist reflections on the national question are simply not considered, as Marxism generally is equated with Soviet communism and, in turn, dismissed as a route to totalitarianism.

There is undoubted substance to each of these approaches. Marx' and Engels' 'great nations bias' did impede their ability to come to theoretical grips with smaller 'minor' nationalities. The Russian chauvinism of the Soviet experience does indeed call into question that regime's commitment, or capacity, to give substance to Lenin's professed dedication to the right of nations to self-determination. And, undoubtedly, an often myopic focus on class as the cornerstone of socialist identity has frequently yielded an untenable marginalization of alternative identities. Finally even the crass equation of Marxism with the aberrations of Stalinism cannot be simply dismissed on grounds that this was somehow 'not real Marxism'. This is not to cede ground to the suggestion that all Marxism leads to Stalin or the Gulag, but, rather that, without a critical awareness of the articulation of Marxism with the failures and excesses of Stalinism, Marxists do little more than bury their heads in the sand. It is precisely in this vein that Marxists must engage with both the inadequacies and the insights of the classics.

Indeed over the years numerous Marxists *have* surveyed the early literature on the national question.[10] Until the mid-1970s, though, much of this work was limited to broad (albeit valuable) overviews of the treatment these issues received in the classics, or to incisive critical assessments of *aspects* of that treatment. Seldom, however, did these engagements push much beyond this. In an effort to address this void, Ephraim Nimni has launched a thoroughgoing critical appraisal of the classic treatments of the national question from a position which is perhaps best typified as 'post-Marxist' (1991).[11]

Nimni contests the received wisdom that Marxism has no theory of the nation, arguing that Marx and Engels' reflections exhibit a deep analytical coherence, a thematic unity whose principal elements – economic reductionism, evolutionism and eurocentrism – can be traced through subsequent Marxist treatments of these issues. These elements, he contends, lend classical Marxist reflections on these issues far more unity and consistency than most Marxist commentators have hitherto allowed. On this basis Nimni embarks upon a sweeping review of the early Marxist literature on the nationalities problem.

Marx and Engels' scattered reflections on 'minor' nationalities have long been a source of some embarrassment for Marxists. Rather than attributing these failings to a lack of theoretical rigour, Nimni argues that against the evolutionist–eurocentric backdrop quite a different picture emerges. Detailing the numerous points at which Marx and Engels touched upon the nationalities question, Nimni casts the two as intensely hostile to many nationalities, and frequently prone to abusive language vis-à-vis those communities not conforming to European patterns of sociopolitical development – patterns dominated by the rise of the national state and which implied the disappearance of minor nationalities. For Nimni, Marx and Engels' chauvinism was firmly rooted in a shared dedication to an evolutionistic theory of human progress in which Europe showed to the rest of the world the image of its future. They were so convinced that the social world was hurtling along a singular, predetermined path, of which Europe represented the leading edge, that they descended into scathing and quite reprehensible reflection on peoples whose nationalistic predilections might impede the unilinear trajectory of historical development. Nimni suggests that it is only with Lenin that cracks begin to show in the deterministic edifice bequeathed by Marx and Engels, and then the break is only partial. Although Lenin's recognition of the specificity of the political is seen as something of a watershed, Nimni argues that he (and Stalin) remained firmly trapped in class reductionism, incapable of accommodating such non-economic aspects of national existence as culture and ethnicity, and prone to consider as viable only those nations capable of forming their own states. Even Gramsci is rejected as having lapsed into reductionism and statism. For Nimni, it is only with Bauer that these inadequacies are ultimately (if incompletely) overcome.

Nimni's assumption of the unity of Marx and Engels' oeuvre is, however, fundamentally problematic. Whether or not Marx's work (let alone that of Engels) can be said to display the sort of unity that Nimni claims for it over a span of forty years is dubious at best.[12] Far more plausible, and potentially fruitful, would be an approach seeking to highlight and contextualise the significant shifts in Marx's treatment of these issues over time. This is not to defend or excuse Marx's or Engels' treatments of these issues,[13] but rather to question Nimni's post hoc construction of theoretical unity. But this is merely symptomatic of some broader weaknesses attending Nimni's argument. In fact, whilst his *nominal* project is to uncover the inadequacies of classical formulations of the 'national question', his *actual* quarrel is with broader theoretical issues/problems attending Marxism generally. Ultimately this leads him to a sweeping indictment of Marxism, with the general theoretical tenability of 'the classics' hinged upon their treatment of the national question. Clearly there is good reason to reject the formulations of the national question contained in many of the classics, but classical Marxism as a whole cannot be expected to stand or fall on its treatment of these issues. Indeed, whilst Nimni makes a powerful case for rejecting many of these formulations, his efforts to base such rejections on a fundamental, debilitating thematic unity of economism, reductionism, determinism and eurocentrism are less convincing. Marxists have, indisputably, been guilty of these charges at many points over the years, and they are manifest in reflections on the national question, perhaps most in the work of Marx and Engels. But Nimni leaves the reader with a profound sense that there is little need to concern ourselves with the baby in this bath water.

Nevertheless Nimni's work is to be commended, not least for leaving no doubt that the 'classics' hold no magic answers to all contemporary sociotheoretical dilemmas, but, more importantly, for reviving the work of Otto Bauer, giving it its due as marking a watershed in Marxist thinking in this area. For Nimni, Bauer represents the way through the problems attending other early Marxist treatments of the national question. Unfortunately, in his effort to recoup Bauer's contribution, Nimni ultimately (and unapologetically) insists upon purging all aspects of Bauer's work which lend it a remotely Marxist hue. The eschewal of economism, reductionism and statism becomes, in a fashion all too typical of much post-Marxism, a deep and debilitating suspicion of any consideration of the place of economy, class and the state, and their historical articulation within various national forms.

It should be added that the suggestion that Marxism must somehow move *beyond* the classic Marxist treatments of these issues is disingenuous, as Marxists *have* gone well beyond the limitations dominating so much of the earlier thinking on the nationalist question. Indeed, as we will see, many of these contributions take the failings of the past as precisely their point of departure.

Recent Reflections

Much of the recent burgeoning theoretical literature on the subjects of nation and nationalism has tended to treat Marxism's contribution to thinking on these issues as having stultified in the classics. Certainly theoretical treatments of these issues have not constituted a hotbed of Marxist scholarship in recent years, but there have been a number of important Marxist interventions. Some of these have gone largely unnoticed in the broader social–scientific literature surrounding the recent revival of interest in this issue, but nonetheless have important insights to proffer with respect to the relations between nation, state, capitalism, socialism and political practice. Still others have had broad-reaching influence, both within, and well beyond, Marxist circles.

The contributions of Debray and Poulantzas lie squarely in the former category. Both have been anxious to avoid any reduction of the nation to capitalist social relations, stressing that the nation is not unique to capitalism, while remaining sensitive to the complex articulation of state and nation in capitalist social formations. Each takes Marxism's underdeveloped theoretical understanding of the specificity of the nation as a point of departure. For Debray, this inadequacy stems from a tendency to overemphasise the universal at the expense of the particular. Marxists, he argues, must recognize the dialectic between these levels, and proletarian internationalism must come to grips with the specificity and determinacy of the particular if socialist struggles are to endure within political consciousness. To press home this point he notes that 'socialist victories have always been linked in one way or another to movements of national liberation' (1977, p. 34). In short, the nation is a force with which socialism must contend. The point is not to abandon socialist internationalism, but rather to abolish the myth that somehow socialism will miraculously usher in a miracle of social homogeneity.

Poulantzas (1978b) seeks to establish the foundations for a theoretical understanding of the specificity of the nation, with particular, although not exclusive, emphasis on the articulation of the nation and the capitalist state. The boundaries of the state do not capture or exhaust the nation, but there is a functional relationship between the *modern* nation and the state. Among its roles, the state 'tries to master the different temporalities and rhythms of social development, re-presses the traditions of subordinate nations, monopolises the national cultural tradition, charts the future of the nation, and so forth' (Jessop, 1985, p. 123). The state, under these conditions, constitutes itself as a 'national' state, and plays a crucial role in the constitution of the 'people-nation' delimited by a complex spatiotemporal matrix. This is a project necessarily, and destined to remain, incomplete, and is, in a very Gramscian sense, a hegemonic articulation.

Both Debray and Poulantzas have been accused of selling out to idealism, abandoning the primacy of class, and attempting to establish the nation as an autonomous, transhistorical force (Blaut, 1987, pp. 63–5). Neither, however, is positing some primordial, transcendent notion of the nation: they seek, rather, to contextualize the nation as a politically constituted element, and an important object of struggle for the organization of the social field. Such criticisms tend to reflect broader tensions within contemporary Marxism, spurred to some extent by an orthodox anxiety over a perceived 'retreat from class' (Wood, 1986) and highlighting many of the problems raised by Nimni regarding the primacy of class in Marxist theory. It is worth noting, however, that neither Debray nor Poulantzas feel it necessary to abandon Marxism in order to articulate a complex theory of the rich ontological depth of the social world.

Whilst the contributions of Poulantzas and Debray seem firmly dedicated to asserting the place of the nation *within* Marxist social theory, other Marxists have made more direct interventions into the broader sociotheoretical debates on the nature of nationalism. Eric Hobsbawm, for one, has made important contributions to the burgeoning literature in the area. Similarly Benedict Anderson's *Imagined Communities* has been widely received as one of the most important interventions in the field. Hobsbawm's contributions to these debates are threefold. First, he stresses the place the 'invention of tradition' has occupied in the constitution of modern national cultures, focusing on the creation of ritual and symbolic practices which have about them a sense of rootedness in the distant past, but actually have quite recent origins. The point is not to deny the existence of long standing social traditions, but rather to stress the remarkable innovation and (often partial) artifice attending the history of many 'traditions', and to problematize the broader historical circumstances which tend to give rise to such 'inventions' (see Hobsbawm and Ranger, 1983).[14] Whilst it is by no means the only source of invented tradition, Hobsbawm suggests that the nation is a particularly poignant source of such 'inventions'. To understand why, we must turn to his characterization of the nation as a particularly *modern* phenomenon.

Capitalism and modernity lend a profoundly transient, unstable quality to social life – one in which it seems (in Marx's famous formulation) that 'all that is solid melts into air'. In these circumstances the nation becomes the symbolic, institutional and practical site for the (re)imposition of some regularity and stability, and moreover, some sense of connectedness with a (however selectively edited) past, in an epoch of otherwise constant change, innovation and social turmoil (Berman, 1982; Harvey, 1989). The elements brought together under the rubric of 'the nation' are not necessarily new or recent (although some certainly are), but their articulation in terms of 'nation' is. In these terms, the nation is very much the offspring of industrial capitalism and the bourgeois revolutions which swept Europe over the past two centuries.

But the heightened globalization of capitalist social relations, and the diminishing capacity of the nation-state to manage the organization of social and economic life in late modernity, lead Hobsbawm to the provocative suggestion that nationalism's place as a major vector of historical development has reached its zenith (1992, pp. 163–92). Hobsbawm suggests that the recent proliferation of nationalist sentiments around the world might not represent the wave of the future at all, but might, rather, represent nationalism's last gasp. Whilst this thesis has proved contentious, both amongst Marxists and within the broader debates (cf. Smith, 1991; Lowy, 1993), it should give us pause for reflection. For implicit in this formulation is a stimulating, if undeveloped, conception of the complex relationship between the nation, the state, capitalism and modernity. Hobsbawm is under no illusions that nations are going to vanish in the near future. His point is, rather, that the place of the 'national' state in the modern world is being profoundly altered by broader social forces, most notably global capital and its impact upon geopolitics. Rather than prematurely consigning the state or nation to the dustbin of history, Hobsbawm is anxious to identify the shifting role and nature of the state in late capitalism, and the decline of a particular project of the nation: one firmly rooted in late eighteenth century Europe, and which contemplates the congruence of state–territory–people. It is not that the nation is a thing of the past, but rather that the nationalist projects which contemplated this combination of elements in a transcendent synthesis are no longer tenable as we enter the twenty first century.

Anderson's *Imagined Communities* takes the subjective moment of nation as its nominal point of departure, something evident in both his title and his working definition of the nation:

the nation . . . is an imagined political community . . . It is imagined because the members of even the smallest nation will never know most of their fellow members, meet them, or even hear of them, yet in the minds of each lives the image of their communion . . . [It] is imagined as limited because even the largest of them, encompassing

perhaps a billion living human beings, has finite, if elastic, boundaries, beyond which lie other nations . . . It is imagined as sovereign
because the concept was born in an age in which Enlightenment and
Revolution were destroying the legitimacy of the divinely-ordained,
hierarchical dynastic realm . . . Finally, it is imagined as a
community, because, regardless of the actual inequality and exploitation that may prevail in each, the nation is always conceived as a
deep, horizontal comradeship. (Anderson, 1991, pp. 6–7).

Thus, for Anderson the nation is constituted at one level through a
subjective sense of communality. But Anderson's concept is hardly as
subjectivist or voluntarist as it might seem at first blush: closer
inspection reveals a firm commitment to the material bases of this
'imagining'.

Central to Anderson's argument is the role that the development of
print capitalism played in the consolidation and promotion of particular vernaculars and the marginalization of others. Also influential
was the routinization of the administrative activities of emerging state
forms which, in turn, facilitated the consolidation of a particular type
of national sensibility – one closely related to the nation-states gaining
ascendancy in Europe with the decline of absolutism. Anderson also
highlights the modern revolutions in the social organization of time
and space, stressing the impact that the introduction of standard times
over delimited spaces had on the routinization and co-ordination of
everyday life, and which, in turn, facilitated the constitution and
consolidation of popular perceptions of communality (cf. Poulantzas,
1978b, pp. 93–120). Finally he notes the important role played by the
media in the consolidation of community and the delimitation of its
boundaries. More recently Anderson has turned his attention to the
place that expatriate nationalists have come to play in the constitution
of national identity. This 'long distance nationalism' is a curious and
seemingly increasingly prominent aspect of the diasporic quality of
late modern life under conditions of heightened globalization –
features closely connected to the geopolitics spurred, in part, by the
transnationalization of capitalist social relations (Anderson, 1992;
1994).

Whilst Hobsbawm and Anderson are widely regarded as valuable
contributors to the broader theoretical debates on the nation and
nationalism, they have come under fire for being both 'modernist'
(Smith, 1986; 1991) and 'eurocentric' (Chatterjee, 1993), but not,
interestingly enough – given the mentioned orientation of the broader

literature – for their Marxism. Indeed, one might be excused for thinking they are received as serious interlocutors in the broader debates *in spite of their Marxism,* as though the latter had no real bearing on their work.

Indeed, while these contemporary Marxists show a sensitivity to the specificity of the nation clearly lacking in the balance of the classic Marxist texts, their interventions do beg the question as to what precisely is distinctively 'Marxist' about their contributions. This is not easy to answer if we take a simplistic reductionist or deterministic account of history to be the legacy of historical materialism. But to do so would be to follow the agenda of Marxism's detractors, invoking a crude caricature, not only of Marx, but of the rich, varied and immanently critical tradition to which he gave rise. If, instead, we take a broader view, seeing Marxism as concerned with elucidating the material conditions of social emancipation, not only from relations of class oppression, but from other forms as well, such as national, colonial, cultural, linguistic, racial, gender, sexual and ethnic, then Marxism seems assured a vital future, and its capacity to inform broader sociotheoretical debates seems secure (cf. Lowy, 1993).

Does this imply relegating class to the status of just one among many equally important foci of analysis? I think not. One of Marxism's great strengths lies precisely in its capacity to help us understand the articulation of these other forms with economic and class oppression: not an insignificant feat. Marxists must not ignore the irreducibility of these other forms but, this said, it can provide valuable foundations for the constitution of counterhegemonic strategies, an advantage largely unrealised by alternative perspectives.

Conclusions: Some Reflections on Theoretical Prospects

As we have seen, the long lamented inadequacy of Marxist reflections on the national question has derived, not from a failure to address the issue, but from the treatment it has received when addressed – particularly where 'the classics' of Marxist theory are concerned. Amidst the current explosion of nationalist sentiment around the globe – indeed when class division and struggle often seem to have given way to struggles for national liberation and/or the assertion of national identity – if Marxism is unable to shake off the weight of its past in order to offer something of value to theoretical reflection in this area, it can only constitute an impediment to critical social thought. Thankfully the prognosis is not so terribly gloomy.

Where the general verdict amongst those Marxists concerning themselves with the issue has been that Marxism does not have a theory of the nation, and that this is a serious failing, we would like to file for appeal. It seems that the continuing anxiety Marxists confront when attempting to come to grips with the 'problem of the nation' is attributable more to the nature of the beast than to any essential or necessary failings on the part of Marxist social theory.

Few aspects of our modern world seem as elusive, and few terms so protean, as the nation. We cannot locate an individual's 'national location' in the way we can, for instance, their 'class location' by virtue of their relationship to the forces and relations of production. Marxists and non-Marxists have been united in a longstanding tendency towards a nominalist convention which ascribes national identity to social actors by virtue of their citizenship of particular national-states: the apparent 'naturalness' of the nation-state as precisely a 'national' state rendered the nation relatively unproblematic. Yet many contemporary 'national' struggles seem increasingly to defy this simple equation of nation and state. Whilst they all bear some relation to a broadly conceived notion of a right of self-determination, the political–institutional implications of such claims are becoming increasingly ambiguous as the role and nature of the state is transformed under conditions of late capitalism. The idea that every nation should have its own state maintains a powerful grip on many contemporary nationalisms, but others attempt to transcend this equation.[15] Efforts to develop a theoretically informed Marxist account of the nation must begin to take these alternative claims seriously.

The quest for 'a theory of the nation' may well continue to elude Marxists if it is driven by a concept of the nation as a relatively static and objective category. As we have seen, some have offered a fixed definition of the nation in terms of a very specific constellation of social elements, but precisely because it is not identifiable by any specific combination of its often assumed elements it tends to defy such objective definition. Indeed no sooner do we settle upon such a definition than we find ourselves marginalizing alternative claims to nationhood, particularly those not driven by the 'nationalities principle'. This is no mere systematic quibble, but a serious point. Claims couched in the language of 'nation' tend not to be as innocuous as those couched solely in terms of culture, ethnicity, language, territory and so on. They are, rather, of a qualitatively different nature. Such claims may not be driven by aspirations to statehood, but they do generally imply a fundamentally politicized notion of collective identity. Failure on the part of Marxists to recognise the very political content of a claim to nationhood or 'nationness', as opposed, say, to a claim to cultural, linguistic or ethnic heritage, threatens to incapacitate Marxism theoretically and, in turn, inhibit its capacity to inform practical social struggles and their articulation with national forms.

In conclusion, a number of points are suggested which must be addressed by Marxists in any future efforts to develop a theoretically informed account of the nation and nationalism. First, *the nation is not definable in terms of a static constant combination of elements, the absence of any one of which would undermine a particular claim to nationhood.* It is important to abandon any conception of the nation defined in terms of a static constellation of elements, and focus, rather, on the way these elements come together, and the political purchase attributed to particular claims to nationhood, in concrete historical conjunctures. Hence the concept might be approached in a fashion similar to that implied by Bauer: as a conjuncturally overdetermined combinatory. However much nationalist discourse would have us believe that nations emerge from the primordial ooze fully formed and constituted by a transcendent essence, nations are social and political products. In turn, understanding the nation requires that we contextualize claims to nationhood against the backdrop of the historical circumstances that have given rise to such claims.

Second, *threshold theories of the nation must be rejected.* Marxists and non-Marxists alike have frequently fallen victim to the seductive simplicity of evolutionist, threshold approaches to the national question, regarding small 'nations' as destined for the dustbin of history, swept aside by the integrative imperatives of larger, more viable, nations. Many small, dispersed nations have shown remarkable tenacity in the face of the pressures to which Marx, Engels, Lenin and others believed they would eventually succumb. Marxists have shown a greater awareness of the inadequacies of such approaches where others have not.[16] Nevertheless the numerous Third World national liberation movements, the burgeoning claims to nationhood pressed by indigenous peoples the world round, and the resurgence of virulent chauvinistic nationalisms in the Balkans, all highlight the need to develop further this sensitivity and sophistication in future analysis.

Third, *the nation is irreducible to class.* The failings of Marxists in dealing effectively with the national question have stemmed, at least in part, from an unwillingness to grant an adequate measure of autonomy to social relations of identity irreducible to class or economic relations. Insofar as class occupies a central place in Marxist theory, this centrality must not impede the attempt to understand the ways in which other social identities such as gender, nation and race are articulated with class: the point being to highlight the specificity of other social relations which cut across those of class, and whose historical articulation has had important implications for class struggle.

Fourth, *the nation is neither exhaustively bounded by the geopolitical space of, nor reducible to, the state.* As an important dimension of the constitution of sociopolitical identity, national projects have always incorporated a homogenizing dimension: the constitution of an 'us' and a 'them'. The geopolitical space of the modern state has offered a seemingly natural home for this sort of politics, but the boundaries of states have never exhausted the national identifications of their subject populations.

Fifth, *the nation is a hegemonic project which has been articulated in very important ways with the politics of the modern state.* There can be little doubt that the nation has been an important feature of the modern state. But, as a hegemonic project, the unity of the people-nation constituted by the modern state has always been open to contestation. In turn this has implied an open character to the nation, one that belies its mythological closure in the discourses of nationalism.

Sixth, *nations are fundamentally political beasts.* As hegemonic projects, nations are always political, but to acknowledge this is not, as some would imply (Nimni, 1991), to descend into the trap of statism. Just as politics is not 'contained' by the state, nations do not rely upon the existence of a state for their continued and/or prospective vitality, although the modern state has proved to be a particularly powerful constitutive force in consolidating nations.

Marxists must eschew dogmatic adherence to orthodoxy for its own sake, and reject the implication that the solutions to all the dilemmas of modern social theory lie in the classics; the blatant inadequacies of the classics on the national question should, it is hoped, put paid to such myths. The suggestion implicit in so much of the classic treatment of these issues – that the nation and nationalism are only of marginal importance for Marxism – threatens to leave us unable to understand one of the most potent features of contemporary social life. Many Marxists have, undoubtedly, underestimated the tenacity of the nation and the important role it plays in the organization of social life. Today it seems increasingly clear that, although the globalizing force of international capital has implied a significant diminution of the capacity of the state to harness, shape and direct the social forces hitherto thought to be 'contained' by it, the nation is as potent a force as ever. Marxists ignore it at their peril.

Notes

1. For their helpful comments and suggestions on various aspects of this chapter I am indebted to Rob Ryan, Colin Hay, Alan Hunt, Charles Lepage, Valerie Peters and Tony Tant. Of course, the usual caveats apply.
2. Whilst Marx is frequently, and correctly, called to task for this chauvinism, it was one that was widely shared among nineteenth century European thinkers, from Hegel to J. S. Mill.
3. Whilst Engels focused particularly upon the 'minor Slav peoples' – Serbs, Slovaks, Czechs, Croats and so on – he does, in passing, include in this category of 'history-less national refuse' the Gaels of Scotland, the Bretons of France, the Basques of Spain and the pan-Slav South Slavs (Engels, 1849b, 221–2).
4. See particularly Rosdolsky (1980).
5. In addition to the contributions surveyed here, Kautsky, Bernstein, Trotsky, Pannekoek, Strasser and Connolly, amongst others, would also make significant interventions.
6. This assumption was not limited to Lenin and Stalin, or to Marxists. Even much of today's literature in this area starts from precisely this premise (cf. Gellner, 1983; Giddens, 1981; 1985; Greenfeld, 1992).
7. Most notably, Karl Renner (1978). For useful discussions of Renner's contribution to these debates, see Kolakowski (1978) and Bottomore and Goode (1978).
8. Traces of both of these resonate strongly in the work of Ernst Renan (1990), whilst the 'will to nation' (nation defined by the conscious solidarity of national agents) lies at the heart of Max Weber's conceptualization (1968).
9. Stalin was particularly scathing in his attacks on Bauer for these reasons. For a recent critique in a similarly orthodox vein, see Blaut (1987, pp. 59–62)
10. Most notably, Rosdolsky (1980), Davis (1967; 1978), Haupt *et al.* (1974) and Lowy (1976).
11. Nimni's formulations draw heavily on the work of Laclau and Mouffe (cf. Laclau and Mouffe, 1985).
12. For a powerful epistemological and methodological critique of the flaws inherent in assuming the unity of 'the oeuvre', see Foucault (1972, pp. 21–30).
13. Whilst 'much can and has been made of Marx and Engels' ethnocentrism and the dominance in their work of an ideology of progress, neither

detailing the doctrine of "history less" people nor debating whether or not Marx and Engels were latent racists will take us very far in understanding the limitations of their theory of the nation' (James, 1993: p. 177). Indeed, without making excuses for some of their excessive language, it should be noted that the underpinnings of Marx and Engels' great-nations chauvinism lay not in some immanent conception of inherent racial-cum-ethnic superiority (or anything of the sort), but rather in a profoundly underdeveloped teleological conception of the nation, one borrowed uncritically from Hegel (cf. Balakrishnan, 1995, p. 60).

14. Here Hobsbawm's work intersects elements of the broader literature dealing with the role of collective memory in the constitution of the nation. As Renan pointed out, the nation is as much about forgetting as it is about remembering (Renan, 1882, p. 11). But where others highlight the selective and partial nature of 'national memory', the thesis of invented traditions highlights the way novel themes, symbols and practices are appropriated and consolidated in the constitution of national identity.

15. We might note here important dimensions of Scottish nationalism (McCrone, 1992), the numerous indigenous peoples' national movements (Jenson, 1993; Purvis, 1995) and many Third World and minority nationalisms (Lowy, 1993).

16. Compare, for instance, the crude evolutionism driving Ernest Gellner's (1983) conception of the nation with the more conjuncturally sensitive treatments of the issue by Poulantzas (1978b), Anderson (1991) and Hobsbawm and Ranger (1992).

12

Marxism and Democracy

Daryl Glaser

Those not well disposed to the Marxist enterprise may see little use, after the collapse of 'communism', in exploring the potential of Marxism as a source of democratic theory. Yet there are at least two plausible reasons why radicals and democrats might continue to seek a place for Marxist ideas in democratic thought, and for democratic thought in Marxism, even after the events of 1989–91. Radicals may judge that Marxism remains a useful source of concepts and methods for explaining social phenomena and bolstering the struggle for needed social changes; that being so, there is a need to show that it can accommodate, better still foster, so important and widely valued a good as democracy. A democrat, on the other hand, may conclude that democratic theory, considered independently of Marxism, exhibits important deficits which Marxist insights can help to remedy. This author holds, if not without certain doubts, both of these convictions. They supply a rationale for exploring, in what follows, the evolution of debates about democracy amongst Marxists, and for offering, towards the end, some arguments of my own about the relationship between Marxism and democratic theory.

This chapter begins with an outline of the Marx and Engels writings on democracy and then explores the late nineteenth and twentieth century fate of democracy-relevant Marxist thought and politics. Subsequently the diverse attempts by Marxists to delineate democratic alternatives to both 'Stalinism' and reformist social democracy are recorded. The chapter concludes with a balance sheet of Marxist democratic theory and some arguments which might assist in its reconstruction.

Democracy in the Writings of Karl Marx and Friedrich Engels

If there is a democratic theory in Marx and Engels it can be extracted from their diverse texts only with some difficulty. The way these writers talked about democracy was influenced by their changing theoretical preoccupations as well as by current political events in Europe. While they exhibited varying degrees of interest in it, democracy was not a central category for the founders of Marxism and they never developed an extended thesis on the subject.

If we begin with what Marx and Engels say directly about democracy, we must, with Michael Levin (1989, ch. 2), note differences of emphasis between these two writers as well as changes in their respective positions over time. In his first writings as a journalist and then critic of Hegel (1842–3), Marx aligned himself with the struggle for democratic freedoms and used the term 'true democracy' to describe his preferred society. From 1844 onwards Marx employs the term only sparingly (as when, in his final draft of the *Communist Manifesto*, he insists with Engels on the need to 'win the battle of democracy'). After the failure of the 1848 revolutions, Marx used democracy mainly as a label for the middle class democrats who had betrayed the revolutionary movement; to designate one weapon amongst others in the struggle for social revolution; or as the name for a liberal political model he judged insufficiently emancipatory.

Engels' trajectory is slightly different: he remained optimistic about democracy until closer to the eve of the 1848 revolutions, viewing it, Levin writes, variously as identical with communism, an important transitional form, or as the name of the general movement for social and political change supported by Marx and Engels. After 1848, Engels joined Marx in downgrading democracy to a mainly instrumental role and in referring to it less frequently (Levin, 1989).

Marx and Engels developed, through their various writings, a powerful critique of then emergent institutions we today associate with democracy – the modern constitutional state, parliamentarism and individual/citizenship rights.

Marx and Engels considered the liberal political order incapable of delivering the human freedom its advocates promised. Marx presented the modern state as a form which, far from transcending civil society and reconciling its competing interests (as Hegel claimed), was subordinate to the civil sphere and its dominant actors (Marx, 1975). While offering an illusory sense of universal community to its citizens within the elevated realm of public life, the state did nothing to alter the competition, isolation and economic exploitation experienced by individuals and groups in the private sphere. State constitutions promoted by liberals as impartial sets of rules reflected in practice the particular (typically class) interests of those who authored and interpreted them. Liberal talk of individual rights gave expression to the egoistic character of bourgeois civil society while masking its economic inequalities. Though supplying an ideological illusion of popular rule, parliaments for their part were manipulated by capitalists or else devoid of real power. While tactical involvement in parliament was often justifiable (as Engels especially came to stress), parliamentarism always threatened to lure insufficiently vigilant revolutionary movements into reformist politics (Pierson, 1986; Levin, 1989).

What, according to Marx and Engels, would replace the bourgeois liberal state following the social revolution which they anticipated? The emancipated condition which lies at the end of the road is communism, a society of well-rounded individuals, freed from imperatives of necessity and the division of labour, from which the state and indeed politics in the conventional sense will be absent – a vision not dissimilar to the anarchist one. For the earlier Marx especially, communism resolves the contradiction between political freedom and civil oppression through the reabsorption of the state into a socially transformed society. Under communism politics no longer constitutes a distinctive sphere or form of activity, cut off from everyday life; it merges with economic management and administration by the collective producers. The disappearance of the political state is made possible by the abolition of class divisions (and thus of class conflicts) and, it seems, the liberation of humanity from scarcity.

To make communism possible post-revolutionary societies must pass first through a stage of socialism in which (in contrast to the anarchist vision) a state remains necessary, albeit under proletarian rather than bourgeois control. This transitional state presides over the expansion of the productive powers of society and defends the revolution politically against the dominant classes of the old order. There is little clarity about the nature of this state, and indeed about whether it will begin to disappear already under socialism. Two suggestions in Marx and Engels' work must stand in for a developed theory here. One is their call for a 'dictatorship of the proletariat' to manage the post-revolutionary transition to a classless society. Proletarian dictatorship here may entail the social dominance of the proletariat rather than authoritarian rule (Kautsky, 1964; Balibar, 1977), although Marx was not averse to advocating centralism for purposes of economic management and was willing to sanction repression to bolster a post-revolutionary order (Levin, 1989, pp. 117, 121).

The other clue we have about the nature of the transitional polity lies in 'The Civil War in France'. In this work Marx upholds the 1871 Paris Commune as a new form of government premised on the abolition of privileged political and bureaucratic castes raised above society. In revolutionary Paris representatives were (so Marx believed) paid skilled workers' wages, performed executive tasks and were subject to recall, while the standing army was abolished (Marx, 1986). There is some uncertainty about whether Marx and Engels viewed the Paris Commune as an incarnation of the dictatorship of the proletariat (as Engels later suggested it was) or as a departure from its precepts. Marx may have felt obliged to defend the Commune simply for its bravery and radicalism, despite his known doubts about its viability and the appropriateness of its democratic political methods. Alternatively he may have pictured the proletarian dictatorship as Lenin later would, a free participatory democracy like the Paris Commune for the working class and its popular allies, a repressive dictatorship towards the bourgeoisie and other anti-socialist classes (Lenin, 1917 [1968], p. 463).

Two theoretical preoccupations provided the compass for Marx and Engels' accounts of the liberal state, socialism and communism. The first was a concern to establish the social and economic basis of political institutions. Marx and Engels were distrustful of all claims to class-transcending universalism and reluctant to take constitutional or legal forms at face value. They set about uncovering the economic forces which influenced the emergence of political institutions and the class interests which, objectively or by design, they served.

Secondly, Marx and Engels were concerned to locate political institutions, including democratic ones, within a narrative of historical progress. In their middle and later work especially they claimed to have discovered, via the method of historical materialism, objective social and economic trends which explained the emergence of capitalism from feudalism and pointed towards its supersession by socialism and communism. This progressive movement of history was not something that could be understood or predicted exactly, nor was its course predetermined; but it generated the possibility and perhaps necessity of replacing liberal forms with higher ones more closely aligned to the interests of the rising proletariat.

Revisions and Reiterations

During the thirty years following Marx's death in 1883 Marxists formed themselves into what can now be seen as three broad schools, each bearing a distinctive interpretation of democracy and its significance for socialism. The revisionist school is most famously identified with the German Social Democratic Party (SDP) theorist Eduard Bernstein. Bernstein argued that a revolution against an increasingly self-stabilizing capitalist order was unlikely to succeed and that the real possibility of further electoral advance by socialist parties rendered it unnecessary. For Bernstein the enfranchisement of the proletarian majority marked the end of political class domination and, together with the growing cartellization of capitalism itself, opened the way to a 'piecemeal realization of Socialism' through parliament, secured in alliance with other, non-proletarian social forces. Untethered from a commitment to class struggle, Bernstein advocated an idealistic or ethical socialism (see Gay, 1962: Chapter 8; Bernstein, 1961).

A second school found its principal voice in the leading SDP theorist Karl Kautsky. Kautsky insisted, against Bernstein, on the inevitability of capitalist breakdown, and he opposed proletarian alliances with classes not sharing an interest in socialism. Nevertheless Kautsky regarded participation in parliament as important, and for more than narrowly tactical reasons. In the first place parliamentary elections gauged popular support for socialism. Without majority backing, Kautsky maintained, any revolution would amount to premature adventurism and, if it succeeded, produce only a minoritarian dictatorship (such as he would later claim the Bolshevik regime to be). The growing size and maturity of the proletariat hastened the day when it would obtain a parliamentary majority which it could use to strengthen parliament against bureaucracy and effect a socialist transformation of society. In the meantime parliamentary politics would unify the proletariat and increase its confidence.

In the second place Kautsky was convinced that parliamentary institutions would play a primary role in the actual government of socialism. While workers' councils were crucial as 'fighting organisations' of the proletariat, their class-exclusive nature, procedural informality and indirect method of election rendered them unsuitable as permanent organs of government. Parliament was indispensable to democracy, and democracy to socialism (Kautsky, 1964; 1971).

The third school of Marxism was the most resolutely revolutionary. Its dominant wing is known as Marxism–Leninism, after its most famous exponent, Vladimir Lenin. Lenin had little time for the pretensions of liberal democracy. While, like Marx and Engels, he favoured tactical participation in parliamentary elections, he argued that parliaments concealed the real loci of bourgeois state power in the executive and repressive branches of the state. He was convinced that democratic capitalism had entered a final or imperialist stage marked by the rule of finance capital, colonial adventures and the violent rivalry of great powers.

To prepare for the coming revolution socialists needed a coherent and effective vanguard party governed internally by democratic centralism – that is to say, by a dialectic of internal discussion and rigid discipline, election of officers and strong leadership (Waller, 1981). At the same time the dramatic upsurges of proletarian activity in 1905 and 1917 brought out a libertarian side in Lenin – one willing to open the party to a mass membership and to envisage, in *State and Revolution*, popular participation in post-revolutionary administration, the replacement of parliamentary rule by the higher democracy of the Commune and the commencement, under the dictatorship of the proletariat, of the gradual withering away of the state (Lenin, 1917 [1968]).

The Leninist Ascendancy

It was, of course, the Leninist current which in 1917 achieved the first revolutionary seizure of power by a Marxist party. The Bolsheviks established their power in a military action backed by the urban working class and its grassroots organisations.

For parts of 1917 and 1918 revolutionary soviets and factory-based worker committees promised to provide the basic cells of a self-managing socialism; at the same time the multi-party elections practised in the soviets and planned for the constituent assembly held out the possibility of government based on consent and political pluralism. These prospects came to naught. Factory committees were soon absorbed into increasingly bureaucratic trade unions while soviets mutated into centralised and ineffectual bodies bereft of internal democracy. The constituent assembly elected in 1918 was quickly dispersed by the government after the Bolsheviks failed to get the electoral mandate they wanted, and within a few years rival political parties had been banned on various pretexts from government bodies and assemblies. During the Civil War a massive apparatus of police terror was set in motion, and in 1921, *after* the end of the War, internal factions were banned from the ruling Communist Party.

There has been much debate amongst Marxists about the extent to which Lenin, faced by the exigencies of civil war, scarcity and encirclement, had any choice but to employ repressive measures on the scale he did; and about the degree of Lenin's responsibility for the brutal and routine oppression practised by later Soviet governments (Polan 1984; Brovkin 1987; Farber 1990). My own view is that the post-October government did have open to it the option of governing non-repressively, but that its chosen revolutionary model – according to which the leading working class party had to hold on to government at all costs rather than cede power to political or class enemies – precluded a pluralistic or participatory politics in a situation where Bolsheviks had only minority support. Lenin's hostility to parliamentary democracy and bourgeois liberties rendered their abolition in the face of adversity much easier to contemplate and justify, just as his technicist approach to socialist economics weakened the ground on which enterprise democracy rested. The ban on factions certainly seems to have been avoidable on any democratic model except one chronically averse to all manifestations of dissent, ill-discipline or disunity.

Again it is likely that the Leninist regime does bear some responsibility for the totalitarianism that subsequently marked the USSR political system. While it is unreasonable to 'blame' Stalin's personal reign of terror on Lenin, it is reasonable to attribute to Lenin some share in authoring the model of a one-party police state which, with or without Stalinist terror, would characterise the regimes of 'real socialism' until the ignominious collapse of most of them between 1989 and 1991. If the absence of political liberty, civil autonomy, grassroots democracy or rule by consent were the central democratic deficits of communist rule, then all of these were features of Soviet Russia by the time of Lenin's death in 1924. Moreover Lenin played a significant role, well before Stalin, in exporting some of the elements of this model to non-Russian parties through his leadership of the Communist International.

Nevertheless it might be mentioned here that some professedly anti-Stalinist Marxists, notably the Trotskyists, identify the origins of authoritarianism under 'real socialism' not in Leninism (or Marxism) but in the betrayal of the Leninist project by those who seized power in the USSR in the late 1920s. For these analysts (see, for example, Cliff, Callinicos, Hallas), if the Soviet Union degenerated into a bureaucratic or distorted workers' state, this was because Stalin and his followers opted for 'socialism in one country', abandoning the world socialist revolution and pursuing the great power interests of an internationally isolated and backward USSR. In pursuing this course Stalinists created conditions in which power could pass to a parasitic bureaucracy for which Marxism played only a legitimatory role.

Social Democratic Roads

On the other side of the Cold War divide a tradition of reformist socialism, known variously as social democracy, labourism or socialism, achieved occasional electoral victories and stretches of governmental office in Europe, Australasia and elsewhere. Operating through parliamentary legislation, complemented in some cases by tripartite corporatism, these governments contributed to the growth of welfare states which ameliorated the harshness of advanced capitalism.

The bulk of socialists came to view the social democratic path as the only alternative to the deeply unattractive one followed behind the 'Iron Curtain', and Marxism fell out of the programmes and vocabularies of social democratic parties. However critics on the left came, especially from the later 1960s, to accuse welfare state capitalism of failing to redistribute wealth effectively and of governing by means of intrusive and unresponsive bureaucracies; still others would, from the 1970s, insist on social democracy's complicity in a politics of economic growth pursued at the expense of the environment and other 'quality of life' concerns. In any case the social democratic parties were, by the mid-1980s, showing every sign of capitulating to a new neo-liberal consensus dedicated to rolling back welfare gains. So, while its ranks were to inflate impressively from 1989 with the conversion of many former Communist Parties, social democracy seemed, by the 1990s, largely exhausted as an ideological programme. Parts of the left continue to search for radical alternatives to both social democracy and 'Stalinism' – alternatives which challenge capitalism effectively while preserving, indeed extending, democracy.

It is for this quest that Marxist democratic theory may remain an important reference point. To assess its relevance we need to look now at the way Marxists themselves have challenged orthodox Marxism–Leninism, and to the democratic alternatives they have advanced.

Critiques of Marxist Democratic Theory

The democratic credentials of Marxism have been fiercely questioned by a wide spectrum of conservative and liberal thinkers. Conservatives consider Marxism to be a rationalist and hyper-reforming ideology that disregards traditional beliefs (including religious ones), natural hierarchies and the practical experiences of particular nations and peoples. Liberals argue that Marxism's collectivist ethic, hostility to private economic activity and demotion of 'bourgeois' freedoms lead inevitably, where Marxists gain power, to totalitarianism. For some extreme economic liberals Marxism is implicated in the more general evils of socialist welfarism (Hayek, 1960). A number of critics have attacked Marxism for its dangerous utopianism (see Geoghegan, 1987, ch. 5). J. R. Talmon treats Marxism as complicit in a totalitarian desire to perfect human beings and abolish all contradiction and conflict (Talmon, 1970). Karl Popper condemned it for seeking radical social engineering guided by a philosophy that is immune to falsification (Popper, 1972). A comparable argument is advanced by Kolakowski (1977). Marxism has even been depicted as the ideology *par excellence* of intellectuals in search of class power (Konrad and Szelenyi, 1979).

While some Marxists will dismiss these critiques as ideological rationalisations of capitalism, they can at their best convey important insights. Nevertheless our own concern in this section will not be with liberal or conservative critics of Marxism, except in passing, though some liberal assumptions influence the present approach. Nor will we take up further the Trotskyist critique of the Stalinist 'aberration'. Instead we will focus on democracy-relevant critiques of Marxism – and especially of the classical work of Marx, Engels, Lenin and the Second International – advanced by Marxists themselves.

A fairly wide range of writers have traced classical Marxism's main democratic deficit to its *reductionism* or *essentialism*: its tendency to treat social and political phenomena as causally determined by a limited range of primary structures and processes, or as outer expressions of (often unobservable) essences (Cutler *et al.*, 1977–8; Laclau and Mouffe, 1985). The structures/processes typically granted causal primacy (or the status of essences) in Marxism are the economy (forces and relations of production, laws of motion), economic classes and class struggles.

Marxists of Eurocommunist or radical liberal orientation argue that reductionist or essentialist Marxisms downgrade institutions, organisations and values which are crucial to democratic life and effective democratic politics. Conceptually reducing parliaments and rights to their (allegedly bourgeois) class causes or essences, Marxism can too easily sanction a politics which negates these democratic goods or uses them only where they serve a (proletarian) class-instrumental purpose (Hunt, 1980). Analytical reduction of civil society to a sphere of capitalist economic activity and egoism obscures the democratic role of non-state associations and opens the way to repressive attempts to fuse state and civil society under socialism (Cohen, 1983). Finally class reductionism fuels a sectarian tendency to undervalue progressive social forces outside the working class, and underestimates the cultural and ideological creativity required to win mass support for socialist positions.

Humanist Marxists criticise classical (and structuralist) Marxism for treating individuals as mere 'bearers' of social relations or structures. This objectivism, humanists claim, can have a variety of negative consequences specifically for democratic practice since, for example, it encourages a view of individuals as secondary in importance to collectivities, or as obliged to give way to supposed forces of historical progress; it also renders less important individual subjective assent to governments and programmes. Further, objectivism closes off the possibility of ethical or normative discussion, which assumes that individuals, however constrained by structure, have some room to make choices of moral significance. Courses of actions – say, Lenin's disbanding of the constituent assembly – are not necessarily predetermined, and require justification other than by recourse to supposedly objective necessities (see, for example, Lukes, 1985).

The charge of objectivism or determinism is sometimes joined to another, that of positivism or scientism. Some critics hold that a certain type of Marxism – classically that associated with the Second International – places an excessive faith in the capacities of science and, more specifically, in the possibility of developing a science of history and society akin in methodology and precision to natural sciences. Exaggerated belief in the power of Marxist science to disclose objective truths about the world carries several dangers for democracy. The most serious one is that it might grant unaccountable authority to a scientific elite, be it one of Marxist theorists or socialist technocrats, and devalue the non-scientific judgements of ordinary people (who might for example be held to be suffering from false consciousness). Insofar as it threatens to reduce inherently contestable political decisions to merely technical ones, scientism conspires in the undemocratic hope that politics itself might one day be superseded by forms of administration insulated from controversy and debate (Corrigan *et al.*, 1978; Polan, 1984).

For some Western Marxist critics (notably those of the Frankfurt school, and eco-Marxists), the charge of scientism overlaps in turn with that of productivism. Marxism attaches great importance to the emancipation of humans through creative appropriation of the material world and the expansion of labour productivity. When joined to scientism, critics suggest, a focus on labour encourages an instrumental rationality which regards nature as an Other to be quantified and mastered by humans. Apart from its potentially ruinous ecological consequences, instrumental rationality spills over into human relationships, where it sanctions technocracy, treatment of people as means to ends, amoralism and the disruption of authentic communication (Held, 1980, ch. 5; Eckersley, 1992).

According to one line of criticism, scientistic productivism encourages the view that expertise and top-down managerial techniques (such as Taylorism) are more important to socialist economic progress than is industrial democracy, thus offering apparent justification for workplace regimes which depend, like their capitalist counterparts, on alienated labour (Corrigan *et al.*, 1978; Sirianni, 1982). A different line of criticism calls into question the whole tendency to locate oppression and liberation centrally in the workplace, arguing that the preoccupation with work privileges producers over consumers, local communities and the non-employed, devalues struggles against domination in other spheres such as the household, and deflects attention from the needed struggle for free time and liberation *from* work (Gorz, 1983).

A final major accusation, based upon, for example, Marx and Engels' endorsement of economic centralisation, is that classical Marxism is statist. A number of classical Marxist writings appear to justify or sanction a strong state: the emphasis on centralised revolutionary effort rather than a plurality of struggles for social change, scepticism about civil society, undiscriminating hostility to the market, Lenin's vanguardism, the anticipated termination of politics in communist 'administration'. Others argue that Marxism's statism consists not in its advocacy of a strong state as such but rather in its failure sufficiently to champion institutions – parliaments, liberties and rights, local and economic democracy – capable of rendering centralised state power accountable or limiting its scope (see, for example, Wohlforth, 1981).

Alternative Directions

Marxists have addressed Marxism's democratic deficits broadly in two ways. One involves a more positive reassessment of liberal–democratic institutions and, more hesitantly, a critically sympathetic engagement with liberal–democratic theory. The other way may be described, for want of a more satisfactory umbrella label, as anti-technocratic libertarianism. Sometimes these tendencies are developed in opposition to each other, sometimes as complementary.

The Engagement with Liberal Democracy

The first alternative found its most famous expression in the 'Eurocommunism' of the Italian and Spanish Communist Parties of the 1970s. It proceeds from the view that parliamentary democracy and its associated political liberties are, firstly, powerfully entrenched features of the Western political landscape which Marxists must use tactically and strategically if they wish to secure radical change and, secondly, desirable components of any kind of democratic government, socialist or otherwise. The latter position takes Marxism beyond the instrumental parliamentary participationism of Marx, Engels and Lenin, and most clearly distinguishes this current. It is a line of thinking which (re)opens the way to a principled Marxist acceptance of parliamentary democracy.

According to this approach, representative institutions and liberties were achieved in part through the struggles of the labour movement, enjoy widespread legitimacy in the working class and must be defended against those (such as capitalist counterrevolutionaries) who might in future seek to suppress them. Parliamentary institutions have no essential bourgeois class character which might be counterposed to the 'proletarian' soviets. The institutions of so-called 'bourgeois democracy' enjoy a relative autonomy from class and economic determination, their class significance being open to political contestation. They can play a crucial role, alongside other organs, in ensuring democratic socialist government (Hodgson, 1977; Hunt, 1980; Hindess, 1980).

Such views have obvious antecedents in the arguments of Bernstein and Kautsky. Eurocommunists preferred, however, to avoid association with Bernstein's reformism or with Kautsky's workerism and anti-Bolshevism. Instead the Communist Party of Italy (PCI) and British Eurocommunists chose as their principal prophet the Italian communist thinker Antonio Gramsci (McLellan, 1983).

Gramsci never repudiated the insurrectionary strategy employed by the Bolsheviks in Russia, but he suggested that the conditions of the West, where the state was less imposing and civil society stronger, required a different, more complex, political strategy. In the West more so than in Russia bourgeois rule depended on popular consent; the Western bourgeoisie's hegemonic leadership was secured and reproduced in significant measure through institutions of civil society (such as the Church in Italy) rather than via a Russian-style coercive state. A successful revolution in the West required, according to Gramsci, a 'war of position' in civil society aimed at winning for socialist revolution a wide popular consent encompassing the proletariat and its allied classes. Proletarian hegemony could only be secured via a protracted cultural, political and ideological struggle (Gramsci, 1971b; Ransome, 1992). In such arguments the PCI claimed to find justification for popular alliances against monopoly capital, the seeking of popular consent via elections and a political dialogue with the Church, and pursuing a road to socialism distinct from the USSR's.

While Eurocommunist parties argued for a radical challenge to monopoly capitalist power and for a deeper democratisation of the state, the practice of the PCI in particular tended towards accommodating the existing political establishment. Mainstream Eurocommunism's parliamentary legalism and gradualism elicited opposition not only from defenders of a more traditionally Leninist politics, but also from, for example, 'left Eurocommunists' like Nicos Poulantzas. The state, argued Poulantzas, was a terrain of class struggles rather than an instrument readily available to an elected socialist government. A socialist breakthrough would inevitably involve showdowns with the ruling class and its allies, and for these the working class needed to establish non-parliamentary as well as parliamentary bases. While vigorously defending the democratic role of representative institutions, Poulantzas stressed the importance of building grassroots democracy outside the state and of winning the allegiance of non-elected personnel within it (Poulantzas, 1978a, 1978b).

While Eurocommunism is now eclipsed, there has continued a longer-standing Marxist engagement with the liberal political and philosophical tradition, evident in a variety of writings and practices. In the 1960s and 1970s the Marxism-influenced Canadian C. B. Macpherson appeared to envisage a democratic politics which realised the egalitarian promise of liberalism in a way that acquisitive individualist liberalism could not (1973). In 1980, Alan Hunt, the British Eurocommunist, could assert that 'the project of socialism has as its goal the completion or realization of the democratic project initiated by the bourgeois revolutions of the eighteenth and nineteenth centuries' (Hunt, 1980, p. 17). Activists on the left of the British Labour Party, some Marxist-influenced, today join with radical liberalism in a debate about rights and radical constitutional reform under the rubric of movements like Charter 88 (see, for example, Blackburn, 1992). There is every sign that this critical exchange will continue.

Anti-technocratic Libertarianism

Other Marxists have found alternatives to Stalinism and social democracy in forms of politics which we have labelled libertarian and anti-technocratic. Advocates of this politics identify the democratic deficits of classical Marxism above all in those elements of it – especially the central role it accords the forces of production – which legitimate bureaucratic, hierarchical forms of organisation and the rule of experts.

It is necessary to distinguish two main currents of Marxist anti-technocratic libertarianism. The longer-standing one espouses workplace democracy and frequently presents economic or producer democracy as the foundation of political representation in the wider polity. It is a libertarian position because it envisages self-government by the exploited majority class of capitalism, the proletariat; and it is anti-technocratic insofar as it looks forward to a blurring of the division of labour in the workplace and to replacing alienated labour with creative labour freed of domination by experts (Coates and Topham, 1974; Kardelj, 1978; Mandel, 1979b; Sirianni, 1982; Crocker, 1983; Gluckstein, 1985; Shipway, 1988).

Workers' council democracy borrows from some sources which are not specifically Marxist, like French and Italian syndicalism and British guild socialism. There are also Marxist antecedents. Marx, as we have seen, veered between urging commune-type and centralised economic control; he offered no theory of workplace democracy except implicitly in his critique of alienated labour and the social division of labour. Trotskyists identify precursors in writings of Lenin championing soviet democracy and participatory administration. Left Communists sceptical of Leninism look to the Gramsci of *L'Ordine Nuovo*, Rosa Luxemburg and council communists like Anton Pannekoek, Herman Gorter, Karl Korsch and Karl Renner. Though attributing an important role to the proletarian party, these latter thinkers were more consistently concerned than Lenin to defend the centrality of workers' councils to socialism (Pannekoek, 1950; Williams, 1975; Gramsci, 1977; Renner, 1978; Riddell, ed., 1986; Gorter, *circa* 1989; Schecter, 1994).

Participants in the other strand of Marxian libertarianism advocate a sustained anti-technocratic struggle in which economic growth and waged work are played down and new political causes of a non-class kind – those of women and minorities, gays, peace and environmental activists – are married to the traditional concerns of the labour movement. In this world view the focus is on restoring authentic human life-worlds freed of technocratic rationality and on searching for more harmonious relations between people and nature, both external nature and inner human nature. In terms of democratic models this approach can point down two main paths: towards a politics of grassroots social movements fighting for cultural change and co-operative self-government on the terrain of civil society, or towards a reorganisation of modern industrial society around small, self-sufficient, low-technology communes. It connects with a wider, and not necessarily Marxist, deep ecology movement (Habermas, 1981, 1989; Gorz, 1983; Bahro, 1986; Frankel, 1987; Eckersley, 1992). The most prominent Marxist precursors to such thought are to be found amongst writers of the Frankfurt school of critical theory (Adorno and Horkheimer, 1972; Marcuse, 1966; Held, 1980; Habermas, 1989; 1990a).

While Leninism achieved ascendancy through its revolutionary victories and association with Soviet-style communism, the anti-technocratic libertarians were not bereft of reference points in the world of 'real socialism'. Some supporters of worker self-management looked to Yugoslavia after 1950; a few advocates of commune-based, decentralised and rustic socialism defended Mao's Cultural Revolution. However worker self-management did not survive the unravelling of the Yugoslav state, and Maoism has long since been exposed as a violent and oppressive interlude in Chinese history. Like orthodox

Marxist–Leninists, anti-technocratic libertarians today grapple with a record of failed experiments.

Marxist Democratic Theory: the Balance Sheet

What conclusions can we draw concerning the possibility of a plausible and distinctive Marxist democratic theory? Have the alternative approaches here described – the reassessment of liberal democracy and anti-technocratic libertarianism – successfully addressed the deficits of classical Marxism? Can these rival sets of solutions be reconciled? A few general concluding thoughts are offered below.

It seems essential that the Marxist engagement with representative democracy and liberal democratic theory continue. The casual assumption that representative democracy can be dispensed with in the name of higher forms of democracy is not defensible. Representative democracy, for all its limits, offers a relatively stable minimum of government by popular assent able to function moderately effectively in a quite wide range of circumstances. Whatever one thinks of a given parliamentary set-up or electoral system, it is difficult to see how any democracy can today be defended which is not based on universal adult franchise, (more or less) equal-counting votes, multi-party competition and direct election of representatives to centres of power.

Again liberal democracy defends political liberties, such as freedom of expression and association, without which democracy becomes meaningless, a police state attacking not only the bourgeoisie and pro-capitalist parties but, inevitably, the political, trade union and other rights of the working class as well. It follows that a plausible Marxist democratic theory will have to be reconstructed to acknowledge the politically and ideologically indeterminate, non-class character of representative democracy and political liberties. Of course such acknowledgement would not, in itself, offer a distinctively Marxist contribution to the theory of liberal democracy. That must be sought in other arguments of Marxist provenance.

Firstly, Marxism exposes the contradiction between capitalism and any form of democracy aspiring to deliver to its citizens an approximately equal distribution of politically relevant resources. The concentration of economic power in capitalist hands, and social inequality more generally, may not negate the democratic benefits of universal franchise and political liberty, but it does skew their operation in favour of the moneyed few. Marxism insists, rightly, that the abolition of systemic social inequality is a precondition of flourishing democracy.

Secondly, Marxism properly calls into question claims for a public/private division between the state on the one side and the economic enterprise on the other. Marxists join socialist liberals like Robert Dahl (1985) in insisting on the public character of the economic power exercised by owners and managers in 'private' workplaces. Mandatory and binding democracy does not, for Marxists, belong exclusively to the state, but is required in the economic enterprise too.

Finally, though damaging if it leads to their repudiation, the Marxist critique of formal democracy can, in the right context, offer a healthy corrective to naive legalism. The liberal constitutionalist assumptions that the state is a neutral instrument in the service of the government of the day and/or that it operates exactly as its constitution says it does, cannot be sustained in the face of any serious look at the world. Like other forms of realist political sociology, Marxism insists on examining actual political processes, and on treating the executive branch of government and parliament, their sovereign status notwithstanding, as one set of actors amongst others in the political and wider social system. For such an approach Marxists argue that we need a theory of the state and of its relationship to the class structure. In making that case, Marxism draws attention to many concerns relevant to democratic theory which are only dimly or recently present in other paradigms of political science: the threat to democracy from executive power and the security services; the class interests represented in particular state apparatuses; the external veto exercised by capital over government policies and programmes. Marxist political sociology underlines the importance of democratising state administration. Strategically it reminds those seeking radical change that winning governmental power is never itself equivalent to winning state power, and that democratising the state involves complex, protracted struggles never reducible to electoral ones.

The anti-technocratic libertarian currents of Marxism make their own contribution to democratic theory, but their legacy is more problematic. The council and commune models do not, as they are most commonly presented, offer a convincing vision of socially inclusive, ideologically pluralistic self-government. Councils and communes are often imagined – or have in practice functioned – as organic communities committed to common goals, walling out social groups and values alien to their purpose. The council state typically involves inherently controversial features: class-bounded electorates, disproportionate representation of the employed or organised, pyramidal representation with direct popular election only of local assemblies and, on some accounts, the exclusion of openly pro-capitalist parties. Its democratic vitality depends on a very high degree of both popular participation at all levels and of political decentralisation; where the former ebbs or the latter is not feasible, council democracy threatens to mutate into a bureaucratic and highly indirect system of representation (Wohlforth, 1981; Sirianni, 1983; Glaser, 1994).

The anti-technocratic libertarians' celebration of grassroots social movements is more obviously defensible. However the more ambitious accounts of social movement democracy pose their own problems. Many fail to offer an adequate theory of state-level political representation, offering only the quite inappropriate – for both state and civil society – suggestion that social movements or associations should themselves take over state functions, enter an institutionalised relationship with the state or between themselves actually recompose the state. It should be clear that this sort of radical corporatism would result in state co-option of autonomous movements and interpose a layer of (often self-appointed) organisational leaders and community spokespeople between the people and lawmakers.

Nevertheless a distinctive Marxist democratic theory must make the case for combining representative democracy with directly democratic and participatory forms. Classical Marxism never committed itself to pure direct democracy on the Athenian model; but Marx, Engels and Lenin did speak against the alienation of political functions from society and praise the efforts of the Paris Commune to prevent the formation of a permanent political class. Since the combination of representative and direct democracy is best effected within localities and workplaces, Marxism should also commit itself, wherever doing so is compatible with its egalitarian principles, to a very substantial decentralisation of political power. Radical devolution of power on the model of an anarchist-style contractual federalism is not realistic: some centralised power is necessary to redistribute wealth, achieve economies of scale and permit free movement of people and ideas over large territories. Even so, decentralisation is a good, other things being equal, bringing government closer to the people and helping polities cope with complexity. A normative ideal of decentralisation is a necessary underpinning to any Marxist commitment to participatory democracy.

There is another useful legacy of the anti-technocratic libertarian strand of Marxism: it alerts democratic theory to the political nature of many choices usually considered technical and affirms the capacities of ordinary people to perform tasks traditionally left to experts. Of course any attempt to reduce technology and economics to their political content can generate its own disasters, as Maoism illustrates. A credible Marxist democratic theory will insist on the endemically political character of major decisions about social goals and the means to achieve them, but refuse any reduction of the technical to the political. It will require that expertise be made accountable and that it be shared as widely as possible.

A final useful contribution of Marxist democratic theory, and a reasonably distinctive one, lies in its understanding of the political role of the working class. If proposals for proletarian rule are best dropped from Marxist democratic thinking, concern for proportional representation of the working class at all levels of government – which will in some cases entail, de facto, a leading role for that class – remains salutary and needed. The rules of political representation *can* be shaped in ways that allow and encourage political parties to offer candidate lists which are microcosmically representative of the class (and also race and gender) composition of the population (multi-member constituencies, for example). Priority can be given to achieving effective universal education and to abolishing the economic inequalities which impede the working class, women and minorities from achieving sufficient political representation and clout. Industrial democracy can be radically extended.

Civil society and its social movements can also benefit from the infusion of a kind of class politics: much of the new politics (feminist, ethnic, ecological) is dominated by a new middle class of students and the university educated, state-employed professionals, voluntary sector employees and 'alternative' people outside the mainstream working class. It seems clear that these movements can only move beyond a rather marginal position on the political scene when they find ways of addressing and incorporating the working class; and that only when they do so will the active civil society now so often celebrated on the left come to embrace the larger part of the society in whose name it often speaks.

Conclusion

This chapter has surveyed the diverse ways in which Marxists have attempted to come to terms with democracy, and suggested the outlines of a distinctive Marxist contribution to democratic theory. To questions as to whether there is a point, today, in trying to rehabilitate Marxist democratic thought, or whether a rehabilitated version will still be Marxist, no definite answer has been found. We *can* say that liberalism has not until now delivered a democratic theory which takes satisfactory account of the limits imposed on democracy by capitalism and technocracy, or which can match the participatory aspirations of classical democratic theory. If Marxism needs reconstruction, a reworked Marxism can in turn supply valuable insights to the reconstruction of democratic theory.

13

Marxism and Ecology

JOHN BARRY

From the vantage point of the late twentieth century it is curious to look back on the previous century as in some ways a better time, when things were simpler, less threatening and the ever onward march of the industrial revolution was taken for granted. Indeed the Marxist critique was essentially that capitalism was a fetter holding back the inevitable tide of progress, denying its fruits to be enjoyed equally by all. How different things seem now, after almost two centuries of industrialisation. Western societies are characterised as 'risk societies' (Beck, 1992), increasingly sensitive to a widespread sense of power-lessness in the face of forces outside their control. A large part of this has to do with the growing sense that nature is taking its revenge, as the ecological life-support systems of the planet are degraded and destroyed. Globally, after four decades of 'development', the vast majority of the world's human population go with basic needs unfulfilled and, perhaps for the first time in human history, there is a widespread feeling that things will not be better in the future. As the new millennium approaches, for a growing number, progress simply ain't what it used to be.

The organisation of this chapter is as follows. The historical relationship between Marxism and ecology is discussed in the first section, together with a brief overview of recent engagements between Marxism and ecologism. In the second section, a recent Marxist understanding of the ecological crisis as the 'second contradiction of capitalism' is elaborated. In the third section this thesis is used as the starting point for an ecological reconstruction of Marxism. The conclusion argues that the ecological critique does require a reassess-ment of Marxism and that for Marxism to be relevant in the next century it must (and can) evolve as an ecosocialist and ecofeminist political project.

Marxism and Ecology: Historical Overview

Despite the perception that ecological issues are new, there is a history of the relationship between Marxism and ecology.[1] It is fair to say that historically classical Marxism, being a product of its time, did not address the range and significance of ecological issues that have come to play such an important part of late twentieth century political and ethical discourse. Indeed, insofar as ecology stresses natural or absolute limits to economic development, early Marxist theory was vehemently anti-ecological. It is in the Marxist attack on Malthus' theory of population and his argument for subsistence wages that we can trace the predominant reaction of Marxism to ecological theory up to recent years.

Marx's attack on Malthus' ideas set the tone, and often the parameters within which the interaction between Marxism and ecology took place. In this encounter are all the main ingredients which marked, and continue to mark, the relationship between ecology and Marxism. First, there is the Marxist perception of ecology as anti-enlightenment in general and anti-industrial in particular. Secondly, and following on from the latter, is the equation of anti-industrial with anti-working class, so that even to this day the first reaction of some Marxists to political ecology is to see it as an intrinsically bourgeois ideology (Enzensberger, 1974). Thirdly, we have the importance of science and technology on both sides. On the one hand, we have Marx completely optimistic in the ability of technology, once free of capitalist relations, to transcend so-called 'natural limits'. On the other, we have Malthus' claim that his theory was fully supported by scientific and statistical data, which led to the opposite conclusion from that of Marx and indeed was at odds with the dominant belief in progress that characterised the early development of industrialisation under capitalism. In this way ecology from a classical Marxist perspective was another fetter holding back the onward and inexorable rise of the revolutionary proletariat. In many ways ecology was worse than bourgeois political economy because, unlike the latter, ecology was held to be anti-industrial and anti-modern, to desire a return to a pre-modern, agrarian, social order. Where ecological thought was expressed as a romantic defence of the natural world against industrialisation, as in Wordsworth, Carlyle or J. S. Mill, this merely confirmed its regressive, conservative, elitist, and anti-democratic character for Marxists.[2]

A dominant Marxist response to the rise in ecological concerns in the early 1970s typified by the (in)famous *Limits to Growth* report (Meadows *et al.*, 1973), was largely negative. For many Marxists this report and the nascent environmental movement which concurred with it were simply ecological versions of Malthusianism. And the reaction by Marxists to ecology was more or less within the paradigm set by Marx's critique of Malthus. Ecological talk of 'postindustrialism', and the necessity for a 'steady state-economy', replacing the premodern complexion of nineteenth century political ecology, was nevertheless still taken to express the anti-working class, anti-socialist character of ecological politics. In opposition to the ecological argument for a less expansionist, simpler lifestyle, Marxists still held the domination and control of nature as a precondition for the creation of a free and equal society. A typical example of this was Markovic's view that 'Man must master the forces of nature in order to develop freely all of his creative powers. For this reason, Marx is aware of the historical significance of industrialisation, private property and reification (which are necessary consequences of an intense struggle with the natural environment). He understands that *there is no other road to universal human emancipation*' (1974, p. 149, emphasis added). Again, just as in the debate between Marxism and ecology in the previous century, talk of limiting human technological control over nature, either because of natural constraints as revealed by ecological science, or circumscribing human control and use of nature, on normative grounds to do with the intrinsic value of the non-human world, was regressive from the Marxist theory of historical materialism.

However there were also discernible signs of a more positive Marxist engagement with ecological issues. The origins of this dialogue are to be found in the early Frankfurt school and especially in Adorno and Horkheimer's *Dialectic of the Enlightenment*, the New Left, and its humanist interpretation of Marxism, both of which constituted some significant revisions of 'scientific' and classical Marxism. In this New Left tradition we find authors such as Gorz (1980) and Marcuse (1992) seeking to incorporate ecological concerns. In a nutshell, the Frankfurt school and the New Left held that the domination of nature (the means) undermined Marxism's emancipatory ends.

Thus we come to the basic dichotomy within Marxists' responses to ecology. On the one hand, there are those for whom its central political message is regressive and what is of value within ecology can be easily incorporated within Marxism. A recent example of this negative

Marxist reception to ecology is Costello, who claims that 'The "green awareness" of the last decade was, in fact, a product of conservative and anti-industrial ideology radicalized due to the absence of a left political alternative' (1991, p. 8–9). On the other hand, in terms of Marxist theory there has been a greater willingness to examine the ecological critique of industrialism and see if Marxism could learn anything from ecology. Here British writers such as Benton (1989; 1993b), Hayward (1992; 1995), Soper (1991) and Mellor (1992, 1995) have accepted core aspects of the ecological critique (but not all of it) and on this basis reconstructed a more ecologically sensitive Marxist political theory, while others such as O'Connor (1994) have begun to flesh out an ecological expansion and reinterpretation of Marxist political economy. This ecological reconstruction of Marxist political economy and politics will be developed within and from the context of the eco-Marxist analysis of the ecological crisis as the 'second contradiction of capitalism'.

The Ecological Crisis as the 'Second Contradiction of Capitalism'

The dominant Marxist analysis of the ecological crisis begins from a search for its underlying economic causes within capitalism. From a Marxist perspective the ecological crisis can be analysed either as an economic crisis *within* capitalism or the more complex process whereby the ecological crisis becomes a crisis *of* capitalism.[3] As a crisis within capitalism, the ecological crisis reveals itself as an increase in the costs of production, lower profits due to ecological sinks filling up, 'polluter pays' legislation, more expensive raw materials as resources run out and so on. In response to this capitalism attempts to restructure itself both ideologically and economically, as discussed below. However, in its attempts to incorporate ecological externalities, pollution, loss of biodiversity and global climate change, all of which it has produced, by 'displacing' rather than solving these problems, this restructuring process comes up against both absolute ecological limits and increasing social and ethical resistance. In other words, the ecological crisis *within* capitalism cannot be contained by the logic of displacement and this results in an ecological crisis *of* capitalism.

Whereas the first contradiction of capitalism is premised on the contradiction between the forces and relations of production, the second contradiction of capitalism has to do with the disjuncture between the capitalist mode of production (both forces and relations) and what James O'Connor (1991) has called the 'conditions of production'. Following Marx, he holds that there are three such conditions: the 'personal condition' that is, human labour power, 'communal general conditions', that is urban space, communications and infrastructure, and 'external conditions', that is nature or environment. From this perspective the ecological crisis can be regarded as a crisis of the 'external conditions' of capitalist production. Capitalism destroys the very natural basis upon which it exists. Since this external condition is not 'produced' by capitalism (or by any form of human social agency for that matter) the capitalist state secures and regulates capital's access to them. The capitalist state ensures the availability of these essential productive conditions to capital.

The first contradiction referred to the inability of capitalism to sustain itself internally owing to the contradiction between socialised production and individual appropriation, and can be seen as a crisis engendered by capitalism being parasitic upon the *non-capitalist social world*. The second contradiction, on the other hand, is caused by capitalism being parasitic upon the *non-human world*. It is this viewpoint which distinguishes the Marxist analysis from those green or ecological analyses which locate the crisis in the anthropocentrism (human-centredness) or particular world view or 'paradigm' that characterises Western societies. From the Marxist position the ecological crisis is part of the wider economic and political contradictions of capitalism. It is for this reason that an ecological analysis and politics by themselves are *necessary* but not *sufficient* for dealing with ecological problems. Without making the link between the crisis tendencies of capitalism and these problems, ecological politics may ameliorate the effects of some environmental risks without addressing the structural causes and contexts which give rise to those problems. What the second contradiction of capitalism thesis shows is that one cannot have an adequate political ecology without political economy.

Marxist political economy would not say that the ecological crisis arises from capitalism running up against natural or absolute limits. The ecological crisis within capitalism arises in the form of higher costs of production as the collective conditions of production are degraded, made scarce and thus more costly, as a result of the actions of individual capitals. In a sense, this system irrationality of capitalism is similar to the 'tragedy of the commons', where individual capitals systematically destroy the 'capitalist commons' that are its 'conditions of production'. As O'Connor puts it, ' "Limits to growth" thus do not appear, in the first instance, as *absolute shortages* of labor power, raw materials, clean water and air, urban space, and the like, but rather as *high-cost* labor power, resources, infrastructure and space' (1994, p. 163, emphasis added). When the conditions of production become scare and thus costly, the system responds to the short-sightedness and collective ecological irrationality of the rational actions of individual capitals seeking to maximise profits, by the state (and supra-state agencies) taking a more interventionist stance in regulating access to the conditions of production. Basically the economic system causes ecological damage which as a 'market failure' becomes the responsibility of the state. Witness the growth in environmental legislation: for example, the creation of state agencies to regulate water, air, soil, forests and urban space, analogous to the expansion of the welfare state to regulate personal conditions of production, such as health, education and housing. In managing the ecological crisis the capitalist state takes it upon itself to manage the collective and long-term interest of capital in cheap and available conditions of production. State regulation of environmental conditions of production acts to displace potentially system-threatening economic and ecological–economic crises into the political realm (Hay, 1994, p. 219). Ideologically the way the state does this is via the extension of economic rationality to encompass ecological goods and services, as can be seen in the recent development of environmental economics, discussed below. The state's 'crisis management' function is extended to cover ecologically based economic crises.

Logics of Displacement within the Ecological Restructuring of Global Capitalism

Together with the increase in state intervention in the regulation of access to environmental conditions of production, which displaces potentially system-damaging crises from the economic to the political sphere, there are other more logics of displacement at the heart of capitalism's response to the ecological crisis.

Capitalist responses to pollution problems, for example, do not seek solutions, since solutions would require the restructuring of the economy and the transformation of capitalism. Rather 'displacement strategies' are deployed: from one media to another (water pollution becomes solid waste), from one place to another (the export of toxins from the North to the South), or in time to future generations.[4] So rather than 'problem solution' we have 'problem displacement'

(Dryzek, 1987, p. 10): instead of dealing with the causes, the negative effects are simply 'removed', both from individual subjective experience and from the national accounts. But herein lies the rub: the strategy of displacement presupposes that there is an 'away' where environmental pollutants can be sent, but within the confines of a small planet there is no 'away' in the long term. At the present time one can say that the ecological restructuring of global capitalism arises from the necessity of addressing the 'ecological crisis' as a series of discrete problems, and thus to some degree 'displaceable', in order to prevent this crisis from inducing a total breakdown in the whole system. The reason for this is quite simple and is related to the globalised options available to capitalism (see Bromley, Chapter 14 of the present volume). Just as the imperialist expansion of the core capitalist nations permitted them to overcome realisation crises domestically by finding new markets and sources of cheap raw materials in those parts of the world they colonised, domestic ecological problems may for a time be 'exported', displaced to another part of the world, or viewed as a 'technical/bureaucratic' problem, or a problem for the future but not for the present.

Just as capitalism is systematically unjust with regard to the distribution of the goods it produces, so from a Marxist perspective it continues this pattern in respect of ecological risks or 'bads'. The externalities of capitalist economic growth are distributed in such a way that it is the marginalised in the core capitalist nations in the North, the southern hemisphere, women and ethnic minorities that suffer the most. This is not new. From the earliest evolution of capitalism the rich have always been able to insulate themselves from the inevitable 'externalities' of capitalism, whether those externalities be crime, urban decay or worsening ecological conditions. It is at this point that Marxist political economy demonstrates its effectiveness in diagnosing the causes of the ecological crisis. Not only is it the poor who suffer from the inegalitarian distribution of ecological bads, but poverty and inequality are causes of global ecological degradation. As Weston remarks,

> It is the accumulation of wealth and its concentration into fewer and fewer hands which creates the levels of poverty that shape the lives of so many people on our planet, thus making it a major determinant of the environment which people experience. It is poverty which forces people to place their own short-term interests above the long-term interests of the Earth's ecology. (1986, p. 4–5)

This is particularly true in the South, where the penetration of capitalism has displaced non-capitalist, sustainable forms of social–environmental metabolic exchange. Neo-colonialism forces the 'developing nations' into adopting forms of industrialised and monocultural agriculture for the global market which are environmentally destructive, such as large scale deforestation leading to soil erosion and desertification. These indebted, hard currency-starved nations are also obliged to offer themselves as convivial sites for footloose capital, competing with each other to lower pollution and health controls, wages and taxes in a desperate effort to attract investment.

It is within the context of ecological restructuring that Marxists would place the recent rhetoric of 'sustainable development' as a way in which global capitalism seeks to alter its conditions of production in order to reduce costs and gain legitimacy as a viable social form. At the global institutional level, especially since the 1992 Rio summit, there has been much debate about 'sustainable development' as the way to reconcile ecological and economic (read 'capitalist') imperatives. That the logic of this discourse is a bureaucratic one of the undemocratic management of the global ecological commons is one of the many points of overlap between green and Marxist critiques. For example, according to Gorz,

> In the context of industrialism and market logic . . . recognition of ecological constraints results in the extension of techno-bureaucratic power . . . It abolishes the autonomy of the political in favour of the expertocracy, by appointing the state and its experts to assess the content of the general interest and devise ways of *subjecting* individuals to it. (1993, p. 5–7), emphasis in original)

This suspicion is also shared by those in the green movement for whom the 1992 Rio summit marked the rise of a new 'global ecocracy' (Sachs, 1995). What the rise in global environmental governance portends is nothing less than the creation of global institutions functionally similar to welfare-state institutions at the national level. Hence the emphasis on such abstract, quantitative concepts such as 'biodiversity', 'carrying capacity' and, above all else, 'population control' which peppers the new global discourse of the 'ecocrats'.

That this whole global ecology discourse and practice is in the interests of the core capitalist nations of the affluent North is something both Marxists and greens agree upon. Where Marxists differ from some ('deep') greens is in refusing to see the global ecological crisis in terms of an undifferentiated 'humanity' making excessive demands on an equally undifferentiated 'nature'. It is not 'humanity' as a whole that is destroying the web of life on earth, but the capitalist system and those classes within that global system who gain most from it. To simply say that human population growth is the major cause of the ecological destruction of the planet lumps together the marginalised, who are forced to precipitate soil erosion by clearing forests to survive, and those who consume for luxury. To adopt this ideological stance is to adopt the perspective of the global ecocracy for whom 'No matter if nature is consumed for luxury or survival, no matter if the powerful or the marginalized tap nature, it all becomes one for the rising tide of ecocrats' (Sachs, 1995, p. 435).

At the national level Marxists would argue that there is an 'ecological restructuring' process underway and point to the institutionalisation of the quasi-corporatist strategy of 'ecological modernisation' (Weale, 1992, Young, 1993) by capitalist states in the West as evidence of this. At the same time, proponents of 'green social democracy' (Eckersley, 1992) are regarded as the other side of the same coin; both are essentially reformist strategies the basic aim of which is to increase the scope of the liberal nation-state in managing the ecological commons. Indeed, from a Marxist perspective, the success of ecological modernisation is positively related to the extent to which the interests of domestic capital and reformist parts of the green movement coincide. In this way the 'greening' of some European states along the lines of 'ecological modernisation' can from a Marxist position be seen as a compromise brokered and mediated by the state between sections of domestic capital, the organised labour movement and the 'realist' wing of the green movement. Green social democracy can be regarded as a way in which the green movement influences the state's ecological regulation of society. Hence this 'realist' green project does not 'break with the social democratic project of "managing capitalism"' (Ryle, 1988, p. 30).

One of the most notable instances of this restructuring process is at the ideological level. The recent growth in influence of 'environmental economics', together with the debate about 'sustainable development', can be regarded as a part of the ecological restructuring of capitalism at the ideological level. It is the core ideological component of ecological modernisation. Environmental economics attempts to 'green' capitalist economic theory by putting an economic value on the goods and services that nature provides 'free' to the economy. By doing so it is hoped that externalities such as pollution emissions can be lessened by an economic value being placed on the absorption facility of the environment. Environmental economics does not advocate the actual exchange of environmental goods and services on the open market in order for their value to be revealed. Rather, by the creation of a 'virtual market' using economic techniques such as contingent valuation, cost–benefit analysis, and 'willingness to pay' experiments, it seeks to adduce the market value of ecological goods and services (Pearce *et al.*, 1993).[5] It is by recourse to this virtual market that ecological modernisation is regarded as a quasi-planning approach by the state to deal with environmental problems. In this way capitalism responds to the ecological crisis by socialising access to external conditions of production. The ecological restructuring of the capitalist state under ecological modernisation is from a Marxist viewpoint simply the state introducing some degree of planning into the management of the ecological conditions of production.

What environment economics aims for is to render nature a source of capital. The imperative of environmental economics is to solve ecological problems by *capitalising nature*. Hence the recent elaboration of 'strong sustainability' in terms of non-declining 'natural capital' (Pearce *et al.*, 1989). In the ecological stage of capitalism the solvent of exchange value is the means by which the capitalisation of nature occurs; economic valuations are placed on the services provided by nature. Thus money and capital flows become integral to the life of ecosystems under capitalism as much as energy and matter flows (Harvey, 1993). This capitalisation of the external world reaches from the global level of the entire planet, in the form of global warming, to the micro level where the patenting of DNA, the very stuff of life itself, and the development of biotechnology imply that capitalism, Midas-like, turns everything it touches into capital (Shiva, 1992).

The various economic techniques used by which nature is capitalised enhance the capitalist state's perceived capacity to deal with the *ecological crisis* by portraying it as series of discrete *environmental problems* to be managed. For Marxists what is important in this is not just that the rigid and bureaucratic managerial rationality of the administrative state simply cannot deal with the complex, non-predictable nature of ecological problems (Dryzek, 1987, 1994, pp. 181–2). More importantly ecological modernisation, and particularly environmental economics, *depoliticises* the ecological crisis by turning it into a matter of extending the state's crisis management functions. Market-based corporatist strategies systematically preclude the formulation of any genuine *democratic* solutions. Ecological modernisation is thus deployed as the exclusive *means* by which the ecological crisis *qua* 'market failure' is dealt with *on behalf of society*. That the resolution of the ecological crisis requires a more radical questioning of the very *ends and organisation of the economy by society as a whole* is 'crowded out'. In this way the capitalist state reacts to the ecological crisis with a complex, and ultimately contradictory, quasi-socialised strategy. The logic of displacement can be seen in different aspects of this admixture: firstly, in the disaggregation of the 'ecological crisis' into a series of pollution or resource problems that are to be managed by non-democratic global institutions and corporatist domestic arrangements; secondly, by displacing the particular issue to another place, media or into the future.; thirdly, by blaming the 'global ecological crisis' on Southern population growth; and finally, the sum total of the logics of displacement within capitalist responses to the ecological crisis is to systematically prevent the full elaboration of the democratic and planning imperatives that are already implicit within its responses at the domestic level.

Towards the Ecological Restructuring of Marxism

This section suggests the ways in which the ecological crisis, under-stood as the second contradiction of capitalism, suggests the revising of certain core aspects of Marxism. This thesis maintains that the ecological crisis of capitalism arises from the collective inability of capitalism as a global and national socio economic system to regulate sustainable access to the 'conditions of production'. These productive conditions are (i) 'external conditions': environmental or non-human contributions to production, (ii) 'personal conditions': human labour power, including reproductive labour, and (iii) 'communal, general conditions': urban space, communication and infrastructure. For reasons of space, and also because there is a large body of Marxist work on the final condition, we concentrate below on the way the integration of the first and second conditions within Marxism necessi-tates the revision of some central Marxist concepts and the revision of its emancipatory political project.

External Conditions of Production

The first revision suggested by ecology for Marxism relates to the Marxist self-understanding of its political project as intimately related to the development of the forces of production. What an ecological view requires is a reassessment of the Marxist idea that the post-capitalist social order is premised on material abundance. The central Marxist thrust about the production of material wealth in order to satisfy the needs of all, which is systematically impossible under capitalism, needs to be tempered by devoting more attention to the question of distribution. An ecologically sensitive Marxism is one which accepts the green argument about the existence of ecological limits to growth. In another sense this revision of Marxist economism suggests that Marxism can be reconciled with the *desirability* and not just the *necessity* of this revision. This has recently been discussed by eco socialist writers who have suggested that the 'Promethean myth' of Marxism, understood as the premise that human emancipation is built upon the 'domination of nature' and the production of the material abundance, must be radically revised. Writers such as Benton (1993b; 1989) and Hayward (1995) have suggested that the claim that only by transcending natural limits (both external and internal) can humans be emancipated needs to be seriously questioned. What needs to be assessed is that the expansion of the forces of production *without reference to the conditions of production* can no longer be taken as conducive to social progress in general and human well-being in particular. Indeed it may be, as outlined in the next section, that social progress and human emancipation require shifting attention away from liberating the forces of production towards altering their development within the context of securing the conditions of production. Whereas the forces of production are *instrumental* to human well-being, the conditions of production are *constitutive* of human well-being.

A Marxism that accepts limits turns its attentions to issues of social or distributive justice, both globally and nationally (Pepper, 1993). For example, an eco-Marxist position would be that the industrialised North is 'overdeveloped' and what is required is an ecological redirection of material development in the North, and ecologically rational forms of economic development in the South. *This may be cashed out as a shift from (capitalistic) undirected, undifferentiated economic growth to (socialistic) democratically planned, differentiated economic and social development across the globe.* One of the implications for Marxist theory of this ecological analysis is the abandoning of productivity as the primary criterion by which to judge economic performance, and the notion of maximum consumption as the criterion of human well-being. Self-limitation, sufficiency and greater stress on reproductive activities and the realisation of the internal goods of work rather than the external rewards of labour point the way towards the vision of a better society. Marxism must evolve into a project of self-limitation, part of which involves the democratic limitation of economic rationality (Gorz, 1994). Both market and administrative logics disempower citizens from collectively and democratically deciding the direction, composition and ends of economic activity. Ecology and economy can only be brought back into synch via a self-conscious, democratic organisation of the economy. However the main point here is that any choice between indiscriminate economic growth and economic self-limitation is precluded at the present time. Whereas continuous economic growth is a structural requirement of capitalism, it is not a requirement of socialism.

A second issue that ecology calls into question is the orthodox Marxist understanding of historical development. The claim that each society must pass through the capitalist historical stage in order to develop the preconditions for an emancipated society has increasingly been criticised. If the relationship between forces and relations of production are no longer the primary focus of Marxist historical materialism, it becomes free of the linear and rigid logic implied by classical Marxism's narrative of the progression of societies through changes in the mode of production. Introducing the conditions of production as a third category of historical materialism which emphasises ecological sustainability as a precondition for a free and equal society may permit Marxism to endorse non-capitalist, non-western models of economic–ecological metabolism. Thus, rather than the linear historical model of classical Marxism, the way is open to seeing *non-capitalist* as opposed to *post-capitalist* forms of socio-economic organisation as possible frameworks for emancipation.

The third major change ecological considerations bring to Marxism is methodological. As outlined above, the second contradiction of capitalism thesis highlights how in the ecological stage of capitalism Marxism needs to place the forces and relations of production (that is, the mode of production) within the context of the conditions of production. For O'Connor (1992) Marxist political economy is necessary to make capitalist relations of production transparent while ecology (as the study of nature's economy) makes the forces of production transparent. The green critique of capitalist forces of production has shown that capitalist forces of production degrade nature. However analysing the forces without looking at their place in the capitalist mode of production, that is, in connection with capitalist social relations, mistakes the *effects* of ecological destruction for *causes*. Simply laying the blame on industrial forces of production, technology and science offers a shallow and mistaken critical analysis. Many green analyses simply 'naturalise' the forces of production, as if there is some inherent anti-ecological dynamic within them, so that irrespective of prevailing social relations industrial productive forces are by their very nature (independent of productive relations) ecologically damaging. An understanding of the source and meaning of this anti-ecological assumption must be sought within social relations. And this involves greens generating a critique of capitalist relations of production, rather than abstracting their critique of the productive forces and reifying it as a super-ideology of 'industrialism'.

Expanding the analysis to include the conditions of production as a third explanatory category alongside the forces and relations of production suggests a way in which both green and Marxist concerns can be combined. This third category can be understood as the 'natural limits of both human and non-human nature which regulate the metabolism (of humans and nature) from the side of nature' (Hayward, 1995, p. 120). This metabolic interpretation of economy–ecology exchanges opens the way towards a reconceptualisation of Marxism. On the one hand, recognition of the limits and contributions of 'internal nature', that is the reproductive conditions of labour, to economic activity is long overdue, as feminists and ecofeminists have argued. This will be dealt with in more detail below. On the other hand, the introduction of the analytical category of the conditions of production reveals that the human economy is a sub-system of the wider natural economy.

Personal Conditions of Production: Reproduction, Time and Dependency

As noted above, one of the conditions of production is what Marx calls 'personal conditions' or human labour. It is one of the advantages of Marxist political economy that it sees the metabolic relationship between humans and external nature as mediated by social labour, that is, *productive* labour. However, as feminists have pointed out, this social/environment metabolism is predicated upon a deeper metabolism, that of reproducing human labour. Together with the contradiction within the 'production' of the external natural conditions of production, the contradictions inherent within the *reproductive* preconditions of social labour in the context of both capitalist and standard Marxist political economy combine to mark a radical departure in the way to theorise economic activity. It is worth noting that what these two conditions of production share is the fact that capitalist production does not 'produce' them. Capitalism is parasitic upon both the natural world and the reproductive work involved in meeting necessary human biological and emotional needs.

What the ecological critique of capitalism highlights is capitalism's indifference to 'time'. Working on the imperative of short-term gain, rapid rates of accumulation and valorisation in exchange, capitalism works with an 'unnatural' sense of time which is inimical to human flourishing and is at the heart of its dislocation from nature. The demands of capitalism require a systematic distortion of the metabolic character of social/environment–material interaction. The temporal, finite, characteristics of human beings have been explained by Benton as meaning that 'Humans are necessarily *embodied* and also doubly, ecologically and socially *embedded*, these aspects of their being are indissolubly bound up with their sense of self and their capacity for the pursuit of the good for themselves' (1993a, p. 103). It is the quality of the embodied nature of human beings which gives rise to the question of our finite needy nature and dependency upon each other and nature, while, as noted above, our ecological embeddedness represents our collective dependence upon the natural world.

Our embodiedness can be said to correspond to 'biological time', the recognition that we are finite beings, not just in the sense that we are not immortal, but in the more important sense that we are vulnerable, require sustenance from others of our species, particularly our immediate conspecifics, especially during our relatively long weaning and development period, and that on a daily basis we require the support of others. *Biological time and the labour/relations that are subsumed under this category ultimately refer to the inescapable neediness of human beings and our dependence upon others.* It is only by bracketing this neediness that we get the liberal view of the *autonomy* of the liberal citizen in the 'public sphere', self-determining and self-defining without reference to the biological relations within the sub-stratum of the 'domestic/private sphere' upon whose labours and relations this 'autonomy' is predicated.[7] But equally, if Marxist political economy does not take into account the sub stratum of female reproductive labour underpinning personal conditions of production, that is, labour power, its analysis of the conditions of production and thus of the capitalist economy will be flawed. (See Jackson, Chapter 2 of the present volume.) Sensitivity to the personal conditions of production can help rectify this gender-blindness within traditional Marxism.[8]

What can be called 'ecological time', referring to the limited and finite ecological conditions upon which the economy is premised, has already been discussed above. Ecological time highlights the reality of economic production as a stage, 'moment' in the process of collective reproduction, and also refers to the 'economy' as a subsystem embedded within the ecosystem.

An *ecofeminist* analysis forces a radical root and branch rethink of Marxist economic categories and modes of analysis.[9] Essentially, materialist ecofeminism question the category of 'production' within both Marxist and orthodox economic theory. According to Hayward, 'There is a tendency for Marx to negate the sociality and historicity of reproductive activities, to view them either as natural and historical or else as historical effects of changes in productive relations, and so to accord them a subordinate or marginal role' (1995, p. 123). Taking full account of the personal conditions of production requires nothing less than an expansion of the category of production to include reproduction. Economic production then represents only *one* aspect of the human species' metabolism with nature, perhaps the most historically specific of this existential metabolic human condition, but only one dimension of the conditions necessary for human flourishing. Ultimately economic production can be seen as a moment in the wider and more fundamental process of species reproduction. The materialist ecofeminist aim is to overcome the traditional ordering and understanding of production and reproduction. An expanded notion of reproduction within which production was included would imply that norms of reproduction, which include but are not determined by biological conditions, rather than production would be the main regulating criteria of the human metabolism with external nature. And this would demand a completely different type of economy and economic organisation, one based on subsistance and sufficiency rather than maximisation.

It is only by reintegrating production and reproduction that Marxist political economy can transcend the flawed gender and ecological logic of capitalism which creates a false understanding of economy, production and freedom. As Mary Mellor notes, 'By separating off production from reproduction and from nature, patriarchal capitalism has created a sphere of "false" freedom that ignores biological and ecological parameters' (1992, p. 51). Unless Marxist political economy takes seriously the point about human ecological embeddedness and biological embodiedness it may simply perpetuate this false understanding of emancipation, and a one-sided political economy. Emancipation means freedom from capitalist and other exploitative social relations, but not 'freedom from' our natures as vulnerable, needy beings, or freedom from our ecological contexts. Real emancipation is an embedded and an embodied freedom *within* external and *consistent with* internal nature.

The upshot for Marxist politics is that it needs to give more attention to the position, experience and norms of those whose labour and time are exploited within the sphere of reproduction, that is, women. According to Sallah, 'if women's lived experience were . . . given legitimation in our culture, it could provide an immediate "living" social basis for the alternative consciousness which [radical men are] trying to formulate as an abstract ethical construct' (1994, p. 121). As Mellor (1995) points out, the radical transformation of society to an ecological, non-exploitative, emancipated social order is not a matter of getting from 'here' to 'there', because women's experience within the sphere of reproduction offers a readily accessible model of a non-capitalist 'there'.

Conclusion

The upshot of the engagement between Marxism and ecology is profound, setting out as it does the necessity for major revisions within Marxist political economy and the Marxist political project. The ecological critique of capitalism reminds socialists that capitalism is a *mode of production* and not simply a set of property relations. Capitalism is also a particular, historically-specific *metabolism* between society and nature. Ecology reveals these modes of social/ environment interaction as having a definite material content, not just in the usual Marxist sense of material, but in the ecological and biological sense of physical, emotional and psychological material interaction. Thus ecology requires a deeper understanding of *materialism* within Marxism, such that 'historical materialism is the ecology of the human species' (Benton, 1989, p. 54). But as the ecofeminist critique demonstrated, this ecological interpretation of historical materialism requires a further understanding of capitalism as a mode of production which is also a *mode of reproduction*. The import of ecology for Marxist politics is also profound. What the ecological perspective calls for is nothing less than a complete reconstruction of its emancipatory political project. As noted above, an eco-Marxism would have to reconceptualise emancipation not as freedom *from* but freedom *within* our ecological and social embeddedness and our embodiedness.

As regards the ecological moral critique of the capitalist mode of production in terms of its purely instrumental view of nature (internal and external) as simply a storehouse of resources (from raw materials to genetic information) or a waste bin, an ecologically updated Marxism is sufficiently flexible to accommodate the thrust of the green moral position. However, unlike some deep green moral critiques, Marxism sees the moral problem as arising from the 'capitalisation of nature', rather than the 'humanisation of nature'. For many greens the blame for the ecological crisis is to be found within this humanisation of nature project, 'industrialism', modernity's 'disenchantment of nature', all of which are held to be morally underpinned by an anthropocentric (human-centred) moral outlook. They therefore advocate an 'ecocentric' or non-anthropocentric moral position to rectify what they see as the 'arrogance of humanism' (Ehrenfeld, 1978). The aim of this ecocentric politics is the 'emancipation of nature' (Eckersley, 1992). Eco-Marxists, on the other hand, would see the moral problem as residing within the particular capitalist interpretation and implementation of humanism. Unlike radical green theory eco-Marxism is firmly anthropocentric, and sees the 'arrogance' rather than 'humanism' as the main problem to be addressed. A reconceptualisation of humanism, one that sees human beings and their emancipation as resting within rather than against nature can be made compatible with the basic ethical thrust of ecocentrism. A new vision of human emancipation which is premised upon the idea that humans are *part of* as well as *apart from* nature, in the sense that humans represent a *differentiation within* rather than a *separation from* the non-human world would have as a practical consequence the flourishing of that non-human world (Barry, 1995). At the same time, as recent ecosocialist writers have shown, a revised Marxism provides a compelling and practical normative framework within which human moral concern can be extended to the non-human world (Benton, 1993a, Hayward, 1995, O'Neill, 1993. Kovel, 1988). But as indicated above, emancipation would have to break with the assumption of material abundance premised on the domination of nature. Marx's goal of the 'humanisation of nature' from an ecological perspective is not compatible with the domination of nature, or with the limiting of its moral critique of capitalism to its destructive effects on human beings alone.

At the cusp where the ecological crisis becomes a crisis of capitalism we can place the green critique of capitalism in terms of its unjustified abuse of the natural world, its inability to ensure the global meeting of human needs, and its inbuilt bias against future generations. It is the political–normative task of new social movements such as the green movement, the peace and the anti-nuclear movements, together with socialists and Marxists and, above all, women to render the opaque economic view of the ecological crisis *within* capitalism publicly visible as a crisis *of* capitalism. It is at this point that capitalism becomes not just economically unsustainable, but, having so disrupted the metabolism between human societies and their environments, both ecologically and socially unsustainable. In capitalising more and more parts of nature, including human nature, capitalism runs up against social resistance of those for whom the environment is not simply a set of resource inputs or a waste sink but constitutive of who and what they are both individually and collectively. That is, it is a matter of identity. In a sense, capitalism threatens the very life-world of individuals in its attempt to render all that exists as capital. Thus both science and ethics are necessary in order to elaborate and comprehend when ecological crisis becomes a crisis of rather than within capitalism; it is only when these two perspectives are brought together politically and internationally that a political project aimed at the transition to a postcapitalist, socially just and ecologically rational, global order can be created. But, the first step of an ecologically updated Marxism requires the reconceptualisation of 'progress' and 'emancipation'. With a whole world potentially at risk, the human (and other) species (and not just 'workers of the world') has more to lose than its chains.

Notes

1. As used here, 'ecology' will refer to both the science of ecology and the more recent constellation of political and ethical ideas which constitute what has come to be known as the green or ecological critique.
2. A missed opportunity for a more positive engagement between ecology and Marxism came in the late nineteenth century. The Russian *narodnik* Podolinski was the first Marxist to attempt a more positive dialogue between Marxist political economy and ecological science, trying unsuccessfully to persuade Marx of the necessity to incorporate an energy or entropic perspective into his political economy (Deléage, 1994). Writing in 1880 he asked, 'According to the theory of production formulated by Marx and accepted by socialists, human labour, to use the language of physics, accumulates in its products a greater quantity of

energy than had to be expended to produce the power of the workers. Why and how does such accumulation take place?' (1880, p. 353). Podolinski's attempt to incorporate a thermodynamic view of the economy, to see the economy as a material process of energy exchange and conversion, was rejected by Marx and later Marxists.

3. Here I follow Hay (1994) who uses Habermas' 'legitimation crisis' analysis, in distinguishing between 'systems' or structural crisis (for example, overproduction and realisation crisis) and 'identity' or agency crisis (for example, when the 'life-world' is threatened and individuals become aware of the irrationality and destructiveness of the system). In these terms a structural crisis is a crisis *within* capitalism while an agency crisis is a crisis *of* capitalism.

4. Another dimension of this temporal myopia of capitalism concerns the in-built bias within contemporary liberal democracies to look no further than the next general election. Add this to the existence of a positive rate of interest within capitalist economic theory, and it is not difficult to see how the future is systematically discounted under capitalism. Since there are neither votes nor money to be made in being concerned about the future, a generalised belief in the capacity of science and technology to find 'solutions' to environmental problems is promoted, which removes the future as a consideration affecting economic decisions today. Sustainability under capitalism becomes the rate at which capital can be economically realised as human capital; we discharge our obligation to the future by bequeathing it enough human capital to compensate for the degradation of natural capital. This is the approach adopted by environmental economics which seeks to 'save' the world by turning it into a range of exchange values, which were previously ignored by the market. That is, we save nature by capitalising it, treating it as a commodity even though it is neither a commodity nor even produced by humans.

5. According to Mulberg (1992) this recourse to planning on behalf of the state in response to ecological problems demonstrates the efficacy and necessity of a fully-planned approach to dealing with the crisis. In this sense ecological modernisation highlights the *necessity* for a planned approach, as Weale notes: 'If national planning does not exist its alternative will have to be invented' (1992, p. 149). Marxists on the other hand have long advocated the desirability of a democratically planned economy, and recent ecosocialist writers have used this point to argue that the resolution of the ecological crisis requires planning (O'Neill, 1993; Hayward, 1995, Pepper, 1993).

6. The importance of incorporating the the third condition of production within the eco-Marxist critique is that it allows a more theoretically and politically fruitful understanding of the ecological crisis. Most greens understand 'ecology', 'environment' and 'nature' as synonymous with the 'non-human world', a perspective which influences their explanation of the 'environmental crisis'. For greens, then, the ecological/environmental crisis is the crisis of the world. However, from an eco-Marxist viewpoint, the environmental crisis is a crisis across all the conditions of production/ reproduction. Thus the degradation of urban areas – the commodifica-

tion of cultural heritage are as much a part of the environmental crisis as the destruction of the Amazonian rainforests. The same destructive system, capitalism, causes both human and natural environmental degradation. The importance of this for any political ecological project is obvious. Including the human-built environment (urban, work) within the concept of 'environment' means that a politics of the environment is not simply about preserving the natural world but about preserving the human social world.

7. It is because of this distinction between human and 'animal' within the notion of autonomy that the liberal view is anxious to distance itself from anything as messy and sensuous as emotional or ecological contexts. The ultimate bedrock for the liberal notion of autonomy is freedom from our animal/natural needs/relations/practices.

8. It is interesting to note that the ecological crisis has revealed not only the dangerous truth that humans can never fully know the external world and the possible effects of our actions upon it: in many respects capitalist technology is like a blunt instrument shoved into a delicate watch, which we do not and perhaps could not ever fully understand. According to Beck (1992) the ecological crisis also reveals our nature as vulnerable beings. In 'risk society' we are vulnerable and, in respect to the invisible threats to our health and well-being, we are passive objects rather than active subjects. Such ecological threats/risks bring home to us our *embeddedness* in nature and our *embodiedness*.

9. As we understood here, ecofeminism refers to materialist ecofeminist theory, which combines feminist political economy and ecological insights. It is distinguished from 'spiritual' or 'essentialist' ecofeminism.

14

Marxism and Globalisation

SIMON BROMLEY

This chapter will argue that much of the current discussion of the theme of globalisation suffers from an indeterminate characterisation of the process and that there is a need for a determinate historical and theoretical specification of the global system. Such a specification must be able to account for the particular intensity of modern globalisation as compared with the more general interaction across space that has characterised much of world history. We will see that there are close connections between discussions of globalisation and those of modernity. Specifically we argue that Marx has some claim to the status of the first major theorist of globalisation. Against this background, the chapter argues that, while other approaches have added refinements to Marx's account and have suggested alternative lines of enquiry, they all rest on an unacknowledged starting-point – Marx's. For these reasons, the argument concludes that the work of Marx and Marxism provide an indispensable point of departure for the study of globalisation.

What is Globalisation?

The current discussion of globalisation has become exceptionally difficult, not to say confused, because there are at least two quite distinct but overlapping positions which are often run together; indeed in many cases they are not even seen to be different. The positions share what might be called a general and abstract theoretical definition of 'globalisation', understood as referring 'both to the compression of the world and the intensification of consciousness of the world as a whole' (Robertson, 1992, p. 8), or as 'the intensification of worldwide social relations which link distinct localities in such a way that local happenings are shaped by events occurring many miles away and vice versa' (Giddens, 1990, p. 64). Understood in these general and abstract terms, globalisation involves the disembedding of social interaction from particular local contexts and its generalised extension across space through a combination of abstract mechanisms and the reflexive monitoring of intentional conduct. This much is more or less common ground.

The difficulties and the differences begin once we ask, not what in general is globalisation, but rather what are the mechanisms and agencies of globalisation, what are its characteristic social forms, institutions and practices and how it is best understood as a concrete and particular phenomenon or set of phenomena. On the one hand, there is a case for saying that globalisation has a long history, stretching back at least to the interchanges between Europe and the other major civilizations in the early modern period, if not to the cultural cross-overs between the great world religions and especially the three monotheisms of Judaism, Christianity and Islam. A related argument is found in the extension of world systems theory backwards to periods before the emergence of the modern world system in the Europe of the long sixteenth century, and the postulation of cycles of regional hegmonies similar to those said to be characteristic of the capitalist world economy as a whole. On these counts, globalisation is at least five hundred years old. On the other hand, there are a number of substantive characterisations of globalisation which typically relate it to the incipient transcendence of the modern nation-state and of its corresponding political, economic and cultural forms. In this latter sense, globalisation is seen as a relatively recent phenomenon and is associated with claims that we are witnessing the end of sovereignty, the supersession of national economies by a transnational global economic order and the fragmentation of unified nationalisms based on linguistic and ethnic homogeneity. Globalisation is thus a condition of at most several decades.

Globalisation and Modernity

Yet another axis of debate around which globalisation revolves is its relationship to the question of modernity. If globalisation is given a distant historical reference, there is a tendency to reckon it as prior to and in part separable from modernity. Globalisation is seen as the matrix within which modernity is able to develop. Thus Roland

Robertson has argued that 'globality is the general condition which has *facilitated* the diffusion of "general modernity", globality at this point being viewed in terms of the interpenetration of geographically distinct civilizations' (1995, p. 27). By contrast, if globalisation is located in the context of contemporary changes, it is more likely to be associated with the notion that we are moving towards a postmodern society, beyond the practices, institutions and cultures of modernity. Globalisation is thus portrayed as a product of the reaching beyond modernity, or at least as a change in the form of modernity and its self-understanding. Barry Smart, for example, argues: 'The ideas of globalisation and postmodernity have come to the fore during the twentieth century as the process of modernisation has expanded to take in virtually the whole world' (1993, p. 173).

Faced with this range of interpretation, from globalisation as the ever-present if always changing condition of modern history to the notion of globalisation as the movement beyond modernity, how are we to respond? This is a matter of some importance: for if it is the former, the question can hardly be said to be new; and if it is the latter, there needs to be clear evidence of substantial social change. Virtually without exception, where they are noticed at all, these problems are avoided, either by an assertion that multiple tendencies are at play and only time will tell which is in the ascendant, or by hedging one's bets and refusing to offer any genuine substantive claims concerning the present. Perhaps these responses represent no more than an appropriate prudence and modesty, respectively. After all, claims to have identified fundamental change in the global system are far from new and have regularly been confounded.

On one level, therefore, such caution is admirable, a helpful warning against exaggerating the significance of the 'new' while neglecting the continuities with the past. However adjudicating this balance can never be simply an empirical matter, a question of sober historical judgement. For an assessment of whether we are seeing a fundamental change in the *kind* of (global) society, or merely a developmental shift *within* it, must have the means to distinguish alterations which partake of the abstract and general sense of globalisation, which merely evidence the contingent flux of social interaction across space, and those which signify a basic shift in the structure(s) of society, which inaugurate a new form of globalisation. Put somewhat less abstractly, such a judgement must involve being able to differentiate between those developments which serve to maintain the global system in its present form and those which might contribute to its transformation.

In turn, these considerations strongly argue the need for a theoretical and historical specification of the structure(s) of the global system, since an apprehension of social structure is the key to differentiating between the mere fact of globalisation and the existence of basic, system-wide change.

Another way of approaching these questions is to notice that 'globalisation' is in fact being employed in two very different ways in the approaches distinguished above. On the one hand, there is what we might call 'weak' globalisation, since it 'refers merely to the existence of a global field of reference, to access beyond local communities, territories, states and regions to a wider arena' (Friedman, 1995, p. 77).[1] On the other hand, there is a 'strong' sense of 'globalisation' which suggests that the mechanisms and agencies of (weak) globalisation have themselves become globalised. From this point of view, the question becomes: what is it that brings about a change from weak to strong globalisation in the concrete structuring of the world system? What is the nature of the global processes which make possible the transition from weak to strong globalisation? In sum, what we need is an approach which provides a determinate historical and theoretical specification of the global system and, thereby, enables us to understand the shift from weak to strong mechanisms and agencies of globalisation within it.

But if 'globalisation' is to be understood as a particular and concrete set of processes and phenomena bringing about a shift from weak to strong globalisation, if it refers to a distinct quantitative and qualitative compression and intensification of worldwide social relations as well as the consciousness thereof, it cannot really be dated much before the eighteenth and nineteenth centuries, and its really explosive growth occurred only after the mid-nineteenth century, especially from the 1870s onwards.[2] In this strong sense, globalisation is more or less coterminous with the advent of modernity. And many of the themes that are currently subsumed under the term 'globalisation' are also to be found in attempts to characterise 'modernity'. Indeed many of these issues were central both to classical social theory and to its forerunners in the Scottish Enlightenment and in continental European Enlightenment thought. Ideas and practices connected to the emergence and spread of a commercial society based on private property and free exchange, of constitutional states governed by the rule of law and of secular reason guided by experiment and analysis all raised questions about the potential universality and global compass of these new forms of society. While such ideas and practices were to a large extent (seen as) European in origin, there was no reason to suppose that in time their reach would not be global. Indeed much of the power of these new, or *modern*, forms derived from the fact that they were simultaneously changing the 'internal' character of European societies from within as well as the 'external' relations between Europe and the rest of the world from without. Thus although the term 'globalisation' did not enter the social science lexicon until the 1980s, there is a strong case for saying that both as a theory and as a practice it has its origins in the societies of Enlightenment Europe.

To be sure, these intimate connections between modernity and globalisation have been obscured and confused by the supposition that the 'global' and the 'national' are in conflict, or that they are contradictory or alternative principles of structuring the world system. This way of thinking has been reinforced by the somewhat paradoxical fact that, while the major social and political theories originating in the Enlightenment were (implicitly at least) of universal scope and applicability, most actual analysis assumed that societies were *nationally* bounded (Shaw 1994). As a result, 'sociology (as well as anthropology) came to deal, often *comparatively*, with [national] societies; while international relations (and portions of political science) dealt with them *interactively*, with relations between nations' (Robertson, 1992, p. 16). That is to say, at precisely the time when determinate social relations were in fact becoming increasingly global in scope, 'society' came to be equated to, or seen as coincident with, the nation-state. (We will see below that the paradox is explained by the fact that one of the main products and agencies of globalisation has been the consolidation of the nation-state system, especially in its liberal capitalist form, and that it is therefore a deep mistake to see the national and the global as alternatives or in contradiction with one another.)

Marx, Marxism and Global Capitalism

If these general considerations are apposite, then there is no anachronism involved in considering the relationship of Marx and Marxism to the problematic of globalisation. Indeed one might even argue that Marx was the first significant theorist of globalisation. Consider, for example, the well known passages from the *Communist Manifesto*:

> The bourgeoisie cannot exist without constantly revolutionizing the instruments of production, and thereby the relations of production,

and with them the whole relations of society. . . . The need of a constantly expanding market for its products chases the bourgeoisie over the whole surface of the globe. It must nestle everywhere, settle everywhere, establish connections everywhere. The bourgeoisie has through its exploitation of the world market given a cosmopolitan character to production and consumption in every country. . . . In place of the old local and national seclusion and self-sufficiency, we have intercourse in every direction, universal interdependence of nations. And as in material, so also in intellectual production. . . . The bourgeoisie, by the rapid improvement of all instruments of production, by the immensely facilitated means of communication, draws all, even the most barbarian, nations into civilization. . . . It compels all nations, on pain of extinction, to adopt the bourgeois mode of production; it compels them to introduce what it calls civilization into their midst, i.e., to become bourgeois themselves. In one word, it creates a world after its own image. (1848/[1973], pp. 70–1)

Marx's particular contribution to the analysis of globalisation was twofold: first, he attempted to anchor and explain the transformations described in the *Manifesto* in terms of the historical emergence and consolidation of a definite form of society, centred on the development of capitalist forms of production; and second, Marx placed the creation of 'universal interdependence' (strong globalisation) at the centre of his conception of the new capitalist world. Some care is needed in specifying Marx's views on these matters, since he also often assumed the existence of nationally bounded societies as defined by the borders of the nation-state. For example, Marx appeared to analyse the development and nature of capitalism as a phenomenon of *national* societies, as illustrated by the fact that *Capital* takes as its empirical point of reference a national society, England, and by the focus on national events and processes in Marx and Engels' political writings. But at a deeper level Marx's theoretical and historical analysis of capitalism did not take the national formation of societies as given. On the contrary, Marx's theory of capitalism had no necessary national reference and his historical depiction of its emergence and consolidation was explicitly global in scope. Most importantly, not only were Marx's analyses unconfined to the national level, but they provide the means for seeing how the national organisation of modernity, embodied above all in the form of sovereign nation-states, is in fact both a product and an agent of globalisation. In short, Marx's theory of capitalism dispels the illusion that modernity and globalisation are fundamentally different phenomena, since both are shown to be aspects of the social forms through which the worldwide expansion of capitalism has been constructed and reproduced. And it is through the particular social forms of capitalist society that 'universal interdependence' is established.

How, then, does Marx's theory of capitalism supply an understanding of globalisation which both explains its national form and shows how it establishes 'universal interdependence' (strong globalisation)? Marx's argument can be broken down into a number of steps (for a different but complementary formulation, see the important work of Rosenberg, 1994). To begin with, Marx shows how the particular organisation of production in capitalist society is based on a form of property which has some unique characteristics when compared with all pre-capitalist forms. In particular, Marx argues that the separation of labour from direct access to the means of production and money, as well as the constitution of those means as 'private', that is the emergence of generalised commodity production on the basis of 'free' wage-labour, gives to capitalist production an unparalleled dynamism and mobility. Wherever capitalist relations of production obtain, where labour power is commodified and where productive assets are privately owned, competition enforces systematic improvements in the productivity of social labour and capital can flow unhindered by ties to specific locations.

Next Marx argues that as property lost its communal, social and political functions, thereby freeing itself from the constraints imposed by particular, spatially-located populations, so a new form of territoriality developed, centred on the 'purely political' state. The argument was first advanced in Marx's *Critique of Hegel's Doctrine of the State*: 'The abstraction of the state *as such* was not born until the modern world because the abstraction of private life was not created until modern times. The abstraction of the *political state* is a modern product' (1843a/[1975], p. 90, original emphasis). In his essay 'On the Jewish Question', Marx explained this as follows:

> The old [feudal] civil society had a *directly political* character . . . The political revolution which overthrew this rule and turned the affairs of state into the affairs of the people . . . inevitably destroyed all the estates, corporations, guilds and privileges . . . The political revolution thereby *abolished* the *political character of civil society*. . . . The *establishment* of the *political state* and the dissolution of civil

society into independent *individuals* – who are related by *law* just as men in the estates and guilds were related by *privilege* – are achieved in *one and the same act*. (1843b/[1975], pp. 232–3, original emphasis)

In general, there is a repeated insistence throughout Marx's early writings that the 'modern' or 'purely political' state is 'an historical phenomenon, coterminous with the establishment of a "civil society" of "independent individuals" whose mutual relations depend on law' (Sayer, 1987, p. 98). Moreover this process occurred on the ground of a pre-existing patchwork of feudal regulation and parcellised sovereignty. Accordingly it was not a transformation whose origins and effects can neatly be demarcated as 'domestic' or 'internal', for 'In securing the uniform rule of the national currency and the national legal system these developments simultaneously defined the national sovereignty of the state against all particularistic powers within its boundaries, on the one hand, and against the sovereignty of other nations beyond its borders, on the other' (Clarke, 1988, p. 177).

If, finally, we bring these considerations together, we can see that the emergence and reproduction of capitalist relations of production, and hence the capitalist forms of the economic and the political, give rise to a type of market that is not directly constrained by politically constituted communities and to a kind of polity which defines its rule in equally exclusive terms internally and externally. For these reasons, the conjoint consolidation of the nation-state system and the world market mean that capital mobility is not confined within national borders. On the contrary, precisely because of this redefinition of the forms of economic and political power, the birth of the national market was *coincident* with the potential internationalisation of capital. Underpinning both was the expanding spread of capitalist relations of production. In sum, for Marx, the differentiation of the capitalist 'market' and the political state, and with them the world market and the system of states, as distinct institutional orders is accounted for by the emergence and consolidation of capitalist relations of production on an increasingly global basis. It is, therefore, the historical spread and social reproduction of these new types of social relations which accounts both for the national form and for the universal interdependence of global capitalism. As Marx was to put it in his *Critique of the Gotha Programme*: 'the "framework of the present-day national state" . . . is itself in its turn economically "within the framework of the world market" and politically "within the framework of the system of states"' (1875/1974b, p. 350).

In Marx's own account, the global spread of capitalist society was seen as an increasingly transnational, if uneven and conflict-ridden, process, driven above all by the dynamics of modern industry. (Marx, however failed to theorise the international consequences of the uneven development of global capitalism – this was a task carried forward with great insight by Trotsky: see Rosenberg, 1996.) By 'modern industry' Marx referred, not to a specific kind of technology, but rather to a phase of capitalist development characterised by the real subordination of labour to capital, by the predominant role played by improvements in technology and organisation in enhancing the productivity of social labour and by the subordination of trade and circulation to the rhythms of production. Together with the technological advances in transport and communications based on steam and electricity,[3] Marx saw modern industry as driving the world market, and with it the bourgeoisie, beyond its European and North Atlantic origins towards an increasingly global sway. But this expansion also involved a historically specific process of conflict and transformation which Marx referred to as 'primitive accumulation', in which the concentrated force of the state played a central role. That is to say, the destruction of pre-capitalist forms of rule and production in order to provide the basis for the creation of the market economy and the abstraction of the modern state were, in general, violent and forcible processes: internally the dynamic of the world market was given by modern industry, and the latter could only develop fully on the basis of the complete commodification of labour-power which presupposed the separation of workers from direct access to the means of subsistence and hence their dependence on the market; and externally the expansion of modern capitalism into its periphery generally demanded the forcible destruction of pre-capitalist or 'natural' modes of production – what Rosa Luxemburg (1976) later called 'the struggle against the natural economy'.

Not only was Marx the first systematic theorist of globalisation in the strong sense of the term, but the first international debate about the character of globalisation, a debate that took place in what Robertson has described as its 'take-off' phase, was also Marxist – the classical Marxist debate on the character of imperialism. (Imperialism was, of course, itself a major vector of globalisation, bringing the world market and the states system to vast reaches of the non-European world.) Many of the themes originally suggested by Marx were further developed in these debates, albeit in a changed international context. For example, Trotsky considered the pattern of uneven and combined development which arose from the unification of global politics by the spreading reach of the world market and the competitive pressures transmitted through the states system; Luxemburg insisted that the processes of primitive accumulation persisted throughout the expansion of capitalism at the margin where it reached pre-capitalist forms, and that this margin was not just geographical, involving the spread of capitalism into new spaces, but also social, based on its further development through commodification within already capitalist societies; Hilferding (1940) argued that the strategies of monopoly and protectionism, based upon a growing concentration and centralisation of capital, constituted new forms of international competition which involved political as well as economic means; and Bukharin (and then Lenin) further developed these arguments by conjoining themes taken from Marx and Luxemburg (on the global spread of capitalist relations of production) with those adopted from Hilferding (on processes of monopolisation and protectionism organised on the terrain of the nation-state).

Marx and Marxism, then, depict globalisation as a definite historical process inextricably linked to the formation of the world market and the rise of liberal sovereign nation-states in the nineteenth century. This globalisation of social relations is understood to be both consequence and cause of the rise of a distinct form of capitalist *society* embodying new forms of economic and political power. The ramifications of globalisation are to be explained within the context of a theoretical account of the workings of capitalist societies, which are constituted by the emergence of new property forms and 'purely political' states, and their interaction with each other.

Alternative Theories of Globalisation

Alternative accounts of globalisation offer a range of different historical, theoretical and methodological starting points. Whatever position is taken on the historical purchase of 'globalisation', its mechanisms and agencies of operation can also be characterised in a number of different ways, with correspondingly different implications for the way it should best be theorised. Globalisation may be seen as primarily an economic, a political or a cultural process, or as involving changing combinations of these elements. Globalisation may also be studied primarily as a process with specific societal origins which then expands on an increasingly worldwide basis, or as a feature of systemic interaction from the outset. Thus, for example, Immanuel Waller-stein's world systems theory (see, e.g., Wallerstein, 1974, 1980, 1989) and the 'civilisational' analysis of Robertson agree in dating the origins of globalisation at least as far back as early modern Europe, but their emphases are in other respects distinct. World systems theory focuses on the material dynamics of the capitalist world market and the multicentric states system, it is materialist in its method and systemic in its focus; whereas, according to Robertson, 'globalization theory turns world-systems theory nearly on its head – by focusing, first, on *cultural* aspects of the world 'system' and, second, by systematic study of *internal* civilizational and societal attributes which shape orientations to the world as a whole and forms of participation of civilizations and societies in the global–human circumstance' (1992, p. 133). Equally, among those who argue that globalisation is a recent phenomenon, related to the emergence of a range of transnational practices involving the activities of transnational corporations, poli-tical elites, non-state actors and consumer cultures, there is much disagreement as to which practices act as the principal bearers of disembedded and reflexively monitored social arrangements, as well as contrasting emphases on the societal and systemic determinants of these phenomena. (See Waters, 1995, for a review of the debates.)

As these brief reflections suggest, there are many different ap-proaches to the problematic of globalisation. Indeed we have already suggested that Enlightenment thought, classical social theory and Marxism were making sense of globalisation *avant la lettre*. This is important to recognise, since much of the most interesting work done on the subject of globalisation has not been explicitly identified as such. Outside Marxism, there has been a huge range of work which we do not have space even to summarise. Rather we will consider a small number of key contributions in order to assess the extent to which they provide alternatives to the Marxist approach briefly sketched above.

If we confine our attention to postwar social theory, then arguably the first major contribution to the study of globalisation was made by the theorists of modernisation. In terms of the classification of approaches offered above, the approach of modernisation theory was primarily cultural and societal. For example, Walt Rostow's famous work, *The Stages of Economic Growth* (1960), took growth to be 'one manifestation of a much wider process of modernisation', in which the emergence of new forms of property and markets, together with the 'building of an effective centralised national state', were of central importance (1960, pp. 174–7). But what was distinctive about developments in Europe in the seventeenth and eighteenth centuries was primarily a cultural shift, an acceptance of the view that the physical world was both knowable and subject to human manipulation, and it was 'this which distinguishes the modern world from all previous history' (ibid., p. 173). While European – and especially British – in origin, this process of modernisation was of worldwide significance, since modernisation is 'forced upon more backward nations by the consequences of failing to modernise in an inherently competitive and contentious arena of world power' (ibid., p. 174). Thus Rostow contends:

> The strongest force that has operated to induce and diffuse the impulse to growth has been the intrusion of the more advanced nations on the less advanced. . . . The profit motive played its part in the spread of modern growth; but it was Alexander Hamilton's insight that was critical in one nation after another down to the present day: 'not only the wealth but the independence and security of a country appears to be materially connected with the prosperity of manufactures'. (Ibid., p. 174)

Modernisation thus brings about global transformation through the competitive spread of mercantilist policies, driven forward by the impetus of reactive nationalism in the backward regions of the world. The principal feature of the globalisation process, then, is the progressive expansion of the number of modern societies in the international system and their convergence on a relatively peaceful model of development focused on consumer-oriented growth and social welfare. In this conception, globalisation is a result of the expansion and induced replication of processes of modernisation such that the direction of development is towards an increasingly homogeneous set of national societies linked together through economic independence and the sharing of a common secular, rational and democratic culture. Francis Fukuyama (1992) provided an updated version of this thesis appropriate to the post-Cold War world.

The world systems theory developed by André Gunder Frank (1978) and Wallerstein (1974, 1980, 1989) can best be understood as a direct critique of and alternative to modernisation theory. (Indeed at times it reads as a simple inversion of the main tenets of modernisation theory.) Thus where modernisation theory was culturalist, world systems theory is materialist; where modernisation theory focused on societal transformation, world systems theory looks to systemic processes; and where modernisation theory anticipated material and cultural convergence, world systems theory predicts uneven development and growing inequality on a world scale. Specifically world systems theory argues that modernisation theory was wrong to assume (as Rostow and others for the most part did) that the backward regions would repeat the stages of growth of the developed world, both because contact between the advanced and the backward regions changed the internal nature of the latter and because the developmental priority of the developed world altered the external context within which backward countries could develop. In addition, world systems theory claims that the relations between the developed and what it called the 'underdeveloped' world were not merely contingent and historical, but that they functioned to reproduce and increase global inequality between core and periphery, were 'an essential part of the structure and development of the capitalist system on a world scale as a whole' (Frank, 1970, p. 5). Globalisation in this sense is a feature of the operation of the system from the outset, and it functions to expand the system but at the same time to deepen its inequalities and contradictions.

Drawing on the insights of both modernisation and world systems theory, Anthony Giddens has offered a rather more abstract theory of globalisation. On the one hand, Giddens is critical of the endogenous models of change found in modernisation theory, with their evolutionary and unilinear characterisations of modernity, but he accepts that there are meaningful contrasts to be drawn between 'traditional' societies and 'modernity'. On the other hand, he welcomes the break with endogenous models of change and the focus on the world system pioneered by Wallerstein and others, but distances himself from their more or less functionalist account of the system as well as its effective reduction to the world *economy*. Giddens starts by noting the prolific 'dynamism of modernity' as compared with that of traditional societies, a dynamism which makes modernity 'inherently globalising'. This dynamic and globalising character of modernity derives from the 'facilitating conditions' of those historical transformations which themselves constitute modernity, thus these conditions 'are involved in, as well as conditioned by, the institutional dimensions of modernity' (1990, p. 63).

The first condition consists in the potential separation of the timing and spacing of human activities and their recombination in forms stretched across time–space in a process of 'zoning'. In traditional societies, by contrast, the bulk of human activities required the direct maintenance of face-to-face interaction for their routine reproduction. The second condition is closely linked to this, as it involves the '*disembedding* of social systems' as local practices are linked with globalised social relations by means of 'abstract systems' involving impersonal symbols (such as money) and anonymous others (experts). In combination, these facilitate conditions wherein 'larger and larger numbers of people live in circumstances in which disembedded institutions . . . organise major aspects of day-to-day life' (ibid., p. 79). The third condition facilitating the dynamism of modernity is the reflexive character of social interaction itself. Once traditional forms of conduct have eroded, social action is increasingly (and routinely) carried out by means of the employment of knowledge of the conditions of reproduction of that conduct.

Understood thus, globalisation is the product of the radicalisation of modernity as the latter is universalised by the global spread of its distinctive institutions: 'On the one hand there is the extensional spread of modern institutions, universalized via globalizing processes. On the other, but immediately bound up with the first, are processes of intentional change, which can be referred to as the radicalizing of modernity' (Giddens, 1994, p. 57). The connection between these two processes is forged by the disembedding of social interaction resulting from the emergence of abstract systems. Along the way, traditional cultures are inevitably corroded by this globalisation of modernity as the conditions for the (re)production of tradition are undermined and they 'are called upon to "explain" and justify themselves' (ibid., p. 105).

Then there is so-called 'globalisation theory' itself, the work of Robertson. Globalisation theory appears to differ, at least in part, from all of the above treatments.[4] To begin with, Robertson suggests that the debate between modernisation and world systems theories involves an unnecessary polarisation, something of a false dichotomy:

something like a middle ground should be established between those who emphasize world systematicity and those who tend to think of current trends towards world unicity as having issued from a particular set of societies, as an outgrowth of the shift from 'the traditional' to the 'modern' . . . [for] what has come to be called globalization is . . . best understood as indicating the problem of *the form* in terms of which the world becomes 'united' . . . Globalization as a topic is, in other words, a conceptual entry to the problem of 'world order' in the most general sense – but, nevertheless, an entry which has no cognitive purchase without considerable discussion of historical and comparative matters. (Robertson, 1992, pp. 14, 51)

We have already seen that Robertson also differentiates his own approach from that of Wallerstein by reference to its focus on culture and internal civilisational and societal attributes. Yet Robertson is perhaps closer to world systems theory than he cares to admit when he asserts that 'Different forms of societal participation in the globalization process make a crucial difference to its precise form. . . . [but that] there is a general autonomy and "logic" to the globalization process, which operates in *relative* independence of strictly societal and other more conventionally studied sociocultural processes' (ibid., p. 60).

Next Robertson takes issue with the close identification of globalisation and modernity offered by Giddens. Thus:

the problem of modernity has been expanded to – in a sense subsumed by – the problem of globality. Many of the particular themes of modernity – fragmentation of life-worlds, structural differentiation, cognitive and moral relativity, widening of experiential scope, ephemerality – have been exacerbated in the process of globalization (. . .) without denying that certain aspects of modernity have greatly amplified the globalization process, I insist that globalization of the contemporary type was set in motion long before whatever we might mean by modernity. (Ibid., pp. 66, 170)

In contrast to Giddens, Robertson suggests that time–space distanciation, disembedding and reflexivity are not specific to the institutional forms of modernity, but rather are features of globalisation per se. Globalisation for Robertson thus becomes the overarching framework for making sense of the modern world. Within this framework, the path of globalisation is traced through the forms, individual and collective, by which actors understand and orient themselves to the world. According to Robertson, there are four such reference points: the abstract individuals of the modern citizen-state; national systems composed of nation-states; the international system or society of states produced by the interaction of national systems; and conceptions of a global humanity developed from abstract individualism without reference to specific national belongings: one earth, one humanity.

Closer in spirit to the original analyses of Marx, at least in part, are those considerations of globalisation which are to be found in radical geography and international political economy, approaches which seek to make sense of many of the phenomena identified by Giddens, Robertson and others. These approaches typically focus on the concrete institutionalisation across time and space of the circuits of capital – money capital and finance, productive capital and investment, commercial capital and commodities and even labour power – and argue that both the spatial scope and the temporal velocity of circulation have increased, especially under the impact of new electronic forms of communication. Some have suggested that this heightened scope and rapidity of circulation has outgrown the confines of nationally organised social structures and is shaped by global networks of information and communication, such that 'the flows of subjects and objects are progressively less synchronized within national boundaries' (Lash and Urry, 1994, p. 10). The rise of global cities, on the one hand, and of regional economies organised either above or below the level of the nation-state, on the other, lead to a 'hollowing-out' of the nation-state. Another version of this argument can be observed in the increasingly influential 'management' literature. Kenichi Ohmae, for example, has argued that 'nation states have been a transitional form of organization for managing economic affairs' and that as a result of the decreasing importance of control over military power, natural resources and even political independence in the face of global markets and corporations, governments must 'cede meaningful operational autonomy to the wealth-generating region states that lie within or across their borders' (1995, p. 141–2).

Finally there are certain schools of thought which question the assertion that growing levels of economic, social and technological interdependence are undermining the role of the nation-state. Realist theory in international relations, most notably in the neo-realist school inspired by Kenneth Waltz's work (1979), and some of the new historical sociology, such as the work on state power and autonomy by Michael Mann (1983) and Theda Skocpol (1985), have questioned whether interdependence undermines either the functionality of a general public, authoritative power for other actors operating in and between societies or the specific effectiveness of the state institutions as a bureaucratic means of mobilising power. According to these otherwise diverse theorists, states remain the predominant political organisations and actors both in relation to the structuring of an increasingly interdependent international society and in terms of the authoritative allocation of domestic resources and values.

Where does all of this leave our understanding of the modern global system? Let us start with a rather obvious, if generally overlooked, question: what fact or set of facts about the world is presupposed, or taken for granted, in these diverse attempts to make sense of the modern, global condition? Rostow takes modern growth to be capitalist growth, based essentially on private property and markets; argues that territorially unified and centralised national states are of vital importance; and sees the dynamics of modernisation as driven by the competitive interaction of these features on an international scale. Wallerstein and world systems theory *define* the 'capitalist world-economy' as consisting of an unevenly structured world market and a multiple states system. Giddens asserts that the institutional dimensions of modernity cluster around those of capitalist production, industrialism, surveillance and the monopolisation of the means of violence, configured in the form of industrial capitalism and the nation-state. Robertson's focus on the progressive thematisation of the four reference points of the global condition presupposes the joint consolidation of the nation-state system and a form of economy consistent with a more or less abstract individualism. The new departures in radical geography, international political economy and management theory take the changed nature of the international economy as their starting point, even if they then reach conclusions about the supersession of the nation-state that Marx and the earlier Marxist tradition did not share. And the realist accounts of state power and autonomy continue to insist on the centrality of the nation-state and the states system, interacting with, yet in some respects causally independent of, the world economy, to the character of the global order.

In short, *all* of these post-Marxist accounts presuppose precisely those features of the global system that Marx argued to be central to its constitution as an expansion of capitalist society, capitalist markets and the system of sovereign, or purely political, states, aspects which Marx *explained* in terms of the expanded reproduction of a historically novel type of property and its accompanying forms of economic and political power. If, then, the unacknowledged starting point of subsequent theories of globalisation is that of Marx, do any of these later accounts either offer an alternative explanation of the constitutive features of capitalist society or develop a different account of the dynamics of globalisation? Of the approaches reviewed above, only the work of Giddens and Robertson, on the one hand, and of the realists, on the other, could be said to mark significant new departures.[5]

Giddens offers a valuable account of the dynamic and reflexive character of modern institutions, based on notions of distanciation, disembedding and reflexivity. He is able to show how these aspects of modern institutions give rise to a form of society characterised by 'historicity', in contrast to what Lévi-Strauss called the 'cold' character of traditional society, and he can account for the phenomenon of globalisation in the strong sense by the universalisation of the institutions of modernity. However the very generality of this treatment of the facilitating conditions of modernity/globalisation, together with the form of the organising contrast between traditional and modern societies, does leave the argument empty of substantive specification of concrete and particular historical processes. At this point we must return to Giddens' institutional specification of modernity. In contrast to Marx and the Marxist tradition, Giddens claims that modern societies cannot adequately be characterised as *capitalist*. Instead modernity is argued to consist of four basic 'institutional clusters': capitalist production based upon private ownership of the means of production and the commodification of labour power; the created or built environment produced by industrialism; the administrative power which results from the control of information as focused through surveillance; and the military power which derives from monopolising the means of coercion. Giddens recognises that these clusters are substantively intertwined, but wants to keep them distinct for analytical purposes. Indeed, in substantive terms, Giddens avers: 'If capitalism was one of the great institutional elements promoting the acceleration and expansion of modern institutions, the other was the nation-state' (1990, p. 62; see also 1985). But this was Marx's argument.[6] At most, then, we can say that Giddens has added a general and abstract theory of the dynamic and recursive character of modern institutions to the substantive focus on the mechanisms and agencies of globalisation given by Marx.

Robertson's contribution is of a rather different kind. To begin with, he explicitly takes for granted much that a Marxist account would focus on, such as the creation of a capitalist international economy and the global consolidation of the nation-state system. Next, like Giddens, Robertson is keen to emphasise the multidimensional character of the current global condition – its progressive thematisation around the four reference points – but he says little about their substantive relations to one another. Instead Robertson's distinctive focus is on the *cultural* aspects of the processes of globalisation and the role of culture as the medium of globalisation. Indeed perhaps Robertson's central substantive thesis is the claim that, though the world has been economically unified through the capitalist world market and politically unified through the spread of the states system, it has *not* been culturally unified. Cultural plurality characterises the contemporary state of globalisation, as it did earlier intercivilizational encounters, and the 'independent dynamics of global culture', in circumstances where 'cultural pluralism is itself a constitutive feature of the contemporary global circumstance', defines the central mechanism and agency of globalisation (Robertson, 1992, p. 61).

Clearly Robertson's focus on the cultural aspects of globalism adds substantially to the main concerns of Marxist work on the topic, but recall the *Communist Manifesto*: 'In place of the old local and national seclusion and self-sufficiency, we have intercourse in every direction, universal interdependence of nations. *And as in material, so also in intellectual production*' (1848/[1973], p. 70, emphasis added). To be sure, Marx and Marxism have until recently had little to say about these questions, but the point is hardly new. (Frederic Jameson, 1984, and David Harvey, 1989, for example, have developed powerful Marxist theories of some of the central aspects of the cultural dimensions of globalisation.) More importantly Robertson's postulation of a general cultural means of globalisation conflates the weak and the strong senses of the term identified earlier, it therefore presupposes global mechanisms for the diffusion of culture. As Jonathan Friedman has pointed out:

> The prerequisite for strong globalization is the homogenization of local contexts, so that subjects in different positions in the system have a disposition to attribute the same meaning to the same globalized objects, images, representations, etc. . . . [and therefore] In order to comprehend the differences in kinds of globalization it is necessary to understand the nature of the global process itself, that is, as a social process that transforms social conditions of the production of meaning attribution. (Friedman, 1995, pp. 77–8)

This social process remains unspecified by Robertson. Again, as in the case of Giddens, Robertson's valuable reflections on the cultural features of globalisation remains parasitic on a specification of what it is about the form of modern societies that makes strong globalisation possible.

Realist and statist accounts provide a clear theoretical alternative to Marxist positions, though their substantive conclusions are often closer than might at first be apparent. The sources of state power and state autonomy are differently located as compared with Marxism: on the one hand, realists tend to locate the necessity and effectivity of the state in the anarchical character of a global political system characterised by an absence of an overarching authority; and on the other, statists argue that the autonomy of the state derives from its monopoly of coercion combined with the functional role it plays in relation to expanding the infrastructural powers of society. While these are different accounts of state power and autonomy from that found in the Marxist tradition, it is not clear that they are inconsistent with elements of Marxist thinking. In terms of substantive, empirical explanation, such accounts are often very similar to those developed in the Marxist tradition.[7]

Finally there is the question of where globalisation is headed. We noted above that some have argued that globalisation is bringing about a supersession of the nation-state in the process of a move beyond the institutional forms of modernity. Thus Camilleri and Falk contend: 'If they persist, the twin trends of globalization and its corollary, domestic fragmentation, are likely to weaken the conceptual and practical foundations of sovereignty' (1992, p. 254). This view is strongly supported by Ohmae (1995). Giddens is sceptical of such claims and argues that globalisation is a product of the universalisation and hence radicalisation of modernity. Specifically Giddens agrees with the realist and statist theorists that it is an illusion to think that growing interdependence 'fosters a submerging of sovereignty' (1985, p. 284). Robertson, by contrast, suggests that multiple tendencies are at play, especially in relation to the progressive importance of action and culture oriented towards 'global humanity', and that a movement towards a new form of globalisation may well be under way. Lash and Urry (1994) take a somewhat similar stance to Robertson's.

In order to assess these different views we need a theory of sovereignty and its relation to the major mechanisms and agencies of globalisation. And we have argued above that only Marx even attempts to provide a concrete and substantive theory of the particular form of sovereignty and property in capitalist societies, a form which enables globalisation to co-exist with the persistence of the nation-state. (Realists and statists recognise the fact of sovereignty, but rarely seek to explain it – an exception being Mann, 1983.) Historically speaking, the formation of nationally unified sovereign states and the creation of the national markets of industrial capitalism were coincident with the expansion of the nation-state system and the construction of a world market in the international economy (see, for example, Hobsbawm, 1975; 1979). The latter did not follow the former.

The specific institutions through which these processes have been accomplished have, of course, changed over time, as have the non-state actors and kinds of inter-state regulation which accompany them, but there is precious little evidence to suggest that any of these mark a qualitative departure towards non-capitalist forms of the 'economic' and the 'political', or a diminution of the importance of sovereignty and the rule of law (for a helpful discussion, see Hirst and Thompson, 1996). Indeed the growth of regulatory bodies and practices has, on the whole, served to provide the conditions for the expanded reproduction of capital on a global scale, thereby *underwriting* the sovereign form of political power that is the basis of the liberal capitalist states system. For in its liberal form it is not quite accurate to say that sovereignty is exclusive externally, since from the outset capitalist states have evolved 'a network of bilateral arrangements for the mutual support of national jurisdiction . . . [and] specific functional multinational organisations for the co-ordination of state functions' (Picciotto, 1991, pp. 219–20). The fact that the reproduction of capitalist social relations is in part mediated and effected through a states system reinforces the mobility of capital vis-à-vis any particular state, and hence incursions on the market-based regulation of accumulation by the state are limited by the operation of capitalist competition upon individual nation-states. Once the relation between the international mobility of capital and the sovereign form of the state is properly understood, it becomes clear that the converse of the conventional wisdom is a more accurate depiction of the relation between globalisation and the nation-state. In an era when the state socialist alternative to capitalism has collapsed, when the national regulatory project of social democracy is in widespread, if uneven, retreat, and when the imposition of liberal state forms on the Third World has become the international project of the dominant capitalist powers, the increased globalisation of capital can be seen to have reinforced, not undermined, the sovereign (liberal) form of the state.

Conclusion

As for the foreseeable future of globalisation, then, Giddens is right to argue that the institutions of modernity are being globalised, rather than that globalisation is superseding the forms of modernity, as Robertson and others suggest. But the explanation for this is to be found, not in the abstract character of the 'facilitating conditions' of modern institutions *as such*, nor even in the speed of transactions made possible by electronic media, but in the specific social form taken by economic and political power in liberal capitalist societies. For this reason alone, while Marxism has much to learn from other perspectives and while its range of attention has been too narrowly 'economic' for too long, Marx remains an indispensable starting point for any serious study of globalisation.

Notes

1. Friedman is in fact speaking only of the cultural aspects of globalisation, but his distinction between a weak and a strong sense of the term is of wider relevance.
2. Indeed the leading modern theorist of globalisation, Roland Robertson, has argued that, while it is not specific to modern history, 'the concept of globalization *per se* is most clearly applicable to a particular series of relatively recent developments concerning *the concrete structuring of the world*', developments whose 'key take-off' phase he dates as the 1870s – mid-1920s (1992, p. 53). Unfortunately Robertson is somewhat cavalier in his use of 'globalisation', since he argues strongly for its 'civilisational' sense and distinguishes it sharply from 'modernity'.
3. Marx described railways as the 'crowning achievement' of industrial capitalism and said of the telegraph that it finally represented the means of communication adequate to modern means of production'.
4. I say 'appears' deliberately, since Robertson uses the term 'globalisation' in so many different ways that it is different to pin down his position with any accuracy.
5. Beyond a stress on the importance of secular reason to advance of Europe, Rostow does not offer a distinct *theory* of modernisation and what he has to say of the processes and mechanisms of modern growth is more or less consistent with a Marxist position, if the latter is separated from teleological assumptions about the course of class conflict and capitalist crisis. Wallerstein's theory of the capitalist world system takes its global form for granted, since it is built into the very definition of the modern world system. Lash and Urry's work takes much from Marx and also provides an interesting, if controversial, critique of Gidden's work.
6. A number of critics have pointed out that Giddens' account of the relation of the nation-state to capitalist production is much closer to that of Marx than Gidden's caricature of Marx's position allows (see, for example, Bromley, 1991; Sayer, 1990).
7. See, for example, the difficulty experienced by the realist Stephen Krasner (1978) in differentiating realist from structural accounts of United States foreign policy. See, especially, Cammack (1989) and Skocpol (1985) for further discussion of this point.

15

Marxism, Communism and Post-communism

NEIL ROBINSON

Marxism should have played a considerable part in enriching our understanding of communist systems. As a theory traditionally concerned with the relationship and interaction between economy/society (base) and the state (superstructure) Marxism's analytical focus should have complemented and filled out the concern with politics that dominated liberal Soviet and communist area studies. However a dialogue between liberal communist area studies and Marxist approaches never emerged. Both sides were to blame for this. Much of liberal communist area studies – particularly as they began to develop as an academic discipline after the Second World War (Cohen, 1985, pp. 8–19) – was influenced by security concerns and was thus unsympathetic to, and frequently ignored, the work of Marxists. This was made all the easier to do by the fact that Marxism critical of the Soviet bloc developed in a specific, political fashion.[1]

Most Marxist analysis of Soviet-type systems has been produced by analysts working from within the same revolutionary traditions (particularly variants of Trotskyism) that created the communist states of Eastern Europe, the USSR and the People's Republic of China. Post-Gramscian 'Western Marxists' had a vestigial interest in events in the Eastern bloc(s), as a brief perusal of the contents page of *New Left Review* or *Telos* over the years shows. But in general the attitude adopted by the mass of 'Western' Marxists was that 'Marxism has nothing to do' with what happened in the one-party states of East–Central Europe and Asia (Miliband, 1991, p. 9). Instead of developing an extended critique of communist states, 'Western' Marxists contented themselves with assaults on the intellectual progenitors of Soviet-type systems (see, for example, Colletti, 1972; Poulantzas,

1978b). This served to distance them from the horrors of 'really existing socialism' but meant that the theoretical ideas and increased appreciation of politics which emerged as Marxists moved away from economic reductionism and essentialism in response to the changes in Western capitalism after the Second World War did not impinge either on area studies in general, or on the bulk of Marxist writing on the Soviet bloc. There were, of course, exceptions to this general rule. But these are rare and cannot be taken as representing the main explanatory effort of Marxists and neo-Marxists writing about Soviet-type systems.

The Origin of Marxist Critiques of Communist Regimes: Trotsky and the 'Degenerated Workers' State'

Marxist analysis of Soviet-type systems developed largely from the work done in exile by Leon Trotsky.[2] Trotsky, like the Marxists who have followed in his tradition, was concerned to develop a strategic theory of Soviet-type societies, a theory that both defended the idea of proletarian socialist revolution and provided a guide to the way the USSR should be treated by the international revolutionary movement. Gradually, as the political influence of Trotskyism declined, so the need to deduce how to treat the USSR also declined in importance. Contempt for the socialist claims of the Soviet bloc was seen as enough to distance oneself from charges of sympathy or shared beliefs with the ruling communist parties of the 'second world'. But the desire to vindicate Leninist ideas on proletarian revolution led by a vanguard party remained to limit their analysis by channelling it only in set directions to 'repeat and codify the classic period of Leninist practice', as one of Trotsky's critics was to put it (Castoriadis, 1988, p. 8). For Trotsky and his followers this meant explaining the perversion of the revolution by focusing on the backwardness of the Russian economy and the inadequacy of international support for the 1917 Bolshevik uprising.

Trotsky's best known summary description of the Soviet Union is the label 'degenerated workers' state' (Trotsky, 1973, p. 210). In his main work on the distortion of socialism in the USSR, *The Revolution Betrayed* (written in 1936), Trotsky (1972, pp. 254–5) characterized this state as a 'transitional, or intermediate' regime, 'halfway between capitalism and socialism'. This hybrid socio-economic system had been created, Trotsky argued, by the need to 'regulate the antagonism between the proletariat and the peasantry, between the workers' state and world imperialism' (cited in Bellis, 1979, p. 66). This degeneration of socialism was in many ways natural given the incidence of revolution in an economically underdeveloped country and the failure of international revolution, and not caused by, or even remotely a function of, Bolshevik ideas on political organization.

This conclusion followed from Trotsky's theories of 'combined and uneven development' and 'permanent revolution', which he had begun to formulate after the failed 1905 revolution in Russia and which found their fullest expression in his work of the late 1920s. Trotsky (1969) postulated that socialist revolution was most likely to occur in a country like Russia which was late developing capitalism. Late development produced an advanced proletariat very rapidly because industry used the most modern techniques available (large-scale factories, modern production processes and so on), rather than developing slowly by accumulating capital on a national scale and gradually evolving technological and industrial organization appropriate to advanced capitalist production. This advanced proletariat was numerically small, however, and isolated in a generally undeveloped socioeconomic and political environment. Being isolated, the only modern class in a primitive society and polity, the proletariat was unlikely to be diverted by bourgeois reformism because there were few channels for the incorporation of the labour movement into bourgeois interest politics. Instead its clashes with authority were extreme, its sense of alienation more complete, and it was more likely to develop a revolutionary consciousness and support a revolutionary party than the proletariat of advanced capitalist states. However, because it was isolated, the working class could not be successful in constructing socialism following a revolution. The small proletariat would be able to co-operate with the larger peasantry and overthrow the old regime. But the peasantry would not support the construction of communism: as a class it was ultimately bourgeois in outlook and interested in the protection of its own property rights. Trotsky therefore theorised that a split would develop between the revolutionary workers and an increasingly reactionary peasantry. Without the aid of foreign proletarians in power because of international revolution, the working class of a late developing country could not hope to settle its conflict with the peasantry in favour of socialism and consolidate the revolution because of its numerical weakness.

This theoretical schema seemed to Trotsky to have been proved by the isolation of the Russian proletariat after 1917 and the subsequent debasement of the revolution. The failure of workers' revolutions in Europe after the First World War meant that international support, the necessary condition of a successful transition to socialism in a backward country, was not forthcoming. Consequently the Russian proletariat was left isolated, without the material wealth to build socialism or the means to end the division between town and village. Instead of trying to secure aid for the workers' state by promoting revolution, the state apparatus (bureaucracy) led by Stalin adopted a centrist position and advanced the idea that socialism could be built 'in one country.' This developmental strategy secured the continued existence of the USSR, but at a high cost. Workers were led to believe that they were engaged in constructing socialism, but the bureaucracy's power grew as it directed the economy through 'planning'. Both worker and peasant were placed under state/police control, and the impetus to promote international revolution was lost.

Trotsky named this rise of centrism and decline of revolutionary zeal the 'Soviet Thermidor', a reference to the decline of Jacobinism in the French Revolution (Trotsky, 1972, pp. 87–89, 105–14). The 'Soviet Thermidor' created a 'Bonapartist' regime in which state power became independent of society and based on 'a police and officer corps, and allowing of no control whatever' (ibid., pp. 277–8). Stalin, with his dictatorial powers, was the personification of this Bonapartist trend. But, Trotsky argued, the rise of a Bonapartist bureaucracy did not change the essential character of the Soviet system since it had not led to the restoration of private property:

> The nationalisation of the land, the means of industrial production, transport and exchange, together with the monopoly of foreign trade, constitute the basis of the Soviet social structure. Through these relations, established by the proletarian revolution, the nature of the Soviet Union as a proletarian state is for us defined. (Ibid., p. 248)

The nationalization of the economy made the proletariat the dominant class in terms of property rights so that in form, if not in content, the Soviet system was socialist. However production relations, and hence social and political dynamics, were only socialist in appearance since the rise of the Bonapartist bureaucracy had 'expropriated the proletariat politically' (ibid. p. 249). Socialist democracy had been curtailed and the institutions of popular rule, the Soviets, were a sham; the withering away of the state had been subverted by the development of a powerful bureaucracy; the working class were subjugated to the plan which inhibited workplace democracy.

The combination of the bureaucratic political power and nationalized economy made the USSR a hybrid system, neither capitalist nor socialist. The Soviet bureaucracy was 'similar to every other bureaucracy, especially the fascist' and had a higher degree of autonomy from the 'dominating class' than any other bureaucratic stratum in history. This made it 'in the fullest sense of the word the sole privileged and commanding stratum in Soviet society' (ibid. pp. 248–9). But despite these privileges the bureaucracy could not be a class and make the Soviet Union a capitalist state. Although it controlled the means of production because the 'means of production belong to the state . . . [and] the state 'belongs' to the bureaucracy', the bureaucracy was forced to perpetuate the myth that the Soviet Union was really a workers' state (ibid., p. 249). This prevented it from creating 'social supports for its dominion in the form of special types of property' (ibid.), and meant that it could only reproduce itself as a social stratum defined by administrative position, not as a class:

> The bureaucracy has neither stocks nor bonds. It is recruited, supplemented and renewed in the manner of an administrative hierarchy, independently of any special property relations of its own. The individual bureaucrat cannot transmit to his heirs his rights in the exploitation of the state apparatus. The bureaucracy enjoys its privileges under the form of an abuse of power. . . . All this makes the position of the commanding Soviet stratum in the highest degree contradictory, equivocal and undignified, notwithstanding the completeness of its power and the smoke screen of flattery that conceals it. (Ibid., pp. 249–50)

Ultimately, therefore, the social nature of the Soviet Union depended for Trotsky on the bureaucracy's social position. While it remained a stratum unable to transform itself from being the controller to the owner of the means of production the social nature of the USSR would remain in a state of flux. Trotsky (ibid., pp. 252–5) put forward three possible alternative scenarios that would determine how transition would be resolved.

His first scenario outlined the optimal solution to transition for socialist development. If the Bonapartist regime was 'overthrown by a revolutionary party having all the attributes of old Bolshevism' the bureaucracy would be replaced through a political revolution and social differentiation once more attacked. If this first scenario came to pass, there would be no need for a social revolution like that of October 1917 because property would not need to be renationalized. A 'bourgeois restoration', on the other hand, would restore private property through compromise with the bureaucracy and would entail social revolution against the working class, who would lose their formal rights over property. But the USSR did not necessarily have to move back to capitalism through social revolution *or* return to a true socialist path of development by the political overthrow of bureaucracy. It was also possible for the bureaucracy to maintain itself in power as an administrative stratum. If this occurred, Trotsky considered that the bureaucracy would try to convert its management and use rights of state property into ownership so as to become a 'new possessing class' of capitalists. But until it achieved this, or was overthrown by the proletariat, social relations would not jell and the USSR would be in locked into a permanent transitional state.

This last developmental scenario of Trotsky's was the source of the debate over the nature of the USSR between later Trotskyites. There was some very limited debate over the extent to which it was isolation or backwardness that had caused the USSR's deviation from socialism. But essentially the fault lines between Trotsky's followers developed over the question of the bureaucracy's success in transforming itself into a 'new possessing class' without a bourgeois social revolution. These debates focused on two interrelated issues: the nature of accumulation and the production of value, and the nature of the USSR's ruling group as a function of its extraction and use of value produced through accumulation. The different positions adopted on these issues were based only infrequently on detailed examination of the actual operation of the Soviet political system and economy. More generally the antagonists were motivated by a desire to maintain or claim their Trotskyite lineage, or by their more general position on the state of the world.

Developments after Trotsky

Ernest Mandel

The 'transitional society' model was defended after Trotsky's death by Ernest Mandel. For Mandel, as for Trotsky, Soviet society was an immature 'transitional society', one unable to develop proper socialist relations in production because of isolation from international revolution (Mandel, 1974a, p. 8).[3] Distortions in socialism had therefore developed, but these were not capitalist in form. Mandel did not just repeat Trotsky's model, however. He attempted to update it and develop it as Marxist economic theory by theorising the nature of value produced in the Soviet economy. For Mandel, planning by the state maintained the 'fundamental social characteristics of the economy' and ensured that 'Soviet accumulation is an accumulation of means of production as *use-values*': production did not lead to the accumulation of capital for capital's sake, but for the further development of production (Mandel, 1968, p. 561). 'Use-values' were thus different from the surplus value sought by capitalists for the purpose of capitalist accumulation. Mandel's innovation was, however, rejected by opposing Trotskyite schools of thought and other Marxists critical of 'really existing socialism'.

State Capitalism and its Variants

The first objection to the 'transitional society' model, propagated in particular by Tony Cliff (1964, p. 119), stated that the USSR had developed into a 'bureaucratic state capitalism' system. The grounds for making this claim rested, not on an analysis of the USSR, but on perceived changes in the international system as the Second World War ended. Towards the end of his life, Trotsky saw the capitalist system as being on the verge of collapse because of economic depression and the outbreak of the Second World War. Cliff and his followers argued that this position was mistaken because the postwar confrontation between the USSR and the West had alleviated the prewar crisis of capitalism. The Cold War had caused an expansion in arms budgets and military industrial production that created a dynamic of competition and capital accumulation in a 'permanent war economy' (Cliff, 1957; Hallas, 1979, pp. 101–2; Callinicos, 1991, p. 39). This competition broke down the differences between West and East. On both sides of the Cold War divide, ownership of the means of production became less important than controlling production and the state, the allocator of resources in the 'permanent war economy'. These developments, and the continued lack of worker power in what was supposed to be a workers' state, made the USSR capitalist rather than socialist. The Soviet bureaucracy, as controller of the state and economy, was no different from any other exploiter class, and was in competition with its rival Western power elite as an alternative capitalist class.

Although this new description of the Soviet Union was generated by ideas about the Cold War, Cliff and his followers attempted to supplant Trotsky's analysis completely by dating the onset of 'bureaucratic state capitalism' from the late 1920s. The roots of a militarised economy, they argued, lay in the policy of rapid industrialization adopted after Lenin's death and the defeat of Trotsky and the Left Opposition. The coercion and exploitation of society at this time by the bureaucracy made it 'the personification of capital in its purest form' (Cliff, 1964, p. 118; Callinicos, 1991, p. 29). Free of the constraints imposed by stockholders and investors, the Soviet bureaucracy was able to dedicate more of the surplus product extracted from the population to accumulation. It was therefore at once a 'partial negation of the traditional capitalist class', because it did not rely on ownership to control the expropriation of surplus product, and 'the purest personification of the historical mission of [the capitalist] class', since it was unconstrained in its pursuit of surplus value and hence more capital. The fact that the bureaucracy could not pass on ownership of the means of production from generation to generation in the form of stocks and bonds – as Trotsky had insisted was necessary for the emergence of a capitalist class – was an irrelevance to Cliff. Control over production and redistribution, and 'accumulation for accumulation's sake' were more important than formal ownership. Moreover this control, along with the access to privilege that it brought, *was* increasingly inherited, owing to the general slowing down of social mobility and the restriction of access to education, and hence advancement, by the Soviet ruling class.

The idea that the USSR and the other communist states that emerged after the Second World War were governed by a new ruling class that had capitalist characteristics (at least) was not exclusive to neo-Trotskyite thinkers like Cliff. Variants of 'state capitalism', like the 'bureaucratic collectivist' model, became a feature of much Western Marxist writing on Eastern Europe and are still being generated in an endless, and sometimes ridiculous, attempt to pin down the composition of the Soviet ruling class precisely (Carlo, 1974, 1980; Resnick and Wolff, 1995). Maoist versions of the 'state capitalist' thesis emerged to supplement the neo-Trotskyite account following the split between China and the Soviet Union in 1950s. For the Maoists, the USSR became 'state capitalist' because of its 'economism', faith in the primacy of economic development, and consequent lack of attention to developing socialist relations through such devices as cultural revolution (Bettelheim, 1976).[4] This fault in the Soviet system became worse, and more apparent, after the death of Stalin when Khrushchev stabilized the position of the Soviet elite.

Versions of the 'state capitalist' thesis also appeared from within eastern Europe (Bahro, 1978; Djilas, 1957; Kuron and Modzelewski, undated; Rakovski, 1978). As one might expect, these arguments sometimes questioned revolutionary Marxism in a way that the Maoist and Trotskyite models did not, and often based their arguments on a more sophisticated sociology of communist states. This made them more widely read amongst Western Marxists, but neither they nor the Western variants on 'state capitalism' radically altered Marxist analysis of communist states, or advanced it much further than Cliff's analysis.[5] The differences between the Western and East European 'state capitalist' models were of degree and terminology, rather than important substance. Much time and paper was used in explicating the differences between models, but to no noticeable intellectual effect.

The Critique Group

The second neo-Trotskyite position put forward as a counter to the 'transitional society' thesis was developed by the *Critique* group. The main objections of the group to the 'transitional society' model were that the Soviet system could not be described in any way as a 'workers' state', and that the Soviet economy was not a planned economy, but an administered, command system. Superficially these differences look, as Mandel (1974b, p. 23) argued, to be 'of an essentially semantic nature'. But from them the group developed an alternative version of Trotsky's idea that 'social relations will not jell' in the absence of proletarian political revolution or bourgeois restoration, a version which questioned the stability of 'transitional society' and its economic productivity.

The main theorist of the *Critique* group, Hillel Ticktin (1973), described the USSR (and by implication other Soviet-type systems) as having an unviable mode of production because 'its drive' was 'self-contradictory'. Unlike Cliff, Ticktin (ibid., pp. 20–1) reached his conclusions about the USSR from an analysis of its internal workings. The main economic feature of the Soviet system was, Ticktin argued, 'enormous wastefulness and probably a tendency to increasing waste' (ibid.). Waste was created by the state's attempts at forcing capital accumulation through bureaucratic planning based on orders passed down the administrative hierarchy, rather than through socialist planning based on workers' democratic participation in economic decision making. Bureaucratic planning was a logistical impossibility. Information about what went on in the economy could not be efficiently gathered or effectively used to plan production. One layer of the bureaucracy played off other layers. In the absence of a market, particularly a labour market, it was impossible to control workers effectively. Their 'negative alienation',[6] expressed in lack of attention to work, absenteeism, theft and rapid turnover in jobs, was accepted by bosses who sought to maintain a steady supply of labour so as to fulfil changes in plan targets arbitrarily ordered from above. The result was low quality production, a slow rate of technological change and innovation, and waste in the form of underutilization of productive capacity, underemployment of labour, low labour productivity and misuse of materials.

This description of the Soviet economy was not very different from explanations of the shortcomings of Soviet planning produced by economists from across the political spectrum. But as used by Ticktin it mocked attempts to describe Soviet-type systems as either capitalist or stable in its 'transitional' pattern. The stress on wastefulness as a factor of production denied that the Soviet economy could in practice create meaningful amounts of surplus value that could be appropriated by a 'state capitalist' class, or 'use-values' that could be deployed to develop productive capacity. The bureaucracy was not the personification of capital or a developer of productive capacity as Cliff and Mandel argued. Rather it was an inefficient allocator of resources desperately struggling to control economic activity through senseless political orders and administrative procedure. Accumulation was forced and coerced to feed the inefficiencies of the system; more was demanded, so that ever greater amounts could be pumped into an economic system that was going nowhere. Ticktin recognised that growth in the economy did occur, of course. But this was due to the large amounts of materials and labour power that could be directed into production and was finite. Eventually the system would seize up like one of the poorly produced machines that it manufactured. The costs of materials would grow higher owing to shortage, the labour pool would diminish and labour productivity would not rise because there were no means of ensuring worker compliance for any significant length of time.

An idea that instability was inherent in the Soviet system was thus at the core of Ticktin's analysis. This was carried through to his description of the USSR's social structure, which he portrayed as unique and unsettled because of the way in which the plan and its demands perverted all economic relations. At best, Ticktin seems to argue, Soviet social structure was immanent and latent. Objectively class could be identified according to the position occupied by aggregations of individuals in the system of production. But these aggregations could not become or act as classes since social groups could only relate to one another politically because of the absence of market mechanisms of exploitation and exchange which create mutual interest and solidarity. The result was social confusion. Labour power was not bought or sold through the market, but the worker was compelled to work and suffer alienation. This alienation was controlled politically by repression so that workers could not see themselves as a distinct social group or act as one, even though they were individually aware of their subjugation to the system.

Instead of being created as a proletariat by the shared experience of the labour market, Soviet workers had 'to fight to become a class' (Ticktin, 1992, p. 87). Control of the means of production was not expressed through property ownership but depended upon administrative position. As a result, the Soviet elite was 'in a state of constant flux, insecurity and competition, with no title to anything' (Ticktin, 1978, p. 43). The formal power that the elite had was constantly depreciated by the phenomenon of wastefulness which deprived them of control over any surplus product that might be produced. In sum, social relations were one-dimensional and incomplete, and atomization in the Soviet system was far higher than in any other social order. The elite maintained its exploitation of the people 'in the form of direct political measures, involving the use of the state' and strove to extend this exploitation by political means to overcome its 'partial control' (ibid., p. 55). But, ultimately, all of its efforts were in vain. It could only issue orders to its subject population in the hope of controlling them but could not ensure compliance, and the wastefulness of planning would always contradict attempts to create surplus.

Politics and Marxist Analysis of 'Really Existing Socialism': the Crisis in the Soviet Bloc and Beyond

Ticktin's analysis captured more fully than those of his rivals the frustrations and futility of the Soviet system. The *Critique* group's intervention and modification of the 'transitional society' model in the 1970s was the only one of the Trotskyite models to have any impact on area studies in general. The group's stress on examining the actual formation of economic relations in the USSR, rather than abstracting them from Trotsky's original theory or the USSR's international position, meant that they shared concerns about the need for detailed empirical work with the wider area studies community. This led to their having a larger readership, particularly in the field of labour history and relations, than their neo-Trotskyite rivals (see, for example, the work of Arnot, 1988; Filtzer, 1986, 1992, 1994; Smith, 1981). But overall the *Critique* group was often as insular and as unable to go beyond a set series of reference points to develop their analysis as their rivals, with whom they had a common ideological heritage and concern over protecting the idea of a revolutionary road to socialism. Their work was used for its empirical insights, but did not force any substantial qualification of non-Marxist approaches to communist systems.

The vast majority of Marxist writing on communist systems thus revolved around a few definitional points. The major failing that this produced was in the analysis of politics. Sociologically Marxists could hold their ground with other approaches (although they were never called upon to do so because there was effectively no debate between them). But their analysis of politics was almost universally weak and one-dimensional. The strategic orientation of theory, the desire to protect the concept of proletarian social revolution and defend the idea of the vanguard role of the Leninist revolutionary party and its theories of the revolutionary period, made it impossible to account fully for the development or operation of the Soviet system. The deformation of socialism in the USSR could only be explained in terms of backwardness and/or the failure of international revolution because the role of Leninist theory and ideology in the construction of the Soviet system was not subject to critical analysis (Robinson, 1995, pp. 4–6). Nor could Leninist theory be recognised as having any lasting influence on the function and structure of the Soviet system since this would have honoured the Soviet elite with Marxist credentials.

This self-imposed limit on what could be given a place in explanatory schemata resulted in a set of very one-sided explanations of the operation and faults of the Soviet system. Political history was reductionist, as continuity between the early revolutionary period and Stalinism had to be discounted or severely played down. The intellectual and institutional sources of social atomization in an exclusionary class-based politics, the anti-democratic political practices of the early Soviet period and the imperfect nature of Soviets as representative institutions were all ignored in favour of a monocausal explanation focused on physical terror. Distinctions between the party and the state were seldom drawn since it was not possible to argue fully that the party's claims to power were created and sustained by appeal to the ideological principle of Leninist vanguardism. It thus proved difficult to develop a nuanced assessment of the relative powers of party and state, and/or to describe the interaction of both sets of institutions. Institutional differences and relations were subsumed by the idea that there was a class or stratum or generalized bureaucratic interest that underpinned and superseded conflict. Differences in the Soviet ruling group, when recognized, were either personalized or explained in terms of crude struggles over resource allocation.

The explanation of politics in Marxist models of Soviet-type systems was thus fairly barren, if it existed at all. The ruling group, whether seen as a class or a stratum, was assumed to be more homogeneous as a social group than other classes and to possess a high degree of autonomy, even if the power given by its autonomy was always to be thwarted, as in Ticktin's description of Soviet social structure. This image of power was not very different from that presented by crude totalitarian models. (Trotsky in fact frequently used the term 'totalitarian' to describe the USSR under Stalin.) Power was seen as concentrated and mediated only by logistical limits and economic performance, and even these were often seen as being a minor hindrance that could be overcome by political will and the total coercive power of the state. The effects of modernization and urbanization, ideological constraint and conditioning, policy and institutional complexity, ethnic variation and culture, were left out of Marxist writing in much the same way as they were left out or marginalized in totalitarianism. As a result, the main Marxist models failed to change and develop over time. They became less attractive as 'liberal Sovietology' expanded its intellectual reach against the totalitarian paradigm so that there seemed nowhere theoretically for Marxist analysis of Soviet-type systems to go by the 1980s.[7]

There were, as was pointed out at the beginning of this chapter, some exceptions to this general rule. The three clearest examples are the work of Herbert Marcuse, of Cornelius Castoriadis and Claude Lefort, and of Ferenc Fehér, Agnes Heller and György Márkus. Unlike the majority of Marxist writers on Soviet-type systems, these authors focused on political processes rather than social structure. Marcuse (1958), in a brief foray into communist studies, wrote one of the most thorough early critiques of Soviet Marxism as a body of theory. Examining its practical influence on politics as a new form of rationality, Marcuse's work is almost unique amongst Marxist writings for taking Soviet thinking seriously and attempting to examine the way in which the regime's own rhetoric could be dangerous to it. Lefort (1986) and Castoriadis (1988), founder members of the French *Socialisme ou Barbarie* ('Socialism or Barbarism') group, produced concepts of totalitarianism that are intellectually richer than – and radically different from – those usually employed by Western Sovietologists, through a critical engagement with the work of both Trotsky and Marx. Again their examination of ideology is distinctive, particularly Lefort's theoretical attempt to discern the way in which ideological discourse affects institutional structures and practices and creates hierarchies of power within bureaucracies. Fehér *et al.*, (1983) offer a very different account of Soviet bureaucracies and their relationship to society. Describing Soviet-type systems as dictatorships 'over need', they produce a theory of bureaucracy that elides the debate on class structure and concentrates instead on the way in which power was created and maintained in communist systems by the control over definition of needs and their satisfaction by the party-state.

However, despite the distinctiveness of these authors' work, only the work of Fehér, Heller and Márkus (1983) has had any real impact on communist area studies thus far.[8] Marcuse's work suffered from the long neglect of Soviet ideology by scholars from across the political spectrum; the work of Lefort and Castoriadis has only had a very limited and recent circulation in area studies.

But despite the existence of some Marxist writing on the USSR which appreciated ideology and political processes, the general lack of concern with politics made it difficult for Marxist analysts to explain the crisis that overtook the regimes of the Eastern bloc in the late 1980s. Indeed there was some slippage backwards. Gorbachev's *perestroika* (reconstruction) was an attempt to revitalize the moribund Soviet and East European systems by having ruling communist parties live up to at least part of their socialist rhetoric. They were supposed to work in a 'true Leninist' fashion, lead the people politically and integrate them into the system so that it would once more be productive and legitimate.

The importance of ideas and the institutional reforms to which they led was lost, however, on nearly all Western Marxists.[9] Little new thinking was done and the image of the Soviet system as driven by an unconstrained elite was endlessly reproduced. Indeed, and despite the rifts over the nature of the Soviet ruling group between Marxists and some occasional sniping at the opposition, there was a high degree of agreement on the nature of reform in the USSR. Writers from supposedly diverse backgrounds built on their common perception of the Soviet elite as a social group with a high degree of autonomy and no socialist characteristics to describe *perestroika* and Gorbachev's high (in the Soviet context) moral rhetoric and talk of democratization as a placebo given to the Soviet people whilst the modernizing elite that came to power under Gorbachev normalized its hold over the political and economic system and saved itself from the prospect of economic collapse.

Ticktin (1989, p. 91) described attempts at changing the scope of worker participation in factory life during *perestroika* as 'little more than a cosmetic exercise . . . in propaganda and possibly also . . . an attempt to further the incorporation of the skilled working class by putting them on more committees'. Overall, *perestroika* was little more than an attempt to introduce market economics so as to secure the elite's position (Ticktin, 1992, pp. 156–64). Castoriadis (1989) described *perestroika* as being nothing more distinctive than a sign of the bureaucracy's desire for social self-reproduction that was empty of any real, socialist content and driven by militaristic concerns. Fehér and Heller (1989, p. 35) described it as a response to economic and demographic crisis and a crisis of the ruling stratum initiated by a new modernizing elite that differed from previous elites in that it had 'no internalised ideological taboos'. Mandel (1989, pp. 48, 50) described Gorbachev as representing 'the technocratic–modernising wing of the bureaucracy' that was motivated to reform in the interests of the entire bureaucratic stratum. Alex Callinicos, a follower of Cliff's 'state capitalism' thesis, described reform as 'authoritarian . . . an attempt to preserve the Stalinist system by modernising it from above' that was made necessary by the international 'obsolescence of the bureaucratic state-capitalist model' (Callinicos, 1991, p. 49).

If anything, then, the state of Marxist writing on Soviet-type societies probably worsened during the *perestroika* period as much of what was distinctive about the various models of the Soviet system was worn away. Analysis of the growing crisis in the USSR and eastern Europe did not change the appreciation of politics amongst Marxists, nor did it rectify their failure to appreciate the radical nature of the changes that Gorbachev proposed or their source in Marxism–Leninism. Political fragmentation at the centre and in the regions and subject nations, the effect of institutional innovation and the nature of opposition to the party-state were either unexplained or related back to elite politics in a simplistic fashion. The sheer enormity of change was consequently only rarely captured. The political crises of the late Soviet period were reduced to economics so that the sweep of historical change became a matter of capitalist restoration and little else. Not surprisingly, therefore, at this moment of general uncertainty when dialogue and exchange of information were more than ever needed, there was no greater engagement between Marxism and area studies than before.

It is thus ironic that Marxist analysis of post-communism might actually be very healthy. The collapse of the communist states frees Marxists from the need continually to go over old and stale ground. Interest in the changes in the former Soviet Union and eastern Europe is attracting Marxist, neo-Marxist and post-Marxist scholars who were not involved in the earlier debates and faction fights (see, for example, Habermas, 1990b; Offe, 1991). There are also signs of a critical Marxism developing in the East which might eventually help to refresh analysis.[10]

But the increased attention being paid by a broad cross-section of Marxists to the former Soviet Union and eastern Europe and the emergence of a critical 'native' Marxism are not the main factors that might revitalize Marxist analysis of the old Eastern bloc. What is happening in the former Soviet bloc concerns things that Marxists have long analysed and are equipped to help explain: capital accumulation for capitalist production, social differentiation, class formation and its relationship to state formation, economic interest representation and mediation. This, plus the chance to work with scholars from the East, make the possibility of good, empirically aware and conceptually rich Marxist work appearing more likely. Indeed some excellent work is already appearing and has been doing so for several years. So far most of this work, starting with Michael Burawoy's comparison of production regimes under capitalism and late socialism, and continuing with his and Simon Clarke's work with East European and Russian scholars on privatization, has focused largely on the micro level changes that are taking place in industry (Burawoy, 1985; Burawoy and Hendley, 1992; Burawoy and Lukács, 1992; Clarke, 1992; Clarke *et al.*, 1993, 1994).

Further, as Burawoy (1995) has argued, the possibilities of going beyond micro level analysis and studying the fate of the Soviet bloc as a part of comparative political economy are large and potentially highly informative. This, however, can only be done if the old rigid approach to class that dominated much of Marxist writing is abandoned and politics are more appreciated. The new writing that has begun to appear has so far managed to do this. As with the earlier work of the *Critique* group, the focus on microprocesses has led to theory being built on appreciation of the internal workings of industry and the power relations that are beginning to be formed between worker and management. The politicized nature of economic reform, the growth of lobbying and the more visible linkage between politicians and industrialist groupings have also led to increased attention being paid to political processes. Finally, as a result of the combination of micro-level work and increased attention being paid to politics, the gap between Marxist-inspired analysis of the societies and economies of the transitional states and area studies has begun to close. It is too soon to say that an actual debate about the merits of Marxist approaches has begun. But as both Marxist analysis and area studies expand and try to come to terms with events in the former Soviet bloc the prospects for cross-pollination are better than at any time previously.

Notes

1. For alternative surveys of Marxist analyses of Soviet-type systems, see Lane (1976, pp. 28–43), Bellis (1979), Nove (1986), Westoby (1981, pp. 286–94, 304–55; 1985, pp. 220–3), Fehér *et al.* (1983, pp. 1–44). For a description of the theoretical development of non-Marxist communist studies, see Almond and Roselle (1989).

2. There is a large Marxist literature, much of which is cited below, that discusses Trotsky,s views on the Soviet Union. For a survey of disagreements amongst Trotskyites on the nature of the Soviet Union, see Bongiovanni (1982). The two best, but politically very difficult, accounts of Trotsky's analysis of the Soviet Union can be found in Knei-Paz (1978, pp. 367–441) and Bellis (1979, pp. 56–92).

3. For specific arguments against Mandel, see the work of Ticktin cited below, as well as Ticktin (1979) and Buick (1975). Mandel's response to Tickin can be found in Mandel (1974b, 1979a).

4. For a critique of Bettelheim, see Tickin (1976), Miliband (1983, pp. 189–201). A less well known, but more interesting, Maoist critique of Bolshevism can be found in Corrigan *et al.* (1978).

5. Djilas' model was warmly received by non-Marists since it came from a former senior Yugoslav official and Politburo member, and because he later recanted his Marxism (Djilas, 1969). Bahro's description of social stratification in Eastern Europe was more influential amongst Western Marxists. See, for example, Wildt (1979).

6. As opposed to 'positive' alienation where workers are able to express their grievances through strikes, the organised labour movement and social revolution.

7. This is not to say that 'liberal' Sovietology, the antipode to both orthodox totalitarian theory and reductionist Marxism, always managed to explain the influence of such variables or the operation of Soviet-type systems fully, and did not become involved in debates that were as obtuse and unproductive as the Marxist contest over the class nature of the Soviet system. But the fact that 'liberal' Sovietology attempted to deal with themes and explanatory variables other than the economy and class gave it a plurality and dynamism that Marxist approaches to communist states generally lacked.

8. For example, it has been used to inform studies of Soviet local government (Urban, 1988) and as the basic framework for the study of state–society interaction during the collapse of the USSR (Fish, 1995).

9. The exception, unfortunately, would be those writers who saw Gorbachev's policies as possibly leading to the renewal of socialism in the Soviet Union. This line failed to see the limits of Gorbachevian reformism and the depth of popular antagonism to the CPSU. See, for example, Ali (1988).

10. The most widely read work of a native Marxist so far is that of Boris Kagarlitsky (1990; 1992; 1995). Kagarlitsky's work is not always theoretically interesting, but has a political urgency and focus that is missing from much of the recent Western work written from within orthodox Marxist frameworks.

16

Resurrecting Marxism

DAVID MARSH

Some claim that Marxism is dead and the list of potential killers is quite long, although possible collaboration between them is not denied. The collapse of communism, the triumph of capitalism, New Right ideology and postmodernism have all been credited with a hand in the quick death of Marxism. There is certainly no doubt that Marxism is in crisis to the extent that it is out of fashion; even university sociology degrees these days are likely to feature more courses drawing on postmodernist thought than on Marxism. At the same time, many intellectual Marxists have changed their position, again often embracing post modernism and pluralism. However, as Andrew Gamble emphasised in Chapter 1, such crises are not new. Marxism, like other theories, has always developed in this way, responding to intellectual challenges from sympathisers as well as critics and attempting to explain and understand changes in the social world which it is analysing. Nevertheless there are some important questions which this book has addressed. How well is Marxism responding to this challenge? Is it still a coherent position? Is it still a relevant position?

This book analyses how Marxism engages with various critiques, including postmodernism, New Right theory and feminism, and illuminates substantive issues such as the state, culture, ecology and globalisation. In this conclusion, it will be argued that (i) Marxism is a thriving tradition, which has evolved in response to criticism and to changes in the 'real' world; (ii) although there are many variants of Marxism it does have a coherent core, which centres around a rejection of economism and determinism and a commitment to realism as an epistemological position; (iii) it still has great utility as a critical analytical framework, and the collapse of communism and, even more importantly, the changes which have occurred in capitalist society, have revitalised, rather than diminished, its role.

A Thriving Tradition?

Marxism has changed out of all recognition in the last twenty years. Classical Marxism was questioned not only by non-Marxists, but also by Marxists. This led to a rejection of economism, determinism and structuralism. This section looks at the problems of classical Marxism and at the critiques which have been made of it. The second section will then examine the recent developments within Marxism which respond to those critiques.

The Problems of Classical Marxism

The history of twentieth century Marxism can be seen in terms of a struggle with economism, determinism and structuralism. Of course all these 'isms' are crucially connected. Economism emphasises that economic relations determine social and political relations and, thus, focuses on structural explanation, allowing very little space for agency.

Certainly Marx's analysis of capitalism concentrated upon the economy, which analytically he separated out from everything else. He saw it as inevitable that political institutions, laws, belief systems, and even the family, would conform to the basic requirements of the economic system. So the main function of the law was to protect private property and, as such, the state was an agent of the ruling class. The economy thus caused or determined how the rest of the social system evolved and functioned. This formulation is clear in the 'Preface to a Contribution to a Critique of Political Economy' (1859):

> In the social production of their life, men enter into definite relations that are indispensable and independent of their will; relations of production that correspond to a definitive stage of development of their material productive forces. The sum total of these relations of production constitutes the economic structure of society, the real foundation, on which rises a legal and political superstructure and to which correspond definitive forms of social consciousness. The mode of production of material life conditions the social, political and intellectual life process in general. It is not

the consciousness of men that determines their being, but on the contrary, their social being that determines their consciousness.

Here, the economic 'base' determines the 'superstructure' and agents have little, if any, autonomy; the mode of production of material life determines consciousness. Of course, Marx's work was not always as economistic, determinist and structuralist and in the 1970s and 1980s there was an industry in interpreting or 'reading' Marx. At the same time, there were Marxists who opposed economism throughout the century, particularly, although certainly not exclusively, within the Second International; here Kautsky, Lukács and, especially, Gramsci are crucial. However, there is no doubt that the 'base/superstructure' model dominated readings of Marx for most of the first two-thirds of this century and it was this view that most of its adherents took and its opponents attacked.

Such formulations are now almost universally rejected by Marxists. There are three broad reasons for this change. First, Marxists have responded to theoretical critiques from both inside and outside the Marxist tradition. Second, such an economistic formulation has proved unable to explain economic, social and political developments. Third, economic, social and political changes in the world have stimulated new theoretical development. Obviously we can only deal with these three points briefly here.

Theoretical Critiques

Marxism has constantly been under challenge and critique from within and outside the tradition. If we consider the internal critiques first, and take the development of Marxist state theory as an example, the point is easily made. As Hay shows, the work of Gramsci was crucial. Gramsci's emphasis upon the role of political or hegemonic struggle, the importance of ideology and the significance of agents, in his case parties, worker's councils and intellectuals, marked a break with economism, determinism and structuralism and such themes have been taken up and developed in modern Marxist state theory. Gramsci was influenced by some of the non-economistic arguments within the Second International, but it is also worth emphasising that he drew upon the tradition of Italian social and political thinking which goes back to Machiavelli. Subsequently, and this point is again well made by Hay, the work of Poulantzas, and particularly his attempt to theorise the relative autonomy of the state, was also crucial in the development of Marxist state theory. In both cases, modern Marxists, taking issue with the Marxist orthodoxy, have moved the debate on the theory of the state significantly forward.

It is equally easy to illustrate the influence on Marxism of critiques from outside that tradition. So, as an example, Johnston and Dolowitz show how Weberian ideas on class have influenced contemporary Marxist theory. Similarly, Jackson shows the way in which feminist critiques have influenced Marxist analyses of gender and Barry shows how Marxism has responded to ecological arguments. Jackson's argument is particularly interesting as it has broader resonance. Feminist thought has had a significant influence across the broad gamut of Marxist theory. As an example, it has strongly affected Marxist state theory. Feminism raises important questions about the definition of politics, revolving particularly around the distinction between the public and the private and the nature and sites of political power. In addition, it emphasises that gender is a, perhaps the, key basis of structured inequality which is reflected in definitions of politics and the nature and exercise of power. As Jackson shows, Marxist or socialist feminists attempt to incorporate class and gender into their analysis. However, more significantly, most Marxist theorists not directly concerned with gender (see, for example, Jessop, 1982) have also acknowledged that gender is a crucial basis of structured inequality which cannot be reduced to class and which is reflected in the form and actions of the state.

Explaining Economic, Social and Political Change

Of course, one of the major reasons both for the theoretical critique of classical Marxism and for its resonance was that economism, determinism and structuralism did not offer a convincing explanation of economic, social and political developments. Empirical analysis indicated that economic relations of production did not *determine* culture and ideology or the form and actions of the state. So, for example, developed capitalist countries at similar stages of economic development and with comparable relations of production had different, more or less democratic or authoritarian, state forms. Similarly, any examination of the politics of capitalist states showed that policy decisions did not always and clearly advance the interests of the owners and controllers of capital. States clearly had autonomy, even though such autonomy was constrained, and, increasingly, Marxists aimed to theorise that autonomy, first by developing the concept of relative autonomy and, subsequently, by dropping notions of deter-minancy altogether.

The Effect of Economic, Social and Political Change

It is also clear that economic, social and political change has had a major effect on the development of Marxism. At the economic level, the changes in advanced capitalism since Marx wrote have been phenomenal. Most important has probably been the internationalisa-tion of capitalism. The current vogue is to talk of globalisation as though it has sprung upon us, and also to overestimate its effects in a way which has strong economistic overtones, but that is the subject of another paper. However the British economy at least has had a strong international orientation throughout the twentieth century and, in-deed, many have argued that the international orientation of the British banking/financial sector has been a major cause of Britain's relative economic decline. Be that as it may, and accepting the point that the constraint that globalisation exercises on government policy can be overestimated, it is nevertheless clear that such developments have, as both Bromley and Kenny show, led to a major reinterpreta-tion of Marxist political economy.

Social change has also clearly shaped the development of Marxism. Here, we will take just two illustrative examples. First, changes in the social structure, including the growth of the public sector, the decline of the manufacturing sector, the rise of white-collar employment and the increase in the female labour force, have all had a significant affect on the Marxist conceptualisation of class, as is clear from Johnston and Dolowitz's chapter. Second, the changing role of women, which owes something to economic changes but also much to the growth of feminism, has provided a major stimulus to Marxism's attempt to conceptualise more adequately the role of gender.

Political changes have also played a role. For a long period Marxist analysis of politics was affected by the situation in the Soviet Union. For over fifty years, most Marxists felt it necessary to defend political practice in the Soviet Union. In addition, many Marxist intellectuals in Europe were attached to Communist parties with close links to Moscow and few questioned Moscow hegemony; although even here there were exceptions, so that the PCI (the Communist Party of Italy) took a more independent line even from 1945. As a consequence, few Marxist intellectuals wrote about politics and Ralph Miliband could claim when he published *The State and Capitalist Society* in 1968 that it was the first Marxist account of the state since Lenin's *The State and Revolution*. This claim ignored Gramsci's work, but nevertheless had some validity. The death of Stalin in 1953 and the invasion of Hungary in 1956 were important events which led some Marxist intellectuals to question the practice of the Soviet Union and the next decades saw individuals and even domestic Communist parties follow this road, moving away both from unquestioning support of the Soviet Union and from the ideological economism imposed by Moscow.

Here again it seems that the work of Gramsci was crucial. Stalin failed to stop him thinking heretical thoughts, but Mussolini imprisoned him for over ten years. As a consequence, his major work, *The Prison Notebooks* (1971), was not published in Italy until after the Second World War and only became widely available over the next two decades; indeed they had virtually no influence in the English-speaking world until they were published by Lawrence & Wishart in 1971. Then, given the social and political changes there had been, and given the poverty of Marxist economism, they found a receptive audience.

A Coherent Position?

Marxism is a living theoretical tradition. We cannot find all truth in the work of a German intellectual writing 150 years ago, but Marxism is a rich tradition and one which has undergone substantial change as it has struggled to reject economism, determinism and structuralism. Any critic of Marxism must confront these modern variants rather than setting up a more economistic view as a straw man.

At the same time, Marxism is a broad tradition; in an important sense we no longer have Marxism but Marxisms and this volume indicates that different authors, who in different ways acknowledge their debt to the Marxist tradition, use that tradition in significantly different ways. So, for example, Tant advances an argument which many other authors in this collection would find problematic; he reassesses the claim that Marxism can be viewed as scientific, in the light of contemporary definitions of science. In contrast, Daly would reject any such claim, instead arguing that the world is discursively constructed and that, as such, there is no objective truth 'out there' to be discovered. To him both science and Marxism are discursive constructs. As such, Marxism is a discourse which can be used as an element in the construction of an emancipatory hegemonic project.

However Daly's view, which has postmodernist overtones, would hold little resonance for McMahon, who argues strongly against post-Marxist, postmodernist, interpretations of culture. At the same time, Jackson's view is different again. She argues that we need to develop a materialist feminism which acknowledges its Marxist antecedents and takes from the Marxist tradition its emphasis upon the existence of crucial structural, and material, inequalities which constrain the actions of agents.

Despite the diversity which exists within modern Marxism, its broad response to the critiques and changes already identified is clear. In this section two themes will be developed. First, we argue that, in contrast to its classical variants, most modern Marxism rejects economism; rejects determinancy, emphasising contingency; rejects structuralism, accepting a key role for agents; no longer privileges class, acknowledging the crucial role of other bases of structured inequality; and, to an extent, privileges politics. All these developments will be illustrated by a brief consideration of the changes in Marxist state theory over the last thirty years. Second, we contend that almost all Marxists broadly share a realist epistemological position, that is, a view of the status of knowledge, although, as we will see, this epistemological position has changed over time, again in response to criticism. In both cases there are exceptions. So there are some Marxists, like Cohen (1978) or Geras (1988), who still embrace major aspects of economism, and perhaps even more Marxists who flirt very heavily with relativism, although most of the latter, like Daly, would regard themselves as post-Marxists. Nevertheless, it is the contention of the present writer, which will not be shared by all Marxists, that these two themes reflect the core of contemporary Marxism.

In Praise of Flexibility, Contingency and Politics

In the 1970s, Poulantzas' (1969) formulation of the relative autonomy of the state was seized upon by Marxists trying to escape economism because it allowed the state autonomy while retaining the determinance of economic relations in the last instance. Poulantzas' conceptualisation had strong functionalist undertones. The state needed relative autonomy to advance the interests of 'capital in general'. More specifically it: (i) mediated between the interests of the different fractions of capital (for example, preventing or defusing conflict between industrial and banking capital); (ii) mediated between classes in order to reduce the class tensions inevitable in a capitalist society (for example, by ensuring welfare state provision and manipulating ideology); and (iii) intervened in economic relations (for example, by establishing corporatist structures which incorporated labour in order to emasculate it).

In Poulantzas' view, the state enshrines class interests because its form reflects the outcome of past class struggles, a process Poulantzas calls 'structural selectivity'. In addition the state knows best what is in the interest of capital and any concessions to other social forces, even if they are opposed by capital, are designed to advance the long-term interests of capital in general, if necessary as against the interest of particular capitals.

There are considerable problems with this conceptualisation, even if we reject the Popperian, positivist, notion that the theory is non-falsifiable because the last instance never comes. First, Poulantzas offers no explanation of how the state knows best and no exposition of the mechanisms by which this knowledge is achieved. What is more, it is perhaps easier to point to examples of state failure than to examples of state success in economic management. Second, the theory is still essentially economistic and deterministic, if only in the last instance. The concept of structural selectivity merely moves the economic determinancy back temporally; the outcome of past class struggles is reflected in the present state form and political outcomes. Third, Poulantzas still privileges social class and ignores the fact that the state reflects gender and race inequality as well as class inequality. Fourth, the position is structuralist; there is little or no space for agency.

Jessop's response (1982) to these criticism offers an excellent example of the way modern Marxism has attempted to move away from economism, determinism and structuralism. He develops the concept of strategic selectivity as an alternative to Poulantzas' concept of structural selectivity (Poulantzas, 1978). To Jessop the state form is inscribed with the outcomes of past strategic struggles between social forces. There are two immediately obvious differences between the two concepts. First, Jessop talks of strategy which implies calculating subjects. Structures do not determine outcomes; agents are not simply bearers of structures. Rather the relationship is dialectical; structures constrain and facilitate agents whose actions constitute and reconstitute the structures. Second, class is not privileged. Instead it is acknowledged that gender, race, knowledge and so on are crucial bases of structured inequality which are inscribed in the state and which shape, while not determining, its actions.

At the same time, Jessop's approach also highlights the three other developments mentioned earlier. Most fundamentally, he rejects economism and determinism by arguing that no theory of the state is possible and, consequently, outcomes are contingent. In Jessop's view the concept of relative autonomy is untenable; the state is autonomous and the extent to which its actions are constrained by the outcome of past strategic struggles is an open question. To Jessop then, a state may be a capitalist state, advancing the interests of capital, but such a relationship is contingent, not necessary, and is a matter for empirical investigation, not theoretical assertion. In addition, Jessop, like much of modern Marxism, is essentially politicist. This does not mean that he takes the state as a starting point for any analysis; rather his notion of strategic selectivity suggests that the form and actions of the state are the product of hegemonic, and essentially political, struggles. Obviously this development is even clearer in post-Marxist writers such as Laclau and Mouffe (1985; see Daly, above).

Overall, then, modern Marxism is characterised by diversity, but most Marxists share a rejection of economism, determinism and structuralism. Of course it might be argued, and indeed has been argued, that the modern variants are no longer Marxist precisely because they reject economism, the primacy of class and the Marxist theory of history. If one defines Marxism in such narrow terms then this assertion is true by definition. However, Marxists like Jessop take the work of Marx and others in the Marxist tradition as their point of departure and, in so doing, are Marxists. Similarly, some would argue that the diversity of approaches within Marxism is a weakness, that there is now no such thing as a Marxist position. On the contrary, this is rather a strength. Marxism has developed considerable flexibility in response to both criticisms and changes in the 'real' world; its utility should be judged in terms of its capacity to help us explain and understand those changes.

In Praise of Realism

Most Marxists are realists in epistemological terms, although there have been major changes in this position over time, largely as a response to relativist critiques of the sort discussed by Daly. The core of Marx's own classical realist epistemology lies in three propositions (for a fuller discussion see Furlong and Marsh, 2000, forthcoming): (i) unlike the relativist who believes that the world is socially constructed, the realist shares with the positivist the view that the world exists independently of our knowledge of it; (ii) to the realist, however, unlike the positivist, many of the relationships between social phenomena in which we are interested cannot be directly observed; (iii) unlike the relativist, and in common with the positivist, the realist believes there is necessity in the world; so social phenomena do have causal powers and we can make causal statements.

The epistemological position of most modern Marxists, however, would also rest on two other propositions which, while in some readings they can be traced back to the work of Marx, owe a great deal to relativist critiques. First, unlike positivists, while they acknowledge that social phenomena exist independently of our interpretation, they acknowledge, *pace* relativism, that it is our interpretation and understanding of these social phenomena which affects outcomes; the production and interpretation of knowledge is theory-laden. Second, and consequently, structures do not determine the actions of agents, rather they constrain and facilitate them. Social science involves the study of reflexive agents and these agents can deconstruct and reconstruct structures.

This is not the place to examine the validity and problems of this epistemological position; here, we merely wish to argue both that this shared epistemological position informs Marxist analysis and that most Marxists, as such, share a similar approach to some of the key problems in social science. Modern Marxists acknowledge that there is an external world which is independent of our knowledge of it and that the discursive construction of this external world has a crucial effect on political outcomes, but that the nature of this external world constrains and/or facilitates that construction.

The position is easily illustrated if we take as an example the phenomenon of globalisation which has become increasingly important in British politics over the past two decades. As far as the critical realist is concerned, there are real processes of globalisation going on but it is the discursive construction of these processes which has shaped policy. So, there has been an increase in the internationalisation of trade and the flexibility of capital and there has been a globalisation of American culture and an increase in the ease of global communication and the role of the global media. Of course, there are significant arguments about the extent of that globalisation, but there is little doubt that some has occurred. At the same time, however, the way that globalisation affects national policy making is mediated by its discursive construction by economists, businessmen and politicians particularly. In the British case, for example, the extent of globalisation, using the usual economic measures, is not as great as the dominant rhetoric about globalisation suggests, yet this rhetoric, rather than the reality, has shaped government economic policy over the last decade (see Watson, 1999, forthcoming). Nevertheless the logic of the position is that the gap between the reality and the dominant discursive construction allows space for the construction of an alternative discourse which, in the long run, would have more resonance to the extent that it more accurately reflected that reality.

This critical realist position underpins much of modern Marxism's approach to key problems in social science. This point will be illustrated with reference to two issues, the relationship between structure and agency and the relationship between the material and the ideational, drawing upon recent debates about British politics.

A Dialectical Approach to the Structure/Agency Problem
The structure/agency debate is one of the most crucial within social science (for an excellent discussion of this literature, see Hay, 1995). However there is a tendency throughout the social sciences for authors to favour structural or agency explanations. The literature on Thatcherism amply illustrates the point: a large amount of material explains change in this period to a large extent in terms of the role of Margaret Thatcher (see Marsh, 1995). She was a strong, decisive, leader with a definite ideological position and some strongly held policy preferences. As such, she broke the mould of British politics, moving Britain away from the postwar consensus towards a market-dominated economy, less state intervention and more self-reliance. In a sense, this view was well summed up in the two slogans beloved of Thatcher and many analysts, particularly in her first two terms: 'The Lady's Not for Turning' and 'There is No Alternative'. In contrast, many analysts give priority to structural factors. For example, many argue that Thatcherism was a response to economic crisis; that the move towards privatisation and the market represented an attempt to restore capitalist profitability after the failure of Keynesianism and corporatist policies.

This is not the place to analyse such contentions. However, such explanations suffer from the fact that they take a simplistic approach to the relationship between structure and agency. In contrast, Marxist critical realism views the relationship between structure and agency as dialectical. Agents are, in a sense, 'bearers' of structural positions, but they interpret those structures. At the same time, structures are not unchanging, they change in part because of the strategic decisions of the agents within the structure. Certainly outcomes cannot be explained solely by reference to structures; they are the result of the actions of strategically calculating agents. However, those agents are located within a political and broader social–structural context. Significantly, agents do not control that structured context. At the same time, they do interpret that context and it is as mediated through that interpretation that the structural context affects the strategic calculation of the actors.

This dialectical view has significant implications for the interpretation of Thatcherism; it argues against partiality in both senses of the word. First, it emphasises that any analysis must consider change over a considerable period of time, as a dialectical approach necessitates a longitudinal analysis; it cannot take a partial snapshot of one brief period. So, any analysis of Thatcherism which does not trace how it emerged over time cannot assess the interaction between structural factors, like the nature of economic relations, and agency factors, like the role of Thatcher. Second, it emphasises that we need to examine the interaction between economic, political and ideological factors; we cannot undertake a partial or unidimensional analysis.

The Material and the Ideational

There are analyses of postwar British political economy which emphasise material factors, while others stress ideational factors. The literature on Britain's relative economic decline amply illustrates this point (see Johnston, 1999). A number of authors see decline as an inevitable result of capitalist crisis, of the tendency for the rate of profit to fall under capitalism. Here the material relations lead to decline and are not affected by any ideational representation of that crisis. In contrast, others see decline as a response to the peculiarities of the British culture; the cultural construction of the British elite involved, among other things, a devaluing of the competitive ethic which affected economic performance. Of course, some other authors would see the effect of the two sets of factors as additive; that is, decline resulted from a combination of material and ideational factors.

In contrast, Marxist critical realists would conceptualise outcomes as a result of an interactive, or again dialectical, relationship between the two. The material world does have an affect, but it is mediated through its ideational construction and that affects the material world. So, there may be an economic crisis, which we can establish by reference to broadly agreed economic indicators. However, such a crisis only has an effect on economic policy to the extent that it is perceived as being a crisis by key political and economic actors and in a way which reflects the nature of that discursive construction. What is more, that discursive construction will have an influence on the crisis, as measured by these indicators. For example, investors may disappear as the result of a decline in business confidence. In addition, the decisions taken by economic policy makers will probably also affect the crisis. Overall, then, the outcome reflects the ideational construction of the material and that outcome, in turn, affects the material level, which is then discursively constructed, and so on.

What Has Marxism to Offer?

If we equate Marxism with historical materialism, economism, determinism and structuralism then it has little to offer. However, if we acknowledge Marx's own work as the source of a rich, varied and immanent critical tradition, the answer is much more positive. Purvis makes the point very well (see above p. 233):

> [If we see] Marxism as concerned with elucidating the material conditions of social emancipation, not only from relations of class oppression, but from other forms as well, such as national, colonial, cultural, linguistic, racial, gender, sexual and ethnic, then Marxism seems assured a vital future, and its capacity to inform broader sociopolitical debates seems secure.

The emphasis here is on three crucial points. First, Marxism offers an explanation of how and why the capitalist system is prone to periodic crises which offer space for alternative political projects. Second, it also shows how and why society is characterised by structured inequality and how that structured inequality constrains and facilitates outcomes; this is perhaps the key feature of contemporary capitalism and needs to be explained. Third, in normative terms it denounces this inequality and the exploitation it produces. In addition, it asserts that something can be done about it. As Marx himself said in the *Theses on Fuerbach*: 'The Philosophers have only interpreted the world, in various ways; the point however is to change it.' Marxism at its best is a humanity-centred and activist philosophy. As Worsley (1982, p. 119) argues, it contains a vision of ending 'a long stretch of human history in which the exploitation of many has been possible because the few have monopolised the means of production'.

The contributions to this volume have indicated what the Marxist tradition has to offer both in engagement with other theoretical traditions and as an approach to various substantive issues. However, many would still argue that it is in decline, in part because of the collapse of the Soviet Union, the triumph of New Right ideology and modern changes in capitalism. It is possible to take issue with those claims. First, the collapse of the Soviet Union removes a constraint on Marxism, the need to justify development in central and eastern Europe, which was very damaging to the development of Marxism for most of this century. Second, the changes in modern capitalism, which have resulted in the current economic crisis and related increases in inequality, make the Marxist explanation and critique more relevant. These points are important enough to deserve brief consideration.

Marxism and Post-communism

There is no need to deal with this issue at any length because it is the focus of Robinson's chapter. However it is important to reiterate one of Robinson's main conclusions (see above, p. 317):

> It is thus ironic that Marxist analysis of post-communism might actually be very healthy. The collapse of the communist states frees Marxists from the need continually to go over old and stale ground. Interest in the changes in the former Soviet Union and eastern Europe is attracting Marxist, neo-Marxist and post-Marxist scholars who were not involved in the earlier debates and faction fights . . . There are also signs of a critical Marxism developing in the East which might eventually help refresh analysis.

The point here is both that the collapse of communism frees Marxism from an inhibiting legacy and that, at the same time, it offers fruitful new fields of study.

The Current Capitalist Crisis and the Challenge to Neo-Liberalism

At the international level, the last two decades have witnessed the rise of neo-liberal discourse to a position of dominance and, against this background, critical discourses have found it difficult to find any space or resonance. Neo-liberal ideas and US-style capitalism seemed to have carried all before them; indeed, many talked of the end of ideology, and even the end of history, as all apparently converged towards a view which suggested that the market was a good and the state a bad, the private good and the public bad. Fortunately, there is abundant evidence that unfettered capitalism causes more problems than it solves and, while the neo-liberal discourse continues to dominate, there are signs that it, too, is likely to be questioned.

The current global financial crisis began in Pacific Asia. It started in Thailand in late 1997 when a mixture of internal economic problems and imprudent engagement with the free-wheeling Western financial system resulted in a run on the local currency and a collapse of the local stock market. However, the crisis now threatens to spread systemic instability. From Thailand, the financial contagion swept on to embrace South Korea and Indonesia. As the financial panic continued to run through the region it became clear that even the mighty Japanese economy was in trouble. A widespread regional economic downturn ensued which has had severe political conse-quences and has caused extensive social dislocation, with millions in the poorer countries thrown into poverty.

Initially, the crisis was dismissed in the West as a peculiarity of Asian capitalism and, indeed, was seen by some observers as offering a opportunity to force the structures of the Asian economies more into line with those of the West. However, the crisis soon spread to all those areas of the global economy which Western investment bankers have defined as 'emerging markets'. The Russian currency collapsed and the country's banks defaulted on foreign loans, to be followed by Brazil, the most powerful of the Latin American economies. It was at this point that alarm bells finally began to ring in the capital cities of the metropolitan capitalist heartlands of the West.

In Asia it was primarily Japanese and EU banks which were exposed; in Russia almost exclusively banks from EU countries. However, in Brazil and Latin America it was US banks which were heavily committed. At this stage, Washington, the home of neo-liberalism and the base from which the US government had endeavoured, in the years following the end of the Cold War, to organise global neo-liberal settlement became seriously concerned (see, Sachs, 1998). Doubts were also beginning to be expressed in respect of the technical competence of the financial institutions of Western capitalism, the World Bank and the International Monetary Fund (Wade and Venerosa, 1998).

Nevertheless, perhaps the collapse of the giant hedge-fund, the Long-Term Capital Management Fund (LTCMF: the irony of this name hardly needs emphasising), is the best reflection of the state of contemporary capitalism. Hedge-funds were devised to ensure that big players in the international currency market can't lose: if we are living through a period of casino capitalism, hedge-funds attempt to fix the roulette wheel so the big players don't lose. The LTCMF involved two Nobel Prize economists and a supposedly foolproof system. It lost, or more accurately gambled away, $100 billion dollars and had to be bailed out by the US government.

Of course, even if there is an economic – and, in particular, a financial – crisis this does not mean that the dominant discourse will quickly and inevitably be undermined. However, not only are world markets currently far from the state of equilibrium predicted by neo-classical economics, but the credibility of the international institutions which have done much to promote neo-liberal orthodoxy – notably the World Bank and the IMF – has been destroyed. Even *The Times*, hardly a radical newspaper, claimed that 'the IMF reputation has sunk to its lowest since the body was set up ... in 1944' (quoted in Hobsbawm, 1998, p. 4).

Actually, it seems to me that not only the creditability of the World Bank and the IMF, but also the whole of the dominant neo-liberal discourse, is under threat. As Kaletsky (1998, p. 30) puts it:

> All over the world extreme free market ideology is now in retreat and is likely to retreat much further in the years ahead. The reason is obvious. Even though global capitalism will recover from the present crisis, the ideological claim that markets work best when left to their own devices has been exposed as a myth. Capitalist economies do not automatically maintain full employment. Instead of relegating politics to the sidelines and mandating minimal government, advanced capitalism requires conscious management by government, central banks and international regulators in order to prosper or even perhaps to survive. Without a certain amount of government intervention, global capitalism generates booms, busts and crises. As for unfettered financial markets, it is simply risible to claim they can always be relied on to allocate resources in an optimal, or even in a prudent, way. In short, the global financial crisis is exposing the 'magic of the market' as a myth.

This view is endorsed by the person who has probably benefitted most from playing the financial markets, George Soros. He argues:

> Unless we review our concept of markets, our understanding of markets, they will collapse, we are creating global markets without understanding their true nature ... We need some international

regulation to match the globalisation of markets. Because what is lacking is the ability of society to impose constraints on the market. (Giddens and Pierson, 1998, pp. 225–6)

At the same time, Soros recognises (p. 225) that the global competition which characterises contemporary capitalism is socially divisive: 'with the accumulation of wealth there comes increased social division and the majority of people don't benefit from the global economy'. More specifically (p. 223), he argues:

> What global competition has done has been to benefit capital at the expense of labour, and to benefit financial capital to the detriment of fixed investments. Because capital is more mobile than labour, and financial capital is the most mobile of all, more mobile than direct investment.

In the context of increased evidence of the weaknesses, and even the contradictions, of contemporary capitalism, there appears to be a growing space for radical socialist ideas, and indeed more radical politics, and Marxism can, indeed must, contribute to this renewed debate.

The Increase of Structured Inequality

At the domestic level there can be little doubt that developed capitalist countries are characterised by structured inequality or, indeed, that in many it has increased over the last two decades. This section briefly considers three key bases of structured inequality, class, gender and race, in the British context (for a fuller discussion, see Marsh, 1997); however there is evidence that such structured inequality is a characteristic of most modern societies. Of course, the effect of these three structures on political outcomes is mediated through both education and knowledge and access to political power. So, although there is no simple relationship between social structural factors and political outcomes, these patterns of structured inequality are reflected in access to the three key resources actors use in trying to shape political outcomes: money, knowledge and political power. My argument is not a determinist one; rather it is contended that these factors interact to constrain and facilitate, that is to shape, political outcomes and that modern Marxism, unlike more mainstream approaches such as pluralism, focuses on these structural constraints, thus offering more interesting insight into explaining the operation of modern capitalism.

In Britain, structured inequality is clearly reflected in each of these three resource dimensions. There are significant inequalities of wealth and income: in 1994, the most wealthy 10% of the population owned 48% of the marketable wealth and the figure rose to 63% if the value of houses was not included (see Marsh, 1997). In addition, these inequalities have increased significantly in the last two decades. Thus, the Rowntree *Inquiry into Income in Welfare* (1995) found that between 1977 and 1990 there was rising inequality in France, West Germany, Norway, Australia, Holland, Japan, the USA, Britain and New Zealand. More specifically only in New Zealand was the rise greater than in Britain. Indeed, during Thatcher's tenure in Downing Street, average income rose by 36%, but the income of the bottom 10% fell by 14% ,while that of the top 10% rose by 64%. It is also clear that these inequalities in wealth and income are related to gender and race. So, for example, the average earnings of women in Britain in 1995 were 72% of those of men, while the average wage of non-manual women was only 64% of non-manual men (see Marsh, 1997).

At the same time, although there is considerable debate about the concept of an underclass, there is certainly a significant section of the population which is caught in a poverty trap. The British government's own figures show that 14% of the population (eight million) is totally dependent on welfare. Similar figures show 24% of the population living in poverty, 17% receiving income support, 19% of households with no working adults, and so it goes on. Children from such backgrounds do much worse at school, are one and a half times more likely to have a long-standing illness and twice as likely to have a disability. They are much more likely to be black and women who are lone parents: for example, between 1979 and 1993 the proportion of lone parents in poverty in Britain increased from 19% to 58% (see Marsh, 1997).

Of course there is social mobility, but while there is evidence to suggest that it is greater now than previously (see Saunders, 1996; and, for a critique of this work, Marshall *et al.*, 1997), it is still limited. In particular, upward social mobility is more common than downward social mobility. Origins still shape, but do not determine, destinations.

Structured inequality is also reflected in education. The English public school system is a clear bastion of privilege as is Oxbridge, and here figures are hardly necessary. In a less extreme form the education system generally reflects similar patterns of privilege. Working class children are less likely to stay on at school or to attend university. As far as race is concerned, Asian achievement is very similar to that of whites, but blacks are only a third as likely to obtain 'O' and 'A' levels or to go to university as other groups. In contrast, the educational achievement of men and women is similar. Here one of the chief differences is in subjects studied, with some researchers arguing that the fact is that boys are much more likely to study maths and science, a choice which benefits them on the labour market (see Marsh, 1997).

Moving to access to positions of political power, the underrepresentation of the working class, women and blacks in the political elite hardly needs demonstrating, although the percentage of women in the House of Commons has increased significantly since the 1997 election. The dominant political elites in Britain are overwhelmingly white, male and middle class, if not by birth, then by education (see Marsh, 1997).

A similar pattern exists in the United States. In 1976 the wealthiest 1% of America owned 19% of all the private material wealth in the United States. By 1995 they owned 40% of the wealth and their share is greater than that owned by the bottom 92% of the population combined (see Wolff, 1995). While average earnings have risen, inequalities of earnings have grown much faster. So, between 1979 and 1995, the bottom 60% of the population saw their incomes decrease. The income of the next 20% showed modest gains, while the top 20% saw an 18% increase in income (see United for a Fair Economy Website, http://www.stw.org.html/popular-education). Most dramatically, the income of the wealthiest 1% grew by 92% (see Wolff, 1995). One consequence has been an increase in poverty. In 1996 the US Census reported 14% of the population in poverty; up from 9% in 1972 because of the erosion of welfare programmes.

These inequalities are strongly related to gender and race. So in 1995 the Census reported that female average earnings were only 58% of male average earnings while black average earnings were 75% and hispanic 66% of white average earnings.

In the US, structured inequality is also reflected in access to education and political positions. So, in 1996 while 83% of whites had completed 4 years of high school, the same level had been reached by 74% of blacks and only 53% of hispanics. In education terms the difference between the sexes was negligible. Education was in turn related to income; those without a high school education earned less than half of average earnings. As far as access to positions of political power are concerned, women fare particularly badly in the United States. Women make up only 22% of the membership of State legislatures; there have only been 174 female members of Congress in its history to date; there are currently 55 female members of the 105th Congress; while the only two women who have been Supreme Court Justices are currently among the nine encumbents. In racial terms, blacks and hispanics are also significantly under-represented at federal level; so there were only 37 blacks in the House of Representatives in 1997–8 and 1 in the Senate (*Congressional Quarterly Almanac*, 1998).

Thus, there can be little doubt that there is a persistent structural inequality which is reflected in access to money, knowledge and power; and these are the key resources used in the struggle for political influence. This structural inequality provides actors with various structural possibilities, but any explanation of the outcomes must be in terms of both those structural possibilities and the strategic calculations of the actors. In addition, if we are to understand the operation of contemporary capitalism we need to: (i) acknowledge that structured inequality exists; (ii) examine how it is reflected in the balance between social forces in society, the resources available to political agents and the institutions and processes of governance; (iii) recognise that there are a variety of structural constraints which cannot be reduced to one and which, while they may reinforce one another, may also be contradictory; and (iv) recognise that these are constraints, not determinants. Agents operate within these constraints but their knowledge of these constraints is contingent; they have knowledge of a number of different constraints relevant to them; this knowledge is mediated by frames of meaning or discourses; they are reflexive, so the relationship is not mechanical – rather the actors strategically calculate their interests given their knowledge of the constraints; and, finally, agents affect structures.

The main point here is that, while such structural inequalities have always existed, they are more evident in a society like Britain as a result of the changes of the last two decades. Of course, Marxism is not the only theoretical position which can account for the continuance and even increase in structured inequality; radical Weberianism also has much to offer. However the move away from economism, determinism and structuralism means that modern Marxists are confronting the issues raised here in a way that more mainstream social science is not. Certainly, as Glaser argues, Marxism is particularly well placed to identify both the inequalities in society and the consequences of these inequalities for democracy. Similarly, as Pierson contends, Marxism offers particular insights into the way in which the problems of the modern welfare state are underpinned by the nature of modern capitalism, We need to acknowledge, and build upon, such insights.

In Conclusion

This book is to an extent a polemic. It has argued that Marxism still has a great deal to offer to social scientists. Marxists have continued to confront their critics from within and outside that tradition. Marxism is a vibrant and developing tradition; it is also a broad church. This book demonstrates that fact as the contributors engage with Marxism to different extents and in differing ways. Most importantly, Marxism is a crucial perspective because it focuses upon the problems of capitalism and upon structured inequality which is the key feature of modern society at both the national and the international level. Finally, for all those who believe that the purpose of social science is not just to understand society but also to change it, it offers an agenda and a series of putative ways forward which we do not have to accept, but with which we should engage. Such engagement is particularly important at present because we live in times which have been dominated by the discourse of the market; the cry abroad is that what is good for ICI or Ford or Nissan is good for Britain, the USA or Japan. However, while the 'haves' benefit from the dominance of this discourse, the 'have-nots' suffer. It is therefore crucial for all those who believe in a more just and equitable society to challenge this discourse, to assert and demonstrate that such large inequalities are destructive to the social fabric of a democratic society. Marxism can help in that struggle both because it identifies and attempts to explain structured inequality and because it is emancipatory, holding out the hope of something better.

Bibliography

Adams, Parveen, Beverley Brown and Elizabeth Cowie (1978), 'Editorial' *m/f*, 2: 3–5.

Adams, Parveen, Rosalind Coward and Elizabeth Cowie (1978), 'Editorial' *m/f*, 1: 3–5.

Adkins, Lisa (1995), *Gendered Work: Sexuality, Family and the Labour Market* (Milton Keynes: Open University Press).

Adkins, Lisa and Diana Leonard (1995), *Sex in Question: French Feminism* (London: Taylor & Francis).

Adorno, T. and M. Horkheimer (1972), *Dialectic of Enlightenment* (New York: Herder and Herder).

Aglietta, M. (1979), *A Theory of Capitalist Regulation* (London: New Left Books).

Ali, T. (1988), *Revolution from Above: where is the Soviet Union going?* (London: Hutchinson).

Allen, J. (1990), 'Does Feminism Need a Theory of the State?', in S. Watson (ed.), *Playing the State: Australian Feminist Intervention* (London: Verso).

Almond, G. and L. Roselle (1989), 'Model fitting in communist studies', in T.H. Remington (ed.), *Politics and the Soviet System* (Basingstoke: Macmillan).

Althusser, L. (1969), *For Marx* (London: Allen Lane).

Althusser, L. (1974), *Essays in Self-Criticism* (London: New Left Books).

Althusser, L. (1985), 'Ideology and ideological state apparatuses', in V. Beechey and J. Donald (eds), *Subjectivity and Social Relations* (Milton Keynes: Open University).

Althusser, L. and E. Balibar (1970), *Reading 'Capital'* (London: New Left Books).

Altvater, E. (1973), 'Notes on Some Problems of State Interventionalism', *Kapitalistate,* 1: 97–108; 2: 76–83.

Amin, A. (1994), 'Post-Fordism: Models, Fantasies and Phantoms of Transition', in A. Amin (ed.), *Post-Fordism: A Reader* (Oxford: Blackwell).

Anderson, B. (1991), *Imagined Communities: Reflections on the Origin and Spread of Nationalism* (rev. edn) (London and New York: Verso).

Anderson, B. (1992), 'The New World Disorder', *New Left Review*, 193 (May/June): 3–13.

Anderson, B. (1994), 'Exodus', *Critical Inquiry*, winter.

Anderson, C.H. (1974), *The Political Economy of Social Class* (New Jersey: Prentice-Hall).

Anderson, P. (1976), *Considerations on Western Marxism* (London: New Left Books).

Arnot, B. (1988), *Controlling Soviet Labour. Experimental change from Brezhnev to Gorbachev* (London: Macmillan).

341

Aron, R. (1979), *Main Currents in Sociological Thought*, Vol. 1 (Harmondsworth: Penguin).

Aronson, H. (1995), *After Marxism* (New York: Guilford Press).

Avineri, S. (1968), *The Social and Political Thought of Karl Marx* (Cambridge: Cambridge University Press).

Avron, H. (1973), *Marxist Esthetics* (Ithaca: Cornell University Press).

Bahro, R. (1978), *The Alternative in Eastern Europe* (London: New Left Books).

Bahro, R. (1986), *Building the Green Government* (London: GMP).

Balakrishnan, G. (1995), 'The National Imagination', *New Left Review*, 211 (May/June): 56–69.

Balibar, E. (1977), *On the Dictatorship of the Proletariat* (London: New Left Books).

Ball, T. and J. Farr (eds) (1984), *After Marx* (Cambridge: Cambridge University Press).

Barker, Diana Leonard and Sheila Allen (eds) (1976), *Sexual Divisions and Society: Process and Change* (London: Tavistock).

Barnes, B. (1982), *T. S. Kuhn and Social Science* (London: Macmillan).

Barrett, Michèle (1980), *Women's Oppression Today* (London: Verso).

Barrett, Michèle (1991), *The Politics of Truth: From Marx to Foucault* (Oxford: Polity).

Barrett, Michèle (1992), 'Words and things: materialism and method in contemporary feminist analysis', in M. Barrett and A. Phillips (eds), *Destabilizing Theory: Contemporary Feminist Debates* (Oxford: Polity).

Barrett, Michèle and Mary McIntosh (1979), 'Christine Delphy: towards a materialist feminism', *Feminist Review*, 1: 95–106.

Barrett, Michèle and Mary McIntosh (1980), 'The family wage: some problems for socialists and feminists', *Capital and Class*, 2: 51–7.

Barrett, Michèle and Mary McIntosh (1982), *The Anti-Social Family* (London: Verso).

Barrow, C. W. (1993), *Critical Theories of the State: Marxist, Neo-Marxist, Post-Marxist* (Madison: University of Wisconsin Press).

Barry, J. (1995), 'Deep Ecology, Socialism and Human "Being in the World": A Part of, Yet Apart from Nature', *Capitalism, Nature, Socialism*, 6: 3.

Barthes, R. (1967), *Elements of Semiology* (London: Cape).

Barthes, R. (1973), *Mythologies* (London: Cape).

Baudrillard, J. (1980), *Selected Writings* (Cambridge: Polity).

Bauer, O. (1978a), 'The Concept of the Nation', in T. Bottomore and P. Goode (eds), *Austro-Marxism* (Oxford: Clarendon).

Bauer, O. (1978b), 'Socialism and the Principle of Nationality', in T. Bottomore and P. Goode (eds), *Austro-Marxism* (Oxford: Clarendon).

Baxendall, L. (1968), *Marxism and Aesthetics* (New York: Humanities).

Baxendall, L. and S. Morowski (1973), *Marx and Engels on Literature and Art* (New York: International General).

Beardsley, P. (1974), 'Political Science: The Case of the Missing Paradigm', *Political Theory*, 2 (1).

Beck, U. (1992), *Risk Society: Towards a New Modernity* (London: Sage).

Becker, J. (1973), 'Class Structure and Conflict in the Managerial Phase, Part 1', *Science and Society*, 37:3.

Becker, J. (1974), 'Class Structure and Conflict in the Managerial Phase, Part 2' *Science and Society*, 37:4.

Beechey, Veronica (1979), 'On patriarchy', *Feminist Review*, 3: 66–82.

Bellis, P. (1979), *Marxism and the USSR: the theory of proletarian dictatorship and the Marxist analysis of Soviet society* (Basingstoke: Macmillan).

Belsey, C. (1980), *Critical Practice* (London: Routledge).

Benjamin, W. (1973), *Understanding Brecht* (London: New Left Books).

Bennett, T. (1979), *Formalism and Marxism* (London: Methuen).

Benston, Margaret (1969), 'The political economy of women's liberation', *Monthly Review*, 40:

Benton, T. (1984), *The Rise and Fall of Structuralist Marxism* (London: Hutchinson).

Benton, T. (1989), 'Marxism and Natural Limits: An Ecological Critique and Reconstruction', *New Left Review*, 178.

Benton, T. (1993a), 'Animal Rights', in A. Dobson and P. Lucardie (eds), *The Politics of Nature: Explorations in Green Political Thought* (London: Routledge).

Benton, T. (1993b), *Natural Relations: Ecology, Social Justice and Animal Rights* (London: Verso).

Berman, M. (1982), *All that is Solid Melts Into Air: The Experience of Modernity* (New York: Penguin).

Bernal, J. (1969), *Science in History* Vol. 1 (Harmondsworth: Penguin).

Bernstein, E. (1961), *Evolutionary Socialism* (New York: Schocken Books).

Bertramsen, R. B., T. P. F. Thomsen and J. Torfing (1990), *State, Economy and Society* (London: Unwin Hyman).

Bettelheim, C. (1976), *Class Struggles in the USSR: first period: 1917–1923* (Brighton: Harvester).

Bhaskar, R. (1975), *A Realist Theory of Science* (Brighton: Harvester).

Bhaskar, R. (1989), *Reclaiming Reality* (London: Verso).

Bhavnani, Kum-Kum and Margaret Coulson (1986), 'Transforming socialist feminism: the challenge of racism', *Feminist Review*, 23: 81–92.

Blackburn, Robin (1991), 'Fin-de-Siecle: Socialism after the crash', *New Left Review*, 185: 5–67.

Blackburn, R. (1992), 'The Ruins of Westminster', *New Left Review*, 191: 5–35.

Blaut, J. M. (1987), *The National Question: Decolonizing the Theory of Nationalism* (London: Zed).

Bloch, E., T. Adorno, W. Benjamin and G. Lukács (1977), *Aesthetics and Politics* (London: Verso).

Block, F. (1987a), 'The Ruling Class Does Not Rule: Notes on the Marxist Theory of the State', in *Revising State Theory: Essays in Politics and Postindustrialism* (Philadelphia: Temple University Press).

Block, F. (1987b), 'Beyond Relative Autonomy: State Managers as Historical Subjects', in *Revising State Theory: Essays in Politics and Postindustrialism* (Philadelphia: Temple University Press).

Bonefeld, W. (1993), 'Crisis of Theory: Bob Jessop's Theory of Capitalist Reproduction', *Capital & Class*, 50: 25–48.

Bongiovanni, B. (1982), 'The dissolution of Trotsky', *Telos*, 52.

Bottomore, Tom (1973, rpt 1979), *Karl Marx* (Oxford: Blackwell).

Bottomore, Tom (ed.) (1988), *Interpretations of Marx* (Oxford: Blackwell).

Bottomore, T. and P. Goode (ed.) (1978), *Austro-Marxism* (Oxford: Clarendon).

Bottomore, T. and M. Rubel (eds) (1956, rpt 1990), *Karl Marx: Selected Writings in Sociology and Social Philosophy* (Harmondsworth: Penguin Books).

Bottomore, T. and M. Rubel (eds) (1978), *Selected Writings in Sociology and Social Philosophy* (Harmondsworth: Penguin).

Bourdieu, P. (1979), *Distinction: A Social Critique of the Judgement of Taste* (London: Routledge).

Bowles, S. D., M. Gordon, and T. E. Weisskopf (1986), 'Power and Profits: The Social Structure of Accumulation and the Profitability of the Postwar US Economy', *Review of Radical Political Economy*, 18, 1/2: 132–67.

Boyer, R. (1986), *La Flexibilité du Travail en Europe* (Paris: La Découverte).

Boyer, R. (1990), *The Regulation School: a Critical Introduction* (New York: Columbia University Press).

Boyer, R. and J. Mistral (1982), *Accumulation, Inflation, Crises* (Paris: Presses Universitaires de France).

Bradley, Harriet (1989), *Men's Work, Women's Work* (Cambridge: Polity).

Brah, Avtar (1992), 'Question of Difference and International Feminism', in J. Aaron and S. Walby (eds) *Out of the Margins: Women's Studies in the Nineties* (London: Falmer).

Brannen, Julia and Gail Wilson (eds) (1987), *Give and Take in Families: Studies in Resource Distribution* (London: Allen & Unwin).

Brantlinger, P. (1990), *Crusoe's Footprints* (London: Routledge).

Braverman, H. (1974), *Labor and Monopoly Capital: The Degradation of Work in the Twentieth Century*, (New York: Monthly Review Press).

Brenner, R. and M. Glick (1991), 'The Regulation Approach: Theory and History', *New Left Review*, 188: 45–120.

Breuilly, J. (1993), *Nationalism and the State* (2nd edn) (Manchester: Manchester University Press).

Bromley, S. (1991), 'The Politics of Postmodernism', *Capital & Class*, 45: 129–150.

Brovkin, V. (1987), *The Mensheviks After October: Socialist Opposition and the Rise of the Bolshevik Dictatorship* (Ithaca: Cornell University Press).

Brown, W. (1992), 'Finding the Man in the State', *Feminist Studies*, 18 (1): 7–34.

Bruegel, Irene (1979), 'Women as a reserve army of labour: a note on recent British experience', *Feminist Review*, 3: 12–23.

Buick, A. (1975), 'The myth of the transitional society', *Critique*, 5.

Bukharin, N. I. (1921 [1926]), *Historical Materialism: A System of Sociology*. (London: Allen & Unwin).

Burawoy, M. (1985), *The Politics of Production: Factory regimes under capitalism and socialism* (London: Verso)

Burawoy, M. (1995), 'From Sovietology to comparative political economy', in D. Orlovsky (ed.), *Beyond Soviet Studies* (Washington: Woodrow Wilson Center Press).

Burawoy, M. and K. Hendley (1992), 'Between *perestroika* and privatization: divided strategies and political crisis in a Soviet enterprise', *Europe–Asia Studies*, 44 (3).

Burawoy, M. and J. Lukács (1992), *The Radiant Past: Ideology and reality in Hungary's road to capitalism* (Chicago: University of Chicago Press).

Burrows, R. and Loader, B. (1994), *Towards a Post-Fordist Welfare State?* (London: Routledge).

Butler, Anthony (1995), *Transformative Socialism* (London: Macmillan)

Butler, Judith (1990), *Gender Trouble: Feminism and the Subversion of Identity* (New York: Routledge).

Callinicos, A. (1976), *Althusser's Marxism* (London: Pluto Press).

Callinicos, A. (1989), *Against Postmodernism: A Marxist Critique* (London: Lawrence & Wishart).

Callinicos, A. (1991), *The Revenge of History: Marxism and the East European Revolutions* (Cambridge: Polity).

Camilleri, J. and J. Falk, (1992), *The End of Sovereignty?* (Aldershot: Edward Elgar).

Cammack, P. (1989), 'Bringing the State Back In: a Polemic', *British Journal of Political Science*, 19 (2).

Carby, Hazel (1982), 'White women listen! Black feminism and the boundaries of sisterhood', in Centre for Contemporary Cultural Studies (eds), *The Empire Strikes Back: Race and Racism in 70s Britain* (London: Hutchinson).

Carchedi, G. (1975), 'On the Economic Identification of the New Middle Class', *Economy and Society*, 4.

Carchedi, P. (1977), *On the Economic Identification of Social Classes* (London: Routledge).

Carlo, A. (1974), 'The socio-economic nature of the USSR', *Telos,* 21.

Carlo, A. (1980), 'The crisis of bureaucratic collectivism', *Telos,* 43.

Carnoy, M. (1984), *The State and Political Theory* (Princeton, NJ: Princeton University Press).

Carr, E. H. (1992), *What is History?* (Harmondsworth: Penguin).

Castoriadis, C. (1988), 'General introduction', *Political and Social Writings* Volume 1, *1945–55: From the Critique of Bureaucracy to the Positive Content of Socialism* (Minneapolis: University of Minnesota Press).

Castoriadis, C. (1989), 'The Gorbachev interlude', in F. Fehér and A. Arato (eds), *Gorbachev: the debate* (Cambridge: Polity).

Chalmers, A. (1982), *What is this thing called Science?* 2nd edn (Milton Keynes: Open University Press).

Charles, Nickie and Marion Kerr (1988), *Women, Food and Families* (Manchester: Manchester University Press).

Chatterjee, P. (1993), *The Nation and Its Fragments: Colonial and Postcolonial Histories* (Princeton: Princeton University Press).

Clarke, S. (1986), 'Overaccumulation, class struggle and the regulation approach', *Capital and Class*, 36: 59–91.

Clarke, S. (1988), *Keynesianism, Monetarism and the Crisis of the State* (Aldershot: Edward Elgar).

Clarke, S. (1992), 'Privatization and the development of capitalism in Russia', *New Left Review,* 196:

Clarke, S., P. Fairbrother, V. Borisov and P. Bizyukov (1994), 'The privatization of industrial enterprises in Russia', *Europe–Asia Studies,* 46 (2).

Clarke, S., P. Fairbrother, V. Borisov, M. Burawoy and P. Krotov (1993), *What about the Workers? Workers and the transition to capitalism in Russia* (London: Verso).

Cliff, T. (1957), 'Perspectives on the permanent war economy', *Socialist Review,* 6 (2).

Cliff, T. (1964), *Russia: Marxist Analysis* (London: International Socialism).

Coates, K. and T. Topham (1974), *The New Unionism: The Case for Workers' Control* (Harmondsworth: Penguin).

Cohen, G. A. (1978), *Karl Marx's Theory of History: A Defence* (Oxford: Clarendon Press).

Cohen, J. (1983), *Class and Civil Society: The Limits of Marxian Critical Theory* (Oxford: Martin Robinson).

Cohen, S. (1985), *Rethinking the Soviet Experience: Politics and history since 1917* (Oxford: Oxford University Press).

Colletti, L. (1972), *From Rousseau to Lenin: Studies in Ideology and Society* (New York: Monthly Review Press).

Colletti, L. (1981), 'Introduction' *Karl Marx: Early Writings* (Harmondsworth: Penguin).

Connell, R.W. (1990), 'The State, Gender and Sexual Politics: Theory and Appraisal', *Theory and Society,* 19: 507–44.

Coonz, Stephanie (1988), *The Social Origins of Private Life: A History of American Families 1600–1900* (London: Verso).

Corrigan, P., H. Ramsay and D. Sayer (1978), *Socialist Construction and Marxist Theory: Bolshevism and its Critique* (Basingstoke: Macmillan).

Costello, A (1991/2), 'The Ecology of Failure', *Analysis,* Winter.

Coulson, Margaret, Branka Magas, and Hilary Wainwright (1975), 'The housewife and her labour under capitalism: a critique', *New Left Review,* 89: 59–71.

Coward, R. and J. Ellis (1977), *Language and Materialism* (London: Routledge & Kegan Paul).

Cox, Robert (1987), *Production, Power and World Order* (New York: Columbia University Press).

Craig, D. (ed.) (1975), *Marxists on Literature* (Harmondsworth: Penguin).

Crocker, D. (1983), *Praxis and Democratic Socialism* (Brighton, NJ: Humanities Press).

Crompton, Rosemary and Michael Mann (eds) (1986), *Gender and Stratification* (Cambridge: Polity).

Cutler, A., B. Hindess, P. Hirst and A. Hussein (1977), *Marx's Capital and Capitalism Today* (London: Routledge & Kegan Paul).

Dahbour, O. and M. R. Ishay (eds) (1995), *The Nationalism Reader* (Atlantic Highlands: Humanities Press International).

Dahl, R. (1985), *A Preface to Economic Democracy* (New Haven and London: Yale University Press).

Dalla Costa, Mariarosa and Selma James (1972), *The Power of Women and the Subversion of the Community* (Bristol: Falling Wall Press).

Daly, G. (1991), 'The Discursive Construction of Economic Space', *Economy and Society*, 20: 79–102.

Daly, G. (1993), 'The Discursive Construction of Economic Space', PhD thesis.

Daly, G. (1994), 'Post-metaphysical Culture and Politics: Richard Rorty and Laclau and Mouffe', *Economy and Society*, 23 (2), May: 173–200.

Daly, H. (1977), *Steady State Economics*, (San Francisco: W. H. Freeman).

Davis, Horace B. (1967), *Socialism and Nationalism* (New York: Monthly Review Press).

Davis, Horace B. (1978), *Towards a Marxist Theory of Nationalism* (New York: Monthly Review Press).

De Vroey, M. (1984), 'A regulation approach interpretation of the contemporary crisis', *Capital & Class*, 23: 45–66.

Debray, R. (1997), 'Marxism and the National Question', *New Left Review*, 105: 25–41.

Deleague, J. P. (1994), Eco-Marxist Critique of Political Economy', in M. O'Connor (ed.), *Is Capitalism Sustainable? Political Economy and the Politics of Ecology* (London: Guilford Press).

Delphy, Christine (1976), 'Continuities and discontinuities in marriage and divorce', in D. Leonard Barker and S. Allen (eds) *Sexual Divisions and Society* (London: Tavistock).

Delphy, Christine (1977), *The Main Enemy* (London: Women's Research and Resources Centre).

Delphy, Christine (1979), 'Sharing the same table: consumption and the family', translated by Diana Leonard, in C. C. Harris (ed.), *The Sociology of the Family: New Directions for Britain* (Keele: Sociological Review Monographs).

Delphy, Christine (1980), 'A materialist feminism is possible', *Feminist Review*, 4: 79–104.

Delphy, Christine (1981), 'Women in stratification studies', translated by Helen Roberts, in H. Roberts (ed.), *Doing Feminist Research* (London: Routledge & Kegan Paul).

Delphy, Christine (1984), *Close to Home: A Materialist Analysis of Women's Oppression*, translated and edited by Diana Leonard (London: Hutchinson).

Delphy, Christine (1988), 'Patriarchy, domestic mode of production, gender and class', in C. Nelson and L. Grossberg (eds), *Marxism and the Interpretation of Culture* (London: Macmillan).

Delphy, Christine (1992), 'Mothers' Union?', translated by Diana Leonard, *Trouble and Strife*, 24: 12–19.

Delphy, Christine (1993), 'Rethinking sex and gender', translated by Diana Leonard, *Women's Studies International Forum*, 16 (1): 1–9.

Delphy, Christine (1994), 'Changing Women in a Changing Europe: Is Difference the Future for Feminism?', *Women's Studies International Forum*: 27 (2): 187–201.

Delphy, Christine and Diana Leonard (1986), 'Class analysis: the family', in R. Crompton and N. Mann (eds), *Gender and Stratification* (Cambridge: Polity).

Delphy, Christine and Diana Leonard (1992), *Familiar Exploitation: A New Analysis of Marriage in Contemporary Western Societies* (Cambridge: Polity).

Demetz, P. (1964), *Marx, Engels and the Poets* (Chicago: University of Chicago Press).

Derrida, J. (1988), *Limited Inc* (Evanston: Northwestern University Press).

Derrida, J. (1994), *Spectres of Marx* (London: Routledge).

Devine, F. (1996), 'The Process of Class Mobility in Post-Industrial Societies: Studying Changing Opportunities and Constraints', ASA Annual Meeting, New York.

Djilas, M. (1957), *The New Class: An analysis of the communist system* (London: Thames & Hudson).

Djilas, M. (1969), *The Unperfect Society: Beyond the New Class* (London: Methuen).

Dobb, Maurice (1937), *Political Economy and Capitalism* (London: Routledge).

Docherty, T. (ed.) (1993), *Postmodernism: A Reader* (Brighton: Harvester Wheatsheaf).

Domhoff, G. W. (1967), *Who Rules America?* (Englewood Cliffs, NJ: Prentice-Hall).

Domhoff, G. W. (1970), *The Higher Circles: The Governing Class in America* (New York: Vintage Books).

Domhoff, G. W. (1979), *The Powers That Be: Processes of Ruling Class Domination in America* (New York: Vintage Books).

Domhoff, G. W. (1980), *Power Structure Research* (Beverly Hills: Sage).

Domhoff, G. W. (1990), *The Power Elite and the State* (New York: Aldine de Gruyter).

Draper, H. (1977), 'Karl Marx's Theory of Revolution', Volume 1, *State and Bureaucracy* (New York: Monthly Review Press).

Dryzek, J. (1987), *Rational Ecology: Environment and Political Economy* (Oxford: Basil Blackwell).

Dryzek, J. (1994), 'Ecology and Discursive Democracy: Beyond Liberal Capitalism and the Administrative State', in M. O'Connor (ed.), *Is Capitalism Sustainable? Political Economy and the Politics of Ecology*, (London: Guilford Press).

Dunford, M. (1991), 'Theories of Regulation', *Environment and Planning D: Society and Space,* 8 (3): 297–319.

Dunleavy, P. & B. O'Leary (1987), *Theories of the State: The Politics of Liberal Democracy* (London: Macmillan).

Dunn, J. (ed.) (1994), 'Contemporary Crisis of the Nation State'? Special Issue of *Political Studies,* 42.

Eagleton, T. (1976), *Marxism and Literary Criticism* (London: Methuen).

Eagleton, T. (1983), *Literary Theory* (Oxford: Basil Blackwell).

Eagleton, T. (1984), *Ideology* (London: Verso).

Eagleton, T. (1986), *Against the Grain* (London: Verso).

Eagleton, T. (1991), *Ideology: An Introduction*, 2nd edn (London: Verso).

Easlea, B. (1980), *Witch Hunting, Magic and the New Philosophy* (Brighton: Harvester).

Eckersley, R. (1992), *Environmentalism and Political Theory: Towards an Ecocentric Approach* (London: UCL Press).

Economy and Society (1995), 'Special Feature: local political economy – regulation and governance', 24: 3.

Edholm, Felicity, Harris, Olivia and Young, Kate (1977), 'Conceptualizing Women', *Critique of Anthropology*, 3:101–130.

Ehrenfeld, D. (1978), *The Arrogance of Humanism* (Oxford: Oxford University Press).

Ehrenreich, B. and J. Ehrenreich (1971), 'The Professional–Managerial Class', *Radical America,* 11: 2.

Ehrenreich, B. and J. Ehrenreich (1979), 'The Professional–Managerial Class', in P. Walker (ed.), *Between Labour and Capital* (Brighton: Harvester Press).

Eisenstadt, S. N. (1969), *The Political Systems of Empires* (New York: Free Press).

Elam, M. (1994), 'Puzzling out the post-Fordist Debate: Technology, Markets and Institutions', in A. Amin (ed.), *Post-Fordism* (Oxford: Blackwell).

Elson, Dianne (1988), 'Market Socialism or Socialism of the Market', *New Left Review* 172 3–44.

Engels, F. (1844 [1975]), 'Outline of a Critique of Political Economy', in K. Marx and F. Engels, *Collected Works,* Volume 3 (London: Lawrence & Wishart).

Engels, F. (1849a [1973]), 'Democratic Pan-Slavism', in D. Fernbach (ed.), *Marx: The Revolutions of 1848* (pp. 226–45) (Harmondsworth: Penguin).

Engels, F. (1849b [1973]), 'The Magyar Struggle', in D. Fernbach (ed.), *Marx: The Revolutions of 1848* (pp. 213–26) (Harmondsworth: Penguin).

Engels, F. (1852 [1969]), 'Panslavism – The Schleswig-Holstein War', in K. Marx (ed.) *Germany: Revolution and Counter-Revolution* (New York: International: Publishers).

Engels, F. (1866 [1973]), 'What Have the Working Classes To Do With Poland?', in D. Fernbach (ed.), *Karl Marx, The First International and After: Political Writings, Volume III* (Vol. III, pp. 378–88) (Harmondsworth: Penguin).

Engels, F. (1878 [1947]), *Anti-Dühring* (Moscow: Progress Publishers).

Engels, F. (1884 [1978]), *The Origin of the Family, Private Property and the State* (Peking: Foreign Language Press).

Enzensberger, H. M. (1974), 'A Critique of Political Ecology', *New Left Review*, 84.

Erlich, V. (1981), *Russian Formalism: History, Doctrine* (New Haven: Yale University Press).

Errington, Frederick and Deborah Gewertz (1987), *Cultural Alternatives and a Feminist Anthropology* (Cambridge: Cambridge University Press).

Farber, S. (1990), *Before Stalinism: The Rise and Fall of Soviet Democracy* (Cambridge: Polity).

Fehér, F. and A. Heller (1989), 'The Gorbachev phenomenon', in F. Fehér and A. Arato (eds), *Gorbachev: the debate* (Cambridge: Polity).

Fehér, F., A. Heller and G. Márkus (1983), *Dictatorship over Needs* (Oxford: Blackwell).

Femia, J. V. (1981), *Gramsci's Political Thought: Hegemony, Consciousness and the Revolutionary Process* (Oxford: Clarendon Press).

Féministes Collective (1981), 'Variations on common themes', translated by Yvonne Rochette-Ozzello, in E. Marks and I. de Courtivron (eds), *New French Feminisms* (Brighton: Harvester).

Ferguson, Ann (1989), *Blood at the Root: Motherhood, Sexuality and Male Dominance* (London: Pandora).

Fernbach, D. (1973), 'Introduction', in K. Marx (ed.), *The Revolutions of 1848* (pp. 9–61) (Harmondsworth: Penguin).

Feuer, L. S. (1984), *Marx and Engels: basic writings on politics and philosophy* (London: Fontana/Collins).

Feyerabend, P. (1975), *Against Method: Outline of an Anarchistic Theory of Knowledge* (London: New Left Books).

Filtzer, D. (1986), *Soviet Workers and Stalinist Industrialization* (London: Pluto).

Filtzer, D. (1992), *Soviet Workers and De-Stalinization* (Cambridge: Cambridge University Press).

Filtzer, D. (1994), *Soviet Workers and the Collapse of Perestroika* (Cambridge: Cambridge University Press).

Finch, Janet (1983), *Married to the Job: Wives' Incorporation into Men's Work* (London: George Allen & Unwin.)

Finegold, K. and T. Skocpol (1995), 'Marxist Approaches to Politics and the State', *State and Party in America's New Deal* (Madison: University of Wisconsin Press).

Fiore, G. (1970), *Antonio Gramsci: Life of a Revolutionary* (London: New Left Books).

Firestone, Shulamith (1972), *The Dialectic of Sex* (London: Paladin).

Fish, M. Steven (1995), *Democracy from Scratch: Opposition and regime in the new Russian revolution* (Princeton: Princeton University Press).

Flax, Jane (1990), 'Postmodernism and gender in feminist theory', in L. Nicholson (ed.), *Feminism/Postmodernism* (New York: Routledge).

Forgacs, D. (1986), 'Marxist Literary Theories', in A. Jefferson and D. Robey (eds), *Modern Literary Theories* (London: Batsford).

Forgacs, D. (1993), 'National-popular: genealogy of a concept', in S. During (ed.), *The Cultural Studies Reader* (pp. 177–90) (London and New York: Routledge).

Foucault, M. (1972), *The Archaeology of Knowledge* (London: Tavistock).

Frank, A. G. (1970), 'The Development of Underdevelopment', in Robert Rhodes (ed.), *Imperialism and Underdevelopment* (New York: Monthly Review Press).

Frank, A. G. (1978), *World Accumulation, 1492–1789* (New York: Monthly Review Press).

Frankel, B. (1987), *The Post-Industrial Utopians* (Cambridge: Polity).

Fraser, Nancy (1995), 'From Redistribution to Recognition? Dilemmas of Justice in a "Post-Socialist" Age', *New Left Review*, 212: 68–93.

Freedman, F. (1975), 'The Internal Structure of the Proletariat: A Marxist Analysis', *Socialist Revolution*, 26.

Friedman, J. (1995), 'Global System, Globalization and the Parameters of Modernity', in Mike Featherstone *et al.* (eds), *Global Modernities* (London: Sage).

Fukuyama, F. (1992), *The End of History and the Last Man* (Harmondsworth: Penguin).

Furlong, P. and D. Marsh, (2000), 'Epistemology and Political Science', in D. Marsh and G. Stoker (eds), *Theory and Methods in the Social Science,* 2nd edn (Basingstoke: Macmillan).

Gamble, A. (1995), 'The New Political Economy', *Political Studies,* 43 (3): 516–30.

Gamble, Andrew (1996), *Hayek: The Iron Cage of Liberty* (Cambridge: Polity).

Gamble, Andrew and Gavin Kelly, (1996), 'The New Politics of Ownership', *New Left Review* 220: 62–97

Gardiner, Jean, Susan Himmelweit, and Maureen Mackintosh (1975), 'Women's domestic labour', *Bulletin of the Conference of Socialist Economists,* 4: 1–11.

Gay, P. (1962), *The Dilemma of Democratic Socialism: Eduard Bernstein's Challenge to Marx* (New York: Collier Books).

Gelb, S. (1991), 'South Africa's economic crisis: an overview', in S. Gelb (ed.), *South Africa's Economic Crisis* (London: Zed Books).

Gellner, E. (1964), *Thought and Change* (London: Weidenfeld & Nicolson).

Gellner, E. (1973), 'Scale and Nation', *Philosophy of the Social Sciences,* 3: 1–17.

Gellner, E. (1983), *Nations and Nationalism* (Oxford: Blackwell).

Geoghegan, V. (1987), *Utopianism and Marxism* (London: Methuen).

Georgescu-Roegen, N. (1971), *The Entropy Law and the Economic Process* (Cambridge, MA: Harvard University Press).

Geras, N. (1977), 'Althusser's Marxism: An Assessment', in *Western Marxism: A Critical Reader* (London: Verso).

Geras, N. (1987), 'Post-Marxism?', *New Left Review,* 163: 40–82.

Geras, N. (1988), 'Ex-Marxism without substance', *New Left Review,* 169: 34–61.

Giddens, A. (1981), *A Contemporary Critique of Historical Materialism* (vol. 1) (London: Macmillan).

Giddens, A. (1984), *The Constitution of Society* (Cambridge: Polity).

Giddens, A. (1985), *The Nation-State and Violence* (Cambridge: Polity).

Giddens, A. (1985), *The Nation-State and Violence:* vol. 2 of *A Contemporary Critique of Historical Materialism* (Berkeley and Los Angeles: University of California Press).

Giddens, A. (1990), *The Consequences of Modernity* (Cambridge: Polity).

Giddens, A. (1994), 'Living in a Post-Traditional Society', in Ulrich Beck *et al.* (eds), *Reflexive Modernization* (Cambridge: Polity).

Giddens, Anthony (1971, rpt 1991), *Capitalism and Modern Social Theory: an analysis of the writings of Marx, Durkheim and Weber* (Cambridge: Cambridge University Press).

Giddens, A. and C. Pierson (1998), *Conversations with Anthony Giddens* (Cambridge: Polity Press): 218–26.

Giddens, A., D. Held, D. Hubert, S. Loyal, D. Seymour and J. Thompson (eds) (1994), *The Polity Reader in Cultural Theory* (London: Polity Press).

Giddens, Anthony (1973), *The Class Structure of the Advanced Societies* (London: Hutchinson).

Ginsburg, N. (1979), Class, Capital and Social Policy (London: Macmillan).

Glaser, D. (1994), 'The Paradoxes of the Council State', *Studies in Marxism,* 1 (1): 143–77.

Gleick, J. (1988), *Chaos: Making a New Science* (New York: Viking).

Gluckstein, D. ₍(1985), *The Western Soviets: Workers' Councils Versus Parliament 1915–1920* (London: Bookmarks).

Gold, D. A. *et al.* (1975a), 'Recent Developments in Marxist Theories of the Capitalist State: Part I', *Monthly Review,* 27 (5): 29–43.

Gold, D. A., C. Y. H. Lo and E. O. Wright (1975b), 'Recent Developments in Marxist Theories of the Capitalist State: Part II', *Monthly Review,* 27 (6): 36–51.

Gorter, H. (c. 1989), *Open Letter to Comrade Lenin* (Wildcat).

Gorz, A. (1980), *Ecology as Politics* (London: Pluto Press).

Gorz, A. (1983), *Farewell to the Working Class: An Essay on Post-Industrial Socialism* (London: Pluto).

Gorz, A. (1989), *Critique of Economic Reason* (London: Verso).

Gorz, A. (1993), 'Political Ecology: Expertocracy versus Self-Limitation', *New Left Review,* 202.

Gorz, A. (1994), 'Politics, Ecology: Expertocracy versus Self-Limitation', *New Left Review.*

Gouldner, A. (1979), *The Future of Intellectuals and the Rise of the New Class* (New York: Seabury Press).

Gouldner, A. (1980), *Two Marxisms* (London: Macmillan).

Graham, Hilary (1987), 'Being poor: perceptions and coping strategies of lone mothers', in J. Brannen and G. Wilson (eds), *Give and Take in Families: Studies in Resource Distribution* (London: Allen & Unwin).

Graham, J. (1992), 'Post-Fordism as politics: the political consequences of narratives on the left', *Environment and Planning D: Society and Space:* 10: 393–410.

Gramsci, A. (1971a), 'Americanism and Fordism', *Selections from the Prison Notebooks* (London: Lawrence & Wishart).

Gramsci, A. (1971b), *Selections from Prison Notebooks* (London: Lawrence & Wishart).

Gramsci, A. (1977), *Selections from Political Writings (1910–1920)* (London: Lawrence & Wishart).

Greenfield, Liah (1992), *Nationalism: Five Roads to Modernity* (Cambridge, MA and London: Harvard University Press).

Guillaumin, Colette (1981a), 'The practice of power and belief in nature. Part 1: The appropriation of women', translated by Linda Murgatroyd, *Feminist Issues* 1 (2): 3–28.

Guillaumin, Colette (1981b), 'The practice of power and belief in nature. Part 2: The naturalist discourse', translated by Linda Murgatroyd, *Feminist Issues* 1 (3).

Guillaumin, Colette (1995), *Racism, Sexism, Power and Ideology* (London: Routledge).

Habermas, J. (1975), *Legitimation Crisis* (London: Heinemann).

Habermas, J. (1981), 'New Social Movements', *Telos,* 49: 33–7.

Habermas, J. (1989), *The Structural Transformation of the Public Sphere: An Inquiry into a Category of Bourgeois Society* (Cambridge: Polity).

Habermas, J. (1990a), *Moral Consciousness and Communicative Action* (Cambridge: Polity).

Habermas, J. (1990b), 'What does socialism mean today? The rectifying revolution and the need for new thinking on the left', *New Left Review*, 183:

Hachen, D. and E. O. Wright (1982), 'The American Class Structure', *American Sociological Review*, 47.

Hall, S. (1981), 'Cultural Studies: two paradigms', in T. Bennett *et al.* (eds), *Culture, Ideology and Social Processes* (London: Batsford).

Hall, S. (1985), 'The rediscovery of "ideology": return of the repressed in media studies', in V. Beechey, and J. Donald (eds), *Subjectivity and Social Relations* (Milton Keynes: Open University Press).

Hall, S. (1986), 'Introduction', in S. Hall and J. Donald (eds), *Politics and Ideology* (Milton Keynes: Open University Press).

Hall, Stuart (1988), *The Hard Road to Renewal* (London: Verso).

Hall, S. (1992), 'Introduction', in S. Hall and B. Geiben (eds), *Formations of Modernity* (Cambridge: Polity).

Hall, S. and M. Jacques (eds) (1990), *New Times* (London: Lawrence & Wishart).

Hallas, D. (1979), *Trotsky's Marxism* (London: Pluto).

Harding, Sandra (ed.) (1987), *Feminism and Methodology* (Milton Keynes: Open University Press).

Harland, R. (1987), *Superstructuralism* (London: Routledge)

Harrison, John (1973), 'The political economy of housework', *Bulletin of the Conference of Socialist Economists*, Winter: 35–52.

Hartmann, Heidi (1976), 'Capitalism, patriarchy and job segregation by sex', *Signs*, 1: 137–68.

Hartmann, Heidi (1981), 'The unhappy marriage of marxism and feminism: towards a more progressive union', in L. Sargent (ed.), *Women and Revolution: the Unhappy Marriage of Marxism and Feminism* (London: Pluto Press).

Harvey, D. (1990), *The Condition of Postmodernity* (Oxford: Blackwell).

Harvey, David (1982), *The Limits to Capital* (Oxford: Blackwell).

Harvey, D. (1989), *The Condition of Postmodernity: An Enquiry into the Origins of Cultural Change* (Oxford: Blackwell).

Harvey, D. (1993), 'The Nature of Environment: The Dialectics of Social and Environmental Change', *The Socialist Register 1993*.

Haupt, G., Löwy, M. and C. Weill (eds) (1974), *Les Marxistes et la question nationale* (Paris: François Maspero).

Hawkes, T. (1977), *Structuralism and Semiotics* (London: Methuen).

Hay, C. (1994), 'Environment: Security and State Legitimacy', in M. O'Connor (ed.), (1994), *Is Capitalism Sustainable? Political Economy and the Politics of Ecology* (London: Guilford Press).

Hay, C. (1994a), 'Environmental Security and State Legitimacy', *Capitalism, Nature, Socialism*, 5 (1): 83–97.

Hay, C. (1994b), 'Werner in Wunderland: Bob Jessop' s Strategic–Relational Approach', in F. Sebai and C. Vercellone (eds), *Ecole de la Régulation et*

Critique de La Raison Economique (Paris: Futur Anterieur, Editions L'Harmatton).

Hay, C. (1995a), 'Social regulation after Fordism: regulation theory and the global–local nexus', *Economy and Society,* 24 (3): 357–86.

Hay, C. (1995b), 'Structure and Agency: Holding the Whip Hand', in D. Marsh and G. Stoker (eds) *Theory and Methods of Political Science* (London: Macmillan).

Hay, C. (1996a), *Re-stating Social and Political Change* (Buckingham: Open University Press).

Hay, C. (1996b), 'Rethinking Crisis: Narratives of the New Right and Constructions of Crisis', *Rethinking Marxism,* 8 (2): 59–76.

Hay, C. (1996c), 'Narrating Crisis: The Discursive Construction of the Winter of Discontent', *Sociology,* 30 (2): 253–77.

Hay, C. (1996d), 'From Crisis to Catastrophe? The Ecological Pathologies of the Liberal Democratic State', *Innovation: The European Journal of Social Science,* 9 (4): 421–34.

Hay, C. (1997), 'Marxist Theories of the State: Horses for Courses?', *Muirhead Working Papers in Politics,* University of Birmingham.

Hay, C. and B. Jessop (1995), 'The Governance of Local Economic Development and the Development of Local Economic Governance: A Strategic–Relational Approach', *Lancaster Working Paper in Political Economy,* 53.

Hayek, Friedrich (ed.) (1935), *Collectivist Economic Planning* (London: Routledge).

Hayek, Friedrich (1937), 'Economics and Knowledge', *Economica,* 13 (2): 33–54.

Hayek, F. A. von (1960), *The Constitution of Liberty* (London: Routledge).

Hayward, T, (1992), 'Ecology and Human Emancipation', *Radical Philosophy,* 62.

Hayward, T. (1995), *Ecological Thought: An Introduction* (Cambridge: Polity).

Held, D. (1980), *Introduction to Critical Theory: From Horkheimer to Habermas* (Cambridge: Polity).

Held, David (1992), 'Democracy: From City-States to a Cosmopolitan Order?', *Political Studies,* 40 (Special Issue): 10–39.

Held, David (1996), *Democracy and the Global Order* (Cambridge: Polity).

Hennessy, Rosemary (1993), *Materialist Feminism and the Politics of Discourse* (New York and London: Routledge).

Hilferding, R. (1940), 'State Capitalism or Totalitarian State Economy'.

Hills, J. (1994), *The Future of Welfare* (York: LSE/Rowntree).

Hindess, B. (1980), 'Marxism and Parliamentary Democracy', in A. Hunt (ed.), *Marxism and Democracy* (London: Lawrence & Wishart).

Hindess, B. and P. Hirst (1977), *Mode of Production and Social Formation* (London: Macmillan).

Hirsch, J. (1978), 'The State Apparatus and Social Reproduction: Elements of a Theory of the Bourgeois State', in J. Holloway and S. Picciotto (eds), *State and Capital: A Marxist Debate* (London: Arnold).

Hirsch, J. (1983), 'The Fordist Security State and New Social Movements', *Kapitalistate,* 10/11: 75–88.

Hirsch, J. (1991), 'From the Fordist to the Post-Fordist State', in R. Jessop (ed.), *The Politics of Flexibility: Restructuring State and Industry in Britain, Germany and Scandinavia* (Brookfield, VT: Edward Elgar).

Hirst, P. (1994), *Associative Democracy* (London: Sage).

Hirst, P. and G. Thompson (1996), *Globalisation in Question* (Cambridge: Polity).

Hirst, P. and J. Zeitlin (1990), 'Flexible Specialisation versus post-Fordism: theory, evidence and policy implementation', *Economy and Society*, 54: 1–56.

Hobsbawm, E. (1975), *The Age of Capital, 1848–1875* (London: Weidenfeld & Nicolson).

Hobsbawm, E. (1979), 'The Development of the World Economy', *Cambridge Journal of Economics*, 3.

Hobsbawm, E. (1998), 'The Death of Neo-Liberalism', *Marxism Today*, pp. 4–8.

Hobsbawm, E. and T. Ranger (eds) (1983), *The Invention of Tradition* (Cambridge: Cambridge University Press).

Hobsbawm, E. and T. Ranger (eds) (1992), *Nations and Nationalism since 1780: Programme, Myth, Reality* (2nd edn) (Cambridge: Cambridge University Press).

Hodge, R. and G. Kress (1988), *Social Semiotics* (London: Macmillan).

Hodgson, G. (1977), *Socialism and Parliamentary Democracy* (Nottingham: Spokesman).

Hodgson, Geoff (1988), *Economics and Institions* (Cambridge: Polity).

Hoggart, R. (1957), *The Uses of Literacy* (Harmondsworth: Penguin).

hooks, bell (1982), *Ain't I a Woman?* (London: Pluto Press).

Howson, C. (ed.) (1976), *Method and Appraisal in the Physical Sciences* (Cambridge: Cambridge University Press).

Humphries, Jane (1977), 'Class Struggle and the Persistence of the Working Class Family', *Cambridge Journal of Economics*, 1: 241–58.

Hunt, A. (1980), 'Introduction: Taking Democracy Seriously', in A. Hunt, (ed.), *Marxism and Democracy* (London: Lawrence & Wishart).

Hutchinson, John (1994), *Modern Nationalism* (London: Fontana).

Hutton, W. (1995), *The State We're In* (London: Cape).

Hyman, R. (1991), 'The Fetishism of Flexibility: The Case of British Rail', in R. Jessop (ed.), *The Politics of Flexibility: Restructuring State and Industry in Britain, Germany and Scandinavia,* (Brookfield, VT: Edward Elgar).

Irvine, S and C. Ponton (1988), *A Green Manifesto: Policies for a Green Future* (London: Optima).

Jackson, L. (1991), *The Poverty of Structuralism* (London: Longmans).

Jackson, Stevi (1992a), 'Towards a historical sociology of housework', *Women's Studies International Forum*, 15 (2): 153–72.

Jackson, Stevi (1992b), 'The amazing deconstructing woman', *Trouble and Strife*, 25: 25–31.

Jackson, Stevi (1995), 'Gender and Heterosexuality: A Materialist Feminist Analysis', in M. Maynard and J. Purvis (eds) *(Hetero)sexual Politics* (London: Taylor & Francis).

Jackson, Stevi (1996), *Christine Delphy* (London: Sage).

James, P. (1993), 'Marx and the Abstract Nation', *Arena* 1 (1): 172–94.

Jameson, F. (1971), *Marxism and Form* (Princeton: Princeton University Press).

Jameson, F. (1984), 'Postmodernism, or the Cultural Logic of Late Capitalism', *New Left Review*, 146.

Janicke, M. (1990), *State Failure: The Impotence of Politics in Industrial Society* (Cambridge: Polity).

Jefferson, A. and D. Robey (1986), *Modern Literary Theories* (London: Batsford).

Jenson, J. (1989), ' "Different" but not "Exceptional": Canada's permeable Fordism', *Canadian Review of Sociology and Anthropology*, 26 (1): 69–94.

Jenson, J. (1992), 'Gender and Reproduction: Or, Babies and the State', in M. P. Connelly and P. Armstrong (eds), *Feminism in Action: Studies in Political Economy* (Toronto: Canadian Scholars' Press).

Jenson, J. (1993), 'Naming nations: Making nationalist claims in Canadian public discourse', *Canadian Review of Sociology and Anthropology*, 30 (3): 337–58.

Jessop, B. (1977), 'Recent Theories of the Capitalist State', *Cambridge Journal of Economics*, I (4): 353–72.

Jessop, B. (1978), 'Marx and Engels on the State', in S. Hibbin *et al.* (eds), *Politics, Ideology and the State* (London: Lawrence & Wishart).

Jessop, B. (1982), *The Capitalist State* (Oxford: Martin Robertson).

Jessop, B. (1985), *Nicos Poulantzas: Marxist Theory and Political Strategy* (London: Macmillan).

Jessop, B. (1990), *State Theory: Putting Capitalist States in their Place* (Cambridge: Polity).

Jessop, B. (1994a), 'Changing Forms and Functions of the State in an Era of Globalisation and Regionalisation', in R. Delorme and F. Dopfer (eds), *The Political Economy of Diversity: Evolutionary Perspectives on Economic Order and Disorder* (London: Edward Elgar).

Jessop, B. (1994b), 'The Transition to Post-Fordism and the Schumpeterian Workfare State', in R. Burrows and B. Loader (eds), *Towards a Post-Fordist Workfare State?* (London: Routledge).

Jessop, B. (1995), 'The Future of the National State: Erosion or Reorganisation? General Reflections on West Europe', *Lancaster Working Paper in Political Economy*, 50.

Jessop, Bob (1988), *Conservation Regimes and the Transition to Post-Fordism* (Colchester: University of Essex Papers).

Jessop, R. (1988), 'Regulation theory, post Fordism and the state: more than a reply to Werner Bonefeld', *Capital & Class*, 36: 147–67.

Jessop, R. (1990), 'Regulation theories in retrospect and prospect', *Economy and Society*, 19 (2): 153–216.

Jessop, R. (1992), 'Fordism and post-Fordism: a critical reformulation', in A. J. Scott and M. J. Storper (eds), *Pathways to Regionalism and Industrial Development* (London: Routledge).

Jessop, R. (1993), 'Towards a Schumpeterian workfare state? Preliminary remarks on post-Fordist political economy', *Studies in Political Economy*, 40: 7–39.

Jessop, R. (1994), 'Post-Fordism and the state', in A. Amin (ed.), *Post-Fordism: A Reader* (Oxford: Blackwell).

Jessop, R. (1995), 'The regulation approach, governance and post-Fordism: alternative perspectives on economic and political change?', *Economy and Society*, 24 (3): 307–33.

Johnson, R. (1979), 'Histories of Culture / Theories of Ideology', in M. Barrett *et al.* (eds), *Ideology and Cultural Production* (London: Croom Helm).

Johnston, J. (1999), 'Britain's economic decline: cultural v. structural explanations', in D. Marsh *et al.*, *Postwar British Politics in Perspective* (Cambridge: Polity Press).

Johnston, L. (1986), *Marxism, Class Analysis and Socialist Pluralism* (London: Allen & Unwin).

Kagarlitsky, B. (1990), *Farewell Perestroika: A Soviet Chronicle* (London: Verso).

Kagarlitsky, B. (1992), *The Disintegration of the Monolith* (London: Verso).

Kagarlitsky, B. (1995), *Restoration in Russia: Why capitalism failed* (London: Verso).

Kaletsky, A. (1998), 'The Market Myth', *Marxism Today*, pp. 30–1.

Kaluzynska, Eva (1980), 'Wiping the floor with theory: a survey of writings on housework', *Feminist Review*, 6: 27–54.

Kamenka, Eugene (ed.) (1983), *The Portable Karl Marx* (Harmondsworth: Penguin).

Kardelj, E. (1978), *Democracy and Socialism* (London: Sommerfield).

Kautsky, K. (1964), *The Dictatorship of the Proletariat* (Ann Arbor: University of Michigan Press).

Kautsky, K. (1971), *The Class Struggle* (New York, W.W. Norton).

Keat, R. and J. Urry (1982), *Social Theory as Science* (London: Routledge & Kegan Paul).

Kenny, Mike (1995), *The First New Left* (London: Lawrence & Wishart).

Kiernan, V.G. (1991), 'Nation', in T. Bottomore, L. Harris, V.G. Kiernan and R. Miliband (eds), *A Dictionary of Marxist Thought* (pp. 392–3) (Oxford: Blackwell).

Kingdom, J. (1991), *Government and Politics in Britain* (Cambridge: Polity).

Kirk, R. (ed.) (1982), *The Conservative Reader* (New York: Viking).

Knei-Paz, B. (1978), *The Social and Political Thought of Leon Trotsky* (Oxford: Oxford University Press).

Kolakowski, L. (1977), 'Marxist Roots of Stalinism', in R.C. Tucker (ed.), *Stalinism* (New York: W.W. Norton).

Kolakowski, L. (1972), *Positivist Philosophy* (Harmondsworth: Penguin).

Kolakowski, Leszek (1978), *The Main Currents of Marxism*, 3 vols (Oxford: Oxford University Press).

Konrad, G. and I. Szelenyi (1979), *The Intellectuals on the Road to Class Power* (Brighton: Harvester).

Kotz, D.M. (1990), 'A Comparative Analysis of the Theory of Regulation and the Social Structure of Accumulation Theory', *Science and Society*, 54 (1): 5–28.

Kovel, J. (1988), 'Human Nature, Freedom and Spirit', in *The Radical Spirit: Essays on Psychoanalysis and Society* (London: Free Association Books).

Krasner, S. (1978), *Defending the National Interest* (Princeton: Princeton University Press).

Kuhn, T. S. (1970), *The Structure of Scientific Revolutions* (Chicago: Chicago University Press).

Kuron, J. and K. Modzelewski (n.d.), *An Open Letter to the Party* (London: International Socialism).

Laclau, E. (1975), 'The Specificity of the Political', *Economy and Society*, 4 (1): 87–110.

Laclau, E. (1988), 'Politics and the Limits of Modernity', in A. Ross (ed.), *Universal Abandon? The Politics of Post-Modernity* (Minneapolis: University of Minnesota Press): 21–35.

Laclau, E. (1990), *New Reflections on the Revolution of Our Time* (London: Verso).

Laclau, E. and C. Mouffe (1985), *Hegemony and Socialist Strategy: Towards a Radical Democratic Politics* (London: Verso).

Laclau, E. and C. Mouffe (1987), 'Postmarxism without Apologies', *New Left Review*, 166: 79–106.

Laclau, E. and C. Mouffe (1990), *New Reflections on the Revolution of Our Time* (London: Verso).

Laing, D. (1978), *The Marxist Theory of Art* (Brighton: Harvester).

Lakatos, I. (1974), 'Falsification and the Methodology of Scientific Research Programmes', in I. Lakatos and A. Musgrave (eds.) *Criticism and the Growth of Knowledge* (Cambridge: Cambridge University Press).

Landry, Donna and Gerald MacLean (1993), *Materialist Feminisms* (Oxford: Blackwell).

Lane, D. (1976), *The Socialist Industrial State* (London: George Allen & Unwin).

Lane, M. (ed.) (1970), *Structuralism: A Reader* (London: Cape).

Lange, Oscar, and F. Taylor (1938), *On the Economic Theory of Socialism* (Minneapolis: University of Minnesota Press).

Larrain, G. (1983), *Marxism and Ideology* (London: Macmillan).

Larrain, G. (1989), 'Ideology and its Revisions in Contemporary Marxism', in N. O'Sullivan (ed.), *The Structure of Modern Ideology* (London: Edward Elgar).

Larrain, J. (1994), *Ideology and Cultural Identity: Modernity and the Third World Presence* (Cambridge: Polity).

Lash, S. and J. Urry (1994), *Economies of Signs and Space* (London: Sage).

Laurinson, D. T. and A. Swingewood (1971), *The Sociology of Literature* (London: M & K).

Lavoie, Donald (1985), *Rivalry and Central Planning: The Socialist Calculation Debate Reconsidered* (Cambridge: Cambridge University Press).

Lawson, T. (1986), 'In the Shadow of Science', *Social Studies Review*, November.

Lefebvre, H. (1972), *The Sociology of Marx* (Harmondsworth: Penguin).

Lefort, C. (1986), *The Political Forms of Modern Society: Bureaucracy, Democracy, Totalitarianism* (Cambridge: Polity Press).

Lenin, V. I. (1916 [1967a]), *The Socialist Revolution and the Right of Nations to Self-Determination (Theses). Lenin on the National and*

Colonial Questions: Three Articles (pp. 1–19) (Peking: Foreign Languages Press).

Lenin, V. I. (1917 [1968]), *The State and Revolution*, V. I. Lenin, *Selected Works* (Moscow: Progress Publishers).

Lenin, V. I. (1967b), *Questions of National Policy and Proletarian Internationalism* (Moscow: Progress Publishers).

Lenin, V. I. (1968), *Critical Remarks on the National Question: The Right of Nations to Self-Determination* (Moscow: Progress Publishers).

Leonard, Diana (1980), *Sex and Generation: A Study of Courtship and Weddings* (London: Tavistock).

Leonard, Diana (1990), 'Sex and Generation Reconsidered', in C. C. Harris (ed.), *Family, Economy and Community* (Cardiff: University of Wales Press).

Letwin, Shirley (1992), *The Anatomy of Thatcherism* (London: Fontana).

Levin, M. (1989), *Marx, Engels and Liberal Democracy* (Basingstoke: Macmillan).

Lévi-Strauss, C. (1967), *The Scope of Anthropology* (London: Cape).

Lifshitz, M. (1973), *The Philosophy of Art of Karl Marx* (London: Pluto Press).

Lipietz, A. (1986a), 'Behind the Crisis: The Exhaustion of a Regime of Accumulation. A "regulation school" perspective on some French empirical works', *Review of Radical Political Economy*, 18 (1/2): 13–32.

Lipietz, A. (1986b), 'New tendencies in the international division of labour: regimes of accumulation and modes of regulation', in A. J. Scott and M. Storper (eds), *Production, Work and Territory: the geographical anatomy of industrial capitalism* (Boston: Allen & Unwin).

Lipietz, A. (1987a), *Mirages and Miracles: The Crises of Global Fordism* (London: Verso).

Lipietz, A. (1987b), 'Rebel Sons: the Regulation School. An Interview with Alain Lipietz', conducted by Jane Jenson, *French Politics and Society*, 5 (4): 17–26.

Lipietz, A. (1992), *Towards a New Economic Order: Post-Fordism, Ecology and Democracy* (Oxford: Oxford University Press).

Lipietz, A. (1993), 'From Althusserianism to "Regulation Theory"', in E. A. Kaplan and M. Sprinker (eds), *The Althusserian Legacy* (London: Verso).

Lipietz, A. (1994), 'Post-Fordism and Democracy?', in A. Amin (ed.), *Post-Fordism* (Oxford: Blackwell).

Lively, J. and A. Reeve (eds) (1989), *Modern Political Theory from Hobbes to Marx: key debates* (London: Routledge).

Loren, C. (1977), *Classes in the United States* (San Francisco: Cardinal Publishers).

Löwy, M. (1976), Marxists and the National Question, *New Left Review*, 96: 81–100.

Löwy, M. (1993), 'Why Nationalism?', in R. Miliband and L. Panitch (eds), *Socialist Register 193: Real Problems, False Solutions* (pp. 125–38), (London: Merlin Press).

Lukács, G. (1962), *The Historical Novel* (London: Merlin).

Lukács, G. (1963), *The Meaning of Contemporary Realism* (London: Merlin).

Lukács, G. (1972), *Studies in European Realism* (London: Merlin).
Lukács, G. (1981), *History and Class Consciousness* (London: Merlin).
Lukács, G. (1983), *George Lukács: Record of Life* (London: Verso).
Lukes, S. (1985), *Marxism and Morality* (Oxford: Clarendon).
Luxemburg, R. (1976), 'The National Question and Autonomy', in H. B. Davis (ed.), *The National Question: Selected Writings by Rosa Luxemburg* (New York: Monthly Review Press).
Lyotard, J. F. (1984), *The Postmodern Condition* (Manchester: University of Manchester Press).
Macherey, P. (1978), *A Theory of Literary Production* (London: Routledge & Kegan Paul).
MacKinnon, C. A. (1982), 'Feminism, Marxism, Method and the State: An Agenda for Theory', *Signs*, 7 (3): 515–44.
MacKinnon, C. A. (1983), 'Feminism, Marxism, Method and the State: Toward Feminist Jurisprudence', *Signs*, 8 (4): 645–58.
MacKinnon, C. A. (1985), *Toward a Feminist Theory of the State* (Cambridge, MA: Harvard University Press).
Macpherson, C. B. (1973), *Democratic Theory: Essays in Retrieval* (Oxford: Clarendon Press).
Magnus, B. and S. Cullenberg (eds) (1995), *Whither Marxism? Global Crises in International Perspective* (London: Routledge).
Mahon, R. (1991), 'From "Bringing" to "Putting": The State in Late Twentieth-Century Social Thought', *Canadian Journal of Sociology*, 16 (2): 119–44.
Malinowski, B. (1982), *Magic, Science and Religion* (London: Souvenir Press).
Malos, Ellen (ed.) (1980), *The Politics of Housework* (London: Allison & Busby).
Mandel, E. (1968), *Marxist Economic Theory*, Vol. 2 (London: Merlin).
Mandel, E. (1974a), 'Ten theses on the social and economic laws governing the society transition between capitalism and socialism', *Critique*, 3.
Mandel, E. (1974b), 'Some comments on H. Ticktin's "Towards a political economy of the USSR"', *Critique*, 3
Mandel, E. (1979a), 'Once again on the Trotskyite definition of the social nature of the Soviet Union', *Critique*, 12.
Mandel, E. (1979b), *Revolutionary Marxism Today* (London: New Left Books).
Mandel, E. (1989), *Beyond Perestroika: The future of Gorbachev's USSR* (London: Verso).
Mann, M. (1983), 'The Autonomous Power of the State', *Archives Européennes de Sociologie*, 25.
Marcuse, H. (1958), *Soviet Marxism: A critical analysis* (London: Routledge & Kegan Paul).
Marcuse, H. (1966), *Eros and Civilization: A Philosophical Inquiry into Freud* (Boston: Beacon Press).
Marcuse, H. (1972), *One-Dimensional Man* (London: Sphere).
Marcuse, H. (1992), 'Ecology and the Critique of Modern Society', *Capitalism, Nature, Socialism*, 3:3.
Markovic, M. (1974), *The Contemporary Marx: Essays on Humanist Communism* (Nottingham: Spokesman Books).

Marsh D. (1995a), 'Explaining Thatcherite Policies: Beyond Unidimensional Explanation', *Political Studies*, 43 (4): 595–613.

Marsh, D. (1995b), 'The Convergence between Theories of the State', in D. Marsh and G. Stoker (eds), *Theory and Methods of Political Science* (Basingstoke: Macmillan).

Marsh, D. (1997), 'It's Always the Happy Hour for Men with Money, Knowledge and Power', mimeo, University of Birmingham.

Marshall, G. (1997), *Against the Odds: Social Class and Social Justice in Industrial Society* (Oxford: Clarendon).

Marx, K. (1843a [1975]), 'Critique of Hegel's Doctine of the State', in L. Colletti (ed.), *Karl Marx: Early Writings* (London: Pelican).

Marx, K. (1843b [1975]), 'On the Jewish Question', in L. Colletti (ed.), *Karl Marx: Early Writings* (London: Pelican).

Marx, K. (1844 [1975]), 'Introduction to a Contribution to a Critique of Hegel's Philosophy of Law', in L. Colletti (ed.), *Karl Marx: Early Writings* (London: Pelican).

Marx, K. (1848/[1973]), *Manifesto of the Communist Party* (Harmondsworth: Penguin).

Marx, K. (1850 [1978]), 'The Class Stuggles in France: 1845 to 1850', in K. Marx and F. Engels, *Collected Works*, Volume 10 (London: Lawrence & Wishart).

Marx, K. (1852 [1979]), 'The Eighteenth Brumaire of Louis Bonaparte', in K. Marx and F. Engels, *Collected Works*, Volume 11 (London: Lawrence & Wishart).

Marx, K. (1859 [1987]), 'Preface to a Contribution to a Critique of Political Economy', in K. Marx and F. Engels, *Collected Works*, Volume 29 (London: Lawrence & Wishart).

Marx, K. (1867 [1976]), *Capital* (vol. 1) (New York: Vintage Books).

Marx, K. (1870 [1974a]), 'The General Council of the Federal Council of French Switzerland', in David Fernbach (ed.), *Karl Marx, The First International and After: Political Writings vol. III* (New York: Vintage).

Marx, K. (1871 [1986]), 'The Civil War in France', in K. Marx and F. Engels, *Collected Works*, Volume 22 (London: Lawrence & Wishart).

Marx, K. (1875/[1974b]), 'Critique of the Gotha Programme', *The First International and After* (Harmondsworth: Penguin).

Marx, Karl (1935), 'The Critique of the Gotha Programme', in K. Marx and F. Engels, *Selected Works*, (Moscow: Progress Publishers).

Marx, K. (1968), *Karl Marx and Frederick Engels: Selected Works* (London: Lawrence and Wishart).

Marx, K. (1973), *Capital* (Harmondsworth: Penguin).

Marx, Karl (1976), *Capital*, Vol. 1 (Harmondsworth: Penguin).

Marx, K. (1981), *Grundrisse* (Harmondsworth: Penguin).

Marx, K. (1983), *Capital*, Vol. 1 (London: Lawrence & Wishart).

Marx, K. (1984), *Capital*, Vol. 3 (London: Lawrence & Wishart).

Marx, K. and F. Engels (1845/6 [1964]), *The German Ideology* (Moscow: Progress Publishers).

Marx, K. and F. Engels, (1848 [1967]), *The Communist Manifesto* (London: Pelican).

Marx, K. and F. Engels (1968), *Selected Works in One Volume* (London: Lawrence & Wishart).

Marx, Karl and Friedrich Engels (1968a), *The German Ideology* (Moscow: Progress Publishers).

Marx, Karl and Friedrich Engels (1969), *Selected Works* (Moscow: Progress Publishers).

Marx, K. and F. Engels (1975), *Collected Works* (London: Lawrence & Wishart).

Marx, K. and F. Engels (1977), *Collected Works*, Vol. 3 (Moscow: FLPH).

Marx, K., Engels, F. and V. Lenin (1975), *On Proletarian Internationalism and Bourgeois Nationalism* (Moscow: Novosti Press Agency Publishing House).

Maslow, A. (1970), *Motivation and Personality*, 2nd edn (New York: Harper & Row).

Mathieu, Nicole-Claude (1977), *Ignored by Some, Denied by Others: the Social Sex Category in Sociology* (London: Women's Research and Resources Centre).

Mathieu, Nicole-Claude (1980), 'Femininity/masculinity', *Feminist Issues*, 1 (1).

Mayer, M. (1991), 'Politics in the Post-Fordist City', *Socialist Review*, 21 (1): 105–24.

Mayer, M. and R. Roth (1995), 'New Social Movements and the Tranforrnation to Post-Fordist Society', in M. Darrovsky, B. Epstein and R. Flacks (eds), *Cultural Politics and Social Movements* (Philadelphia: Temple Univesity Press).

Maynard, Mary (1990), 'The re-shaping of sociology? Trends in the study of gender', *Sociology*, 24 (2): 269–90.

Maynard, Mary (1995), 'Beyond the "big three": the development of feminist theory in the 1990s', *Women's History Review*, 4 (3): 259–81.

McCarney, J. (1990), *Social Theory and the Crisis of Marxism* (London: Verso).

McCrone, D. (1992), *Understanding Scotland: The Sociology of a Stateless Nation* (London: Routledge).

McDonough, Roisin and Rachel Harrison (1978), 'Patriarchy and relations of production', in A. Kuhn, Annette and A. M. Wolpe (eds), *Feminism and Materialism: Women and Modes of Production* (London: Routledge & Kegan Paul).

McIntosh, M. (1978), 'The state and the oppression of women', in A. Kuhn and A. Wolpe (eds), *Feminism and Materialism: Women and Modes of Production* (London: Routledge & Kegan Paul).

McLellan, D. (1983), 'Theoretical Roots of Liberal, Democratic, National Communism', in H. Machin (ed.), *National Communism in Western Europe: A Third Way for Socialism?* (London: Methuen).

McLellan, D. (1985), *Karl Marx: Selected Writings* (Oxford: Oxford University Press).

McLellan, David (ed.) (1977), *Karl Marx: Selected Writings* (Oxford: Oxford University Press).

Meadows, D. *et al.* (1972), *The Limits to Growth: A Report for the Club of Rome's Project on the Predicament of Mankind* (New York: Universe).

Mehring, F. (1938), *The Lessing Legend* (New York: Critics Group Press).
Mellor, M. (1992), *Breaking the Boundaries: Towards a Feminist Green Socialism* (London: Virago).
Mellor, M. (1995), 'Materialist Communal Politics: Getting from There to Here', in J. Lovenduski and J. Stanyer (eds), *Contemporary Political Studies*, Vol. 3 (Belfast: Political Studies Association).
Metzaros, I. (1980), *The Marxist Theory of Alienation* (London: Merlin).
Mies, Maria (1986), *Patriarchy and Accumulation on a World Scale: Women in the International Division of Labour* (London: Zed Books).
Miliband, R. (1965), 'Marx and the State', *Socialist Register 1965*, 278–96.
Miliband R. (1969), *The State in Capitalist Society: An Analysis of the Western System of Power* (London: Weidenfeld & Nicolson).
Miliband, R. (1970), 'The Capitalist State – Reply to Poulantzas', *New Left Review*, 59: 53–60.
Miliband, R. (1973), 'Poulantzas and the Capitalist State', *New Left Review*, 82: 83–92.
Miliband, R. (1977), *Marxism and Politics* (Oxford: Oxford University Press).
Miliband, R. (1983), *Class Power and State Power: Political essays* (London: Verso).
Miliband, R. (1991), 'Reflections on the crisis of communist regimes', in R. Blackburn (ed.), *After the Fall* (London: Verso).
Miliband, R. (1994), *Socialism for a Sceptical Age* (London: Verso).
Mills, C. (1986), 'Ideology in Marx and Engels', *Philosophical Forum*, XVI (4).
Mintz, B. and M. Schwartz (1985), *The Power Structure of American Business* (Chicago: University of Chicago Press).
Mises, Ludwig von (1936), *Socialism: An Economic and Sociological Analysis* (London: Cape).
Mishra, R. (1984), *The Welfare State in Crisis: social thought and social change* (Brighton: Harvester Wheatsheaf).
Mitchell, Juliet (1975), *Psychoanalysis and Feminism* (Harmondsworth: Penguin).
Modleski, Tania (1991), *Feminism without Women* (New York: Routledge).
Molyneux, Maxine (1979), 'Beyond the domestic labour debate', *New Left Review*, 116: 3–27.
Morris, P. (1994), *The Bakhtin Reader* (London: Edward Arnold)
Mouffe, C. (1993), *The Return of the Political* (London: Verso).
Mouzelis, N. (1991), *Back to Sociological Theory: The Construction of Social Orders* (Basingstoke: Macmillan).
Mouzelis, N. (1995), *Sociological Theory: What Went Wrong?* (London: Routledge).
Mulberg, J. (1992), 'Who Rules the Market: Green versus Ecosocialist Economic Programmes', *Political Studies*, 30: 2.
Mulhern, F. (1981), *The Moment of 'Scrutiny'* (London: Verso).
Mulhern, F. (1992), *Contemporary Marxist Literary Theory* (London: Longmans).
Murray, R. (1985), 'Benetton Britain', *Marxism Today*, November: (166): 54–64.
Nairn, T. (1981), *The Breakup of Britain*, 2nd edn (London: Verso).

Nelson, G. and L. Grossberg (eds) (1989), *Marxism and the Interpretation of Culture* (London: Longmans).

Nelson, G. and P.A. Treicher (eds) (1992), *Cultural Studies* (London: Routledge).

Nicolaus, Martin (1968), 'The Unknown Marx', *New Left Review*, 48.

Nimni, E. (1989), 'Marx, Engels and the National Question', *Science & Society*, 53 (3): 297–326.

Nimni, E. (1991), *Marxism and Nationalism: Theoretical Origins of a Political Crisis* (London: Pluto).

Noel, A. (1987), 'Accumulation, regulation and social change: an essay on French political economy', *Internatonal Organization*, 41 (2): 303–33.

Noel, A. (1992), 'Les fils respecteux de l'économérie', *Cahiers de Recherche Sociologique*, 17: 107–23.

Norris, C. (1990), *What's Wrong with Postmodernism: A Critical Theory and the Ends of Philosophy* (New York: Harvester Wheatsheaf).

Norris, C. (1992), *Uncritical Theory Postmodernism, Intellectuals and the Gulf War* (London: Lawrence & Wishart).

Norris, C. (1993), *The Truth about Postmodernism* (Oxford: Blackwell).

Nove, A. (1986), *Marxism and Really Existing Socialism* (Chur: Harwood Academic Publishers).

O'Brien, Mary (1981), *The Politics of Reproduction* (London: Routledge & Kegan Paul).

O'Connor, J. (1992), 'Socialism and Ecology', *Society and Nature*, 1: 1.

O'Connor, J. (1973), *The Fiscal Crisis of the State* (New York: St Martin's Press).

O'Connor, J. (1991), '"External Natural" Conditions of Production, the State and Political Strategy for Ecology Movements', *Center for Ecological Socialism Working Paper 1*, University of California, Santa Cruz.

O'Connor, J. (1994), 'Is Sustainable Capitalism Possible?', in M. O'Connor (ed.) *Is Capitalism Sustainable? Political Economy and the Politics of Ecology* (London: Guilford Press).

O'Connor, M. (ed.) (1994), *Is Capitalism Sustainable? Political Economy and the Politics of Ecology* (London: Guilford Press).

O'Neill, J. (1993), *Ecology, Policy and Politics* (London: Routledge).

Offe, C. (1974), 'Structural Problems of the Capitalist State: Class Rule and the Political System: On the Selectiveness of Political Institutions', in K. von Beyme (ed.) *German Political Studies* (Beverly Hills: Sage).

Offe, C. (1975), 'The Theory of the Capitalist State and the Problem of Policy Formation', in L. Lindberg *et al.* (eds), *Stress and Contradiction in Modern Capitalism* (Lexington: D.C. Heath).

Offe, C. (1984), *Contradictions of the Welfare State* (London: Hutchinson).

Offe, C. (1991), 'Capitalism by democratic design? Democratic theory facing the triple transition in East Central Europe', *Social Research*, 58, (4).

Offe, C. and V. Ronge (1975), 'Theses on the Theory of the State', *New German Critique*, 6: 137–47.

Ohmae, K. (1995), *The End of the Nation State* (London: HarperCollins).

Olson, M and H. Landsberg (eds) (1973), *The No-Growth Society* (London: Woburn Press).

Pahl, Jan (1990), *Money and Marriage* (Basingstoke: Macmillan).

Painter, J. (1995), *Politics, Geography and Political Geography* (London: Arnold).

Pannekoek, A. (1950), *Workers' Councils* (Melbourne: Southern Advocate for Workers' Councils).

Pateman, Carole (1988), *The Sexual Contract* (Cambridge: Polity).

Pearce, D., E. Barbies and A. Markandya (1989), *Blueprint for a Green Economy* (London: Earthscan).

Pearce, D., K. Turner, T. O'Riordan, N. Adger, G. Atkinson, I. Brisson, K. Brown, R. Dubourg, S. Frankhauser, A. Jordan, D. Maddison, D. Moran and J. Powell (1993), *Blueprint 3: Measuring Sustainable Development* (London: Earthscan).

Peck, J. and Y. Miyamachi (1994), 'Regulating Japan? Regulation theory versus the Japanese experience', *Environment and Planning D: Society and Space,* 12: 639–74.

Peck, J. and A. Tickell (1992), 'Local Modes of Social Regulation? Regulation Theory, Thatcherism and Uneven Development', *Geoforum,* 23 (3): 347–63.

Pepper, D. (1993), *Eco-Socialism: From Deep Ecology to Social Justice* (London: Routledge).

Perrons, D. (1986), 'Unequal integration in global fordism: the case of Ireland', in A.J. Scott and M. Storper (eds), *Production, Work, Technology* (London: Allen & Unwin).

Petty, Celia, Deborah Roberts and Sharon Smith (1987), *Women's Liberation and Socialism* (London and Chicago: Bookmarks).

Picciotto, S. (1991), 'The Internationalisation of Capital and the International State System', in S. Clarke (ed.), *The State Debate* (Basingstoke: Macmillan).

Pierson, C. (1986), *Marxist Theory and Democratic Politics* (Cambridge: Polity).

Piore, M.J. and C.F. Sabel (1984), *The Second Industrial Divide* (New York: Basic Books).

Piven, F.F. and R. Cloward (1971), *Regulating the Poor: The Functions of Public Welfare* (New York: Pantheon Books).

Plekhanov, G. (n.d.), *Fundamental Problems of Marxism* (Moscow: F.L.P.H.).

Plekhanov, G. (1956), *Art and Social Life* (London: Lawrence & Wishart).

Plekhanov, G. (1961), *Collected Philosophical Works,* Vol. 5 (Moscow: F.L.P.H.).

Podolinski, S. (1880), 'Le Socialisme et l'unité des forces fisiques', *Revue Socialiste,* June.

Polan, A.J. (1984), *Lenin and the End of Politics* (London: Methuen).

Pollin, Robert (1996), 'Financial Structures and Egalitarian Economic Policy', *New Left Review,* 214: 26–61.

Popper, K.R. (1963), *Conjectures and Refutations* (London: Routledge & Kegan Paul).

Popper, K. (1972), *Conjectures and Refutations* (London: Routledge & Kegan Paul).

Popper, K.R. (1980), *The Logic of Scientific Discovery* (London: Hutchinson).

Poulantzas, N. (1969), 'The Problems of the Capitalist State', *New Left Review*, 58: 67-78.

Poulantzas, N. (1973), *Political Power and Social Classes* (London: New Left Books).

Poulantzas, N. (1975), *Classes in Contemporary Capitalism* (London: New Left Books).

Poulantzas, N. (1976), 'The Capitalist State: A Reply to Miliband and Laclau', *New Left Review*, 95: 63–83.

Poulantzas, N. (1978a), 'The State and the Transition to Socialism' (interviewed by H. Weber), *Socialist Review*, 38: 9–36.

Poulantzas, N. (1978b), *State, Power, Socialism* (London: New Left Books).

Prawer, S. S. (1976), *Karl Marx and World Literature* (Oxford: Oxford University Press).

Przeworski, A. (1977), 'Proletariat into a Class: The Process of Class Formation from Karl Kautsky's The Class Struggle to Recent Controversies', *Politics and Society*, 7: 4.

Przeworski, A. (1985), *Capitalism and Social Democracy* (Cambridge: Cambridge University Press).

Purvis, T. (1995), 'Aboriginal Peoples and the Idea of the Nation', in L. Smith (ed.) *Issues in Archaeological Management: a Reader* (St Lucia: Tempus Publications).

Putnam, H. (1981), *Reason, Truth and History* (Cambridge: Cambridge University Press).

Questions Féministes Collective (1981), 'Variations on a Common Theme' (editorial to *Questions Féministes*, 1), reprinted in E, Marks and E. DeCourtivron (eds), *New French Feminisms* (Brighton: Harvester).

Rakovski, M. (1978), *Towards an East European Marxism* (London: Allison & Busby).

Ranney, A. (1975), *Governing of Men*, 4th edn (Hinsdale, IL: The Dryden Press).

Ransome, P. (1992), *Antonio Gramsci: A New Introduction* (New York: Harvester Wheatsheaf).

Renan, E. (1882[1990]), 'What is a Nation?', in H. Bhabha (ed.), *Nation and Narration* (pp. 8–22) (London: Routledge).

Renner, K. (1978), 'Democracy and the Council System', in T. Bottomore and P. Goode (eds), *Austro-Marxism* (Oxford: Clarendon Press).

Renner, K. (1978), 'The Development of the National Idea', in T. Bottomore and P. Goode (eds), *Austro-Marxism* (pp. 118–25) (Oxford: Clarendon).

Resnick, S. and R. Wolff (1995), 'Lessons from the USSR. Taking Marxian theory the next step', in B. Magnus and S. Cullenberg (eds), *Whither Marxism? Global crises in international perspective* (London: Routledge).

Riddell, J. (ed.) (1986), *The German Revolution and the Debate on Soviet Power* (New York: Pathfinder/Anchor).

Riley, Denise (1988), 'Am I that Name?', *Feminism and the Category of 'Women' in History* (Basingstoke: Macmillan).

Roberts, Helen (1993), 'The women and class debate', in David Morgan and Liz Stanley (eds), *Debates in Sociology* (Manchester: Manchester University Press).

Robertson, R. (1992), *Globalization* (London: Sage).

Robertson, R. (1995), 'Glocalization: Time–Space and Homogeneity–Heterogeneity', in Mike Featherstone *et al.* (eds), *Global Modernities* (London: Sage).

Robinson, N. (1995), *Ideology and the Collapse of the Soviet System: A critical history of Soviet ideological discourse* (Aldershot and Brookfield, VT: Edward Elgar).

Roemer, John (1994), *A Future for Socialism* (London: Verso).

Rorty, R. (1989), *Contingency, Irony and Solidarity* (Cambridge: Cambridge University Press).

Rorty, R. (1991), *Objectivity, Relativism and Truth* (Cambridge: Cambridge University Press).

Rosdolsky, R. (1987), *The Making of Marx's 'Capital'* (London: Pluto Press).

Rosenberg, J. (1996), 'Isaac Deutscher and the Lost History of International Relations', *New Left Review*.

Rosenberg, R. (1994), *The Empire of Civil Society* (London: Verso).

Roskin, M. G., R. L. Coro, J. A. Medeiros and W. S. Jones (1988), *Political Science* (Englewood Cliffs: Prentice-Hall International).

Rostow, W. (1960), *The Stages of Economic Growth* (Cambridge: Cambridge University Press).

Rowbotham, Sheila (1981), 'The Trouble with "Patriarchy"', in R. Samuel (ed.) *People's History and Socialist Theory* (London: Routledge & Kegan Paul).

Rubin, Gayle (1975), 'The traffic in women: notes on the "political economy" of sex', in R. Reiter (ed.), *Toward an Anthropology of Women* (New York: Monthly Review Press).

Rubin, I. I. (1983), *Essays in Marx's Theory of Value* (Canada: Black Rose).

Ruccio, D. (1989), 'Fordism on a World Scale: International Dimensions of Regulation', *Review of Radical Political Economy*, 21 (4): 33–53.

Rushton, Peter (1979), 'Marxism, domestic labour and the capitalist economy: a note on recent discusssions', in C. C. Harris (ed.) *The Sociology of the Family: New Directions for Britain* (Keele: Sociological Review Monographs).

Rustin, Mike (1985), *For a Plural Socialism* (London: Verso).

Rustin, M. (1989), 'The Politics of Post-Fordism: or, The Trouble with "New Times"', *New Left Review*, 175: 54–77.

Ryle, M. (1988), *Ecology and Socialism* (London: Hutchinson).

Sabel, C. F. (1989), 'Flexible Specialisation and the Re-emergence of Regional Economies', in P.Hirst and J.Zeitlin (eds), *Reversing Industrial Decline* (Oxford: Berg).

Sachs, J. (1998), 'Global Capitalism: Making it Work', *The Economist*, 12 September 1998, pp. 23–5.

Sachs, W. (1995), 'Global Ecology and the Shadow of Development', in G. Sessions (ed.), *Deep Ecology for the 21st Century* (Boston: Shambala Press).

Sallah, A. (1994), 'Ecology and Discursive Democracy: Beyond Liberal Capitalism and the Administrative State', in M. O'Connor (ed.), *Is Capitalism Sustainable? Political Economy and the Politics of Ecology* (London: Guilford Press).

Sanderson, J. (1963), 'Marx and Engels on the State', *Western Political Quarterly,* December.

Sartori, G. (1974), Philosophy, Theory and Science in Politics', *Political Theory* 2 (2):

Saunders, P. (1996), *Unequal but Fair? A Study of Class Barriers in Britain* (London: IEA).

Sayer, D. (1979), *Marx's Method* (Brighton: Harvester).

Sayer, D. (1987), *The Violence of Abstraction* (Oxford: Basil Blackwell).

Sayer, D. (1989), *Readings From Karl Marx* (London: Routledge).

Sayer, D. (1990), 'Reinventing the Wheel: Anthony Giddens, Karl Marx and Social Change', in John Clark *et al.* (eds), *Anthony Giddens: Consensus and Controversy* (London: Falmer Press).

Scheter, D. (1994), *Radical Theories: Paths Beyond Marxism and Social Democracy* (Manchester: Manchester University Press).

Schmitter, P. (1985), 'Neo-Corporatism and the State', in W. Grant (ed.), *The Political Economy of Corporatism* (Basingstoke: Macmillan).

Schoenberger, E. (1988), 'From Fordism to flexible accumulation: technology, competitive strategies and international location', *Environment and Planning D: Society and Space,* 6: 245–62.

Schumpeter, Joseph (1950), *Capitalism, Socialism and Decocracy* (London: Allen & Unwin).

Scott, J. (1996), *Stratification and Power* (Cambridge: Polity).

Scruton, Rodger (1980), *The Meaning of Conservatism* (Harmondsworth: Penguin).

Seldon, R. (1985), *A Reader's Guide to Contemporary Literary Theory* (Brighton: Harvester).

Shaver, S. (1989), 'Gender, Class and the Welfare State: The Case of Income Security in Australia', *Feminist,* 32, 91–108.

Shaw, M. (1994), *Global Society and International Relations* (Cambridge: Polity).

Shipway, M. (1988), *Anti-Parliamentary Communism: The Movement for Workers' Councils in Britain 1917–1945* (Basingstoke: Macmillan).

Shiva, V. (1992), *Staying Alive* (London: Zed Books).

Sirianni, C. (1982), *Workers' Control and Socialist Democracy: The Soviet Experience* (London: Verso).

Sirianni, C. (1983), 'Councils and Parliaments: The Problems of Dual Power in Comparative Perspective', *Politics and Society,* 12 (1): 83–123.

Skocpol, T. (1985), 'Bringing the State Back In', in Peter Evans *et al.* (eds), *Bringing the State Back In* (Cambridge: Cambridge University Press).

Slaughter, C. (1980), *Marxism, Ideology and Literature* (Brighton: Harvester).

Smart, B. (1993), *Postmodernism* (London: Routledge).

Smith, A. D. (1971), *Theories of Nationalism* (London: Duckworth).

Smith, A. D. (1986), *The Ethnic Origins of Nations* (Oxford: Blackwell).

Smith, A. D. (1991), The Nation: Invented, Imagined, Reconstructed?, *Millennium,* 20 (2): 353–368.

Smith, G. A. E. (1981), 'The industrial problems of Soviet agriculture', *Critique,* 14.

Smith, Paul (1978a), 'Domestic labour and Marx's theory of value', in A. Kuhn and A. M. Wolpe (eds), *Feminism and Materialism: Women and Modes of Production* (London: Routledge & Kegan Paul).

Smith, Paul (1978b), *Socialist Courier* (New York).

Smith, Paul (1978c), *Society,* 20, (1) February: 79–102.

Soper, K. (1991), 'Greening Prometheus: Marxism and Ecology', in P. Osborne (ed.), *Socialism and the Limits of Liberalism* (London: Verso).

Spivak, Gayatri Chakravorty (1988), *In Other Worlds* (New York: Routledge).

Stacey, Jackie (1993), 'Untangling Feminist Theory', in D. Richardson and V. Robinson (eds) *Introducing Women's Studies* (Basingstoke: Macmillan).

Stalin, J. (1913), 'Marxism and the National Question', in *Marxism and the National and Colonial Question, by Joseph Stalin: A collection of Articles and Speeches* (New York: International Publishers).

Staten, H. (1985), *Wittgenstein and Derrida* (Oxford: Blackwell).

Steinmetz, G. (1994), 'Regulation Theory, Post-Marxism and the New Social Movements', *Comparative Study of Society and History,* 36 (1): 176–212.

Strachey, John (1932), *The Coming Struggle for Power* (London: Gollancz).

Stubbs, R. and G. Underhill (eds) (1994), *Political Economy and the Changing Global Order* (Basingstoke: Macmillan).

Sum, N.-L. (1996), 'Capitalism and East Asian NICs: A Regulation Perspective', Political Economy Research Centre (Sheffield University) *Occasional Paper No.7* (Brighton: Harvester Press).

Sweezy, P. (1942), *The Theory of Capitalist Development* (New York: Monthly Review Press).

Talmon, J. L. (1970), *The Origins of Totalitarian Democracy* (London: Sphere).

Taylor, G. (1995), 'Marxism', in D. Marsh and G. Stoker (eds), *Theory and Methods in Political Science* (Basingstoke: Macmillan).

Thomas, K. (1971), *Religon and the Decline of Magic* (Harmondsworth: Penguin).

Thompson, E. P. (1963), *The Making of the English Working Class* (London: Victor Gollancz).

Thompson, E. P. (1978), *The Poverty of Theory* (London: Merlin).

Thorogood, Nicki (1987), 'Race, class and gender: the politics of housework', in J. Brannen and G. Wilson (eds), *Give and Take in Families: Studies in Resource Distribution* (London: Allen & Unwin).

Tickell, A. and J. Peck (1992), 'Accumulation, regulation and the geographies of post-Fordism: missing links in regulationist research', *Progress in Human Geography,* 16 (2): 190–218.

Tickell, A. and J. Peck (1995), 'Social regulation after Fordism: regulation theory, neo-liberalism and the global–local nexus', *Economy and Society,* 24 (3): 357–86.

Ticktin, H. (1973), 'Towards a political economy of the USSR', *Critique,* 1.

Ticktin, H. (1976), 'The contradictions of Soviet society and Professor Bettelheim', *Critique,* 6.

Ticktin, H. (1978), 'The class structure of the USSR and the Soviet elite', *Critique,* 9.

Ticktin, H. (1979), 'The ambiguities of Ernest Mandel', *Critique,* 12.

Ticktin, H. (1989), 'The contradictions of Gorbachev', in W. Joyce, H. Ticktin and S. White (eds), *Gorbachev and Gorbachevism* (London: Cass).

Ticktin, H. (1992), *Origins of the Crisis in the USSR: Essays on the political economy of a disintegrating system* (Armonk: M. E. Sharpe).

Torfing, J. (1996), 'Politics, Regulation and the Welfare State', PhD thesis.

Trinh, T. Minh-ha (1989), *Women, Native, Other* (Bloomington: Indiana University Press).

Trotsky, L. (1960), *Literature and Revolution* (Michigan: Ann Arbor).

Trotsky, L. (1969), *Permanent Revolution and Results and Prospects* (New York: Merit).

Trotsky, L. (1972), *The Revolution Betrayed* (New York: Pathfinder).

Trotsky, L. (1973), 'The death agony of capitalism and the tasks of the Fourth International', *Documents of the Fourth International* (New York: Pathfinder).

Tucker, R. C. (ed.) (1978), *The Marx–Engels Reader*, 2nd edn (New York: W. W. Norton).

Turner, B. (1990), *British Cultural Studies: An Introduction* (London: Unwin Hyman).

Turner, B. S. (1988), *Status* (Milton Keynes: Open University Press).

Urban, M. (1988), 'Local Soviets and popular needs: where the official ideology meets everyday life', in S. White and A. Pravda (eds), *Ideology and Soviet Politics* (Basingstoke: Macmillan).

Urmson, J. and J. Ree (1991), *The Concise Encyclopedia of Western Philosophy and Philosophers* (London: Routledge).

Van den Berg, A. (1988), *The Immanent Utopia: From Marxism on the State to the State of Marxism* (Princeton: Princeton University Press).

Van Every, Jo (1995), *Heterosexual Women Changing the Family: Refusing to be a 'Wife'* (London: Taylor & Francis).

Wade, R. and F. Venerosa (1998), 'The Asian Crisis: The High Debt Model versus the Wall Street–Treasury–IMF Complex', *New Left Review*, 228: 3–23.

Walby, Sylvia (1986a), *Patriarchy at Work* (Cambridge: Polity).

Walby, Sylvia (1986b), 'Gender, class and stratification, towards a new approach', in R. Crompton and M. Mann (eds), *Gender and Stratification* (Cambridge: Polity).

Walby, Sylvia (1989), 'Theorising Patriarchy', *Sociology* 23 (2): 213–34.

Walby, Sylvia (1990), *Theorizing Patriarchy* (Oxford: Blackwell).

Walby, Sylvia (1992), 'Post-post-modernism? Theorizing social complexlty', in M. Barrett and A. Phillips (eds), *Destabilizing Theory: Contemporary Feminist Debates* (Cambridge: Polity).

Waller, M. (1981), *Democratic Centralism: An Historical Commentary* (Manchester: Manchester University Press).

Wallerstein, Immanuel (1974), *The Modern World System I: Capitalist Agriculture and the Origins of the European World-Economy in the Sixteenth Century* (New York: Academic Press).

Wallerstein, Immanuel (1980), *The Modern World System II: Mercantilism and the Consolidation of the European World-Economy, 1600–1750* (New York: Academic Press).

Wallerstein, Immanuel (1989), *The Modern World System III: The Second Era of Great Expansion of the Capitalist World-Economy, 1730–1840s* (New York: Academic Press).

Waltz, K. (1979), *Theory of International Politics* (New York: Addison-Wesley).

Waters, M. (1995), *Globalization* (London: Routledge).

Weale, A. (1992), *The New Politics of Pollution* (Manchester: Manchester University Press).

Weber, M. (1968), *Economy and Society*, 3 vols (New York: Bedminster Press).

Weedon, Chris (1987), *Feminist Practice and Poststructuralist Theory* (Oxford: Blackwell).

Weir, A. (1974), 'The Family, Social Work and the Welfare State', in S. Allen *et al.*, *Conditions of Illusion*, pp. 217–28 (Leeds; Feminist Books).

Wesson, R. (1996), *Why Marxism? The Continuing Success of a Failed Theory* (New York: Basic Books).

Westoby, A. (1981), *Communism since World War II* (Brighton: Harvester).

Westoby, A. (1985), 'Conceptions of communist states', in D. Held *et al.* (eds), *States and Societies* (Oxford: Blackwell).

Weston, J. (ed.) (1986), *Red and Green: The New Politics of the Environment* (London: Pluto Press).

Westwood, Sallie and Parminder Bhachu (eds) (1988), *Enterprising Women: Ethnicity, Economy and Gender Relations* (London: Routledge).

Wildt, A. (1979), 'Totalitarian state capitalism: on the structure and historic function of Soviet-type societies', *Telos*, 41.

Williams, G. (1975), *Proletarian Order: Antonio Gramsci, Factory Councils and the Origins of Italian Communism* (London: Pluto Press).

Williams, R. (1958), *Culture and Society* (London: Chatto & Windus).

Williams, R. (1961), *The Long Revolution* (Harmondsworth: Penguin).

Williams, R. (1972), *The Long Revolution* (Harmondsworth: Penguin).

Williams, R. (1977), *Marxism and Literature* (Oxford: Oxford University Press).

Williams, R. (1980), *Problems in Materialism and Culture* (London: Verso).

Wilson, B. (1981), *Rationality* (Oxford: Blackwell).

Wittig, Monique (1992), *The Straight Mind and Other Essays* (Hemel Hempstead: Harvester Wheatsheaf).

Witz, Anne (1992), *Patriarchy and the Professions* (London: Routledge).

Wohlforth, T. (1981), 'Transition to the Transition', *New Left Review*, 130: 67–81.

Wolfe, A. (1974), 'New Directions in the Marxist Theory of Politics', *Politics and Society*, 4 (2): 131–60.

Wolfe, A. (1977), *The Limits of Legitimacy: Political Contradictions of Late Capitalism* (New York: Free Press).

Wolff, E. (1995), *Top Heavy: A Study of Increasing Inequality in America* (New York: Twentieth Century Fund).

Wolff, J. (1981), *The Social Production of Art* (Basingstoke: Macmillan).

Wood, E. (1986), *The Retreat From Class: The New, True Socialism* (London: New York: Verso).

Woods, A. and T. Grant (1995), *Reason in Revolt* (New York: Wellred Publications).

Woolgar, S. (1988), *Science: the very idea* (first published, Chichester: Ellis Horwood Ltd, and London: Tavistock Publications Ltd).

Worsley, P. (1982), *Marx and Marxism* (London: Tavistock).

Wright, E. O. (1976), 'Class Boundaries in Advanced Capitalist Societies', *New Left Review*, 98.

Wright, E. O. (1978), *Class Crisis and the State* (London: NBL Publishing).

Wright, E. O. (1980), 'Varieties of Marxist Conceptions of Class Structure', *Politics and Society*, 9 (3).

Wright, E. O. (1985), *Classes* (London: Verso).

Young, S. (1993), *The Politics of the Environment* (Manchester: Baseline Press).

Index